Being Different

'*Being Different* is a provocative and important book for two distinct reasons. First, the book is one of the few attempts by an Indian intellectual to challenge seriously the assumptions and presuppositions of the field of India and/or South Asian studies *tout ensemble*, including not only the work of European and American scholarship but as well the neocolonialist, postmodernist and subaltern *ressentiment* so typical of contemporary Indian intellectuals. Second, and perhaps of greater significance, is Malhotra's attempt to analyse the meaning and significance of Indic culture from within the indigenous presuppositions of India's own intellectual traditions, including the ontological claims of Indic cosmology, the epistemology of yogic experience, the unique Indic appreciation for complexity, and the nuances of Sanskritic expression. The book will be controversial on many different levels and will undoubtedly elicit rigorous critical response' – **GERALD JAMES LARSON, Rabindranath Tagore Professor Emeritus, Indiana University, Bloomington, and Professor Emeritus, Religious Studies, University of California, Santa Barbara**

'Malhotra writes with passion from within an avowedly dharmic stance, undermining the attempts to domesticate and expropriate Indian traditions in a process of inter-religious dialogue that is ultimately based on a Western cosmological framework. This book is essential reading for Western scholars. It espouses an "audacity of difference" that defends the distinctiveness of Indian thought and reveals the chauvinism of much Western thought in its encounters with other cultures' – **DON WIEBE, Professor of Divinity, Trinity College in the University of Toronto**

'This book is a "must read" for those who care about India and its future' – **MAKARAND R. PARANJAPE, Professor of English, Jawaharlal Nehru University, Delhi**

'Honest, provocative and wide-ranging, this book gives us (westerners) a rare opportunity to see ourselves through the lens of another worldview. It cuts to the heart of the problems created by Christian beliefs about unique historical revelation, and by the West's consistent investment in a set of linear historical narratives purporting to offer universal salvation but fuelled by particular western needs and anxieties. Informed by postmodernism, but moving beyond it, the book levels the playing field for a genuine encounter between East and West and raises issues that any serious revision of Christian theology must address' – **CLEO KEARNS, University of Massachusetts, Dartmouth, and Infinity Foundation**

'Rajiv Malhotra's insistence on preserving difference with mutual respect – not with mere "tolerance" – is even more pertinent today because the notion of a single universalism is being propounded. There can be no single universalism, even if it assimilates or, in the author's words, "digests", elements from other civilizations' – **KAPILA VATSYAYAN, Independent scholar and Member of Rajya Sabha**

'Many Indian spiritual leaders, lacking a profound knowledge of their own culture, and feeling inferior to the West, try to respond to the Western challenge by showing how Indian and Western religions are the same. Rajiv Malhotra's work is a kind of yajna that reverses the gaze upon the West through the lens of Indian categories. This process is traditionally called *purva paksha*, and in Rajiv's work it is given a new mission. Rajiv has devised the very interesting metaphor of *digestion* to explain how the dharmic traditions are being disassembled into parts for digestion into the belly of Western culture. *Being Different* shows how the West's history-centrism drives it into claims of exclusiveness; this causes anxiety over differences which it seeks to resolve through projects of digestion in order to obliterate whatever seems challenging' – **SATYA NARAYAN DAS, Founder of Jiva Institute of Vedic Studies, Vrindavan**

'What I found particularly informative and original in *Being Different* is the discussion on the positive role of chaos in the Indic world as compared to the West's abhorrence of it. The book explains Hegel's deep-rooted fear of chaos and uncertainty. He privileged *order* in Western aesthetics, ethics, religions, society, and politics and classified Oriental traditions into "pantheism", "polytheism", and "monotheism" as "world historical categories". Hegel developed a system of equivalences to assign relative meaning and value to each culture, thereby defining the contours of the "West" and the "Rest." These became the conceptual tools for epistemic subjugation of the non-West in the name of order. The dharmic worldview is more relaxed about chaos, seeing it as a creative catalyst built into the cosmos to balance out order that could otherwise become stultifying' – **SHRINIVAS TILAK, Independent scholar, Montreal**

'With stunning honesty, *Being Different* alerts the reader to the grave dangers of a difference-negating "sameness" that is marketed worldwide by secular and religious streams in Western culture. This is a very important and highly accessible book in the discourse on the interaction between civilizations' – **RITA SHERMA, Executive Director, Confluence School of Faith Studies; co-editor** *Hermeneutics and Hindu Thought: Towards a Fusion of Horizons*

'*Being Different* is a highly successful attempt in exploring the major differences between Indian and Western worldviews, metaphysics, cosmologies and philosophies which have not previously been adequately appreciated by scholars and spiritual seekers' – **SAMPADANANDA MISHRA, Director, Sri Aurobindo Foundation for Indian Culture, Pondicherry**

BEING DIFFERENT

An Indian Challenge to Western Universalism

Rajiv Malhotra

HarperCollins *Publishers* India

First published in India in 2011 by
HarperCollins *Publishers* India
Building No 10, Tower A, 4th Floor, DLF Cyber City, Phase II,
Gurugram – 122002
www.harpercollins.co.in

1 2 3 4 5 6 7 8 9 10

Copyright © Infinity Foundation 2011

rajivmalhotra2007@gmail.com

ISBN: 978-93-5029-190-0

Rajiv Malhotra asserts the moral
right to be identified as the author of this work.

Typeset in 11/3.5 Adobe Garamond Pro by
InoSoft Systems Noida

Contents

Introduction

'I am simply using the dharmic perspective to reverse the analytical gaze which normally goes from West to East and unconsciously privileges the former. This reversal evaluates Western problems in a unique way, sheds light on some of its blind spots, and shows how dharmic cultures can help alleviate and resolve some of the problems facing the world today.

India itself cannot be viewed only as a bundle of the old and the new, accidentally and uncomfortably pieced together, an artificial construct without a natural unity. Nor is she just a repository of quaint, fashionable accessories to Western lifestyles; nor a junior partner in a global capitalist world. India is its own distinct and unified civilization with a proven ability to manage profound differences, engage creatively with various cultures, religions and philosophies, and peacefully integrate many diverse streams of humanity. These values are based on ideas about divinity, the cosmos and humanity that stand in contrast to the fundamental assumptions of Western civilization. This book explores those ideas and assumptions.'

I want all the cultures of all lands to be blown about my house as freely as possible. But I refuse to be blown off my feet by any.

– Gandhi

This book is about how India *differs* from the West. It aims to challenge certain cherished notions, such as the assumptions that Western paradigms are universal and that the dharmic traditions teach 'the same thing' as Jewish and Christian ones. For while the Vedas say, 'truth is one, paths are many', the differences among those paths are not inconsequential. I will argue that the dharmic traditions, while not perfect, offer perspectives and techniques for a genuinely pluralistic social order and a full integration of many different faiths, including atheism and science. They also offer models for environmental sustainability and education for the whole being that are invaluable to our emerging world. The book hopes to set the terms for a deeper and more informed engagement between dharmic and Western civilizations.

In making these arguments, I may be accused of using broad definitions, generalizations and extreme contrasts. When I speak of 'the West' vs 'India', or the 'Judeo-Christian religions' vs the 'dharma traditions', I am well aware that I may be indulging in the kind of essentialism that postmodern thinkers have correctly challenged. I am also aware that such large categories comprise multiple traditions which are separate and often opposed.[1] I view these terms as family resemblances and guides, not as reified or immutable entities. Furthermore, most people do understand them as pointing to actual entities with distinct spiritual and cosmological orientations, even if they can only be defined in opposition to one another. The terms can thus be used as entry points for debate and as foils to contrast both sides, which may help deepen our understanding.

To be more precise, 'the West' is used in this book to refer to the cultures and civilizations stemming from a rather forced fusion of the biblical traditions of ancient Israel and the classical ones of Greece and Rome. My focus here is on American history and culture, because they are most exemplary of the Western identity today. I investigate European history primarily to uncover the roots of the West's self-understanding and approach to India, and I give special attention to the role of Germany in shaping the Western approach to dharma.

'India' here refers both to the modern nation and to the civilization from which it emerged. For reasons to be discussed at length, I do not follow the current fashion for 'deconstructing' Indian identity into its constituent parts, or for 'breaking India', as I have called the process in my previous book.

As for the term 'Judeo-Christian', it is a hybrid which does make some Jews and Christians uncomfortable, because it lumps together very different and often sharply opposed religions. I try to avoid using this hybrid where a distinction is important. Nevertheless, this term is useful in designating a religious paradigm that is common to both, particularly with regard to the central importance given to historical revelation. (This paradigm is also found in a different form in Islam, but I do not deal with Islam in this volume.)

'Dharma' is used to indicate a family of spiritual traditions originating in India which today are manifested as Hinduism, Buddhism, Jainism and Sikhism. I explain that the variety of perspectives and practices of dharma display an underlying integral unity at the metaphysical level which undergirds and supports their openness and relative non-aggressiveness. Dharma is not easy to define, and a good deal of this book is devoted to explaining some of its dimensions. The oft-used translations of dharma as 'religion', 'path', 'law' and 'ethics' all fall short in substantial ways. Suffice it to say that the principles and presuppositions of dharma are available in classical Sanskrit terms that often have no exact translation in English; dharma encompasses a diversity of lifestyles and views that have evolved over many centuries.

As I have just noted, Western foundational concepts and values stem not from one source but from two: Judeo-Christian historical revelations expressed through prophets and messiahs, and Greek reason with its reliance on Aristotelian logic and empirical knowledge. I will argue at length that the resulting cultural construct called 'the West' is not an integrally unified entity but a synthetic one. It is dynamic but also inherently unstable, leading to restless, expansionist, and often aggressive historical projects, as well as anxiety and inner turmoil. This instability has had a devastating effect not only on non-westerners but on westerners themselves. The cultural constructs of India are, by contrast, relatively more stable, flexible and less expansionist. Additionally, the dharma substrate (not without tension and experimentation) obviates the West's conflicting claims of historical revelations and science-versus-religion conflicts.

As will be obvious, my exploration of these two different worldviews does not arise from a neutral, disinterested position (which would be impossible in any case) but from an avowedly dharmic one. However, I am not suggesting that we must return to the kind of imagined golden past often implied by this kind of advocacy. I am simply using the dharmic perspective to reverse the analytical gaze which normally goes from West to East and unconsciously privileges the former. This reversal evaluates Western problems in a unique way, sheds light on some of its blind spots, and shows how dharmic cultures can help alleviate and resolve some of the problems facing the world today.

India itself cannot be viewed only as a bundle of the old and the new, accidentally and uncomfortably pieced together, an artificial construct without a natural unity. Nor is she just a repository of quaint, fashionable accessories to Western lifestyles; nor a junior partner in a global capitalist world. India is its own distinct and unified civilization with a proven ability to manage profound differences, engage creatively with various cultures, religions and philosophies, and peacefully integrate many diverse streams of humanity. These values are based on ideas about divinity, the cosmos and humanity that stand in contrast to the fundamental assumptions of Western civilization. This book explores those ideas and assumptions.

Some of this analysis is highly critical and will perhaps raise hackles not only among westerners but also among Indians who value Western culture (as I do myself). They will point out that Western culture's self-critique is its hallmark and stock-in-trade. However, that self-critique invariably takes place within Western categories and institutions of knowledge production and, as a result, is blind to many of its shortcomings.

There are two extremes that I wish to avoid in positioning dharma vis-à-vis the West. On the one hand, over-emphasizing dharmic wisdom and its precedents can lead to chauvinism (and give rise to some of the same problems that exist in the 'arrogance' of the West) and even to isolationism and a failure to engage globally. On the other hand, if dharma is put forward merely as an eclectic collection of disparate ideas, it will lack the cohesiveness necessary to function as a force for change.

With these concerns in mind, I offer four areas of difference between dharmic and Judeo-Christian traditions:

1. Embodied Knowing versus History-centrism
2. Integral Unity versus Synthetic Unity
3. Anxiety over Chaos versus Comfort with Complexity and Ambiguity
4. Cultural Digestion versus Sanskrit Non-Translatables

These areas of contrast are summarized below and discussed at length in the subsequent chapters.

Embodied Knowing versus History-centrism

Dharma and Judeo-Christian traditions differ fundamentally in their approaches to knowing the divine. The dharma family (including Hinduism, Buddhism, Sikhism and Jainism) has developed an extensive range of inner sciences and experiential technologies called 'adhyatma-vidya' to access divinity and higher states of consciousness. Adhyatma-vidya is a body of wisdom and techniques culled from centuries of first-person empirical inquiry into the nature of consciousness and undertaken by advanced practitioners. These accounts and the individuals who have embarked on these quests are highly regarded, but they are not reified into canons, messiahs or absolute statements of an exclusive nature. They are neither a code of laws nor a history of past revelations but guides for replicating and retransmitting the experience and its transformational powers. Their truth must be rediscovered and directly experienced by each person. I have coined the term *embodied knowing* to refer to inner sciences and adhyatma-vidya.

The Judeo-Christian traditions, in contrast, depend on the historical revelations of prophets who speak of the collective destiny of whole peoples and of humankind. The human condition stems from an act of disobedience or 'sin', beginning with the 'original sin' of Adam and Eve, the forbears of all humanity. Every individual is born a sinner. For this reason, humans are unable to achieve union with the divine (at least not in the dharmic sense); the spiritual goal instead is salvation that can be achieved only through obedience to God's will as understood through a particular set of prophets and historical events. Hence the historical record of that intervention must be carefully maintained, and its truth must be taken forward and aggressively asserted. The goal of this record is to bring humans collectively to obey a specific 'law'. This history must be considered universal, however particular and fallible its agents (both individual and collective) may be. Humanity's collective destiny will be determined and judged at the End of Time.

Such an absolute status of history weakens the authority of individual spiritual explorations (hence, mystics have been regarded with suspicion in these traditions) and becomes the basis for competing claims to truth that cannot be reconciled. Furthermore, those without access to these historical revelations must remain, by definition, in the dark, lacking the most elementary means to make contact with God. I have coined the term *history-centrism* to refer to this fixation on specific and often incompatible claims to divine truth revealed in the course of history. I regard this historical fixation as the major difference between dharmic and Judeo-Christian paths and as a problem which can breed untold psychological, religious and social conflict.

Integral Unity versus Synthetic Unity

The idea of underlying unity in the dharmic traditions differs radically from how unity is understood in the Judeo-Christian traditions. All dharmic schools begin by assuming that ultimately the cosmos is a unified whole in which absolute reality and the relative manifestations are profoundly connected. Western worldviews, by contrast, have been shaped by a tension between the absolute status of Judeo-Christian historical revelations on the one hand and the knowledge produced by a highly dualistic and atomistic Greek metaphysics and Aristotelian binary logic on the other. As a result, the West's sense of unity is profoundly troubled, first by the split between revelation and reason (or between Hebraism and Hellenism, as this divide is sometimes described) and secondly by the inherently fragmented quality of the reasoning and speculation produced by the latter. I will discuss in Chapter 3 how the dharmic traditions draw on a sense of integral unity whereas the Judeo-Christian one is based on various synthetic unities which are inherently unstable and problematic.

The various dharmic schools, despite some profound differences in theory and practice, all attempt to account for some form of unity. Even though ordinary people find this difficult to experience, the resources for its realization are built into the various spiritual disciplines. The sense of an underlying unity is strong and allows for a great deal of inventiveness and play in understanding its manifestations. As a result, there tends to be a great diversity of paths and philosophical understandings without fear of chaos.

Western worldviews, whether religious or secular, begin with the opposite premise: the cosmos is inherently an agglomeration of parts or separate essences. The debates on this subject are not about how and why multiplicity emerges but about how unity can emerge out of the multiplicity. Such a unity is not innate; it must be sought and justified again and again, and the resulting synthesis is always unstable. The Judeo-Christian faiths begin (with some qualifications) by viewing the divine as profoundly separated and infinitely far from the world and the human, each side of the divide entirely distinct from the other. Classical

Western philosophy and the science that emerged from it (again, with some qualifications) begin with the premise that the universe is composed of atomic entities or separate building blocks. Science and religion are both faced with the need to discover or invent a unity, which they do with some anxiety and difficulty. Furthermore, the starting points and conclusions of Western religion and science are in great mutual tension and even contradiction, which essentially makes Western civilization an uneasy and tentative synthesis of incompatible building blocks. Chapter 3 analyses this difference at length.

Anxiety over Chaos versus Comfort with Complexity and Ambiguity

Dharmic civilizations are more relaxed and comfortable with multiplicity and ambiguity than the West. Chaos is seen as a source of creativity and dynamism. Since the ultimate reality is an integrally unified coherence, chaos is a relative phenomenon that cannot threaten or disrupt the underlying coherence of the cosmos. Sri Aurobindo, the great Indian yogi and philosopher of the twentieth century, said that since unity in the dharmic traditions is grounded in a sense of oneness, there can be immense multiplicity without fear of collapse into disintegration and chaos. He went on to say that nature can afford the luxury of infinite differentiation, since the underlying immutability of the eternal always remains unaffected.

In the West, chaos is seen as a ceaseless threat both psychologically and socially – something to be overcome by control or elimination. Psychologically, it drives the ego to become all-powerful and controlling. Socially, it creates a hegemonic impulse over those who are different. A cosmology based on unity that is synthetic and not innate is riddled with anxieties. Therefore, order must be imposed so as to resolve differences relating to culture, race, gender, sexual orientation and so on.

Dharmic traditions, as a result of their foundational texts, epics, archetypes and values, depict order and chaos as belonging to the same family and weave multiple narratives around this idea of cooperative rivalry. The popular myth of *Samudra-manthana*, which tells of the churning of the ocean of 'milk', illustrates this concept, as we shall see in Chapter 4.

Cultural Digestion versus Sanskrit Non-translatables

Western scholars and westernized Indians are accustomed to translating and mapping dharmic concepts and perspectives onto Western frameworks, thereby enriching and perhaps even renewing the Western 'host' culture into which they are assimilated. Chapter 5 will argue that this approach is highly problematic. One does not say of a tiger's kill that both tiger and prey are 'changed for the better' by the digestion, or that the two kinds of animals have 'flowed into one another' to produce a better one. Rather, the food of the tiger becomes a part of the tiger's body, breaking down and obliterating, in the process, the digested animal. Dharmic traditions and wisdom are compromised or even obliterated once they can be substituted with Western equivalents which are not capable of accurately representing the dharma.

While this problem can be a danger in all inter-civilization encounters where the balance of political power is unequal, it is particularly acute when it comes to translating dharmic concepts in written Sanskrit into Western languages. Not only does Sanskrit, like all languages, encode specific and unique cultural experiences and traits, but the very form, sound and manifestation of the language carry effects that cannot be separated from their conceptual meanings.

The sacred sounds that comprise the Sanskrit language were discovered by India's rishis of the distant past through their inner sciences. These sounds are not arbitrary conventions but were realized through spiritual practice that brought direct experiences of the realities to which they correspond. Numerous meditation systems were developed by experimenting with these sounds, and thus evolved the inner sciences that enable a practitioner to return to a primordial state of unity consciousness. Sanskrit provides an experiential path back to its source. It is not just a communications tool but also the vehicle for embodied knowing. Employed by the spiritual leaders of India, South-east Asia and

East Asia for many centuries as a language, Sanskrit became the medium for expressing a distinct set of cultural systems and experiences.

Sanskriti is the term for this cultural framework. It is the lore and repository of philosophy, art, architecture, popular song, classical music, dance, theatre, sculpture, painting, literature, pilgrimage, rituals and religious narratives, all of which embody pan-Indian cultural traits. It also incorporates all branches of natural science and technology – medicine (including veterinary), botany, mathematics, engineering, architecture, dietetics, etc.

Although the Judeo-Christian faiths also have their sacred languages – Hebrew and Latin – and although the claims made for them are sometimes similar to the ones made for Sanskrit, these languages have not served as the basis for unified civilizations in quite the same way. This distinction will become clearer in Chapter 5.

Furthermore, Christianity, from the beginning, was not transmitted through a sacred language but through the vernacular – first the Aramaic that Jesus spoke, then the everyday koine Greek of the Mediterranean Basin. The New Testament, in its numerous translations, promulgates not a direct experience of the divine but a message or 'gospel' (meaning 'good news') *about* the divine. The emphasis here is on the meaning of the words and the historical deeds they recount and not on their sound or resonance or the embodied response they elicit. Christianity does not have a spiritual tradition similar to mantra, and prayer is a petition, conversation or thanksgiving to an external deity, where the conceptual meaning is far more important than the sound or its empirical effects on the practitioner.

The non-translatable nature of Sanskrit and all that this implies are compromised by the cultural digestion of dharma into the West. In the course of this digestion, crucial distinctions and understandings are lost, important empirical experiences foreclosed, and the most fertile, productive and visionary dimension of dharma eradicated and relegated to antiquity.

1
The Audacity of Difference

'There is a way of dealing with difference anxiety that is especially
dangerous, in part because it is largely invisible. ... I refer to the
digestion of one culture by another that is carried out under the guise
of a desire to assimilate, reduce difference, and assert sameness in
place of the less dominant culture. At the level of popular culture,
India and the West may meet as equals, but at the deeper levels,
where the core assumptions of a civilization reside, the playing field
is tilted. Cultural appropriation gives a false impression
of equalization.'

The cultural and spiritual matrix of dharma civilizations is distinct from that of the West. This distinctiveness is under siege, not only from unsustainable and inequitable development but also from something more insidious: the widespread dismantling, rearrangement and digestion of dharmic culture into Western frameworks, disingenuously characterized as 'universal'.

This process of absorption can take place with the best of intentions and even with the cooperation of many individuals immersed in dharma. They ask: Why not assimilate? Aren't we all really 'the same'? What's wrong with a 'universal' point of view? Isn't the large-scale absorption of Indian ideas, arts, sciences, medicine, business practices, and letters a *good* thing? Don't we live in a post-colonial, post-racial, post-ethnic world? Isn't it wonderful that millions of Americans and Europeans practise yoga and that Indian cuisine has gone global? And besides, doesn't the West have something to offer India in exchange, such as scientific advances, social justice and business and political know-how? The obvious answer to all these questions would appear to be 'yes'.

And yet much of what appears to be an explicit Indian influence on the West is actually indicative of a process that threatens to deplete and exhaust the very sources of dharma on which it draws. Talk of global culture and universalism often creates the sunny impression that the fusion of dharmic and Western cultures is always good. This assumption ignores the many distortions and unacknowledged appropriations on the Western side, as well as the highly destructive influences of fundamentalist Christianity, Marxism, capitalist expansionism, and myopic secularism.

It is true that global culture is bridging and blurring boundaries across races, ethnicities, nationalities and faiths. Consumerism is redefining lifestyles and aesthetics by blending components from all corners of the world. The increased mobility of people, goods and capital is taking us closer to a world of true meritocracy (a phenomenon that Thomas Friedman has called the 'flat world'[1]), and economic and ecological integration is helping dismantle localized structures that get in the way. Young people are especially quick to embrace new kinds of global identities, often at the expense of native traditions. At the same time, an appreciation of the exotic, colourful and novel aspects of Indian culture appears to be on the rise, owing to the influence of Indian cuisine, Bollywood, traditional music and dance, and so on. Indian spiritual capital enjoys a special place in the global quest for greater well-being, as evidenced by the popularity of yoga, meditation and Ayurvedic medicine in various forms and by the influence wielded by certain self-help gurus in popular culture. In fact, Americans invest enormous amounts of money in alternative health and spiritual practices of Indian origin.

All this leads many to conclude that the essential differences among civilizations no longer matter. A number of prominent critics have blamed religious, cultural, racial and national divisions for much of the violence and fragmentation that are destabilizing the world today. Identity differences are seen as tribal fidelities which must be diluted, and the boundaries that define them, removed.[2]

The arguments that distinct cultures should melt into something universal are expressed in theories which see modern societies as 'postmodern', 'post-racial', 'post-religious' and 'post-nationalistic'. These fashionable constructs seem to announce the arrival of a flat, secularized world that is not differentiated by collective histories, identities and religious points of view. The anti-modernity movement of the previous century was one such construct, its lofty goal being the rejection of Western aggression which had led to colonialism, genocide, two World Wars, Nazism and Communism. Anti-modernity offered little in the way of a positive affirmation of differences, and little understanding of why it might be valuable and desirable for differences to coexist harmoniously in the world.

What is misleading about the 'flat world' assumption is that, while superficial cultural elements from around the world do seem to have coalesced into a common global culture, the deeper structures that support the power and privilege of certain groups are stronger than ever before. Globalization is often framed in terms and structures that emerged under Western domination of the world in the past 500 years or so, and these in turn are founded on the values and beliefs that emerged from the unique historical and religious experience of the peoples of European origin. When all collective identities are discarded and all boundaries challenged – whether under the rubric of postmodern critique or as a result of a vague and undefined sense that 'all is one' and 'we're all fundamentally the same' – the result is not a world free from dominance but one in which the strongest identities *along with their versions of history and values* prevail.

Modern China offers a good counter-example to the claim that globalization necessarily means westernization, as it has asserted its distinctiveness while engaging with the world on its own terms. (I am not offering China as a model to follow in every respect but rather as an example of how a non-Western culture can represent itself successfully and autonomously in global discourse.) Prof. Weiming Tu of Harvard claims that Chinese civilization has its own distinct paradigm for modernity and globalization, and that this is by no means contingent on China's becoming westernized. In fact, there is a large movement among the Chinese to develop 'Confucian modernity', based, as the name implies, on Confucian ethics. Many Chinese thinkers are offering these and other ideas as alternatives to the well-known Protestant Ethic on which Western modernity was formulated by Max Weber.[3]

In this way, China positions itself and its ancient civilization as being on par with the West. This example shows that asserting difference does not necessarily mean isolation from the rest of the world or remaining hopelessly stuck in pre-modernity. The jury is still out on the broader implications of China's assertion and whether it will be sustainable, but at least it is demanding and receiving respect on its own terms without having to accept every Western standard. The Chinese example also shows that being different from the West does not mean having to bask in an idealized and ancient past.

At a recent conference, one prominent Western scholar criticized my talk on India's differences by saying that asserting those differences would both isolate India and inhibit it from becoming globalized and modern. I responded by stressing that being different need not mean being isolationist. Japan, for example, has preserved its distinct cultural norms and identity while remaining a major global economy, and France similarly has always asserted its language-based distinctiveness with pride. The Arab nations, too, have asserted their distinctive civilization while playing an active role on the world stage. I suggested that his worldview was Eurocentric, according to which only Western paradigms could serve as templates for the universal. Ironically, this scholar promotes Buddhism positively in the Western academy, so I reminded him that the spread of Buddhism emanated from India and did not involve colonizing the local cultures or other lands, nor was it some reversion to the past.[4]

Piercing the Pretence of Pluralism

Interfaith dialogue is one of the major venues in which the assertion that everyone is 'the same' is used to obscure important differences. I will now cite several examples from my own experience which show that essential religious assumptions and cosmologies are at the heart of the problems I am raising.

In the late 1990s, Prof. Karen Jo Torjesen, head of religious studies at Claremont Graduate University, invited me to the inauguration of a major interfaith initiative at her university. Claremont had decided to launch a programme in which every major world religion would be represented by a practitioner. At the same time, inter-religious dialogue and discussions would be encouraged in order to promote harmony among the world faiths. I was invited to speak on Hinduism and serve on the new initiative's Board of Advisors. Enthused at the prospect of working with peers from other religions, I accepted.

The inaugural event itself was a grand affair involving the university's top brass along with dignitaries from various religions and local communities. One of the highlights was the public endorsement by each representative of a statement written to resolve inter-religious tensions and foster better understanding among faiths. Each of the representatives endorsed the resolution which declared that there must be religious tolerance. When it was my turn to speak, I recommended that the term 'tolerance' in the resolution be replaced with the phrase 'mutual respect'. This elicited applause similar to that which had followed the remarks of the other speakers. Then I went on to explain the significance of this change and why this was not a matter of mere semantics.

As I noted, we 'tolerate' those we consider not good enough, but we do not extend our respect to them. 'Tolerance' implies control over those who do not conform to our norms by allowing them some, though not all, of the rights and privileges we enjoy. A religion which involves the worship of 'false gods' and whose adherents are referred to as 'heathens' can be tolerated, but it cannot be respected. Tolerance is a patronizing posture, whereas respect implies that we consider the other to be equally legitimate – a position which some religions routinely deny to others, instead declaring these 'others' to be 'idol worshippers' or 'infidels' and the like.

I wondered aloud if anyone in the audience would like to be told at the upcoming luncheon that he or she was being 'tolerated' at the table. No husband or wife would appreciate being told that his or her presence at home was being 'tolerated'. No self-respecting worker accepts mere tolerance from colleagues. Tolerance, in short, is an outright insult; it is simply not good enough. I pointed out that this notion of tolerance had emerged from religions built on exclusivist claims according to which other religions are false. Hence, tolerating them is the best one can do without undermining one's own claim to exclusivity.

Religious 'tolerance' was advocated in Europe after centuries of religious wars between adherents of the different denominations of Christianity. In many European countries, Churches functioned as religious monopolies according to which the mere practice of the 'wrong' religion was a criminal offence. 'Tolerance' was a positive attempt to quell the violence that had plagued Christianity for centuries in Europe, but it did not provide a genuine basis for real unity and cooperation, and so it often broke down.[5]

My talk was well-received by the audience; I noticed, though, that the speakers who had made a plea for tolerance were a bit aloof. Karen

Torjesen complimented me privately for 'opening up an important topic', one that was appropriate for discussion since 'this is an academic setting'. The following day, she enthusiastically thanked me for causing a 'sensation' and remarked that 'not everyone present could easily accept such a great idea' but that she herself was fully in agreement. It then occurred to me that I might have touched a nerve in the representatives of the Judeo-Christian religions. I decided to experiment with 'mutual respect' as a replacement for the oft-touted 'tolerance' in forthcoming talks and lectures.

My second major attempt at advocating mutual respect among religions came when Prof. Jane Marie Law, chair of the religion department at Cornell University, approached my foundation in the late 1990s to sponsor a world conference on ways to resolve religious violence. Each religion would be represented by its senior or prominent spokesperson, such as the Dalai Lama for Buddhism, well-known officials for each denomination of Christianity, and so on. According to the working draft of the conference paper, the conference would facilitate a joint and forceful condemnation of religious violence and endeavour to remove the tensions that give rise to it. (Such tall expectations are common in interfaith circles.)

I looked at the various examples of religious tension that were listed in the paper and wondered whether it was perhaps too simplistic to identify the 'victims' and the 'culprits' as they had done. I noticed that Islam was listed as a victim in one country but not as an aggressor in others. The same was true of Christianity: its representatives had lodged complaints against other religious groups in places such as East Timor, but there was silence concerning Christianity's own aggressive campaigns elsewhere. Later I realized that such asymmetrical representations are not uncommon in the academy, so I proposed to Prof. Law that we do some pre-conference preparation and research the deep-rooted causes of religious violence. My feeling was that all religious ideologies, without exception, should be open to serious investigation.

My foundation offered to fund a one-year research project in which graduate students at Cornell representing every major religion would closely scan the major books of every religion. They would highlight every line or statement that expressed contempt, intolerance or hatred against non-believers as well as other excluded and marginalized groups such as slaves, women, foreigners, and so on. Since religious violence often gains steam from such hateful speech contained in the very texts believers revere, the conference would endeavour to enumerate these offensive and questionable teachings and call for a resolution against them. In Hindu scriptures, for instance, all statements that are disparaging of 'lower' castes were to be placed on the list. Throughout the process, each religious delegation would have sufficient opportunity to make comments and resolve disagreements on specifics. I felt it would be a watershed event in the cessation of violence if the various religions agreed to discontinue such offensive teachings.

Prof. Law herself supported my proposal but was unsure about how the religious groups would feel; so she set about calling them to gauge their reactions. Some weeks later, she told me that merely raising my suggestion with certain religious heads (whom she did not name) had elicited considerable anger. They could not 'tolerate' the idea of outsiders meddling with their religious texts. These texts, after all, could never be altered nor declared invalid in any manner as they contained the words of God.

Disappointed that the project had stalled, I reiterated to Prof. Law that we would not ask for the offensive statements to be deleted. We would not try to edit the texts themselves but simply ask each religious delegation to declare that they and others under their influence should stop teaching the listed verses. We would not be 'tampering' with sacred scriptures, as some might fear, but emphasizing a less negative and ultimately more gracious interpretation of these texts. Surely God did not intend for his words to become the basis for violence.

But Prof. Law indicated that this, too, was unacceptable to the religious leaders. Especially in the case of the Abrahamic religions, the core texts could only be reinterpreted to revalidate them and not to find flaws of any kind. The podium, then, was to be dominated by the most politically savvy voices pointing fingers at others but refusing to offer up their own controversial beliefs for discussion and debate. I withdrew from the conference as it would not, in my opinion, have had a level playing field. In fact, it never took place.

Meanwhile, in my speaking engagements around the US, I began to tell others of my attempts to popularize 'mutual respect' in place of 'tolerance' and of my efforts to downplay offensive teachings against non-believers and other targeted groups. Soon several Hindu spiritual leaders started to discuss the need for mutual respect at interfaith meetings rather than mere tolerance.

The next big occasion that offered an opportunity to test my position was the United Nation's Millennium Religion Summit in 2000. This was a major gathering in New York City of hundreds of leaders from all religions. It was promoted as a pivotal event which would be a harbinger of harmony among all faiths in the new millennium. This goal was to be partly accomplished by the release of a resolution on the matter. Everything seemed to be going well until the last minute, when the *New York Times* reported serious disagreements over the final language of the resolution that was to be passed. A few days later, the Summit faced the prospect of a collapse with no resolution passed, prompting top UN officials to intervene in an attempt to try to break the impasse.

The Hindu delegation, led by Swami Dayananda Saraswati of the Hindu Dharma Acharya Sabha, had insisted that the term 'tolerance' in the draft be replaced with 'mutual respect'. However, the then representative of the Vatican, Cardinal Joseph Ratzinger, who is now Pope Benedict, had put his foot down in opposition to such a phrase. After all, if religions deemed 'heathen' were to start getting officially respected, there would be no justification for evangelizing and converting their adherents to Christianity. This would undermine the exclusive claims of Christianity which form the justification for the Church's large-scale proselytizing campaigns.

The matter reached a critical stage and there were media leaks that serious fighting had erupted between two factions demanding different terminology in the resolution. Swami Dayananda Saraswati held firm despite a great deal of pressure and the threat that his position would result in the collapse of the high-profile event. He was emphatic that the time had come for the non-Judeo-Christian religions to be formally respected as equals and not just tolerated by the 'religions of the book' (i.e., the three Abrahamic religions). At the very last minute, the Vatican blinked. Cardinal Ratzinger conceded and the resolution declared that all religions would agree to respect one another. This change was big news and was widely broadcast among the non-Abrahamic religions.

However, the matter did not end here. Within a month of the Millennium Summit's conclusion, presumably after an internal analysis of the consequence of this UN-affiliated resolution, the Vatican suddenly made an announcement which shocked liberal Catholic theologians.

The Vatican's *Congregation for the Doctrine of the Faith* (an office which was previously known as the *Inquisition*), responsible for formulating and enacting official Catholic doctrine, issued a new policy to address the issue of religious pluralism. The policy document, called *Dominus Jesus*, reaffirms the historic doctrine and mission of the exclusivity of the Church.[6] Paragraph 4 points out 'the danger to the Church of *relativistic theories which seek to justify religious pluralism....*' Paragraph 22 rejects the notion that one religion is as good as another, stating that while 'followers of other religions can receive divine grace, it is also certain that *objectively speaking* they are in a gravely deficient situation in comparison with those who, in the Church, have the fullness of the means of salvation'. Many religious scholars, including many liberal Christians who favour pluralism, condemned this doctrine, arguing that it was a step backward in the ongoing struggle to foster religious harmony.

My experiments in proposing mutual respect have also involved liberal Muslims. Soon after the events of 11 September 2001, there was a period of increased camaraderie among Hindu Americans and Muslim Americans from the Indian subcontinent. During a trip to Dallas, I was invited to a radio interview by a Pakistani who produced a weekly talk show. I used the opportunity to explain why mutual respect for religions was better than tolerance, and after my talk listeners were invited to call into the station to comment. One caller, later identified as a local Pakistani community leader, congratulated me and expressed complete agreement with my views: 'Rajiv ji', she said, 'we are delighted and honoured that you advocate mutual respect, which we as Muslims fully agree with.'

I was glad to hear this but wanted to make sure she was not merely being politically correct, so I elaborated, for her benefit, the ideas and practices of my faith which she had so heartily agreed to respect. I explained that in Hinduism there was no injunction against worshipping images of the divine (what the Abrahamic religions routinely and wrongly condemn as 'idolatry'). Indeed, I use images myself in my spiritual practice and felt glad that she had agreed to respect this practice. None of my practices, I reminded her, are being imposed on others. Mutual respect merely means that I am respected for my faith, with no compulsion for others to adopt or practise it. Furthermore, Hindus might view the divine in feminine form and believe in reincarnation rather than the notion of an eternal afterlife spent in either heaven or hell. I was clarifying what her promise of mutual respect entailed. The woman hung up.

I have found that people who represent Judeo-Christian faiths are also generally reluctant to reject the mutual respect principle publicly, and yet once the details of the non-Judeo-Christian religions are explained unapologetically, they feel uncomfortable, for deep down they know that their religion demands not only the rejection of such heretical practices and beliefs but their outright destruction.

In early 2007, I was invited to an event in Delhi where a visiting delegation from Emory University in the US was promoting their newly formed Inter-Religious Council.[7] It was a well-staged, professional presentation with all the right buzzwords about the new forum's potential to usher in religious harmony. The leaders from Emory were pleasant, friendly and well-intentioned. The audience in this case did not contribute anything that could deepen the discussion or go beyond the political correctness that is characteristic of such gatherings, so I raised my hand and started a discussion about some issues central to the objectives of such a forum. My first question was how Rev. Susan T. Henry-Crowe, Emory's dean of chapel and religious life and an ordained Lutheran minister herself,[8] was able to declare in such a forum that there was 'no religious difference among religions'. Was this denial caused by her anxiety in dealing with religious differences?

I wanted to know if she was advocating merely a one-sided sameness designed to encourage Hindus in the audience to conceive of their religion in 'generic/universal' terms, or whether this sameness was reciprocal, in which case it also applied to the dean's own Lutheran faith. I asked the dean if her work on the Inter-Religious Council was consistent and compatible with her preaching as a Lutheran minister, and she confidently replied that it was. So I made my question more specific: 'Is the Lutheran doctrine merely to "tolerate" other religions or also to *respect* them, and by respect I mean acknowledging them to be legitimate religions and equally valid paths to God?' She replied that this was 'an important question', one she had been 'thinking about' but which did not have 'easy answers'. In other words, she dodged the real issue, despite my persistent attempts to excavate the deep anxieties between religions.

As part of my homework for the meeting, I had researched the official policies of the Lutheran Church. After all, the dean could not in good faith be preaching one thing in church and representing something contradictory to people in India! I learned that Lutherans are *required* to believe that the Bible is the source of all revealed divine knowledge and that *it alone* (*sola scriptura*) is the final authority for all matters of faith and doctrine. Indeed, it is mandatory for a Lutheran minister to preach that the Bible is the only reliable guide for faith and practice. Lutheran theology demands, as a requirement for membership, the belief that Adam and Eve disobeyed God and that consequently all human beings are saddled with original sin, born sinful and unable to avoid committing sinful acts. Lutherans believe that original sin is the 'chief sin, a root and fountainhead of all actual sins'. This theology is formulated in the *Formula of Concord* (1577), regarded as the authoritative statement of Lutheran faith to this day. Lutherans insist that without divine intervention humans are not capable of doing any good works that can satisfy God's justice, because, no matter what they do, every human thought and deed is coloured by sin and sinful motives emanating from the original sin. Because of this, all humanity deserves eternal damnation in Hell – except, of course, those who are saved. Lutherans teach that salvation is possible only because of the grace of God expressed through Jesus' birth, life, suffering, death and resurrection.[9]

These formal teachings of her church would seem to make it impossible for the dean to *respect* Hinduism. It amazed me how easily the friendly dean could smile away and evade the Christian posture of exclusivity, one of the chief causes of disharmony among religions, while presenting herself as a champion of religious harmony. It is quite possible that she is indeed, as she suggested, torn between the belief that Christianity alone opens the door to salvation on the one hand and a desire for harmony with those belonging to so-called 'false' faiths on the other. The only way to begin to reconcile the underlying contradictions present in such inter-religious settings is to be explicit about the differences that are in fact crucial to Christianity. Many Hindus are either not knowledgeable about theological matters or too timid to probe, which in turn makes them susceptible to the sameness argument. Deception may not have been the goal of the Lutheran delegation, but it is a matter of record that disingenuous preachers in India have often used the pretence of sameness as a ploy to disarm and eventually convert others.

I continued with my questions: 'As a Lutheran minister, how do you perceive Hindu 'murtis' (sacred images) which are often referred to as "idols" by the church, and are there not official injunctions in your teachings against such idols?' 'Do you consider Krishna and Shiva to be God, or among the "false gods" condemned in the Bible?' 'How do you see the Hindu Goddess in the light of the church's claim that God is specifically masculine?' 'How do you see the Hindu concept of self as "sat-chit-ananda" (meaning inherently divine) in the light of the church's notion of the individual self as a "fallen sinner"?' The Emory University delegation deftly evaded every one of these questions.[10]

Such public forums will never resolve the complex, age-old incompatibilities of the world's religions (if there were easy solutions, the problems would have been solved long ago), but we can at least demand that their participants, who presumably are serious thinkers, face and address issues head-on and not cover up differences by pretence. There is today an entire movement built on the notion of sameness – fuelled by political correctness, ignorance and, in many cases, sheer dishonesty. We must tease out the real issues that lie beneath the mask of hypocrisy pervading most interfaith dialogues. Sameness cannot be one-sided: If X is the same as Y, Y must also be the same as X. But how many churches are willing to worship Krishna or Shiva as the same universal God described in the Bible? This gives us a pragmatic method for empirically testing the sameness claim in any instance.

The reactions of the Indians at the Emory presentation in Delhi were typical of most such audiences: lack of interest in examining the deeper issues, suspicion of the motives of those who dare to speak up, and unquestioning support for the proponents of unity and interfaith. At this and other interfaith meetings I've attended, the problem is always the same: speakers pay lip service to 'mutual respect' and 'underlying unity' while failing – or refusing – to grasp what these ideas might mean for some of their cherished beliefs. Consequently, many Hindu spiritual leaders are easily duped into imagining that true respect and unity are on the table (an offer they cannot refuse, so to speak).

Even when they are not overtly claiming sameness, Christians engaged in interfaith dialogue encourage their Hindu interlocutors to participate on the basis of this naive assumption, never spelling out the beliefs that could be contentious. In response to the increasing number of conflict-ridden situations emerging around the globe (especially among the Abrahamic religions themselves), Christians are recognizing the need for harmony and tolerance among religious traditions – if only to demonstrate their bona fides in promoting universal welfare. However, this attitude goes hand-in-hand with the conversion goals of most major denominations, especially once the targeted population has been disarmed by friendly intentions.

Only a minority of Christians agree with the idea of mutual respect while fully understanding what it entails. One such person is Janet Haag, editor of *Sacred Journey,* a Princeton-based journal published by an organization devoted to the unification of all religions through prayer. In 2008, she sought my support for her inter-religious programmes, and when I asked my favourite question – 'What is your policy on pluralism?' – she gave the predictable response: 'We tolerate other religions.' This prompted a discussion about mutual respect and how it was critical. Rather than becoming defensive or evasive, she indicated that this idea could add an important dimension to her work. Our conversation became the theme of her editorial in the following issue of her journal.

She wrote: 'In the course of our conversation about effective interfaith dialogue, he [Rajiv Malhotra] pointed out that we fall short in our efforts to promote true peace and understanding in this world when we settle for tolerance instead of making the paradigm shift to mutual respect. His remarks made me think a little more deeply about the distinctiveness between the words "tolerance" and "respect", and the values they represent.' Haag went on to explain that the Latin origin of 'tolerance' referred to enduring, which, though a laudable idea, did not connote mutual affirmation or support. '[The term] also implicitly suggests an imbalance of power in the relationship, with one of the parties in the position of giving or withholding permission for the other to be.' She then explained that the Latin word for respect meant holding someone in esteem and that the term 'presupposes we are equally worthy of honor. There is no room for arrogance and exclusivity in mutual respect.' She went on to summarize and endorse what I had explained to her.[11]

Difference: Anxiety or Mutual Respect?

The suggestion that difference must be seen as positive and be examined openly by all sides is often met with resistance from Indians and westerners alike. I call this resistance 'difference anxiety'. The term refers to the mental uneasiness caused by the perception of difference combined with a desire to diminish, conceal or eradicate it. Difference anxiety occurs in cultural and religious contexts frequently.

Such an anxiety seeks the relative comfort of homogeneous ideas, beliefs and identity. It runs counter to the natural world, where differences are inherent in the immense variety of animals, plants, flowers, seasons, rocks, and indeed at every level of the cosmos. I will argue that we must not try to erase differences but, rather, respect them – even celebrate them. First, however, these differences must be defined and acknowledged.

As a way of resolving difference, Western civilization is given to isolating the elements of other civilizations and placing them in its own conceptual categories – categories formulated by the 'white', 'Christian', and 'progressive' race. This categorization privileges the Western gaze and enables it to declare itself as the universal norm for others to emulate. It is a system for gaining control. On the flip side, many raised in dharmic cultures suffer anxieties related to being non-white, non-Western, non-Christian, and so on. Their identities are enhanced by imagining themselves in the colonizer's framework. One has become colonized when one starts to locate oneself in the colonizer's account of 'global history', 'universal ideas', language, myths, aesthetics, etc.

It is neither necessary nor desirable to highlight the differences from a position of superiority. Nor need the practice be isolationist. It is simply a way to learn from one another while serving as the basis for harmony and creative evolution. The cross-fertilization among cultures can be sustained longer than the merging of one into another. Indian traditions embody the approach of *difference with mutual respect* based on the radical idea that differences are not a problem to be solved. Differences are merely characteristic of the way things naturally are, and comfort with them is built into dharmic world views – views which encompass 'chaos', doubt and numerous other complexities.

When it comes from a position of superiority, difference anxiety becomes a motive for the more powerful civilization to dominate, assimilate, or even annihilate the less powerful one. When it stems from inferiority, there is psychological pressure to mimic the dominant culture and see oneself in terms of the dominant culture's categories.

Difference Anxiety from 'Above'

The history of the West is replete with assertions of supremacy based on religious, racial and economic factors. The reasons for this obsession with dominance have to do with the nature of the Judeo-Christian faiths and with a pervasive unease and emptiness which have afflicted Western culture for centuries. For the moment I simply want to show that the West reacts with extreme distress whenever there is resistance to its attempts at domination. This distress can become so acute that it motivates all kinds of unethical and duplicitous behaviour towards non-westerners. There are three main ways in which this distress or anxiety manifests itself:

- *Destruction* of the other through outright violence or forced conversions;
- *Isolation* of the other from the mainstream so that it no longer poses a threat; and
- *Inculturation*, which is a form of infiltration of the other's faith in order to dilute its difference and eventually digest it.

Central to the Christian faith is the assertion that the prophetic revelations of the Bible are exclusive and God-given and that the person of Christ is uniquely divine. A feeling of superiority of 'us' over 'them' is bolstered by the importance given to the chronological narrative of prophetic revelations that have resulted in one saviour and one canonized book. These in turn have given rise to a normative set of practices and beliefs which are interpreted and enforced by a powerful Church. This, the Christian project, is seen as a God-sanctioned franchise to bring about religious homogeneity worldwide. Difference anxiety on this scale frequently leads Western societies down the path of outright destruction of other cultures.[12]

But this destruction is only the most visible and dramatic expression of difference anxiety, and it does not pertain to India. Far more insidious are other expressions of difference anxiety, such as isolation, wherein the westerner appears to tolerate or even respect the difference of the other while actually refusing to engage with it. In this way, whole cultures and peoples – alive, active and with much to offer global culture – can be dismissed as old-fashioned, quaint or banal, or as offering little more than an opportunity for a museum exhibit.

A classic example of difference anxiety may be found in the thought and conduct of American philosopher Richard Rorty (1931–2007). A major exponent of postmodernism, Rorty exemplifies a particular kind of racist and condescending attitude emanating, in my view, from an underlying difference anxiety. According to him, India and its traditions of dharmic thought and metaphysical inquiry are so radically different from Western thinking as to be incomprehensible to westerners (and hence to all 'serious' philosophers and modern scientists).[13]

In her book *Cultural Otherness: Correspondence with Richard Rorty*,[14] the Indian philosopher Anindita Balslev makes a persistent attempt at a cross-cultural dialogue with Rorty. She seeks to uphold the assumption that Indian culture is both different from and equal to Western culture. But this is not agreeable to Rorty, who considers the study of Indian thought irrelevant to westerners. He calls his argument 'pragmatic' in that if such study 'doesn't make a difference to what *we* do, it makes no difference at all'.[15]

Rorty maintains that the West simply *cannot understand* the non-West given the disconnections between their respective worldviews. Hence the only option is to ignore those aspects of India that make it different. Any interaction between India and the West would be flawed, as their frameworks are mutually exclusive without any common categories for authentic discussions.

In the same dialogue, he proposes tolerating the differences 'from a distance', which, in effect, privileges Western thought as universal (a claim to which I shall return later in the book). This position justifies ignoring the universal potential of Indian thought. For Rorty, Indian philosophy is 'context-bound' (also discussed later) whereas 'Christian-scientific-technological thought' (a questionable hybrid in itself) is universal. Rorty says Western philosophers cannot take Indian philosophy seriously because 'the Christian-scientific-technological West' does not have the necessarily qualified persons, i.e., 'people who have some sense of the social institutions within which these texts were composed....'

Rorty is not alone here, though he is perhaps more frank about his attitude than most others. The patronizing attitude he expresses has led to the 'ghetto-izing' of Indian civilization into South Asian Studies and similar niches in the Western academy reserved for marginalized peoples.[16]

But Rorty ignores the Indian origins of many so-called Western ideas, a good example being the roots of many elements of modern mathematics which are used in Western science.[17] This is an Indian discipline which is well-understood and which has been assimilated into the West. Indian mathematical concepts of infinitesimal, infinity and infinite series were quarantined in Europe for more than a century as they were seen as heretical and threatening to the finite and controllable cosmos of the Bible. There are numerous similar examples of Indian civilization being selectively appropriated, and in fact, there is usually a cover-up of the Indian source by successive Western intellectuals once the digestion gets completed. When this was pointed out to him, Rorty would only say that 'the only premises common to all cultures are too banal to be of use'. And while he agrees in principle that non-Western cultures should be brought into dialogue, he does not know how such engagement could prove useful.[18]

What troubles Rorty is his inability to reduce the Indian elements to Western universals. Indeed, he is anxious, it would seem, about this irreducible difference. His assumption is that Western philosophy is universal whereas dharmic points of view are limited to strange and odd people, making communication between them virtually impossible. His approach is a ploy to avoid dealing with Indians' difference by declaring them to be incomprehensible. He seems to be saying: 'I cannot understand your accent or your language or your way of thinking, so I will simply ignore you.'

Rorty is a clear example of a person who deals with difference by refusing to engage. Refusal to engage is the exclusive privilege of the dominant partner in such a debate. No such luxury is afforded to those who are asked to accept claims of Western 'universalism'; they must either engage by accepting the terms of the debate established by the West or else continue to be excluded.

Another, perhaps even more insidious way of dealing with difference is for the dominant partner to pretend to adopt the ways and styles of the other – but only in order to disarm and bend the other to its will. This strategy has been practised repeatedly in Christian history in terms of conquest and conversion. In *The Conquest of America*, Tzvetan Todorov explains how the conquistador Hernán Cortés studied the natives for the purpose of erasing their difference:

> Schematically this behavior is organized into two phases. The first is that of interest in the other, at the cost of a certain empathy or temporary identification. Cortés slips into the other's skin ... Thereby he ensures himself an understanding of the other's language and a knowledge of the other's political organization ... But in so doing he has never abandoned his feeling of superiority; it is even his very capacity to understand the other that confirms him in that feeling. Then comes the second phase, during which he is not content to reassert his own identity (which he has never really abandoned), but proceeds to assimilate the Indians to his own world.[19]

Whatever the specifics in a given instance might be, the underlying drive stems from difference anxiety.

A different, somewhat more advanced and sophisticated version of this is practised by the Roman Catholic Church under the rubric of 'inculturation'. The term was first used to describe efforts to indoctrinate and proselytize societies outside the Jerusalem–Rome axis. Rather than risk replacing an entire way of life with another, missionaries cunningly allowed the natives to retain their cultural identities and practices while replacing their deities with Jesus and asserting that the Church was the ultimate authority on spirituality. Inculturation is well accepted in the Catholic tradition as a strategy for gaining entry into regions outside the West. Inculturation makes concessions to the target native culture for the sole purpose of spreading Christianity and not out of any genuine respect for difference. The Catholic Church in Latin America uses it to convert natives, and it has also been used successfully in Africa and India.[20] It is a way of 'tolerating' differences ostensibly while paving the way for the elimination of difference through conversion.

For centuries, church theologians and officials have debated and adjudicated hundreds of specific cases of inculturation experiments by enterprising missionaries in Africa, Latin America and Asia. They determined what to allow and what to ban. These rulings have official authority and are important in understanding how Christians must compete and expand market share through constant adaptation and self-correction.[21]

The inculturation process works in stages. At first, the native tradition is honoured by the missionaries. Some of the natives' practices and symbols are superficially adopted to make them feel proud that their heritage is being appreciated. The short-term intention is to make Christianity seem less alien and hence attractive to the natives. In the long term, however, the indigenous peoples are weaned away from the core of their religious identities. Their traditional identities eventually become an innocuous husk, their very meaning transformed into a pale reflection of Christianity. Once the new member is firmly placed in this ambiguous or hybrid religion, has burnt bridges with native traditions and become dependent on the church, the proverbial knife is twisted. In the case of Hinduism, the Hindu aspects are downplayed and the Christian aspects emphasized. This is done carefully after ensuring that the link with Hinduism is sufficiently softened and that the person's dependency on the missionaries is strong. Hinduism is not yet denigrated openly, but caste, dowry, female 'abuses' and other examples of 'backwardness' are emphasized as the defining qualities. In the final stage, Hinduism is openly blasted, and the person is turned into a solid Christian. It is only after analysing the long-term implications of this transformation that the treachery becomes apparent.

The most notable pioneer and prime exemplar of Christian inculturation was the Tuscan Jesuit missionary Roberto de Nobili (1577–1656), who came to south India in 1608. He proudly documents that he presented himself first as a sadhu (a spiritual man who has renounced worldly dependencies), and when that was found to limit his access to householders, he adopted the guise of a Kshatriya (warrior) in order to win peoples' trust. After a series of false starts and further experimentation, he assumed his most effective role, that of a Brahmin, complete with dhoti and three-stringed thread, which he said represented the Christian Trinity! He assiduously studied Sanskrit and Tamil, publicly adopted the rigorous lifestyle and simplicity of a Brahmin ascetic, and taught the Christian gospel dressed in words and ideas that were Hindu equivalents or approximations to Christianity. He succeeded in converting a large number of Hindus, even from the highest and most learned castes. During his life, the Vatican frequently disapproved of what it considered to be compromises with pure Christianity and closely followed his movements, but today his work is lauded by the Church as a role model for inculturation – even though it involved deception.[22]

In addition to wearing wooden sandals to conform to the Brahmin custom of avoiding leather shoes, he adopted Hindu symbols and customs such as the water pot, vegetarianism, the shaved head except for only a tuft of hair, and so on. He did so in order to enter into the hearts of Hindus with ease. Known as the 'Roman Brahmin', de Nobili had no qualms about faking his personal genealogy to bolster his authority – even to the point of claiming direct descent from Brahma! He even produced an authoritative 'fifth Veda' in which he proclaimed the truths of Christianity. By associating his Christianized Hinduism with the colonizer's supposedly superior civilization, he gave his converts the impression that they were embracing an *improved* version of their own traditions. Roberto de Nobili is mainly responsible for the present-day use of Hindu terms and personal names by south Indian Catholics, especially in Andhra Pradesh and Tamil Nadu. He adopted words like *kovil* (temple) in place of church, 'prasadam' (food offering) for communion, 'aiyar' (Shaiva brahmin) for Catholic priest, 'vedam' (Vedas) for the Bible, and 'puja' (worship) for mass. In imitation of Christ's twelve apostles, he claimed to have acquired twelve eminent Brahmins as his disciples. Ultimately, the only real obstacle that remained was his white complexion.[23]

Over time the Catholic Church expanded its policy of inculturation to accommodate not just non-Christian cultural symbols but also non-Christian religious sentiments. For instance, in 1939 Pope Pius XII reversed a long-standing Vatican injunction against the Chinese Christian custom of ancestor worship, declaring that this was not superstition but an honourable way of remembering ancestors. This type of inculturation pretends respect for other faiths while in fact seeking to prepare them for conversion.

In the Second Vatican Council (1962–65), the policy of inculturation was modified to encourage Indian Christians to pose as being faithful to local beliefs and sensibilities and declare the 'hidden Christ' at the right moment so that heathens would want to convert. Inculturation even led to the building of Hindu temple-like churches wherein Hindu symbols and paraphernalia were used. Christian priests roamed around in the guise of sadhus.

In the 1960s and '70s, dharma began to influence the popular imagination of westerners, and while some American fundamentalists believed then (as they do today) that yoga and meditation undermined Christianity, other Christians responded in a more opportunistic fashion. In the Western home market, the approach was to assimilate selectively those elements that could boost 'liberal' Christianity, which in effect meant mapping Indian spirituality onto biblical religions. This is, in effect, domesticating the pagan in order to remove the threat. At least a hundred quotations from the Vedas, the Yoga Sutras and the Upanishads have been incorporated into the 'Indian Bible' published by the Roman Catholic Church in 2008.[24] Breaking away from the Jesus who suffers, this Indianized Jesus is portrayed as assuming the tribhanga pose characteristic of Lord Krishna playing the flute. The pain and trauma on Jesus' face have been replaced by the ecstasy and joy normally associated with Krishna, Chaitanya Mahaprabhu or Nataraja. Jesus is shown surrounded by Hindu musical instruments traditionally used in 'bhajans', along with a 'tabla' (drum) and 'jalra' (cymbals) at his feet. The words 'He is dancing with joy' appear on the facing page. Such portrayals have the effect of making Indian Christians feel proud of their inherited cultures. On a more practical level, it provides continuity in their relationships with Hindu friends, relatives and neighbours.

A serious problem with Christian inculturation as practised in India is that it seeks to strip Hinduism of what Christians see as baggage, thereby secularizing the culture. This approach fails to take into account the fact that Hinduism consists of innumerable profoundly symbolic images, ceremonies, attitudes, rituals and customs which are fully intelligible only in the light of its core spiritual principles. One especially disturbing example of this stripping-away is the ongoing campaign to divest Bharatanatyam (classical dance) of its core Hindu identity so that its profound and highly codified aesthetics may be used for purposes of evangelization.[25]

Difference Anxiety from 'Below'

Difference anxiety is not confined to the dominant partner in a cultural or political encounter. Those who experience, whether consciously or unconsciously, their cultural identity as stemming from a position of weakness often bear the burden of erasing the differences in order to seem less strange, less inferior, or at least comprehensible within the dominant side's terms of reference.

Some of this behaviour is common to most societies and is internal to India itself. One finds, for instance, that in corporations, junior employees try to live up to the dress code and manners of their superiors, rather than the other way around. Indian village migrants who work as domestic servants in cities suffer from the anxiety of being seen as different from the middle class in language, manners and idiom, and try to imitate the employer who serves as the role model. But the reverse is not true and the attitude is not symmetrical: when the Indian urban elite go for an exotic holiday in a rural village, they are secure in their own identity and sense of superiority and are merely seeking a temporary 'experience'. They are not moved by any anxiety to become villagers.

Anxiety over faith-related differences can spill over into other kinds of differences. For example, the converted and those susceptible to conversion may become increasingly enamoured with Western cultural norms. As a result, some Indians take pride in being easily assimilated into white societies; they remove difference by mimicking white culture in exchange for upward mobility. The Louisiana governor Bobby Jindal (originally a Hindu named Piyush Jindal) and South Carolina congresswoman Nikki Haley (originally a Sikh named Nimrata Randhawa) are prominent examples of Indian–Americans who have converted to Christianity. Their conversion has had the desired effect of reducing their difference from mainstream white culture (and voters), the implication being that this is what it takes to advance in American politics. Many Indians have diluted their distinctiveness in order that westerners may find them less strange. This desire to manifest sameness occurs at levels both deep and superficial – in attempts to eliminate distinctions of dress, speech and self-presentation, especially in the business sphere, and in efforts to think, write and speak only in Western terms in all kinds of discourse, from political to cultural to academic. Such people may find this book's line of inquiry troubling since it perhaps exposes their difference anxiety and cultural inferiority complex.[26]

To cite another example, modelling schools all over India train small-town girls to look less ethnically Indian by changing their body language and dress, speaking English without an Indian accent, and so on. This training is advertised as a way of boosting their matrimonial prospects and professional opportunities. Matrimonial columns in Indian newspapers are filled with descriptions of persons being fair-skinned – if not white, then at least 'wheatish'. Skin creams are sold on the claim that they will make a person fairer. Indian call-centres train employees specifically to remove Indian accents, names and identities, and to replace these with Western-sounding names. Some are even instructed to assume American interests such as claiming to be a fan of the Dallas Cowboys football team, and so forth.

Most people would acknowledge (in theory if not in practice) that aesthetic tensions across cultures are not based on any intrinsic or absolute superiority but rather are shaped by the prevailing power structure of a given time and place. India's Ajanta caves show light-skinned and dark-skinned persons together who appear to be in a non-hierarchical relationship, demonstrating that these are not absolute aesthetic values of superiority/inferiority. Similarly, the plump, pale-skinned women used as models in European Renaissance paintings are not considered alluring by Madison Avenue standards, because slender, sun-tanned bodies are associated with success today.

An Indian is more likely to feel anxious eating with his hands in a Western gathering than a westerner would feel in using silverware at a traditional Indian gathering. Indians are often anxious about their unfamiliarity with other Western cultural norms such as the correct way to wear a necktie or what to order at a fancy Western restaurant, whereas the more confident westerner feels relatively less anxious in situations where the roles are reversed and he is in a traditional Indian setting. It is all right for a westerner to be different amidst Indians (his difference can even give him a position of privilege), but it can be a serious source of anxiety for an Indian to find himself looking and acting different in a Western setting. Once a westerner sets the tone of informality, many an anxious Indian will quickly follow suit, but not until the westerner has taken the lead.

Another example of mimicry from below is that of Hindu gurus who have become 'global' often by diluting their traditions to make them more widely appealing. They claim that all religions are the same when they ought to be saying that religions are *equal but different*. This mimicry, especially of Judeo-Christianity, started during colonial rule when Hindu leaders started to mutate and adapt their traditions in order to accommodate European sensibilities. I will expand on this point later.

White Americans who consider themselves Hindu face a double anxiety of being different. Indian Hindus often find them peculiar, and this is unfortunate because many of them are very sincere in their practice and could be of immense value in explaining Hinduism to the broader society. At the same time, they face prejudices in their own peer groups of Americans who find it disconcerting that they have turned 'native'. This makes them feel a sort of difference anxiety outside the confines of an ashram or community consisting of others like them. Eventually the combination of these anxieties can induce them to return to the Judeo-Christian identity in a way that erases or denies their Hindu experience and obscures their debt to Indian sources.

While the reverse is also true in that many westerners wear traditional Indian clothes and enjoy Indian cuisine and culture, it is important to note that they do not do so with the psychological attitude of inferiority about their own civilization identity, and the motive is seldom to boost their status. When white American youth adopted the Mohawk hairstyle, it was a fashion. It was not intended to resolve a feeling of inferiority to Mohawks, nor was it meant to impress any Mohawks in securing a job, visa or travel grant. American sports teams are often named in reference to Native Americans (such as the 'Washington Redskins' and the 'Cleveland Indians') to celebrate the natives as a sort of ornament or trophy, and not out of love or concern for them.

For a genuine parallel, however, we have to imagine a hypothetical scenario in which China, for instance, comes to dominate the world economically and culturally. Imagine westerners, driven by difference anxiety from below, not only learning Mandarin and becoming embarrassed when caught speaking English in public but emulating Chinese looks, mannerisms and etiquette, perhaps even undergoing plastic surgery to look 'the same' as the Chinese.

Digestion and Assimilation

There is a way of dealing with difference anxiety that is especially dangerous, in part because it is largely invisible. This approach shares many aspects of the strategies discussed above and is in part a consequence of them. I refer to the *digestion* of one culture by another carried out under the guise of a desire to assimilate, reduce difference, and assert sameness in place of the less dominant culture. At the level of popular culture, India and the West may meet as equals, but at the deeper levels, where the core assumptions of a civilization reside, the playing field is tilted. Cultural appropriation gives a false impression of equalization. The less powerful culture is assimilated into the dominant one in such a way that:

1. the dominant civilization dismembers the weaker one into parts from which it picks and chooses which pieces it wants to appropriate;

2. these appropriated elements get mapped onto the language and social structures of the dominant civilization's own history and paradigms, leaving little if any trace of the links to the source tradition;

3. the civilization that was thus mined gets depleted of its cultural and social capital because the appropriated elements are modified to fit the dominant civilization's own history, and these elements are shown to be disconnected from, and even in conflict with, the source civilization; and

4. the depleted civilization enters the proverbial museum as yet another dead culture, ceasing to pose a threat to the dominant one.

After being digested, what is left of a civilization is waste material to be removed and destroyed. The erasure of differences is what makes a culture vulnerable to becoming digested and remade in the image of the host's DNA, as it were.[27] The dominant side superimposes its concepts, aesthetics, language, paradigms, historical template, and philosophy from above, positioning them as the universal worldview. At the same time, the images, symbols, histories and languages of the weaker culture get absorbed, with inevitable distortion, into the dominant one.

There is a counter-argument to this claim which states that the host civilization itself (the West in this case) undergoes mutation as a result of digesting another civilization.[28] Nevertheless, the enhancement of the predator civilization and corresponding depletion of the civilization being preyed upon are interpreted by many historians as the march of world civilization – with the West positioned both at the centre of the world and as the engine driving humanity forward.[29] Non-Western civilizations are considered relevant only as sources of Western civilization (as in 'our past') or as theatres in which the West operates ('our civilizing mission') or as threats to Western interests ('our frontiers'). The interests and identities of those cultures that get digested are of little consequence.[30]

Besides the obvious racism inherent in such arguments, there is the collective loss of human diversity. In harvesting the fruits of other civilizations, the West has also destroyed its roots, thereby killing their ability to produce more bountiful harvests. The elements appropriated are terminal, because the residual skeletons of the digested civilizations are incapable of further creative evolution and contributions. Just as the non-West bequeathed gifts that have already enriched the world (even though, in most cases, these have been reclassified as Western history and progress), there is a great deal more that *would have been* produced from those sources had they not been digested.

We have seen how one means by which a dominant party resolves its difference anxiety is through digestion – much as a predator consumes another as food. The following chart shows the various processes at work. The digestion is analogous to the food consumed by a host in that what is useful gets assimilated into the host while what does not fit the host's structure gets eliminated as waste. The result is that the source tradition, similar the food, ceases to exist, and the host (i.e., the West) gets strengthened. The overall diversity of cultures suffers, because there is greater homogeneity as a result of the loss of the source tradition.

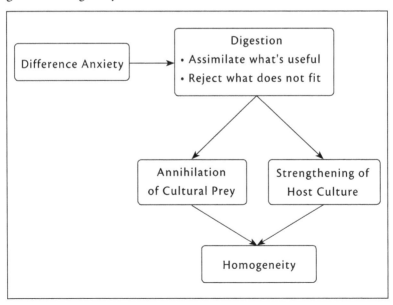

False Resolutions of Difference Anxiety

Dharma and Sameness

Many Indians have internalized the fears that difference causes violence and begun to feel guilty about their own difference from the West. They recoil against religious violence by gravitating towards 'sameness' and diluting their own identities. The Indian elite especially feel comfortable with the 'clean' Westernized version of Hinduism which sameness presents (as was the case in colonial times).

There are a number of philosophical and spiritual stances in the dharma traditions which would seem, on the surface, to agree with this doctrine of 'sameness'. [31] For example, the basic Vedantic proposition that there is only One Reality has caused considerable confusion among those who are drawn to its outlook. 'Oneness' is sometimes cited as if it meant the denial of all difference, but Vedanta actually asserts that there are both the 'One' and the 'many forms of the One' which comprise our cosmos in its infinite diversity. The ultimate or absolute reality is indeed One, but with an internal structure that is understood as a relative reality. While this relative reality does not exist separately by itself and is contingent on the absolute One, it cannot be dismissed as non-existent. For it is in this relative realm that not only karma (the consequences of past actions) but also dharma (the walking of a true path) are manifested and carried out. This relative reality is not pure illusion. Both levels of reality are important, and the relative point of view makes ethical and even political demands on the practitioner.

It is a misinterpretation of Vedanta to say that, since the existence of our world is only relative and not absolute, no worldly outcomes should matter. In truth, no school of dharma calls for the abandonment of the relative world, and every school of dharma encourages responsible action without attachments to the rewards. This is the central theme of the Bhagavadgita, one of the most sacred scriptures of dharma, in which Krishna educates Arjuna not to escape responsibility in this relative world. If differences did not exist in the relative reality, there would be no ethics, because dharma and adharma (valid and invalid ethical conduct) would be viewed with indifference. Often there is a hierarchy of degrees of validity assigned to various forms of conduct, and certainly they are not considered the same. The idea that everything is the same cannot be used to guide our actions in this relative world. Thus, the naive principle of sameness violates dharma teachings which clearly differentiate between 'sat' (truth) and 'asat' (falsity); 'daivika' (the divine) and 'asuric' (the demonic).

Such misunderstanding of dharma is a common safe haven for the many Hindus suffering from difference anxiety and may stem from ignorance of dharma or fear of being associated with 'the Hindu Right' or merely the pressure to be politically correct. Such Hindus approach difference as unreal and the problem itself as illusory, hence as something to ignore. In practice, this passive posture leads to the dilution, distortion and eventual digestion of their dharma.

Indians who misunderstand the teachings of Vedanta are inclined to interpret the Christian mission, especially in the form of inculturation or tolerance, as a form of respect for Hinduism and acceptance of its truth. When a Christian adopts the guise of a Hindu and approaches a Hindu community, Hindus tend to see this as an honest acknowledgement of sameness, and so they respond openly, dropping their guard despite the centuries of duplicity under which they have suffered. This is where the real danger lies – in fooling Hindus into believing there is a level playing field, or even that there is no competitive motive at all.

Simply because the Christian evangelist comes looking like a Hindu and uses Sanskrit terms, Hindu symbolism and gestures, the Hindu assumes that he also accepts Krishna, Shiva and Devi as manifestations of the Supreme Being. The Hindu naively assumes that the Christian considers puja to be a valid prayer service on par with his own biblical prayer, that the Christian respects the murtis as sacred, and that he regards the gurus as enlightened and not just 'wise teachers'. But the hard reality is that most Christian denominations forbid their followers to validate even Judaism or Islam, much less Hinduism or Buddhism.

Among other things, to espouse sameness with Hinduism would be a violation of core Christian injunctions against idol worship and 'false gods' – injunctions which are mandatory conditions for membership at least in the major denominations. Espousing sameness would entail many other revisions as well, including what I call history-centrism (described in Chapter 2) and the mandate to proselytize and convert, as commonly understood. Moreover, it would undermine the fundamental mandates of the Christian Church, namely, the requirement that Jesus be accepted as the literal and only son of God, the belief that Adam and Eve's original sin condemned all humanity to eternal damnation, the mission to convert all humanity, and the demonizing of the religious images of other faiths.

Christian proselytizers deploy inculturation to give the *appearance* that they embrace sameness whereas what they truly believe is that the dharma traditions are illegitimate. If they truly believed in sameness among religions and cultures, there would be no need to convert, since Hindus, Buddhists and Jains would no longer be regarded as heathens. But this would dilute the political power of Christianity and threaten even the survival of institutionalized Christianity. It would make it legitimate for Christians to adopt dharma traditions formally, given that almost every spiritual practice and metaphysical doctrine of Christianity that is prized today has an equivalent available within the dharma traditions. And it would render untenable the Church's claim to be the exclusive bearer of a sacred history that must envelope all peoples of the world as the prerequisite for the Second Coming of Christ.

The assertion of some vaguely Hindu 'sameness' of all religions is a one-way street which perniciously pushes the dharmic traditions towards dilution and assimilation; indeed, this process may lead to their eventual digestion into the belly of expansive institutionalized religions. To give only one example (which I discuss at length in my writings on 'U-turn Theory'), Patanjali's Yoga Sutras, the seminal ancient text of the profound philosophy and psychology on which yoga is based, is in some quarters being reduced to a set of footnotes to the Gospel of John or else treated as a primitive form of Western cognitive science.

When Western seekers enter the Indian spiritual arena, they tend to slip into the common misperceptions about Vedanta noted above and over-prize what is the 'same' in the various religions, conveniently overlooking the very real (and valuable) differences. But the western seeker does not approach this task with a clean slate; there has been past conditioning as a result of his or her collective identity as Jewish,

Christian, or secular. This is an important point that cannot be emphasized enough: the Westerner's mental framework is already wired for certain values, attitudes and categories. Therefore what is termed 'universal' is in effect largely Western in disguise. We shall see how all this leads to contradictions and blockages across various cultures.

Postmodern Evasiveness

Difference and sameness also figure in discourses on postmodernism, a philosophical trend in Western academics to which both secular Indian intellectuals and spiritually inclined Indians are drawn.

Postmodernism has made it fashionable to deconstruct what its adherents called the 'grand narratives' of history, seeing these as little more than the stories of the triumph of Western progress which was largely achieved by suppressing or violently overthrowing other groups. More problematically, postmodernists advocate that *all* identities be dismantled or blurred and view all positively distinctive cultures as being oppressive to weaker or less assertive ones.

This idea might at first seem reasonable, especially when viewed through a postcolonial or subaltern lens, but it opens the door to a pervasive cynicism and narrowness of vision with no workable criteria of value in aesthetics, politics or philosophy. The postmodern insistence on denying such identities as Indian and Western leaves non-Western cultures vulnerable to even further exploitation because they are denied the security of possessing a difference which is real and defensible. Postmodernism, then, tends to undermine the particular reality of the non-Western culture that might be in need of being affirmed, protected and developed. The type of Indian distinctiveness I shall propose is not affected by the problems posed by postmodernists, because (i) it is not based on historical exclusiveness or superiority, be it religious or otherwise, (ii) it makes no claims of finality of knowledge, and (iii) it has no mandate to impose on others.

Many popular writers have adopted the postmodern stance and assumed that today's America exemplifies a society in which hybrid cultures are blurring identities and making all boundaries obsolete. America, according to this view, is on its way to becoming a society free from difference anxiety, because American society is becoming freed from its chauvinistic grand narratives.

But beneath the veneer of popular culture, the foundation of the West, especially with respect to its Judeo-Christian roots, remains largely unchanged. In the Western institutions where power resides, one finds little evidence of boundaries being erased. For instance, the US government's foreign policy is designed to retain superiority and protect what is specifically in its interests. Corporate multinationals fight for market share and maximize their shareholder profits and valuations much in the manner of playing to win a competitive game. Churches fight for 'soul share', not just among denominations but more ferociously in the heathen-filled Third World. Postmodern scholars would do well to go beyond the analysis of pop culture and abstract patterns and attempt to deconstruct the oppressive Western institutions of government, business and Christianity, where the power structure really resides. American socio-political unity has been achieved and maintained from the beginning through a frontier mentality which has always needed an outsider to annex and then effectively eliminate.[32]

Furthermore, the American melting pot has essentially reduced the human being to an interchangeable economic unit – one that may adopt, mix and discard cultural traits as a matter of individual choice. This lures the weaker cultural groups to dissolve into the melting pot, which ironically makes them more vulnerable to the power-hungry groups that retain their superiority. Indeed, when individuals are rendered isolated, rootless and self-centred, the strongly committed power groups such as the evangelical movement or elite financial interests step in to offer direction. Such groups exert tremendous power over both domestic and foreign policy while pretending to be the keepers of multiculturalism. The London-based cultural critic Ziauddin Sardar points out that the postmodern criticism of nation states and their related identities actually empowers imperialism insofar as it 'softens the prey' on behalf of the predator empires by advocating the abandonment of distinctiveness in a one-sided manner. This is so because the West does not practise what it exports. The call to abandon distinctiveness is propagated and promoted through a network of intellectuals in the Third World nurtured and sustained by the First World.[33]

Postmodern philosophers have pointed out that such claims of universalism are in fact parochial and arrogant views of what is actually only one cultural tradition among many. It is perhaps a paradox that the West is simultaneously protecting itself by rewriting its story in a new and renewed chauvinistic mode in which deconstruction itself is seen as the culmination and fruit of its long, singular and ineffably superior philosophical trajectory.

Without an outside perspective on the Western mentalities they seek to deconstruct, the critiques assume an unfolding consciousness in which westerners are the leaders and agents. They tend to project their latest theories back into Western intellectual history, thereby enhancing the Western collective identity rather than dissolving it. Although it decries identity, postmodernism is thus itself the product of a history that has been shaped by particular attitudes towards difference and that marginalize Indian traditions.

The power of the USA and the European Union remains unaffected by the fringe activities of its own liberal postmodern scholars. Ironically, many of the 'leftist radicals' of the counterculture in France and the US later became neo-conservatives – because of the temptations of the marketplace and because the sacrifices required by the left proved unsustainable. Only a few years after participating in strikes and anti-war and civil liberties marches, these radicals found themselves calling for the defence of Judeo-Christian civilization and advocating aggressive but selective humanitarian intervention into other countries. The US military has used liberal social scientists to foment conflict in countries such as Chile and, more recently, Iraq. In fact, much of the research into foreign 'area studies' is done by liberal scholars and ends up serving the interests of the state and/or church.[34] At the same time, the West is secure in its sense of history and identity, and that is because postmodernist thinking in the West is limited to academic cocoons and applied mainly to pop culture.

India's postmodernist scholars who brag about their Western training and connections are encouraged to deconstruct Indian civilization, showing it to be a scourge against the oppressed. The deconstruction of India by Indian thinkers has a destabilizing effect which invites a new kind of colonialism. The most fashionable kind of difference being championed by Indian postmodernists is of the subalterns 'from below', seen as the oppressed underclass. But many of these oppressed minorities have been taken over by global nexuses (churches, Chinese Maoists and Islamists, to name only the major ones) with the result that they are not truly autonomous and independent but satellites serving a new kind of remote-controlled colonialism. Thus, the postmodern posture on difference has had the overall effect of causing native cultural identities to become vulnerable to imperialism – which is exactly the opposite of what the postmodernists claim they want to achieve. This is a serious topic of inquiry outside the scope of this book and which I cover in my book *Breaking India*.[35]

Postmodern deconstruction facilitates the digestion of dharma into the West by disassembling it into a library of random, unrelated components similar to the way clip art is clicked and dragged as useful additions to proprietary frameworks. Some scholars take these components apart so as to de-contextualize them from the rest of the dharma tradition, thereby enabling them to be digested or destroyed selectively. The digestion of Indian civilization by the West is encouraged by arguments that there is no such thing as an Indian civilization, the claim being that the 'Indian' is a construct given, as it were, by the British.[36]

Postmodernism resembles dharma philosophies in several ways. Both, for example, are frameworks for the deconstruction of identity. Also, both approaches share the notion that all concepts are mental constructions which are ultimately empty or devoid of self-existence. Many of the postmodern thinkers have been influenced by these Indian traditions. But there is at least one important difference: Dharma deconstructs the individual ego whereas postmodernism deconstructs the collective cultural identity. Furthermore, postmodernism lacks the yoga of the dharma traditions as a means to achieve a state of consciousness transcending differences experientially. This process is far more challenging than merely a matter of discursive deconstruction as an intellectual exercise. The end-state of postmodernist deconstruction is one of nihilism or indifference. In other words, after deconstructing the meta-narratives of the dominant culture, nothing is left to put in their place, whereas in the Indian approach of 'purva paksha' (defined in the next section), the dharmic notions of selfhood would provide the foundation for a positive existence. This fall into nihilism and indifference can be prevented by utilizing the crucial potential of the dharmic traditions in challenging the Western assumptions.

The table that follows summarizes my responses to a number of issues raised during my discussions with various individuals, including Judeo-Christian, secular westerners and leaders of dharma.

Posture based on Difference Anxiety	My Counter Arguments
Mine is the only one true religion and everyone should convert to it.	This attitude stems from the exclusivism of the Judeo-Christian religions. Indian spirituality not only allows religious pluralism but is built on it.
Religious tolerance shows how good we are towards other religions.	Tolerance is a patronizing way to say that the other's faith is bogus. It is a posture of condescension and an accommodation due to political pressures. We need mutual respect. To respect someone's faith implies that it is seen as legitimate for that person.
Inculturation shows respect for native Indian culture.	It is deception used to gain easy entry. The strategy is to subvert the native faith.
Indian thought is incomprehensible to westerners, hence useless and ignorable.	This is a false assumption meant to retain Western domination in philosophy.
Equality demands that we erase difference.	Only by respecting difference can there be true equality. Indians' mimicry of white/Western culture does not bring equality but servility.
Remaining different would isolate a people from globalization.	People can be different and yet be positively engaged with others, as in the examples of diverse cuisines, women's rights and US black culture.

Difference causes tensions, so we must become the same in order to end tensions.	Difference that is based on supremacy *does* cause tensions, but difference built on unity-in-diversity and harmony does not.
Difference leads to moral relativism and escapism.	Later chapters explain how context-based ethics work while respecting difference.
Cross-cultural fertilization is good and that is why fusion into a single global culture is natural.	Diversity brings deeper cross-cultural fertilization which is sustainable in the long run. Erasing difference will relocate Indian civilization in museums, ending the cross-cultural fertilization, as has happened in the case of Native Americans.
Advaita Vedanta says that everything is One, so why bother with difference.	The relative realm of our existence and actions is based on difference, and the escapist attitude to shun responsibility is not condoned by Vedanta.
Western liberalism has already embraced difference.	In Western liberalism, religious diversity does not enjoy the same place as racial and gender diversity. Religious tolerance is disrespectful of difference. The other common policy is the sameness of all faiths, which dilutes their difference.
Secularism represents progress as defined by the trajectory of Western history.	The West's historical experience is not universal. Forcing all civilizations to follow the West does not bring humanity the benefits of others' experiences.
Hindutva ideology asserts difference the Indian way.	It is too political and reactionary, and has adopted some Western approaches to difference such as emphasis on a unique history.

Purva Paksha: Reversing the Gaze

It is through Western categories, and hence the Western 'gaze', that the people who constitute the Judeo-Christian traditions see the world. This gives the Western perspective a de facto status as arbiter of what is considered universally true. When another civilization is the object of such a gaze, it becomes relative and no longer universal. Indeed, its depiction as the alien makes it interesting precisely *because* it is particular and not universal. Quite apart from the problems already discussed, the universalist pose (which I discuss at greater length in Chapter 6) and the failure to experience itself through different eyes leave westerners themselves blind to their own limitations, failures, idiosyncrasies, peculiarities and exotica. As long as one remains in the privileged position of subject, looking at others and not being gazed at oneself, one can assume that one's positions and assumptions represent the universal norm.

The corrective to this problem in my view is the ancient and powerful Indian practice of 'purva paksha'. This is the traditional dharmic approach to rival schools. It is a dialectical approach, taking a thesis by an opponent ('purva pakshin') and then providing its rebuttal ('khandana') so as to establish the protagonist's views ('siddhanta'). The purva paksha tradition required any debater first to argue from the perspective of his opponent in order to test the validity of his understanding of the opposing position, and from there to realize his own shortcomings. Only after perfecting his understanding of opposing views would he be qualified to refute them. Such debates encourage individuals to maintain flexibility of perspective and honesty rather than seek victory egotistically. In this way, the dialectical process ensures a genuine and far-reaching shift in the individual.

This requires direct but respectful confrontation with one's opponent in debate. In purva paksha one does not look away, so to speak, from real differences but attempts to clarify them, without anxiety but also without the pretence of sameness. There is more to this practice than meets the eye. It involves not only a firm intent but considerable self-mastery (i.e., a movement beyond ego) combined with an understanding of the magnitude of the issues at stake. Reversing the gaze in purva paksha is not painless, and resistance is to be expected.

This method was extensively applied among various schools of Hinduism, Buddhism and Jainism lineages. There are hundreds of volumes of transcripts of these intense debates, and they comprise an important part of the heritage of the dharmic traditions. Advanced training in various schools of Indian philosophy includes a close study of these debates because it was through the purva paksha of the past that each school sharpened itself and evolved over time.

Unfortunately, this tradition was not operative when Islam, Christianity and the European Enlightenment entered India. Rather than engaging in purva paksha with Islam and Christianity, or more recently with Marxism and secularism, the dharmic philosophers tended simply to ignore these foreign entries or else defer to them by adopting the attitude that 'all is one'. This stance, a misreading of the dharmic teachings, became an excuse for abandoning purva paksha, for if there are no differences, there is nothing important at which to gaze. The purva paksha method of engagement can engender sympathy as well as distance, understanding as well as critique. It must, however, retain several qualities not often found today: direct confrontation, clarification of difference, and an assumption of equality. Purva paksha should take place with transparency in as open a forum as possible and in such a way as to benefit each party. Acceptance of the need and potential for change should be a baseline from which to work.

Reversing the gaze in this way should not be confused as 'tit for tat' or 'turning the tables'. Nor is it to be confused with the internal critiques of the West – there are a plethora of those but they are performed from within the West's own closed categories and vested interests. The issue here is not the merits and demerits of the West but the kind of gaze being applied to it. The shift in world power – both financial and political, caused by the rise of China, India and pan-Islam – is already threatening the West's supremacy and self-confidence. This trend, which is likely to continue, underscores the need for the kinds of gaze-reversal and widening of perspectives I am proposing.

Each side has strengths as well as limitations, and these cannot be addressed without each side subjecting itself to the gaze of the other.

The more level, clear and direct the gaze is, the better. Once these differences are understood and refined, we can embark on much more honest, fruitful and productive forms of cultural interaction. Any such programme must, in my view, include:

- a recognition and reduction of difference anxiety on both sides;
- a willingness to articulate and understand major differences both in terms of philosophical/theological debates and actions;
- some negotiation of the thorny issues of history-centrism, exclusivism and aggressive conversion in the West;
- a less passive attitude towards real world issues and religious differences on the part of dharmic practitioners, and a greater direct engagement in discussing the profound differences; and
- an understanding of the need to reform and correct the self-aggrandizing and self-referential institutional networks that produce cultural analysis, including academic institutions, foundations, the media, and publishers.

The kind of respectful, engaged confrontation purva paksha entails is not unprecedented in philosophy or sociology. There is much that dharma scholars can learn from the way other civilizations have attempted to reverse the gaze and look directly at the West from their respective positions. For example, in the 1950s, during Algeria's war of independence from colonial rule, Algerian activist Franz Fanon (1925–61) wrote an influential book on pan-African consciousness titled *The Wretched of the Earth*. In it he makes the point that '(the) colonialist bourgeoisie ... had in fact deeply implanted in the minds of the colonized intellectual [the idea] that the essential qualities remain eternal in spite of all the blunders men may make: the essential qualities of the West, of course.' When Jean-Paul Sartre, the French philosopher of existentialism, read and reviewed Fanon's book, he became acutely conscious of this gaze reversal and its effects.

Edward Said, in his book *Orientalism*, was practising a form of purva paksha when he described in detail how the modern West is a fabricated identity based on its study of others and emphasized the encounter with Arab and Islamic civilizations.[37] That book, highly controversial when it was published in 1978, went on to launch a whole speciality of postcolonial studies in which many Third World scholars joined their white peers to turn their gaze back on the West. Similarly, the Chinese have been gazing at the West for centuries, and there is an extensive literature in Mandarin written from this perspective. Chinese emperors and governments for several centuries funded the translations of important European thinkers into Mandarin specifically for the purpose of understanding the West on Chinese terms.

Indians, on the other hand, undertook no such large-scale study of the West. Starting in the Mughal era, India had sufficient wealth and military power to be able to engage the Europeans who came in small numbers, first as traders. But for a variety of reasons specific to Indian history of that era and which are beyond the scope of this book, Indian rulers did not pursue the serious study of the Europeans on Indian terms. On the contrary, they felt honoured that they were being studied by the West, as if this meant that Indians had become important in the eyes of superior people. The pride which Indians experience whenever the West directs its gaze at them persists even today. They interpret the attention as appreciation of their broad-mindedness, progressiveness, secularism, and so forth.

It is doubly important for Indians and representatives of dharma to challenge the Western view of other civilizations, first by understanding the dharmic point of view on its own terms and then by examining the West from that perspective. There may be some inherent asymmetry in the method, for in this reverse gazing we focus on the highest and best resources available on the dharma side and utilize these in analysing the most fundamental problems on the other side. Still, there is merit in this approach, since it both clears up profound misconceptions (even among Indians) about the dharmic path and unearths and challenges the assumptions buried deep in the Western psyche.

There have been sporadic attempts at using dharmic categories to contest the Western gaze and gaze back, as it were, even though these were not quite purva paksha as I am defining it. For instance, in the 1990s, anthropologist McKim Marriott, in his anthology of academic conference papers, refers to the importance of developing and deploying Indian categories of social thought and analysis, not only to understand the subcontinent better but to refine, develop and render less parochial the study of various cultures in general.[38] Marriott emphasizes how distorting and limiting Western universalism can be, and goes on to note that common distinctions in the West, such as Marx's opposition between material base and superstructure, and Durkheim's separation between sacred and profane, cannot capture the fluid and complex realities one finds in dharmic civilizations. He also points out that the West's constant search for an elusive stability is based on the presupposition that all societies are prepared to accept European and American notions of order rather than other, more fluid categories of social and political identity.

A similar example may be found in the work of A.K. Ramanujan.[39] Ramanujan writes of the limitations of Western ethics by looking at them from an Indian point of view. To see Immanuel Kant (the German Enlightenment philosopher) from the perspective of Manu (the Indian codifier of ethics), for instance, throws into high relief the oddness and inapplicability of the former's 'categorical imperative' and indeed of the whole Western discourse on ethics that tries to remain context-free. (This is discussed extensively in Chapter 4.) Ronald Inden's famous book *Imagining India* (1990) also makes an important contribution by arguing that various ideas and constructs commonly used to describe India are the result of colonialism and that Indian intellectuals have continued down the same path of importing Western theories and applying them to India.

In a related vein, other examples could be cited, but there is a caveat. I have observed that Western anthropologists often seem to be practising something like purva paksha when they 'suspend' their posture of difference as a way of immersing themselves, if only temporarily, in the non-Western culture (or at least to give that impression). This helps them to learn about the other from within, but it is done usually only to gain trust and acquire deeper access before there is a reversion to Western categories and assumptions. The researcher's difference anxiety appears to have disappeared during the data-gathering process but resurfaces when the scholar presents his findings, tailored, as it were, to Western audiences.

I also find that such attempts are too defensive when their focus is merely to rescue the depiction of Indian society from Eurocentrism.

They simply ignore the application of the Indian gaze upon the West itself. Hence, the West's own self-image remains intact as the universal civilization. Such an approach is not a game-changer. The reversed gaze must be fully turned back on the West. A common reaction from intellectually inclined members of dharmic cultures is that 'we should look within and worry about ourselves and our own truth', and therefore, 'why bother with others'? My response is that by remaining introverted and not engaging in purva paksha, dharmic thought stays relegated to an isolated corner. The reverse gazing must be audacious and impossible to ignore. This book is an attempt to begin a dharmic purva paksha of the West.[40] I thus use the dharmic tradition as a kind of mirror, attempting first to wipe it clean of years of misrepresentation and distortion, then using it to reflect Western civilization, in particular its religious and metaphysical substrate.

2

Yoga: Freedom from History

'In the Judeo-Christian traditions, revelation comes 'from above'.
It is initiated by God, and its content is strictly God-given. Human
receptiveness is required, but this alone is insufficient. God is
transcendent and must personally intervene in history from without
in order for human beings to discern the truth. The bedrock of
such religions is this historical event. This leads to an obsession with
compiling and studying the historical details of such interventions
and makes them what I call 'history-centric'. [...]
According to the dharmic traditions, man is not born into original
sin, though he is burdened by his past conditioning, which makes
him unaware of his true nature. Fortunately, he has the innate
capacity to transcend this condition and achieve sat-chit-ananda.
Since the truth about the nature of reality is attained experientially
and passed from practitioner to practitioner, it follows that
knowledge of the divine is varied and that more than one lineage may
be true. It is this concept of the origin and transmission of truth that
I term embodied knowing.'

Two Ways of Knowing the Divine

All civilizations ask such existential questions as: Who are we? Why are we here? What happens when we die? Can we transcend death and if so, how? What is the ultimate reality or truth, and how can we reach it? The distinctions between the Indian and Western approaches to these questions and the answers they offer are sharper than most people realize. I shall now engage with these differences through the practice of purva paksha, that is to say directly, without equivocation and without downplaying the incompatibilities and contradictions that exist.

In the Judeo-Christian traditions, revelation comes 'from above.' It is initiated by God, and its content is strictly God-given. Human receptiveness is required, but this alone is insufficient. God is transcendent and must personally intervene in history from without in order for human beings to discern the truth. The bedrock of such religions is this historical event. This leads to an obsession with compiling and studying the historical details of such interventions and makes them what I call *history-centric*.

The dharmic faiths do not depend on historical events in the same manner or to the same degree as the Judeo-Christian religions. The dharmic traditions posit that truth is not located 'out there' in a heaven, accessible only through the rare intervention of prophets, but resides as the indivisible Self within each person, animal, plant, and indeed each tiniest particle. Theistic dharma traditions such as Hinduism see humanity as a manifestation of God, and the non-theistic ones – Buddhism and Jainism – see humanity's self-realized consciousness as the highest reality. Endowed with the potential for achieving, in this very life, the state of sat-chit-ananda – blissful knowledge of, and unity with, God – anyone may explore and discover autonomously the meaning of our existence. An array of *embodied* approaches such as yoga, shorn of any historical grand narratives or institutional authority, is available to aid the seeker. The path of embodied knowing begins with the sublime idea that humankind is divine, and this is one of India's greatest gifts to humanity.

The Dharma Traditions

The dharmic traditions do not transmit knowledge, values and experience by cultivating a collective and absolute historical identity in the Judeo-Christian sense. Instead, the aspirant is free to start afresh and tap into his potential for discovering the ultimate reality in the here and now. For instance, Sri Ramana Maharshi, a Hindu master of the twentieth century, did not study or rely on any historical events in order to attain self-realization. When the works of Shankara, the Vedanta philosopher, were shown to him, he stated that they merely confirmed the truths he had discovered on his own spiritual journey. All the dharmic traditions share this a-historical and direct approach to knowing the ultimate truth. Sri Aurobindo also found that the study of the Veda confirmed his earlier spiritual experiences. He said: 'The Veda, which I first began to read long afterwards in Pondicherry rather confirmed what experiences I already had than was any guide to my sadhana.'[1]

The potential for sat-chit-ananda exists in all human beings and has been realized, albeit rarely, by exemplars in virtually every age and culture. Thus dharma traditions have flourished without undue concern for history, relying instead on the numerous lineages of spiritual masters who teach from a state of enlightenment. The records of their efforts comprise an enormous, decentralized library of source material available to other seekers, who may in turn serve as guides and teachers to others. Thus, for dharmic practitioners, the experience of Jesus as the embodiment of the divine is easy to accept, yet Jesus cannot be unique since the same state is attainable by all humans.

The critical distinction between dharmic traditions and the Western reliance on history is that the meditative practices of the former remove the layers of conditioning that obfuscate one's true self and the highest truth, while the West lacks both the techniques and the conceptual base to do so. Even if all historical records were lost, historical memory erased, and every holy site destroyed, the ultimate truth could be recovered by ordinary humans through spiritual practices.

Hinduism and Buddhism do not impose their own unique history or claim historical and spiritual sovereignty over the entire world. They are relaxed about the claims of others' spiritual sources and histories, because no privileged period in time or place – nor any person – can exclusively offer access to the divine. Everyone can aspire to, and potentially achieve, divinity. The overarching narratives of dharmic faiths serve as templates and facilitators only.[2]

The scholar Richard Lannoy summarizes my position on the dharmic traditions' ambivalent posture toward history:

> Contrary to the Islamic and Judeo-Christian traditions, history has no metaphysical significance for either Hinduism or Buddhism. The highest human ideal is jivan-mukta – one who is liberated from Time. Man, according to the Indian view, must, at all costs, find in this world a road that issues upon a trans-historical and a-temporal plane ...[3]

The Judeo-Christian Religions

The dharmic emphasis on an individual's ever-present divine potential runs contrary to the Judeo-Christian emphasis on 'salvation from sin'. From the dharmic point of view, the Judeo-Christian fixation on history is strange, if not bizarre. As Sri Aurobindo puts it:

> Such controversies as the one that has raged in Europe over the historicity of Christ, would seem to a spiritually-minded Indian largely a waste of time; he would concede to it a considerable historical importance, but hardly any religious importance; for what does it matter in the end whether a Jesus, son of the carpenter Joseph, was actually born in Nazareth or Bethlehem, lived and taught and was done to death on a real or trumped-up charge of sedition, so long as we can know by spiritual experience the inner Christ, live uplifted in the light of his teaching and escape from the yoke of the natural by that atonement of man with God

of which the crucifixion is the symbol? If the Christ, God made man, lives within our spiritual being, it would seem to matter little whether or not a son of Mary physically lived and suffered and died in Judea. So too the Krishna who matters to us is the eternal incarnation of the Divine and not the historical teacher and leader of men.[4]

In the Judeo-Christian religions, man is born with original sin and therefore lacks the potential to achieve union with God through yoga and other practices right here on earth. In Christianity, it is only through the sacrifice of Jesus on the cross that a path to the divine got opened; hence Christianity's dependence on that unique historical event.

Christianity also endorses what is referred to as 'salvation history', consisting of at least two eras or epochs. The first is the story of the Israelites, God's 'chosen people', who are meant to be a 'light to the nations' and who usher justice and peace into the world. History demonstrates both Israel's faithfulness and unfaithfulness to that calling. Faithfulness is rewarded by freedom from bondage to false gods and by possession of the land of Canaan (which includes present day Palestine). Betrayal is punished by bondage to sin and exile.

Subsequently, the Christian Church came to inherit the mantle of the 'people of God', called upon to bring Israel's, and more specifically Jesus Christ's, light to the nations. The history of the Church is described in terms of the history of faithfulness to that calling. The reward is eternal life and the promise of fruitful possession of the whole earth, not just the land of Canaan. Unfaithfulness is punished by an eternal hell and the destruction of the earth.

These beliefs allow Christianity to insist on and justify missions to guide and reform (sometimes forcefully) other cultures and civilizations. Not all Christians and Jews endorse this project, of course, and both the Old and New Testaments contain voices that call for leadership by example rather than imposition. Nonetheless, this sense of mission has been the *raison d'être* of many aggressive regimes and programmes of expansion worldwide. The result has been violence and a destruction of local and native cultures. Furthermore, converted peoples, after partaking of Christian community and beliefs, end up distancing themselves and even disparaging their own pre-Christian ancestors and traditions.

God has played favourites, these traditions claim. In both cases cited above, one and only one collective entity – Israel and then the Church – was 'chosen' to become the recipient of God's largesse. God reveals his thoughts and plans at unique and dramatic turning points through prophets who belong to particular communities. The written accounts of these prophets have come to be held as the ultimate religious authority, not only for the communities in which they arose, but for all humanity, forever. The entire planet's destiny depends on getting these written accounts right. Organized religion is thus a sort of history club which aims to arrive at the 'right' interpretation of prophetic teachings and instructions. Any questions or misgivings about the sheer unreasonableness of this outlook are denounced by church authorities as a lack of faith and resistance has been known to bring draconian consequences. This collective and historical approach to salvation is quite unlike the individual approach to liberation through dharma. (On the other hand, a lack of political consciousness is more characteristic of dharmic practitioners, in part because of the deficiency of institutions and associations that foster collective and historically rooted religious identities.)

There are serious problems with relying solely on historical records to deliver the truth, let alone the ultimate truth. Not only does it seem unscientific and irrational to do so (the critical claims are not verifiable or reproducible empirically), but the contradictory claims of these events produce conflicts both within religions and among rival ones. Scriptures claiming to be the literal and non-negotiable accounts of history are notoriously opaque in some of their meanings, leading to disastrous consequences on the ground.

For example, Christian Zionists – an influential subgroup of evangelical Protestants and the American religious right – believe Jesus will return (the 'second coming') only when the Jewish temple of David is restored to its original site. But the ground where this temple once stood is now the site of one of the holiest mosques of Islam. Muslims hold that Prophet Mohammed himself had an important, superseding and unsurpassable revelation at exactly the same place, and they are determined that the spot continue to be honoured with a mosque. Each claim is non-negotiable by its respective side and devastating to the other faith. It is this clash of official histories that causes a 'clash of civilizations', most notably in the Middle East. In order for Christian Zionists to fulfil their history-centred duty (as they see it), the mosque must be destroyed.

Explaining Dharma to a Western Audience

Provocative Questions for Westerners

In my own cross-cultural journey, a watershed event was the day these differences finally crystallized in my mind. I was invited, some years ago, to give an informal talk on Hinduism to senior officials of the state of New Jersey, none of whom had more than a cursory knowledge of the subject.[5] I started by asking the audience a set of questions that went as follows: What would happen to your religious lives if all history became inaccessible or falsified? What would you do if you had to live your lives without the knowledge passed down from God through historical events? By what authority would you be able to live a religious life, if at all? In other words, could you discover the spiritual truth for yourselves without dependence on historical sources, or would you be lost if these were unavailable?

To my surprise, this erudite and accomplished group of Jews and Christians were thrown off-guard, disturbed, and in some cases, completely stumped. Many said it would be *impossible* to be religious under such circumstances and stated that humankind lacks the ability to know God's will without the historical prophets. Others asserted that only Jesus' very specific personal sacrifice (a unique historical event) had made it possible for humanity to be redeemed. Some found the very discussion troubling. One man later suggested that I did not have the authority to deny them their history in this way.

My questions seemed to pull the rug from under their religions. Their anxious reactions reflected the profound importance Jews and Christians attach to history, though for slightly different reasons. For Jews, salvation is a collective, not an individual matter, and the redemption of Israel via God's intervention in history is a profound sign of that salvation. Without that redemption (a historic occurrence), the will of God would be impossible to know, and the path toward salvation, inaccessible. The Exodus of the Israelites from Egypt, as recounted in the Bible, is a key event. It is understood as fact and central to the Jewish belief in collective salvation.

Christians say their salvation depends on the occurrence of three historical events: the incarnation, crucifixion and resurrection of Jesus. Christians and Jews can tolerate a good deal of criticism of the actual historical details as per their traditions, but certain historical events are absolutely necessary for salvation. For Jews, this event is usually the Exodus (recollected at Passover), whereas for Christians it is the Resurrection (recollected at Easter).

I proceeded to explain to my audience that my dharma would survive even without historical records. For example, spiritual advancement through yoga techniques and practices is independent of the life history of Patanjali, the author of the Yoga Sutras. The text's teachings have no historical references whatsoever.

Dharma and Direct Experience

In the dharmic traditions, direct experience and empirical testing are important for the acquisition of knowledge. Truth is to be discovered and rediscovered for oneself, an endeavour that requires active inner and outer engagement. The focus therefore is on self-discipline, experimentation with techniques and their means of transmission, adaptation of methods to different temperaments and life circumstances, and the rational defence of the specific tradition – not the pursuit of theory for its own sake.

The practices of tantra do not rely on the personal lives of Hindu saints or deities. Bhajans (devotional songs) are not history-centric, nor are they dependent upon a belief in the lives of the bhakti saints who composed them. Finally, deities were not always seen as historical persons but as ahistorical forces and intelligences, analogous, one could say, to the force of gravity.

For a dharmic practitioner, historical awareness is at best a guide, necessary for those who may not have progressed to learning from their own spiritual experiences. Hence, Hindus and Buddhists often do emphasize the history of a specific 'sampradaya' (lineage) or avatar (God's incarnation). But ultimately, the goal is to move to a state of self-realization without the crutch of past events. Every human being has what I refer to as the 'rishi/yogi potential' borne out by the fact that over time and across the world's cultures there have been innumerable saints who achieved self-realization. Thus, historical awareness is at the most nice to have, but it is not a 'must-have' for achieving an embodied state of divine consciousness.[6]

By contrast, the effectiveness of the prayers and techniques taught by the church depend on the particular circumstances of Jesus' history, namely that he died and rose from the dead. My open-minded, well-educated New Jersey audience seemed shaken, and I wondered: could I have uncovered a serious hidden doubt in their minds about the necessity of history in religion and their own dependence on history? I wondered if my questions had begun to deprive them of their dependence on history and triggered a sort of withdrawal syndrome. Why was their religiosity so contingent and dependent on a few specific historical episodes? Are institutionalized Judeo-Christian religions in *bondage* to history? I began to see the beginnings of what was later to crystallize as my thesis that history-centrism is the key difference between Judeo-Christian and dharma traditions.

It is important at such encounters to provide a clear explanation of dharma, so I provided a brief synopsis of Hinduism in the form of the diagram shown below:

Human Access to First Principles

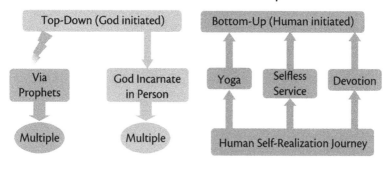

The left half of the diagram depicts the communication of the truth initiated and revealed *by* God, either via intermediaries known as prophets or through his personal incarnation as Jesus. God's incarnation happened only once, as Jesus, according to Christians, though Jews and Muslims do not believe that such an incarnation ever happened. In Hinduism, there is no specific normative list of prophets that is closed, nor did God limit incarnations to any exclusive one.

The right side of the diagram depicts what distinguishes the dharma traditions most dramatically from the Judeo-Christian ones. It shows the human-initiated paths for achieving self-realization. Through the ages, yogis have discovered many such available processes, and none of them has claimed to have discovered the 'only' way, or the 'final' way, or even the 'best' way for all people. Nor do dharma practitioners believe that the ways tried thus far exhaust all possible ways. In other words, the field of spiritual discovery remains open to new approaches.[7]

Itihasa Combines History, Myth and More

Dharma traditions deal with their past through 'itihasa', a Sanskrit term sometimes translated as 'myth' or simply 'narrative'. It is important to clarify the use of the terms 'history' and 'myth' here. In the West, it is common to refer to stories such as those of Lord Krishna and Rama as 'myths'. In popular parlance, the word 'myth' usually refers to that which is imaginary, fantastical, fictional, or even superstitious, primitive or false. What is significant is that it is viewed, at least in the West, as the opposite of truth. European scholars studying Greco-Roman classics and pre-Christian Europe created this normative category and used it to describe the narratives or claims of people and places that were colonized or that existed outside the perimeter of Christianity. The term 'myth' conjures up images of magical gods, goddesses, spirits and demons of the sort one would find in an Indiana Jones movie or fantasy. These may be considered interesting or exotic or even beautiful, but they are not reliable accounts of the truth.

History versus Myth

The Western view that 'history' and 'myth' are mutually exclusive has its roots in Judeo-Christian conditioning. One of the letters to early Christian congregations in the New Testament asserts: 'We did not follow cleverly devised myths when we made known to you the power and coming of our Lord Jesus Christ, but we had been eyewitnesses of His majesty' (2 Peter 1:16).[8]

Until the European Enlightenment, biblical literature was widely accepted as historical fact. Today, while biblical scholarship regards the Bible to be as much a repository of poetry, mythology, and social mores as scripture, those stories that are central to Christian dogma are held to be indisputable *historical facts.*

To a great many westerners, the religious narratives of other cultures are 'myths' (or, more politely put, 'sacred stories'), whereas they regard their own narratives as historically true. The former are depicted as fantasies and often the basis of erroneous views. These other civilizations are believed to lack the West's unbroken continuity with the past and ability to extend successfully into the future. Several years ago, a professor of journalism in the US told me of a course on world mythologies at his college in which non-Western civilizations were interpreted through the lens of their myths. The West itself was excluded in such analysis. When he complained about this exclusion, he was told by a professor that the West is not appropriately taught through 'myths' but through 'history'. He took the matter to higher administrative authorities and was told that the professor had the academic freedom to teach the course as he saw fit. The journalism professor then proposed his own course in which he would interpret various Western narratives, including the Bible, as stemming from their own myths. He was advised that such a course would cause the students to be disturbed about their identity and hence would be inappropriate. He dropped the idea and later moved to another university.

Formal education and even family upbringing in the West are fixated on installing a unique historical identity. This is especially true in the US, where there are thousands of historical societies specializing in all sorts of local histories. These are highly respected as civic organizations and receive massive amounts of public funding and tax exemption. Not only are the Founding Fathers in every child's curriculum; the flag is venerated almost as if it were a deity, and there are formal rules on the proper way to fold and carry it.

Of course, the dharma civilizations too have historical records, and Indians have a long tradition of historical memory – though the dharma is not contingent upon history.[9] The West, aware that literal history is not emphasized in dharmic cultures, continues to insist that the stories of India are entirely mythical with no historical substrate. For example, although the existence of the River Sarasvati – mentioned so prominently in the Vedas – is now established on the basis of satellite imagery and modern geology, and Lord Krishna's city of Dvaraka has been discovered off the coast of Gujarat, the traditional accounts of India remain classified as myths in Western scholarship.[10] It is important to note that, while these discoveries are of some anthropological value, dharmic spiritual practices do not rely on them.

Itihasa

In dharmic civilizations, accounts of the past are not made through *either* myth or history exclusively. Rather, these categories are replaced by itihasa, which combines 'purakalpa' (past narrative) with words of advice regarding all aspects of life.

Truth and not mere history is the concern of itihasa. Itihasa, together with the narrative texts known as the *Puranas*, combine history and myth, and their multiple perspectives make them more open than history. Truth is not dependent on history; rather, history is a manifestation of it. The dharmic relation between history and myth is thus not at all comparable to the Western relation between truth and fiction.

Parables abound in dharmic scriptures, too, but these inspire by the lessons they teach and not by claims of being the exact records of historical events. Hindus participating in rituals in temples do, for the most part, follow a received and codified tradition, and a minority might believe in the narratives they celebrate as literally having happened.

Most Hindus tend to view the historical events in their traditions in a fluid manner. History after all recurs in endless time cycles. However, Hindus recognize that history can be valuable to beginners on the spiritual journey (i.e., as a stage which they will, in time, supersede). The dharma practitioner who studies itihasa explicitly aspires to bring about a change within, emphasizing the virtues illustrated in the narratives and not the historical facts. Lord Rama and Lord Krishna are embodiments of bhavas (attitudes), and their historical significance is superseded by the values they convey. Sri Aurobindo explains the ever-present nature of the Indian narratives, which should not be seen as events in the past in physical space-time: 'The Lila of the Gopis seems to be conceived as something which is always going on in a divine Gokul and which projected itself in an earthly Brindavan and can always be realized and its meaning made actual in the soul.'[11] Yet Sri Aurobindo is convinced of the historicity of Krishna, while making clear that nothing is *contingent* on that historicity.[12]

Itihasa is also fundamentally pluralistic: there are usually a variety of versions. A remodelled account or a new version of a narrative does not nullify all others. There is no burning of old books to erase past versions. What gets rejected is simply ignored, possibly to be revived or revisited at a later time when it might again become contextually relevant. Hence, in India one finds ancient customs coexisting with those from later periods. An open past serves as a creative resource for future generations who might want to explore the roads not taken. The Western unfolding of history, on the other hand, does not have room for parallel streams, finding them threatening and hence believing it safer to display them in museums (i.e., not as living traditions but as dead ones). But collapsing all variations into a mono-history only produces a mono-culture. Such a lack of understanding and insight causes itihasa to get misconstrued as myth vis-à-vis some putative 'reality'.[13]

The West demands that its myths be historicized so that they may be claimed as true. Indians do not carry the burden of history-centrism and so are under no pressure to present their myths as history.

There are multiple stakeholders who compete for their respective versions of history to prevail. Power is always at work in the construction of history. (History is written by the victors, as the popular adage goes.)

More often than not, history is arbitrary in terms of what is included and what is not, what is emphasized, whose point of view is privileged, what values get superimposed, and so forth. In the West, a powerful apparatus and elaborate process have evolved to present history, and the transformation of Western myths into fact remains a major preoccupation of the Western humanities.[14]

The Western Gaze

There are no written records of the origin of the world, shrouded as it is in the haze of prehistory. Myths, however, recount what history cannot. Magda King, a contemporary thinker, writes: 'The myth "hides", puts in what never is in time, ... gives a beginning to what has no beginning, and to what occurred "once upon a time" it gives a significance that is universal and contemporary. Myth uses fiction to convey truth.'[15]

Western scholars, unable to deal with the multiple renditions of itihasa, tend to categorize it all as myth, and myth alone. As noted earlier, their own myths are recounted as history. Indian spiritual texts are subject to interpretive methods which are entirely different from those used to study the tales of Jewish and Christian religions. For example, the West is studied using sociological methods and tools, whereas so-called primitive societies are studied primarily through anthropology and folklore; European and American social units are always described as communities, never tribes.

In both the religious and secular history of the West, major changes have generally involved violence. Every successive stage in evolution has viewed the previous one as threatening and therefore to be either completely consumed or violently eradicated. Hence, the modern era must be rid entirely of the previous medieval or primitive stages in order to establish itself and prevail. The result is an uneasy and inherently unstable synthesis.[16]

Western beliefs of superiority crystallized as a template of universal history; hence, the manifest destiny to lead and to 'civilize' or conquer others. No Indian jati (social group) sees its own past as the universal template through which all communities must pass. There is no Indian sense of manifest destiny to rule the world. There is no notion that the events and chronology of an Indian jati (Punjabi for instance) be the central drama and defining event for all the world's communities. There has never been an Indian expansionism that would make the construction of history an important project the way it has been in the West.

The relationship between itihasa and history is far more complex and multilayered, and India's traditional approach to change has never entailed the destruction or devaluation of past stages. All stages coexist in India and frequently intermingle.

Ramayana and Mahabharata

Itihasa encompasses both history and myth. It is the repository of tales passed down from one generation to the next. The Indian epics, the *Mahabharata* and the *Ramayana*, are outstanding examples of the genre and have been retold in hundreds of versions and variations. The very first 'edition' of the Mahabharata was a recording of an oral recitation by Vedavyasa, the guru and Vedic scribe of ancient times. The Indian storytelling tradition is truly interactive: the storyteller consults his audience about their preferences not only at the start but throughout the narration. An interlocutor speaking for the audience will specify an event, person or a moral or metaphysical topic around which the next round of stories should be woven. Wonder and wisdom cohabit happily with the past in a playful way. The retelling of what has once been heard many times before is never the same when repeated.

The precise story of Rama can never be reproduced, and each attempt involves a combination of reproduction (by supplier), re-narration (often interactive), and re-perception (by audience). Thus itihasa changes, evolves and adapts to circumstances as per the prevailing consensus.

British colonialists in India, however, translated itihasa as history so as to be able to fit India into their own account of world history in a subordinate position. The historian Ranajit Guha remarked that 'in the West, state and historiography came to form the strategic alliance known as World-history … The control of the past is essential to that strategy…. More significantly, the story, as history, was dislodged from civil society and relocated in the state.'[17] Indians gradually accepted being admitted into world history in this way, seeing it as a sign that they too had a past in the European sense. By becoming part of 'world-history', they hoped to make the transition from myth and fantasy to reason. Such confusion reveals this to be an act of epistemic violence, i.e., natives accepting and internalizing categories which are alien to their own traditions and which distort their cultures – just to mimic and impress the colonizers.

Apocalyptic Thinking

The literal events claimed in the biblical religions also include a cataclysmic and violent end of the world known as the End Times. Such thinking has been rife in Christianity throughout its history and is based on an interpretation of the biblical book of Revelation.[18] It foretells a whole series of disasters: the reappearance of Christ and the Anti-Christ and the Day of Judgement with clear distinctions between salvation and damnation. Throughout history, Christians have interpreted (and created) the conflicts of their own times through the prism of the strange, symbolic and veiled prophecies found in the Book of Revelation. This doctrine of the end of history is called *eschatology*. History thus has not only a defined beginning, but also a defined endpoint when Christ will judge all the nations.

Thus the grand narrative of history culminates in a future that is, as it were, frozen. A few years ago, *Time* magazine devoted a cover story to this very idea, in which it was remarked: 'Notions of a divinely choreographed end to history are almost as old as western faith. They appear first in the Jewish Bible's books … Eventually Jewish fascination with a militant restoration of God's kingdom faded. But it was embraced by Christianity.'[19] The article explained that the United States was always seen by many of its leaders in light of this grand narrative:

> From as early as the 17th century, many had seen the New World [i.e., the U.S.A.] as the linchpin of a particularly optimistic End Times scenario. Unlike earlier believers who thought humans were helpless to influence God's cosmic plan, they thought they could trigger Christ's Millennium

by purifying and perfecting America. Ministers preached America as Revelation's New Jerusalem. Many colonists saw the Revolution in millennial terms, with George III as the Antichrist. Those most convinced, whom we would now call Evangelicals, helped shape the nation's culture of civic engagement, founding movements to abolish dueling, drinking, slavery and other sins. By the mid-1800s, some announced confidently that the Millennium might be a mere three years away ...[20]

In recent years, this obsession with the Apocalypse has reached new heights in the US, where many evangelical Christians see everything – especially the Israeli-Palestine wars and the events of 9/11 – as preconditions for the End Times.

How Embodied Knowing Works

According to the dharmic traditions, man is not born into original sin, though he *is* burdened by his past conditioning, which makes him unaware of his true nature. Fortunately, he has the innate capacity to transcend this condition and achieve sat-chit-ananda. Since the truth about the nature of reality is attained experientially and passed from practitioner to practitioner, it follows that knowledge of the divine is varied and that more than one lineage may be true. The truth is transmitted through personal practice and bodily experience as well as by direct contact with a self-enlightened master. It is this concept of the origin and transmission of truth that I term *embodied knowing*.

In his book *Inner Revolution,* Robert Thurman, a prominent Buddhist scholar, notes that a myth prevalent in the West is that only 'hard' science can be objective, in the sense that experiments are carried out, and scientists observe and then report their findings in an unbiased and neutral fashion. In contrast, the disciplines of psychology, philosophy, consciousness studies, ethics, and so forth are, by their very nature, subjective, because they deal with various inner private experiences. Yoga, meditation and other spiritual techniques are even more suspect because of their mystical nature. This dichotomy presupposes that inner experiences do not follow predictable lines of causation whereas the outer world does. It is impossible, then, to study the inner realm scientifically with observations that can be deemed reliable, reproducible and verifiable by others. As per this prevailing myth, only outer revolutions have shaped history, and it is these that have liberated the West by ushering in modernity. The inner disciplines are subjective and well-meaning at best, superstitious or arbitrary at worst. They are 'other-worldly' and offer little benefit to this material/social world apart from making us 'feel better'.[21]

Thurman strongly disagrees with this myth. Scientists, he points out, are limited to studying the world of physical matter and mistakenly see this as objectivity. On the other hand, dharmic practitioners have long discerned the interdependence between object/subject, percept/concept, body/mind, other/self, society/individual, experience/belief, signified/sign, etc., and they have a legitimate claim to using scientific methodology. The inner sciences were developed through observation, experimentation, critical inquiry and debate, and they should not be confused with religious beliefs of the Judeo-Christian genre. Thus, both outer and inner sciences can be scientific. While the inner sciences have a long history in countries such as India, Tibet and China, they have never *rejected* the outer sciences, and there has never been a conflict between dharma and science as there has been between Western religion and science. Thurman explains:

> The enlightenment tradition discovered the micro and macro dimensions more than two thousand years ago by using sophisticated contemplative practices to augment the sixth mental sense of inner vision ... This realm is supernatural only in relation to a constricted definition of natural. It is mystical only when its analytic investigation is not completed. It is magic only when the technique involved is not understood.[22]

Adhyatma-vidya as First-person Empiricism

Adhyatma-vidya is the disciplined and systematic knowledge of the self and the environment attained through precise observation and critical reasoning. It posits that it is possible to achieve a complete knowledge of *all* reality, enabling mastery of the conditions of life and death in order to attain happiness. It further claims that this knowledge can be taught to others. It does not demand blind faith to a dogma or belief but urges practitioners to critique their own beliefs and ideas. This is done using the methods of interior observation wherein the mind itself is employed as an instrument for gaining insight. The inner sciences do not rely on historical evidence of the efficacy of these methods or the desirability of the results.[23]

The first major discovery to be made as a result of such inner observation is that none of the voices in our heads is intrinsically 'ours'.[24] Most dharmic systems came to accept that the entrenched misunderstanding of ourselves and the world is avidya (false knowledge), which gives rise to ruinous views which in turn give rise to destructive and addictive habits ('kleshas') – all of which are the root cause of misery. The superimposition of the mind's prior conditioning and context in order to construct one's perceptions is referred to as 'nama-rupa' (name-form). Nama-rupa is the result of memory traces ('samskaras'), which in turn are the byproducts of past impressions of wilful actions.

One's choices reinforce one's conditioning (samskaras), which in turn serve as a filter for perception. The result is an imagined or illusory world (maya). This theory is the shared foundation of Hindu, Buddhist and Jain traditions which then offer the tools to transcend this conditioning. (This is explored further in Chapter 3 and in Appendix A.)[25]

So the sequence is as follows: *choices/karma* → *samskaras/traces* → *nama-rupa* → *vasana/habits*.

The human limits of cognition can be overcome by refining the internal instruments of investigation, namely the mind, senses, memory and related faculties. The resulting state is free from any mediation by nama-rupa.

Sri Aurobindo explains that the experience of jnana (supramental knowledge) makes it possible for one to know the relative in the light of the absolute: one sees, touches, feels, and knows the infinite by experience. As a result of this extraordinary claim – that the relative limits of the ordinary mind can be transcended – there has been virtually no tension between scientific exploration and dharmic spiritual practice.

The yogi as inner scientist is himself the instrument of observation/ experience, the Sanskrit term for which is 'antah-karana'.[26] Alan Wallace, who has studied the role of meditation in the dharma traditions through the prism of cognitive science, explains that the *primary instrument that all scientists have used to make any type of observation is the human mind.* Therefore, it is the mind that must primarily be fine-tuned and calibrated: 'The untrained mind, which is prone to alternating agitation and dullness, is an unreliable and inadequate instrument for observing anything. To transform it into a suitable instrument for scientific exploration, the stability and vividness of the attention must be developed to a high degree.'[27]

This is the scientific importance of yoga, meditation, *kundalini*, tantra and other dharmic systems for achieving higher states of consciousness and more evolved states of body. These states serve as clean cognitive instruments for discovering the deeper layers of reality:

> Over the past three millennia, the Indic traditions have developed rigorous methods for refining the attention, and then applying that attention to exploring the origins, nature, and role of consciousness in the natural world. The empirical and rational investigations and discoveries by such great Indian contemplatives as Gautama the Buddha profoundly challenge many of the assumptions of the modern West, particularly those of scientific materialism.[28]

These contemplative scientists (rishis, yogis and buddhas) were living human laboratories pursing the methods and techniques needed to refine and develop the inner scientist's capabilities. The great rishi, Patanjali, compiled the famous Yoga Sutras as a system to help humans attain their potential for higher states of consciousness. Shaivism offers powerful methodologies of meditation, optionally combined with theistic devotion, which culminate in complete merger with Shiva. Shiva himself is not a prophet - and is not even God in the Christian sense - but the ineffable ultimate state that includes and *is* everything.

Rishis may be said to have pioneered research in the area of experimental phenomenology. They discovered that in order to increase the resolution and clarity of the inner observations, it is essential to cultivate a simple lifestyle which minimizes mental perturbations and distractions. The more one reinforces mental concepts and desires, the more one strengthens the habitual mind and increases the obstacles to illumination. Hence, a silent mind is the equivalent of a clean laboratory.

Viewing themselves as navigators and explorers, the inner scientists developed, tested and constantly sought to improve the methodologies. Meditation texts were used as guidelines for comparing results and were continually enhanced by new discoveries. Some discoveries were more complete than others, some were better documented and communicated, and some were done with clearer and sharper instruments of knowing. They served as the 'search engines' for various realms not ordinarily accessible to us. Lineages evolved which continued the *adhyatmika* (inner) experimentation across many generations. Over time, this led to the development of many sophisticated conceptual models and epistemologies.

The claims made were subjected to intense peer debates, many of which are well-documented. Such inter-lineage debates laid the foundation for the various *darshana*s (points of view/systems of philosophy). This methodology meets the standards of modern scientific empiricism. By its very nature, the claim of an unmediated state of knowing cannot be deconstructed by socio-political-cultural historical analysis and anthropology.

In summary, the inner sciences combine direct self-observation with jnana yoga (yogic knowing) for accurate understanding and perception, leading to realization and freedom. Such systems might be more accurately referred to as therapies, as opposed to religions. Accurate understanding and perception are possible in human life on earth. This is the hallmark of dharmic thought, and so the development of a clear philosophical 'view', far from being mere metaphysical speculation, is not only possible but necessary for true freedom and happiness.

Modern spiritual leaders claiming similar enlightenment without textual dogma or belief in any prophesy or historical events have included Ramana Maharshi, J. Krishnamurti, Sri Aurobindo and Anandamayi Ma. They all emphasized deconstruction of all contexts and narratives, including both personal and collective identities.

Authority in the Dharma Traditions

While the history-centric approach asserts the centrality of sacred historical texts, the Indian approach generally locates spiritual authority within living spiritual masters. This means an *embodied means of transmission*, usually involving direct interpersonal contact, an approach which differs from the Western emphasis on the 'objective' study of texts, and the transmission of abstract truth.[29] The emphasis on embodied knowing makes the living spiritual master central in dharma traditions.[30]

There are several kinds of embodied masters with varying degrees of authority. Most prominent among them are the rishis, the munis and the gurus. Rishis are prominent in the Rig Veda, which references several dozen of them (both men and women). As a result of their yogic powers, the rishis literally 'saw' the ultimate reality and orally transmitted these visualizations as the four Vedas.[31] The muni was traditionally a wandering ascetic who kept the vow of silence ('mauna'). The muni was also known as the 'shramana', or one who works out his own liberation through self-effort and exertion, acquiring extraordinary yogic powers as a result. To the muni/shraman tradition belong such great exemplars as the Buddha and Mahavira. The guru refers to an extraordinary yogi and teacher who initiates disciples to help them attain self-realization. The 'guru–shishya' (teacher–disciple) relationship is necessary for the transmission of dharma and is representative of the embodied nature of knowing in the dharmic traditions.

The term 'guru' is widely and inaccurately used in the West today. A guru is not a prophet or merely an expert in some field. He embodies what he teaches others. His knowledge is not that of historical events or revelations but of a set of techniques and understandings designed to evoke the practitioner's own experiential wisdom. The relationship between a guru and shishya is much deeper than the relationship between an ordinary teacher and student.[32]

Wherever the dharmic traditions spread, there is a diversity of spiritual exemplars who are recognized as having achieved this state and who then teach others. More such exemplars are always emerging as a result of their ardent practice. This results in a preponderance of local exemplars and reference points, rather than singular reference points which claim universality.

Dharmic traditions thus do not rely on prophets, saints, or a single incarnation of the divine such as Jesus. They are comfortable with the narratives of multiple incarnations, none of whom is deemed to be God's son or daughter in a literal sense. A personal preference for a particular incarnation (avatar or bodhisattva) has never implied the rejection of other incarnations. Nor are those other incarnations seen as threats. More importantly, there was never the imperative of establishing a single correct version based on human testimony of history, an exercise that has become the preoccupation of biblical studies.

Buddha made it clear that the methods and the results he discovered did not constitute the only path available to man, as there was nothing privileged about him or his message. Buddha says, 'You have a right to doubt or feel uncertain,' and continues:

> Do not accept anything on the grounds of revelation, tradition or report or because it is a product of mere reasoning or because it is true from a standpoint or because of a superficial assessment of the facts or because it conforms with one's preconceived notions or because it is authoritative or because of the prestige of your teacher.[33]

His critical attitude is applicable to Buddhism itself:

> If anyone were to speak ill of me, my doctrine or my Order, do not bear any ill-will towards him, be upset or perturbed at heart; for if you were to be so, it will only cause you harm. If, on the other hand, anyone were to speak well of me, my doctrine or my Order, do not be overjoyed, thrilled or elated; for if so it will only be an obstacle in the way of forming a realistic judgment as to whether the qualities praised in us are real and actually found in us.[34]

Sikhism does not rely on prophets either. Its founder, Guru Nanak, never claimed to be God, or an avatar, or the son of God, or his prophet. He claimed to have recovered the divinity through devotion without recourse to orthodoxy, dogma or historical narratives of any sort. The same discovery awaits every human, according to his teachings.

Techniques for realizing truth through the body (including the mind and senses) are abundant in the dharma traditions. Patanjali's Yoga Sutras are among the classic resources for the philosophy and practice of attaining these states. In such texts, philosophy and theology are inseparable from personal spiritual practice.[35]

In Hinduism, classical dance is conceived as an internalized spiritual practice: using movement, sound and emotion to internalize the cosmology and epistemology within the dancer's body. It is the only major world religion to have been successfully transmitted through such embodiment for so long. This is exemplified by the iconographic depiction of Shiva-Nataraja, which is a stylized projection of Shiva manifested as the ascetic master of sacred dance. Similarly, the narratives and iconography of Krishna dancing with his devotees exemplifies, evokes and reinforces the 'rasa' (inner emotional states) of the devotees as they attempt to unite inwardly with their 'ishta-devata' (personal deity). Such expressions are not reserved for use by a spiritual elite; rather, they inform and engage the entire culture and are part of the folk narratives known to every Hindu.

As we shall see at greater length in Chapter 5, mantras are an internal and sacred vibration, a use of sound to manifest energies and intelligences within the body. Such techniques locate experiential truths within the person rather than without. This view is not merely metaphorical, for it is held that creation itself is an emanation of sound. Thus, these designated sounds, discovered and refined through eons of practice and observation, condition us to understand and achieve oneness with the cosmos.

In many forms of yoga, such as 'hatha' (the yoga of 'asana', or posture), the goal of the physical practice, or sadhana, is to prepare the aspirant for greater attainment of knowledge. Representations of truth in the form of texts, conceptualizations, external symbols, rituals, and so forth are merely provisional means to guide the individual toward direct experience. They are pointers only. Higher knowing is actualized in the body. Disciples engage in a variety of practices designed to transform their own bodies into instruments of knowing. All this is impossible in Western religious culture, which, in most traditional formations, treats the body as inherently sinful and the senses as the source of temptation and degradation.[36]

In embodied practices, there are no laws handed down from on high, and there is no closed canon. There is a deposit of wisdom called 'shruti', which is eternal and universal, and there are ever-unfolding interpretations, or 'smriti', which are context-sensitive and cannot be boxed into a closed canon. The student is thus not expected simply to 'believe' blindly but to attain for himself the various states of consciousness and engage in discourse from personal experience. Unlike Western philosophy, which deploys reason without demanding any inner transformation of consciousness through yoga or meditation, Indian philosophical systems are inextricably interwoven with adhyatmika practice.

Even the much-maligned *Manusmriti* (commonly known in the West as the Laws of Manu) was never enforced as the divine and all-encompassing law of Hindus – except by the British rulers who enforced it to show that the colonizers were ruling in accordance with 'Hindu Law' (a canon they had constructed themselves). Moreover, Manu's code is explicit in stating that it is *not* universal. It calls for updates, amendments and rewrites in order to suit different circumstances. (Chapter 4 explains this further.) Given this outlook, the notion of dharmic fundamentalism (or intolerance or exclusivism) is an oxymoron. Behaviour that is inspired and reinforced by personal commitment to a spiritual goal, as in the practice of ethics in the first two limbs of classical yoga (known as 'yama' and 'niyama'), is less likely to fall astray than when ethics are justified only for social cohesion or when morality is imposed by divine fiat.

Although the lives of most ordinary dharmic practitioners are governed by a variety of norms based on group, ritualistic, sectarian and other affiliations, the very multiplicity of these ensures and necessitates context-sensitive negotiation, personal choice, and much latitude for differences.[37] The Bhagavadgita (17.3) explains that everyone develops a particular approach to faith according to the three *guna*s (fundamental qualities or natures). The individual pursuits of self-realization can even override public codes of conduct, which are otherwise recognized as essential for social order. In tantra, we thus encounter the deliberate violation of norms in ritual contexts, disregard for norms in public contexts, reformulation of practices from fresh perspectives, and a host of spiritually derived improvisations.[38]

Dharma shies away from context-free, absolutist 'commandments', which end up as dogma and frozen canons of history. This flexibility in spiritual methodologies often gives rise to charges of moral relativism. However, built into dharmic traditions are many safeguards against moral laxity and relativism, some of which are discussed in Chapter 4.

Transmission in the Dharma Traditions

Knowledge may be said to be disembodied when it is collapsed into conceptual categories and discussed without embodied experience. Hence, while the traditions have developed many highly sophisticated, logical and conceptual systems of discourse, embodied knowing is considered superior to the mere intellectualism of philosophical propositions and the linguistic boundaries of nama-rupa. This is why rishis and yogis are higher in the dharmic pecking order than pandits (priests).

For instance, in Hinduism and Buddhism, mantras, or sacred chants, which encapsulate many of the key insights of the tradition, are taught to children before they can even understand their meaning. Their chanting is considered effective even without this understanding. Through their vibrations, these mantras exert an impact directly on the body down to the cellular or even subtler levels, and become profoundly internalized and transformative. Further discussion of mantras is found in Chapter 5.

The practice of memorizing and reciting ancient scriptures is, in many ways, more accurate than learning via the written word, for an error in recitation can be corrected immediately whereas a scribal error could go unnoticed for centuries.[39] The West tends to think of the oral tradition as a primitive and inefficient means of knowledge transmission, one that was wisely replaced by the invention of writing. Although writing did indeed revolutionize communication, the Indian tradition retains a sense (long gone from the West) that the spoken word carries spiritual energy and is filled with presence. This understanding is reflected not only in the mantra but also in the bhajan, or sacred song.

This emphasis on the spoken word helps us understand why physical proximity to the guru is beneficial – because some knowledge or spiritual essence is passed nonverbally. Such learning is *not* achievable via a hermeneutics of an inert external text, even when the external text provides a supportive framework. *The body of the practitioner is the text.*[40] Instead of the Christian emphasis on belief, there is an emphasis on the attainment of certain inner states of the body through various sadhana or yoga *followed* by a recognition of these states and sharing them with others. Musicians and dancers in the West appreciate this embodied tradition from the points of view of the performer and the fans.

Embodiment is also experienced collectively by a community. For instance, *Ramlila*, the annual re-enactment of the basic story of the Ramayana, has been a popular collective embodiment in many local settings. The ritual has nurtured a sense of community by inviting individuals to assume roles and enact them. Unfortunately, this tradition has largely been replaced by today's TV Ramayana, which is passive, disembodied, and not contextualized for any particular location or time.[41]

Canons of scripture (closed bodies of writing said to be authoritative sources of divine truth) tend to be less influential because of the emphasis given to living masters and their direct transmissions. Vedic mantras, for example, are not considered historical knowledge, and the Upanishads are a-historical treatises for philosophical discourse. The Puranas do use historical narratives and events, but in the form of parables, to teach dharma, and not as indispensable and central strictures. Thus when dharmic traditions come into contact with other cultures, they always respect the local and native spiritual traditions and teachers. This decentralized approach to disseminating spiritual knowledge allows local control by each subculture, which is quite different from having one canon under the control of some institution.[42]

While some would insist that the term 'guru' refers only to those who are fully enlightened, and others might use the word more broadly, it carries a meaning which is foreign to cultures influenced by concepts of prophets and saints. Moreover, because of the huge emphasis placed on individualism in the Western milieu, there are formidable obstacles to recreating this relationship.

Just as external empirical data are the basis for testing a hypothesis in modern science, so inner experiential data are the basis for testing adhyatma-vidya. There are multiple, well-established schools of adhyatmik research. Each offers instruction in its respective theories and practices under the guidance of its gurus. A path is validated if enough subsequent followers of the guru accomplish the same states; otherwise, the truth claims fall by the wayside – rejected by the free market of spiritual claims. There is no need to burn books or violently denounce a rejected school; if followers become scarce and eventually disappear, the school fades away naturally, too.

This method is similar to the way an Indian music guru teaches singing through a process of demonstration and replication, which is different from the use of musical scores. It is the way a hatha yogi reveals the asanas to students through his or her own body and not a historical interpretation of arcane texts. Even the debates among bhakti schools focus on the varied experience of devotional love and on defining it as precisely as possible to cultivate a personal proximity to the divine. A lecture, sermon or discourse in which knowledge is imparted would, by comparison, be a disembodied approach.

Texts serve as supports for the transmission of the teacher's realizations, and disciples can generate new texts by assimilating those core insights into the contexts of their time and place. The great medieval philosopher and cultural theorist Abhinavagupta, in his comprehensive discussion on the nature and validity of traditions as sources of authority, clearly states that they all derive from embodied knowledge and are conditioned by time, place and a host of other factors.[43]

This has encouraged many new start-ups and much creative research and development. It is okay not to conform; in fact the sadhu is considered a spiritual exemplar precisely because he has given up the need to conform.[44]

There is, among many westerners, an assumption that dharmic civilizations are static and lack potential for change and self-reinvention - that their wisdom is frozen in texts unrevised by subsequent revelation and reflection. This impression derives partly from the a-historical basis of the dharmic traditions. Another explanation is that changes in perspective in dharma have seldom resulted in violence, are not based on supersession and displacement, and have not been divided into epochs, eras or periods (at least not in the Western sense).[45]

In fact, there have been numerous innovations in dharmic texts, and they are far from frozen. The Upanishads, for instance, which are later additions to the Vedas, brought a new intellectual approach to dharma. The Ramayana explicates, in elaborate detail, the ideal conduct and duty in various interpersonal relationships and roles. Later, the Mahabharata, as the occasion demanded, turned the spotlight on the role of dharma in social and political conflicts. When Buddhism permeated much of India's population, Shankara's response was to reinterpret old texts using Buddhist insights, which started the revolution of Advaita Vedanta (non-dualism). The bhakti movement within the past thousand years challenged the elite orthodoxy from within the Hindu worldview, thereby enriching it.

What is striking in the long history of the dharma traditions is that innovation has rarely been confrontational. Radical displacement was never the purpose. There were huge shifts from one era to another, but these departures from prevalent views were positioned as a rehabilitation of the teachings from former times or described as the clearer articulation of what was always implicit in the established truths.

In the West, attitudes to change have been influenced by the belief in the biblical advent of the Kingdom of God. The old truths must be confronted and eliminated in order to live in the new. This makes change and the perception of change highly valued and dramatic (Jesus himself said, 'Neither do men put new wine into old bottles', Matthew 9:17). In dharmic traditions, newness is not cherished as a measure of truth, and claiming originality for its own sake is not creditworthy. No innovation has ever justified the deliberate destruction of another civilization or another faith.

The relationship of the past to the present in dharmic civilizations can therefore be characterized as both continuous and changing. Lineages that survive are those that remain effective and relevant to changing times even as they are passed down. Those that cannot simply fade away. For example, India continues to exhibit simultaneously what the West calls pre-modern, modern and postmodern qualities. Change is not discontinuous, nor does it entail defeating prior institutions.

By their very nature, the dharmic traditions are both introverted and open-minded. The spiritual quest has traditionally been given priority over conquest of the external, material world. Many of the finest dharmic practitioners spent their best years perfecting meditation techniques. This explains why dharmic civilizations often lack well-articulated power structures with centralized authority, why their people handle modern scientific and other intellectual challenges rather well, and why there is a relative lack of political will to control others and propagandize.

How History-centrism Works

Christian Religion as Third-person Revelations

Western thought acknowledges that there are human limits to knowing, but it has failed to develop a repertoire of techniques and practices to overcome these limits. In the Bible, God imposes limits on human knowing as symbolized by the divine injunction not to eat from the tree of knowledge of good and evil.

Modern Western secular frameworks in science and philosophy also often claim limits to the mind in a variety of disciplines.[46] The West developed no systematic science comparable to adhyatma-vidya in overcoming these limitations.

Alan Wallace, a scholar in the field of science and religion, notes this deficiency. He writes:

> The first step in developing a science of any kind of phenomena is to develop and refine instruments that allow one to observe and possibly experiment with the phenomena under investigation. The only instrument we have that enables us to observe mental phenomena directly is the mind itself. But since the time of Aristotle, the West has made little if any progress in developing the means of refining the mind so that it can be used as a reliable instrument for observing mental events. And ... there continues to be considerable resistance against developing any such empirical science even today.[47]

The reasons for this resistance lie deep within the Christian psyche. In the Middle Ages, many leading European thinkers believed that extraordinary mental capacities and reliance on empirical verification stemmed from the pagan elevation of reason, as in Greek thought, and thus ultimately from Satan. This view of higher consciousness as demonic precluded the development of a technology of consciousness through free-spirited exploration. European superstitions literally killed the freedom to pursue adhyatma-vidya on a systematic basis. What remained of classical and pagan culture and its pursuits was further destroyed during the Inquisition, from the late fifteenth through to the mid-seventeenth centuries.

Wallace shows that even Christian mystics imposed serious limitations on human potential.[48] Among other things, few of them seemed able to stabilize, refine or categorize mystical states in a consistent way. He points out that there seems to have been a 'widespread conclusion' among Christian mystics:

> that the highest states of contemplation are necessarily fleeting, commonly lasting no longer than about half an hour. This insistence on the fleeting nature of mystical union appears to originate with Augustine, and it is reflected almost a millennium later in the writings of Meister Eckhart, who emphasized that the state of contemplative rapture is invariably transient, with even its residual effects lasting no longer than three days.[49]

In other words, Western thought rejects the concept of samadhi, the state of consciousness in which the mind is continuously and uninterruptedly absorbed in transcendence. Furthermore, struggles between mystics and dogma-based hierarchy almost always resulted in the defeat of the mystics. Christian authorities regarded any rishi or Buddha-type of state as a threat to its historicity. Claims by spiritual adepts were condemned as man-made religions, and human transcendence on earth was viewed as heretical to theological perspectives. The case of St Catherine of Siena, a yogi-theologian in the fourteenth century, illustrates this. Although she was later canonized and declared a 'doctor of the church', during her lifetime she was persecuted and forbidden to practise her sadhana, mainly because she influenced the youth. This pattern of suspicion of direct spiritual experience, sometimes followed by a forced retraction when the mystic demonstrated extraordinary powers even after the death of the body, is not uncommon in Christian mysticism.

Although Protestantism was, in some respects, friendlier to scientific inquiry, Wallace argues that it closed the Western mind even further with regard to serious inner investigations:

> With the advent of the Protestant Reformation and the Scientific Revolution, contemplative inquiry by Christians into the nature of consciousness declined rapidly. Given the Protestant emphasis on the Augustinian theme of the essential iniquity of the human soul and man's utter inability to achieve salvation or know God except by faith, there was no longer any theological incentive for such inquiry. Salvation was emphatically presented as an undeserved gift from the Creator.[50]

Apart from religion, European science remained limited to outer realms, and philosophical speculation did not involve any inner technologies such as yoga. Here, the towering influence of René Descartes (1596–1650) made matters worse. Although he seemed to start from an inner empirical observation – *cogito, ergo sum* (I think therefore I am) – he took this in a radically reductive direction in comparison with adhyatma-vidya. Again, Alan Wallace puts it well:

> Descartes, whose ideological influence on the Scientific Revolution is hard to overestimate, was deeply committed to the introspective examination of the mind. But like his Greek and Christian predecessors, he did not devise any means to refine the attention so that the mind could reliably be used to observe mental events ... Moreover, in a theological move that effectively removed the human mind from the natural world, Descartes decreed that the soul is divinely infused into the body, where it exerts its influence on the body by way of the pineal gland ... This philosophical stance probably accounts in large part for the fact that the Western scientific study of the mind did not even begin for more than two centuries after Descartes.[51]

This limitation extended even to the work of William James (1842–1910), a pioneer of Western religious psychology who himself did not have the required empirical tools. Wallace observes: 'James was well aware of the importance of developing such sustained, voluntary attention, but he acknowledged that he did not know how to achieve this task.'[52]

Wallace sums up the lack of adhyatma-vidya in Western methodology:

> In short, the trajectory of Western science from the time of Copernicus to the modern day seems to have been influenced by medieval Christian cosmology. Just as hell was symbolized as being in the center of the earth, and heaven was in the outermost reaches of space, the inner, the subjective world of man was depicted as being the locus of evil, while the objective world was free of such moral contamination ... And it was only in the closing years of the twentieth century that the scientific community began to regard consciousness as a legitimate subject of scientific inquiry. Why did it take psychology – which itself emerged only after many scientists felt that they had already discovered all the principal laws of the universe – a century before it began to address the nature of consciousness? [53]

Today's academic scholars, for the most part, simply lack this first-person empirical foundation which would enable them to understand the dharma epistemologies.

Jewish and Christian theologians study ancient canons with the same intensity that attorneys might apply to complex commercial contracts. They examine canonical amendments through various covenants from God, look for annexes to various clauses, try to find escape clauses in specific situations, and so forth. Indeed, discussions among theologians often call to mind corporate lawyers in debate. To support this approach to theology, scholars look at evidence to reconstruct the contracts between God and humanity. Hence, legal jurisprudence and historical analysis have dominated much of the scholarship of these religions. These institutions maintain the canons, interpret them, protect them from false claims and threats, control their distribution, and leverage them as assets in expansionist campaigns.

In each given Abrahamic religion, God has bargained *collectively with a specific group.* Jews are the 'chosen' people, Christians are the beneficiaries of God's Son's sacrifice, and Muslims organized as the *umma* that submits to the final and complete words of God sent via his last prophet. Therefore, the focus (as expressed though their institutions) has often been outward. Many important canons are not about *individual* spirituality but about collective salvation, calling for the organizing of society and politics in order to defeat non-believers. Individual salvation is experienced only in an afterlife in Heaven. Too often, success on earth is measured by collective socio-political mobilizations and hence via organized religions.

All this seems strange and irrelevant to most dharma practitioners who fail to see what any of this has to do with spirituality. The core competence that determines the continued success of dharma traditions has been the ability to produce living spiritual masters across the spectrum of space and time so that they may serve specific communities with customized teachings. The *techniques* for achieving embodied enlightenment are what is important – not the history.

No amount of commonality among Abrahamic religions can resolve the conflicts caused by the non-negotiable and proprietary grand narratives of history. Even if the rituals of different religions become common, houses of worship look similar, dress codes become the same, and so forth, there will inevitably be a clash.

Authority in the Prophetic Traditions

In the Judeo-Christian traditions, as we have seen, it is the unique prophetic history of revelation that carries the greatest weight in understanding human access to the divine. Spiritual aspiration here is not primarily about self-realization but about knowing the will of God for individuals and societies on earth. It is important to recognize that this historical and social dimension of these religions is not optional but central. History-centrism is deeply enmeshed in all aspects of these faiths.

According to this worldview, humans are basically sinful and have no innate capacity to transcend their limitations. God intervenes in history so that they may overcome their sinfulness, but transcendence is still limited: human beings cannot 'become' God or achieve identity with God. Furthermore, God's interventions are particular, unique and unrepeatable. Jesus, for instance, is viewed by Christians as possessing the ultimate identity with God, but nobody else can ever achieve the fullness of Jesus' embodiment with God. Indeed, this is the whole point of the Eucharist, the central ritual of orthodox Christianity wherein believers eat a morsel of bread and sip wine in order to connect themselves with the body of Christ. Jesus' body and blood are unique, which makes the Eucharistic ritual the only way for Catholics and Orthodox Christians to share in his embodiment. It also means that the Church, which alone authorizes that transformation and guarantees its reality, effectively controls who may share in it and thus who may have physical contact with the Lord.

The most widely held theory (often called 'substitutionary penal atonement' or 'vicarious atonement') holds that human beings must repay the debt that was incurred as a consequence of their wilful disobedience of God. Since only God can create the conditions necessary to repay the debt, he sent his only son to accomplish this and set things right. Jesus is a sacrifice by God, i.e., Jesus takes the penalty of humanity's sin upon himself and thereby dissolves God's wrath. God thus transferred the guilt of our sins to Jesus, who bore the punishment we deserve. This is why we love Jesus and worship him – because he sacrificed himself for our sake. A central component of this ideology is the element of Jesus' intention to die on the cross as a substitute victim for our atonement.[54]

In these traditions, the human is always subordinate to God, and while unusual individuals or prophets can attain direct contact with the divine, it is always initiated by the divine from without and not through a person's own spiritual practice or discipline. For Christians, the incarnation of Christ is a unique and unrepeatable historical event; so, for Jews, is the giving of the Torah, and so for Muslims, it is the dictation of the Qur'an to the Prophet. Since the prophets are the only channel for knowing God's will, human beings would live in darkness if they do not study the history of the prophets.[55]

Even though the prophets lived a long time ago, we are left with their disembodied history as the exclusive source of authoritative teaching. The critical point is that Christians are asked to accept the principle of embodiment in the case of Jesus (and only in the case of Jesus) but are not asked to embody it themselves in the exact same way. To 'become Jesus' would mean that there would be several others attaining the same state as Jesus, and this would undermine his exclusivity and the exclusivity of the Church based on his uniqueness. Therefore, to lose the historical context and events that framed the prophetic revelations would be catastrophic.[56] The Judeo-Christian approach leads to intensive studies of prophets and their messages, but – despite repeated attempts – theologians have failed to settle matters of doctrine and practice. The historical details of scripture and prophecy are virtually impossible to verify.

In history-centric religions, it is not necessary for prophets to have achieved the highest state of consciousness themselves; they become prophets merely by agreeing to serve as transmitters of the divine will. The Bible itself admits that its prophets are not beyond the limits of cognitive conditioning. The Church claims to be the embodiment of God on earth, and yet its leaders are not known to have attained embodied enlightenment (or if they have, it certainly hasn't been emphasized). The Bible is more culturally conditioned (smriti) than direct wisdom (shruti).

By contrast, the Gita argues that only knowledge that is free from dualism can enable one to see the undivided spiritual nature in all living entities. Knowledge which apprehends all beings as a multiplicity, without underlying unity, is of a lower order. Thus, only a lineage of enlightened masters can transmit authentically.

The authority of a prophet seems to increase with the severity of his message, especially if that message warns of draconian consequences for non-conformers. Fear drives these prophetic campaigns to eradicate the past as dangerous and to burn books, destroy 'idols' of 'false gods', and carry out inquisitions in order to exterminate heretics.

Scientific knowledge, on the other hand, is not history-centric. There is a history of science, but this is entirely different from the role of history in Christianity. Sir Isaac Newton (1642–1727) had a personal history, for instance, but the events in his life did not result in gravitation. He merely discovered what was already there. Even if one proved that Newton never lived, or that he was an impostor, the principles of physics would remain intact, and others could rediscover the same independently. However, the events in Jesus' personal life are *responsible* for God's granting man the ability to be saved from eternal damnation. New covenants are created by God's unique interventions, superseding or voiding prior ones. Newtonian physics is not history-centric because gravitation would not be falsified if one were to falsify, say, the details of Newton's personal life or even prove that he never existed as a historical person.[57]

Unlike the claims made for Jesus, Gautama Buddha emphasized that his enlightenment was merely discovery of a reality that had always existed. He did not bring any covenants from God. He asserted that he was neither God nor a messenger sent by God, and that whatever he discovered was available to every human to discover for himself by following the same process he did. In fact, he stated explicitly that he was neither the first nor the last person to have achieved nirvana. Knowledge of Buddha's life-history is not necessary in order for Buddhist principles to work.[58]

Jewish and Christian religions cannot afford to compromise on their history-centric beliefs, because to do so would be tantamount to surrendering their claims of unique access to knowledge of God's will. Since such knowledge can only come as an intervention 'from above' at a specific point in time, the entire connection of humans to the divine would, in theory, be forfeited. People from dharmic religions tend to find this idea so uncompromising and counter-intuitive that they prefer to overlook it in their exchanges with westerners, considering it a minor obstacle in interfaith dialogue. Such is not the case.

In Jewish and Christian traditions, the institutions – operating in accordance with formal protocols, legalized codes, and closed, canonical texts – control and decide what may be considered authentic and authoritative in their respective faiths. All competitors are relegated to secondary status. Equality and true respect for other faiths are never offered. Interfaith exchanges are a zero-sum game.

To ensure that order prevails, canons of 'authentic' texts are formed, and in Christianity in particular, creeds or condensed forms of crucial affirmations and beliefs are debated, written down and then carefully observed as litmus tests for participation in the religion. The Nicene Creed, for instance, is a list of historical-theological claims. It is recited in most Christian churches as the basic affirmation or mission statement to which Christians must pledge allegiance. For those who doubt the centrality of history in Christianity, it is instructive to read this Creed, first composed in 325 CE when Christianity was endorsed as a state-sanctioned religion of the Roman Empire. The Nicene Creed is official doctrine in Catholicism, Eastern Orthodoxy, most Protestant Churches, as well as the Anglican Communion. It forms one of the bases of Christian unity, the other being the ritual of baptism. The Nicene Creed demands a pledge to the following beliefs, among others:

(i)   'Lord Jesus Christ is the only-begotten Son of God.'
(ii) Jesus had a virgin birth by the 'Holy Ghost of the Virgin Mary'.
(iii) Jesus 'was crucified for us' and 'he suffered', died and was buried.
(iv) 'He rose again on the third day and ascended into Heaven.'
(iv) Jesus sits in heaven on the right-hand side of God.
(v)   Jesus will come again 'in glory' to judge the living and the dead.
(vi) We look for the 'resurrection of the dead'.
(vii) I accept baptism for the remission of sins.

The full text reads as follows:

We believe in one God, the Father, the Almighty maker of heaven and earth, of all that is, seen and unseen. We believe in one Lord, Jesus Christ, the only Son of God, eternally begotten of the Father, God from God, Light from Light, true God from true God, begotten, not made, of one Being with the Father. Through him all things were made. For us men and for our salvation he came down from heaven: by the power of the Holy Spirit he became incarnate from the Virgin Mary, and was made man. For our sake he was crucified under Pontius Pilate; he suffered death and was buried. On the third day he rose again in accordance with the Scriptures; he ascended into heaven and is seated at the right hand of the Father. He will come again in glory to judge the living and the dead, and his kingdom will have no end. We believe in the Holy Spirit, the Lord, the giver of Life, who proceeds from the Father and the Son. With the Father and the Son he is worshipped and glorified. He has spoken through the Prophets. We believe in one holy catholic and apostolic Church. We acknowledge one baptism for the forgiveness of sins. We look for the resurrection of the dead, and the life of the world to come. Amen.[59]

It is clear that belief in each step of Jesus' personal life history has become the official test of being a bona fide Christian and church member (although there are many professed Christians who do not literally believe every word of it). Thus, Jesus' extraordinary personal biography, which would be regarded as extremely inspirational and edifying in all the dharma traditions, gets transformed into the unique and universal means through which God operates.[60]

Major disputes in Christianity, including many that have led to divisions within particular churches, are the result of differences over minute points concerning the historical specifics of his life and its significance.[61] Most of the Abrahamic religious conflicts and wars of today stem from disputes over what exactly God said and how he said it and what exactly it means. For instance, Muslims accept Jesus as a great prophet but not as the son of God. This is critical because Islam denies the very possibility of complete identity with God, who, it insists, has *no* sons *or* daughters. Furthermore, if Jesus were accepted as God's son, it would be difficult to claim that the revelations to Prophet Mohammed supersede the injunctions given by God's only son. One prophet can supersede another prophet, but no prophet could be greater than God's only son. But this downgrading of Jesus from son to prophet is simply unacceptable to Christians, as that would violate the core injunction of the Nicene Creed, and it would mean that Islam supersedes Christianity, having been started by a later prophet with God's latest covenants. The Qur'an is thus not accepted by Christians as God's covenant. Hence, in interfaith dialogue, each side merely tolerates the other, with subtle changes in interpretation which give each side the ability to claim itself as the final religion.

This kind of conflict emerges from claims to unique truth. Sooner or later such claims lead to codes and laws such as the Ten Commandments, and these are regarded as universal, of divine origin, and immutable rather than simply guidelines for ethical human interactions.

Mysticism or the less history-centric aspects of Christianity are similar to, yet distinguishable from, spiritual realization in dharmic traditions. In the latter, spiritual realization is nurtured within specific lineages of teachers who specialize in particular techniques. The transmission of knowledge and authority is marked by formal initiation, accorded only to qualified aspirants. Christian mysticism has tended to be an isolated, spontaneous and discontinuous phenomenon open to much subjectivity in interpreting theological dogmas and one's relationship to the historical Jesus.[62] Without a recognized tradition to protect the newly awakening mystic, such people are also in danger of being marginalized, criminalized, and even forced into mental institutions for exhibiting unusual psychological states. In the Indian context, the typical scenario is for spiritual peers to visit, observe, interrogate, test and even teach the spontaneous mystic before confirming his authenticity.

Since mysticism in Judeo-Christian religions has often been practised in defiance of authority, its clandestine place outside of approved Church doctrine renders it sporadic and wanting in rigorous methodologies, replication, documentation and lineages.

Mainstream Christianity preaches that one should aspire to be like Jesus but that one can never actually achieve Jesus' state of consciousness. The personal experiences of saints and mystics challenge the external authority of institutions, as in the case of Joan of Arc, whose angelic voices led to her being burned at the stake as a heretic (before the Catholic Church recanted and canonized her as a saint). Thus, Meister Eckhart in Christianity was persecuted extensively for bearing witness to the possibility of oneness with the divine.[63] Living spiritual masters tend to subvert institutional power. They have the public credibility to overrule institutional authority in matters of interpretation and practice, even to de-legitimize the institution itself.

In some cases, Western mystics have borrowed directly from contact with non-Western gurus and sources, contributing to the sense that mysticism will adulterate or corrupt the purity of Western religions.[64] In Western secular society, mysticism has occupied a less honourable place than in India. It is often seen as a pre-rational or childlike mental state, prone to aberrations and misinterpretation of experiences.

For all these reasons, mystics were marginalized and sometimes persecuted by authorities. Even today, those who disclose mystical or paranormal experiences are often confined to mental institutions where they are stigmatized or, at worst, deemed possessed by demons.

In Catholicism, a spiritual teacher is formally recognized as a saint only after he or she is dead for a certain number of years, thereby eliminating any threat to institutional authority from the living person. By this formal process, known as canonization, the legacy, example and teachings of the dead person become the property of the Church, which controls the history and the interpretations of the canonized saint's teachings, free from any of the risks associated with the subversive teachings of those who practice and advocate direct contact with the divine.

Transmission in the Judeo-Christian Traditions

In the Abrahamic religions, the list of the most authoritative prophets is closed, as is the canon of their writings. No newer prophecies may supplant existing ones, and the last word has been spoken, whether it be the Old Testament, the New Testament or the Qur'an. While later prophets may arise, they cannot amend or override the official canon for a given tradition. No prophet's word today can have the same status or authority as the Bible or the Qur'an.

Throughout history, Christian mystics have achieved higher states (by accident, as it were), but they attributed these to God's grace since they did not emanate from any formalized practice such as yoga and since no structure was in place for discussion and debate along scientific lines. Martin Luther, who launched the Protestant Reformation, condemned mysticism as un-Christian. Mystical claims were met with disapproval and punishment. Later, the post-Kantian intellectual culture explicitly defined mysticism as being in opposition to rationality and therefore not acceptable to academics. This stereotyping of mysticism and rationality as somehow diametrically opposed to each other persists even today.

Unfortunately, because of these hostile attitudes toward mystical or embodied experiences, there are virtually no sampradayas (traditions or lineages) of inner science in the West. There are certainly none of the rigorous methodologies, replication, documentation, lineages and living masters which we associate with dharma. The inner sciences have been forced underground, i.e., outside the mainstream of approved Church doctrine, and this renders them sporadic as opposed to systematic and sustained. Sadly, there is no 'how to' manual based on rigorous and disciplined practices as there is in the dharmic traditions. Even the great manuals of devotional practice, such as Thomas à Kempis's *Imitation of the Christ* and the works of Francis de Sales, are so out of favour that few Christians know them. A religion with an ever-growing line of enlightened masters, such as exists in the dharma traditions, is less likely to become fossilized into institutional dogma and therefore more difficult to control.

There is an assumption, common in some circles, that Christianity has its own yoga and adhyatma-vidya on par with the dharma. This claim is often supported by attempts to appropriate adhyatma-vidya from dharma into a Judeo-Christian or Western secular-scientific framework. On this basis, even obscure, isolated and unrelated instances from Western history are exaggerated and put into service. Old Western figures are revamped and recast in the role of pioneers, thereby replacing Indian exemplars, and new westerners emerge to claim their own original discoveries, which they have borrowed invariably from Indian sources.[65]

William James is considered a pioneer in the systematic study of mind based on inner observations, yet he was profoundly influenced in all his theories by Buddhist and Hindu thought.[66] It was well known (before it got erased from Western memory) that James not only met and admired Swami Vivekananda (1863–1902), but that he came under the tutelage of the celebrated Sri Lankan Buddhist scholar Anagarika Dharmapala (1864–1933), who was a visitor at Harvard during James' tenure.[67] He was also a close colleague of Josiah Royce (1855–1916), who studied Vedanta rigorously, and Charles Lanman (1819–95), Harvard's learned Sanskritist. There are numerous other instances of pioneering Western philosophers who were influenced by dharmic thinkers such as Nagarjuna, Shankara, Panini and Patanjali (to cite only a few examples).[68] The point being that the influence of dharmic philosophy on Western culture runs deep and yet consistently goes unacknowledged.

In general, however, in spite of these borrowings from India, mysticism in the West lacks the rigorous methodologies, replication, documentation, lineages and living laboratories which we associate with dharma – all for the simple yet astonishing reason that religion, especially in the case of Christianity, marginalized and even killed its mystics as heretics. As we have seen, the Church regards yogic self-realization as a threat, or worse, as heresy punishable by censure, excommunication, denunciation and even death.

Taboos against the Body

Given the differences between Judeo-Christian and dharmic religions, it is not surprising that there is serious resistance to many dharmic views and practices as well as a tendency to downplay their importance – this, despite the remarkable influence of dharmic thought and cosmology on Western philosophy and science, not to mention the widespread popularity of yoga.[69]

Indeed, yoga remains the flash point for serious controversies among many Jewish and Christians leaders. Even today there are attempts to wean practitioners away from what is considered an alien set of practices that may encourage the worship of false gods. Much of this tension is due to the Judeo-Christian fear and anxiety over idolatry, heathenism and taboos of the body.

As we have seen, the disobedience shown by Adam and Eve in eating the forbidden fruit led to mankind's fall and expulsion from the Garden of Eden. In Christian doctrine, Adam and Eve's original sin is transmitted to all humans thereafter. Hence sex, the original temptation, is a sinful act outside Church-sanctioned rituals. Jesus' immaculate conception is critical insofar as it makes him free from original sin. For Roman Catholics and Eastern Orthodox Christians, the Virgin Mary too remains free from the taint of sin. Virgin birth, with its roots in the Garden of Eden, is thus a mandatory claim for Christians.

Throughout the history of the West, the body has been seen as the cause of shame and guilt, which the Enlightenment and its rationalism did little to dispel. Judaism does not entirely share Christianity's obsession with bodily sin, yet there remains an emphasis on obeying God's commandments rather than exploring embodied knowing.[70]

In the Bible, the apostle Paul explains his turmoil concerning the soul/body split, which he considers irreconcilable, saying:

> For in my inner being I delight in God's law; but I see another law at work in the members of my body, waging war against the law of my mind and making me a prisoner of the law of sin at work within my members. What a wretched man I am! Who will rescue me from this body of death? (Romans 7:22–24).

The most extreme form of this sin is to entertain the possibility of finding and communing with the divine within one's own body.

Another taboo is idolatry, i.e., worshipping the 'wrong' deity. In the Old Testament, Moses bans all 'graven images' (statues), to which creative or destructive or magical powers might be attributed. This ban is particularly important in Islam, and the taboo against 'graven images' is more salient to Jews and Protestants than to Catholics and members of the Eastern Orthodox Church, who long ago grew accustomed to venerating images of the Holy Family and the saints.

The dharma traditions are misunderstood for numerous reasons, one being that scholars conflated the use of dharmic images and deities with pre-Christian paganism of the Middle East and Europe. But paganism is quite different from dharmic bhakti.[71] Nonetheless, for centuries, this misunderstanding served as a clever and effective ploy for creating fear and painting dharma as evil.

This suspicion of idolatry is one of the greatest obstacles which Western practitioners of yoga face. The negative association of yoga with idolatry of the body gives rise to odd hybrids such as Jewish Yoga and Christian Yoga. Such derivatives claim to provide a cleaned up yoga, which is free from the dangers of idolatry. (A recent correction in this regard was the historic resolution passed by the Hindu–Jewish Summit in 2008, which removed this condemnation of Hindu image worship by Jews, at least officially.)[72]

Internalized taboos and social prejudices, when left to gestate in dark corners, surface in subtle and unanticipated ways. The individual's latent cultural phobias regarding paganism, heathenism and eroticism

– all stereotypes of dharmic cultures and Hinduism in particular – act as a filter in the interpretation of dharmic traditions and create varied responses to yoga.

Westerners are keen to practice asanas (postures); however, some consider 'pranayama' (conscious breathing practice) to be going too far in its attempt to manipulate consciousness (and, by implication, God's person). Yoga's self-centring silence is seen by some Christians as resisting submission to an external God, and the yogic association of the body with divinity is held to be dangerous. The more conservative and evangelical denominations fear that malevolent supernatural influences tied to Satan may enter the silent mind. Throughout history, as we have seen, many Christian mystics were persecuted because of precisely this fear.

Other practitioners draw the line at the chanting of Aum. Mantra as a system of sympathetic vibrations with primordial energies and frequencies is simply incompatible with conventional biblical theology. It is seen as a heathen threat to the notion that God created the universe *ex nihilo*. Furthermore, in most Christian denominations, God is not immanent, i.e., not manifest *as* the cosmos, but, rather, removed from it. Hence, the notion that mantra invokes divinity *within* one's body is considered suspicious and sacrilegious.

While many Western yoga students agree to chant Aum, others refuse. The typical American yoga teacher may say something like 'please feel free to join me in chanting Aum, or remain silent if you prefer', thereby treating the chant as optional. Many who comply may regard the chant simply as a means of calming and focusing the mind. Most teachers continue to include pranayama and chanting, positioning them as health-related components of modern yoga, and yet this attitude is based, at best, on a shallow understanding of yoga's dharmic roots.

Even students who accept the chanting of Aum in their practice often resist chanting other, more elaborate mantras which appear to resemble prayers. Since the mantra is not sanctioned by the Bible or the Torah, it cannot be a prayer to the One True God, and must therefore be a prayer to a false god(s). This is a violation of the commandment to not worship any other gods. The mantra, then, is seen as a false prayer, sacrilegious and potentially dangerous – a Trojan Horse that may surreptitiously unleash heathenism and hence Satan.

Far more problematic is 'bhakti', or devotional practices in adhyatma-vidya, as this kind of yoga addresses particular deities through verbal means or by visualizing their form. Distinctive bhakti practices thus get generally eliminated from most American yoga classes. The Western teacher may personally have had positive experiences with bhakti yet may find it difficult to navigate his students through these more overtly Hindu or Buddhist practices.

Even more resistance is occasioned by the fact that Christianity imposes definite taboos concerning the body, the female body in particular. Yogic stillness brings mind–body unity and a quiet intimacy, which are seen as sensual and hence sinful. During the Inquisition, European women who practised bodily techniques were demonized as witches and killed. The Catholic Church has assumed the task of protecting humans from this danger, and Protestants, especially evangelicals, have taken up the role as well.[73]

The biblical notions of gender differ from the dharmic notions very centrally: Eve is created from one of Adam's ribs, and this happens after Adam already exists by himself, i.e., woman was derived from man. A competing story in Genesis 1 has them created equally. The first human pair in Sanskrit narratives, Yama and Yami, were co-created as twins. Yami (female) had her own powerful identity which is not subservient to Yama (male). Shiva (masculine) and Shakti (feminine) are often depicted as co-dependent and inseparably intertwined; indeed, the entire cosmos is conceived of as Shakti, or female energy.[74]

In the aesthetics of dharma cultures, a boy or a man can be called beautiful without undermining his masculinity. Traditionally, men in India are not uncomfortable appearing as non-aggressive (quite unlike their American counterparts).[75] Many non-westerners don't even conceive of homosexuality as a distinct category. There is no gay taboo in dharma, and in India, men who are not westernized commonly hold hands and show affection to one another without being self-conscious or fearful.[76]

Table summarizing the contrasts

The table that follows illustrates the contrasts explained in this chapter.

Human bottom-up potential independent of history	God makes top-down history
• Rishis' state of hearing/seeing shruti (eternal truth that is *always* available for access); similarly Buddhist nirvana, Jain exemplars, etc. • Adhyatma-vidya (inner science) empirical claims retested by each generation/culture • Explosion of methodologies, peer debates, and improvements over time	• God sent prophets/son in a concentrated location to bridge the infinite gap between humans and ultimate reality • Miracles required to establish authenticity • Historical interventions are unique, non-reproducible, space-time discontinuities • Narratives of these are canonized as dogma
• Privileged positioning: embodied knowing • Living enlightened masters overrule institutions • Rediscovered/reinterpreted for each time and context by stream of living gurus • Shruti/smriti separation • Empiricism, scepticism, debate, openness • Core competence is adhyatma-vidya • Built-in pluralism and context sensitivity	• Privileged positioning: canon, institutional protectors and promoters • Open exploration seen as threat; mystics persecuted; only dead can become saints, hence no continuity or systematization of adhyatma-vidya • Core competence: exclusive history • Tolerance not based on others' legitimacy but on one's own ultimate superiority
Non-negotiable Grand Narrative of History	**Open Architecture Spiritual Ecosystem**
• Darwinian competition without new start-ups, culminating in monopolistic final goal • Discontinuous advancements, killing the past histories, cultures • Violent expansions glorified as God's work • Undermined by postmodernism	• Gurus as fresh entrepreneurial start-ups • Change with continuity • No monopolistic goals or history of violent expansions • Attributes of tradition, modernism and postmodernism coexist

3

Integral Unity and Synthetic Unity

'The dharmic traditions are steeped in the metaphysics of the non-separation of all reality, physical and non-physical, from the divine – what is referred to henceforth as *'integral unity'*. Their central concerns are how and why seemingly separate entities emerge out of this unity. In spite of important differences in theory and praxis, all dharma schools share the belief in this innate oneness and offer elaborate theories and processes of embodiment for achieving it. This approach is inverted in Western religions, which ... presume intrinsic cleavages: God and humans are separated by sin and utterly removed from one another, the universe is an agglomeration of atomistic particles, and so forth. Furthermore, the reliance on historical and prophetic revelation ties humans to the past while the lure of salvation keeps them fixated on the future, resulting in dissonance in the present moment. Such a worldview may achieve unity but it is a unity that is tentative, tenuous and artificial at best. Moreover, force and domination are often used to achieve it. I refer to this as *'synthetic unity'* ... The cultural assets that are appropriated by violence and deception are then unified in a synthetic fashion, because they were not organically generated from within the cultural ecosystem nor integrated harmoniously.'

The dharmic traditions are steeped in the metaphysics of the non-separation of all reality, physical and non-physical, from the divine – what is referred to henceforth as 'integral unity'. Their central concerns are how and why seemingly separate entities emerge out of this unity. In spite of important differences in theory and praxis, all dharma schools share the belief in this innate oneness and offer elaborate theories and processes of embodiment for achieving it.

This approach is the opposite in Western religions, which start with the assumption of separateness – of matter, life and the divine. The spiritual goal in the Judeo-Christian faiths is to achieve unity or synthesis where none existed before. These religions presume intrinsic cleavages: God and humans are separated by sin and utterly removed from one another, the universe is an agglomeration of atomistic particles, and so forth. Furthermore, the reliance on historical and prophetic revelation ties humans to the past, while the lure of salvation keeps them fixated on the future, resulting in dissonance in the present moment. Such a worldview may achieve unity but it is a tentative unity, tenuous and artificial at best. Moreover, force and domination are often used to achieve it. I refer to this as 'synthetic unity'.

A great deal of Western thought in areas such as human rights, ethics and law regards the separateness and individual existence of entities as de facto, with unity and stability as constructs to be superimposed and applied (even, if necessary, by force). Dharma philosophers would argue that for systems lacking wholeness which is built-in, any attempts at unification are necessarily imperfect with irreconcilable schisms and enduring fault lines.

The distinction between integral and synthetic unity is also deeply related to the distinction between history-centrism and adhyatma-vidya. It is because of their insistence on historical revelation and prophecy that Abrahamic traditions collide so sharply with one another and with scientific discourse even today. Also, as a result of the atomistic and fragmented nature of the Western Enlightenment and its unilateral logic, Western philosophy often ends up resorting to reductionism.

The difference between integral and synthetic unity is illustrated by a conversation that took place between Albert Einstein and Rabindranath Tagore on 14 July 1930. Einstein contended that cosmic existence is independent of consciousness, but Tagore argued that man and the universe are mutually dependent: 'The entire universe is linked up with us ... This world is a human world – the scientific view of it is also that of the scientific man. There is some standard of reason and enjoyment which gives it truth, the standard of the Eternal Man whose experiences are through our experiences.' Einstein disagreed and added candidly: 'I cannot prove that my conception is right, but that is my religion.'[1] Tagore was highlighting the inherent unity of God-Cosmos-Humanity, asserting their inseparability, whereas, in Einstein's worldview, all fundamental building blocks are entities that exist independently of one another.

This quality of fundamental unity is captured by the Sanskrit word 'purna', which has a deep meaning in dharma. It is often interpreted as 'completeness' or 'infinity', and Sri Aurobindo – the prominent twentieth-century expounder of classic Indian thought – translates it as 'integral'. The *Purna Stotra* is one of the most prominent mantras from the Upanishads, and the tradition is to chant it on numerous occasions. It says:

'*Purnam adah, purnam idam purnat purnam udachyate; purnasya purnam adaya purnam evavasishyate.*'[2]

The word occurs seven times in this short text. 'That' transcendent divine and the cosmic macrocosm are purna, and 'this' microcosm is purna. The mathematics of purna are that, 'if you take away purna from purna, you still have purna'. The purpose of chanting this is to attune the listener to integral unity. The micro and macro are each purna and inter-contained, and if you remove purna, what remains is still purna.

By way of contrast, the Western scientific tradition has been reductionist rather than integral. Reductionism attempts to explain wholes in terms of their parts. This works, to a large extent, in ways that are practical, and hence modern science has made major contributions to our lives using this principle.

The unity assumed in most of the dharmic traditions is a unity of consciousness, and matter is merely a form of consciousness. Western scientists and philosophers often ask how consciousness can arise from the chemistry of the brain.[3] In the Indian tradition, we find the reverse problem. Absolute consciousness is understood to be the source of everything. The challenge is to understand our ordinary world of multiplicity. Sri Aurobindo explains that challenge using the concept of the process of *involution* (see Appendix A). He compares our ordinary state with a boy reading a book who is so fully engrossed in it that he forgets everything else. His task of self-awareness is to cultivate dual consciousness and become aware both of the book and of the wider experience of which it is an integral part.

Sri Aurobindo developed his integral yoga based on his own experiences as opposed to intellectual speculations, the goal being to attain the direct experience of purna consciousness, a state he called the 'supramental consciousness'. Purna can only be experienced after intense, long-term concentration of the mind and dis-identification with the body, emotions, desires, and mental processes. One has to *witness* one's own mental processes as a detached outsider and cease identifying with the ego. This process leads to a state beyond the ordinary and habitual. From here one can study one's own psychological processes, like a scientist making empirical observations in a pure and disinterested manner. The next step is to integrate this state of detachment into one's daily life, coming back full circle but with a different and more evolved intuitive unity and outlook.

The dharmic traditions view the essential human condition as one of ignorance, or avidya, liberation from which is achieved through individual practice with techniques of inner science, or adhyatma-vidya. According to the Abrahamic traditions, the human condition is one of sin resulting from disobedience towards God at some distant point in history. Liberation from this state is achieved through repentance and collective understanding of what God has revealed through his prophets. The Abrahamic traditions tend to focus outward; the dharmic ones, inward. The difference between observing historical mandates and discovering the structures of consciousness is stark. I am aware of the centuries of intense intellectual debates among Indian philosophers that clearly demonstrate the vast diversity of views. I do not wish to over-generalize. My integral theory of dharma opposes homogeneity and yet identifies common principles, especially in contrast with Western assumptions.[4] The history-centric worldview results in synthetic unity, not integral unity.

Integral Unity and Synthetic Unity Defined

Integral unity means that ultimately only the whole exists; the parts that make up the whole have but a relative existence. (For a more technical discussion of this complex point, see Appendix A.) The metaphor that has been used to illustrate the nature of this unity is of a smile in relation to a face: A smile cannot exist separately from the face; it is dependent and contingent on the face. However, the face has an independent existence, whether it smiles or not. The relationship of every entity to the cosmic whole is similar: the dependency is unidirectional. Each element, be it physical or non-physical, is inseparable in this manner from the Ultimate Reality. Just as each expression of the face is a form or manifestation of the face, so also everything that exists is a form or manifestation of the single Ultimate Reality. (Though Buddhists may contest this explanation, Buddhism does not allow separate entities, either.)

Synthetic unity starts with parts that exist separately from one another. For example, the parts of an automobile exist separately until they are assembled into a single vehicle. Similarly, in classical physics the cosmos is viewed as an assemblage of separate elementary particles. The problem then becomes how to make them cohere by outside forces (rather than seeking a coherence that is inherent). Given this starting point, it is no accident that Judeo-Christian religious practices such as prayer or obedience are focused outside of the self, because the self, according to these traditions, is independent and separate from others. The way to overcome this essential separateness is to find ways to bond with the other.

There are many terms among the dharmic religions for this unity among the divine, the cosmos, and the human. Hindu philosophical schools use the terms 'tat ekam' (that one), 'sat' (existence) or Brahman (ultimate reality), Bhagavan and Shiva. Buddhists use the phrase dependent co-arising ('pratitya-samutpada') to signify the mutual dependence of all entities. There are important differences among these dharmic systems even as they share the principles of integral unity.

Across the dharma schools and in spite of serious differences among them, integral unity displays the following three common characteristics:

A. All entities (physical, mental, emotional, linguistic, spiritual or anything else), while apparently separate, do not have an actual existence or selfhood independent of the unity. Philosophers refer to this as the absence of 'essences' or 'substances'. Buddhists call this emptiness 'sunyata', though not in the nihilistic sense.

B. The whole is independent and indivisible. Nothing other than itself exists. It is not part of a bigger unity or some other, higher reality.

C. This unity includes within it the potential that generates all phenomena. Diversity is not imported from without but unity is itself pregnant with it.

The precise relationship of unity to diverse phenomena is the subject of intense debate among the various dharmic systems. For example: Shankara used the term maya to describe the experience of multiplicity produced by the unity. Srinivasa Ramanuja, the equally important founder of the school of Vedanta known as Visishtadvaita, says all diversity pre-exists as part and parcel of unity, i.e., unity in diversity is the nature of unity from the very beginning. Sri Aurobindo explains this in terms of the undifferentiated (one) and differentiated (many), the one and the many being aspects of the same Consciousness of the

One. He uses the term 'manifestation' to refer to the process by which the multiplicity inherent in the One expresses itself. The various dharmic systems all agree that Ultimate Reality cannot be fully understood by the ordinary human mind because such a mind is limited and its perceptions consequently deficient. While scripture can communicate something of the concept of unity, one has to advance to a state of unity consciousness in order to grasp it more fully.

Furthermore, in all the dharmic traditions, the interrelated entities are not static but exist in states of flux. Everything – all matter, spirit, humanity, every individual thing down to the tiniest particle, every moment in time and every unit of space – is ever-changing. In Hinduism, creation itself is cyclical. A universe comes into being and eventually passes away, reverting to an un-manifest state, then lies dormant until it emerges again at the commencement of another cycle. This pattern is as natural as inhalation and exhalation and is repeated throughout eternity. Creation is not separate from God. Since the divine manifests itself, in part, as the cosmos (not merely *in* the cosmos), the entire cosmos is intelligent and ultimately One. The divine is thus one with, yet separate from, the cosmos itself. The universe arises out of the Ultimate Reality, not for any reason we can conceptualize but simply because this is its nature.

This view is different both from monotheism, which has one God governing the universe from above, and its antithesis in the West, pantheism, which envisages the cosmos as God but *without* any external God. Dharmic theism includes both of these notions. The Upanishads, for instance, view the divine as simultaneously transcendent (external or untouched), or 'para', and immanent (the very composition of the cosmos), or 'apara'. God is not merely the creator (and hence an external force) of a many-splendoured world; God *is* that world. Everything is ultimately a distinct expression of Brahman. Brahman and the manifestations of Brahman are inseparable. Unity-in-diversity is thus the nature and essence of reality. Western philosophers who got this idea from Hinduism gave it the name panentheism (not to be confused with pantheism).[5]

In Buddhism, too, unity, while understood in a radically different way than in Vedanta, presumes the inherent interconnectedness and interdependence of everything. The perception of separateness – not just of physical entities but even of an idea, feeling or mental object – is illusory. All 'things' that exist, or *appear* to exist, are ultimately understood as transitory, with only a fleeting *apparent* existence. Nothing endures in time, and everything is constantly changing into something else. Each momentary existence is dependent on every other momentary existence in an interconnected web. The central unifying principle is the interconnectedness of everything past, present and future, be it physical or non-physical. This idea of impermanence brings with it infinite diversity, because there are no enduring things at all. Reality, then, is the unity fostered by the interconnectedness of an ever-changing world, its diversity shaped by this very impermanence.

Partly as a result of this metaphysical bedrock, the dharma traditions see no contradiction between the spiritual and the worldly. The two are often superimposed, and even their distinction is blurred.[6]

Hindus and some Buddhists easily blur the human–deity divide, and deify certain actions, attributes, processes and powers. The Sanskrit term *deva*, often translated as 'god', means one who possesses or gives something of value. Sages give knowledge, parents give guidance, the sun gives light – and all of these are devas. Humans, with their infinite spiritual potential, can aspire to become devas with the practice of austerities (*tapas*). Organ, the scholar of dharma traditions, explains:

This Hindu conception of deity is contrary to that held by the Judeo-Christian tradition, where the blurring of the divine-human distinction is not possible. A Western god *is* what he is, and he will not *become* something other than what he is. A changing god is no god. But in India a god may grow or diminish in divinity. The gradation aspect of the *deva* concept gives Hinduism a pattern for integrating all living forms. The separation of animals, men, and gods, so essential to Western religions, is not as absolute and clear-cut. Jainism and Buddhism may be understood to be, in part, alternative attempts to spell out the practical implications of the theory, Jainism concluding that all living beings are to be valued and protected, Buddhism integrating still more by eliminating the concept of beings altogether in a process theory of life.[7]

The relationship between unity and diversity within the Jewish and Christian religions is markedly different. There is one *unique* event, the Creation, which is separate from its creator and before which there is nothing. The Creator/Created dualism does not allow for the idea that God was as all things. Whereas dharma sees all differences as relative modes of the One being, the Judeo-Christian religions see the physical and non-physical entities as having their own ultimate existence, linked only externally by divine fiat.

There are certain philosophical positions and mystical traditions in the West which approximate Hindu or Buddhist insights, but the religions and philosophies that dominate in that civilization do not have as radical a sense of God's immanence as is found in Hindu schools; nor do they embrace the emptiness of all phenomena, as Buddhists do. Many interpretations of Christianity do include the notion of the Holy Spirit as God's immanence, though Holy Spirit has never been worked out as a central idea; furthermore, Christianity has never reconciled good (God) and evil (Satan) or the separation of the sacred and profane.[8]

Significantly, in dharma traditions, integral unity can be discovered and experienced through spiritual practices such as yoga. Since both 'exterior' and 'interior', body and mind, spirit and matter, individual and collective, are mere manifestations or aspects of an integral whole, it becomes natural to start the quest for ultimate truth using what is at hand, namely the embodied self. Sri Aurobindo's interpretation of the *Isha Upanishad* explains nine pairs of opposites and how they are resolved within the integral unity.[9] In Shaivism, Shiva is the ultimate integral unity and inheres within him all the opposites.

In the West, the same quest starts with inherently separate entities – God and Creation, God and humanity, body and mind, spirit and matter, etc. – and attempts to unite them. This underlying separateness is combined with an emphasis on binary either/or propositions and absolute differences. Consequently, differences become a source of anxiety rather than something experienced in relation to integral unity.[10]

Examples of synthetic unity also exist in international politics. The United Nations Organization is a gathering place for sovereign nations with separate identities which have shared interests in matters of trade, legal rights, security, environmental protection, and so forth. None of the UN programmes require that any of the member states sacrifice their individual sovereignty. The G8 likewise is a group of powerful countries which meets to discuss common interests, but their motive is to maximize their own separate interests and not the common good. In Indian politics, the coalition governments are synthetic groups wherein separate political egos come together to pursue common goals until selfish opportunism intervenes and things fall apart.

The health-care industry in the US struggles to keep various tensions in abeyance – tensions among individual doctors, hospitals, insurance firms, employers, politicians and patients. All the stakeholders negotiate from separate self-interests, making the system largely synthetic even though the various contributors are compelled to work together for practical reasons. Modern education, too, is a synthetic portfolio of isolated skills, intended mostly to prepare the child for employment. Even interdisciplinary studies are a form of portfolio management of separate entities which must be brought into unity. The capitalist marketplace is synthetic in that its participants try to optimize their own separate interests, the market's purpose being to enable each party to transact for its own benefit. The same synthetic quality exists in most institutions in modern times – be they national or international. Interfaith dialogue and the notion of tolerance are also examples of how synthetic accommodation may be achieved while preserving one's primacy.

In all these examples, synthesis is a sort of portfolio in which the individual elements retain their identities and interests separately. The whole is merely a collection of independent parts. Indian secular democracy is synthetic as well – a unifying arrangement which could be applied to any random collection of peoples who adopt a constitution and live by it. Synthetic unity is, at best, a convenience; it misses out on the much deeper bonds that hold people together across the boundaries of hierarchies and diversities of various kinds. One of the goals of this book is to help uncover this deeper unity.

A tighter form of synthetic unity can acquire an organic quality wherein the overarching interests of the whole override the separate interests of the various parts. The whole takes priority and the parts are subservient to it. The relationship of a biological cell to the entire human body and of a tree to an ecosystem are examples of complex organic entities. A holistic or organic health-care system (such as Norway has) would look at the collective health interests of all citizens and develop roles and functions for the various components of the system. Doctors, lawyers and medical institutions would all have to fit into the collective system without trying to optimize their individual interests. Confucianism and communism are political systems which strive for a *functional* and *pragmatic* unity but which do not have integral unity. Collective farming and cooperatives are also structured as pragmatic unities.

Environmental coalitions attempt to unite people across the world in order to solve problems that affect the entire planet. Some regard this task as reflective of a selfish, pragmatic need to conserve resources while others take a more organic approach, seeing the need for unity in the cosmos. These movements struggle against synthetic institutions, laws and treaties, i.e., those things that were built on the self-interests of separate groups.

Yet all such organic systems, regardless of how intertwined they become over time, fall short of full integral unity in the dharmic sense. That is because their building blocks still exist separately and exert separate powers. It is rare for a synthetic collection to become so integrated that the parts permanently relinquish their own self-interest. In most cases, even when the self-hood of parts becomes dormant, the truce is temporary and tenuous; self-interest will eventually resurface. In integral unity, there is no question of a merely tentative coalition.

Comparison of Cosmologies

The following chart highlights ways in which the dharmic and Judeo-Christian cosmologies differ from each other. These differences will be explained further in this chapter.

	Dharma	Judeo-Christian
The Ultimate Reality	Some lineages demand a priori belief. Others are process-driven.	A priori belief is mandatory.
	Supreme Being could be male or female or both or neither. Ultimate Reality could be impersonal. Multiple representations and access methods to the One.	Belief in One Supreme Being, described as male and father.
	Brahman is both transcendent and immanent. The world is sacred.	God and World are distinct. World is dependent on God and World is separate/profane unless redeemed by grace.
	Integral unity of everything; ultimately no separate essences or things exist.	Separate souls and world of objects ultimately exist.
	Ishvara includes everything, good and bad. Deal with bad internally.	Evil is a principle with its own self-existence. It is an external force as well as an internal innate inclination to cooperate with that force as a result of sin.
	No doctrine about non-believers is enforced. Let others be. Worry about one's own spirituality.	Elaborate mandates about need to save others. Salvation is collective, hence institutional; also, there is a personal mandate to proselytize others.

The Human	Individual = sat-chit-ananda; must self-realize.	Individual = Sinner; must be saved.
	Reincarnation.	One life only.
	Circumstances are based on karma, hence self-made destiny, not fatalism.	No explanation for individual's good/bad circumstances by birth.
	Many adhyatma-vidyas (processes for advancement). Belief is a working hypothesis. Supreme is present within adhyatma.	Less stress on inner sciences/technologies. Salvation dependent on God's grace with varying roles for belief and 'work'. Works mean any activity, including ritual activity, undertaken for the purposes of salvation.
	Karma and release.	Salvation: Retribution and Redemption.
The World	Time is Beginning-less. Infinite cycle of Creation-Sustenance-Dissolution. Time and causation are non-linear.	Time and space had a beginning and are linear. This affects all history writing.
	No End-Times or Finality. Moksha is individual, not collective.	End-Times = Day of Judgement for all of humanity.
	History not critical because: many Avatars; adhyatmika experience of rishis as shruti; humans rewrite smritis.	Unique historical intervention of God. Hence, history is all-important in order to know God.
	Perennial access here and now. Independent of any history.	Spiritual authority contingent on God's revelation in history.

Indra's Net

The conceptual matrix of integral unity is illustrated in the metaphor of Indra's Net, which is common to many dharmic traditions. The Vedic deity Indra is said to have an infinite net consisting of a jewel in each node, arranged so that every jewel reflects all the other jewels; there is no separate self-existence of any jewel. Each is unique in its reflection of all others. Indra's Net symbolizes a universe with infinite dependencies and relations interwoven among all its members, none of which exists apart from but only in the context of this collective reality. The original idea of Indra's Net is found in the Atharva Veda (one of the four Vedas), where the world is seen as the net of the great Shakra or Indra. Later, Buddhist texts use the metaphor of Indra's Net to describe an infinite universe with no beginning or end, in which every member is mutually related to every other member.[11]

The metaphor of Indra's Net also suggests a creative intelligence which is omnipresent, permeating all life. All appearances of separateness are maya (illusory). The capacity of one jewel to reflect the light of every other within this infinite net is difficult for the linear mind to comprehend, but it serves as an apt precursor to an understanding of multidimensional theories which have emerged in physics and metaphysics.

Thus, long before modern science, Indra's Net provided an excellent metaphor for what is now recognized as the main quality of the hologram, which is that every area of the hologram contains information on the whole. This metaphor explicitly inspired Michael Talbot's recent theory of the holographic nature of the physical universe. He proposes that a holographic model might provide a scientific foundation for understanding various yogic 'siddhis'. These are certain spiritual powers achieved as a result of yogic practices, which Western scholars have renamed 'paranormal', 'supernatural' and 'anomalous' phenomena. The unified 'citta' (consciousness) or unified shakti was thus reconceived as the 'unified field that ties all things in the universe together'.[12] The Indra's Net concept also inspired Douglas Hofstadter's work on the complex relationships among the parts of a system which may be physical, symbolic or conceptual.[13] It has influenced models of the human brain's interconnectedness and models of the way in which the Internet functions. It also offers an ancient correlation to Bell's Theorem in theoretical physics, according to which there are no local events or local causes, because everything in the cosmos is inherently interconnected.

The dharmic notion of integral unity is summarized in Chapter Seven of the Bhagavadgita, in which Lord Krishna explains that the entire cosmos is his own self. From the lowest levels of inert matter all the way to the highest forms of life and intellect, everything material and spiritual, good or bad, is only Lord Krishna's energy in manifest form. He explains:

Earth, water, fire, air, ether, mind, intelligence and false ego – all together these eight constitute my separated energies.

Besides these, there is another, superior energy of mine, which comprises the living entities who are utilizing the resources of this material nature.

All created beings have their source in these two natures. Of all that is material and all that is spiritual in this world, know for certain that I am the creator, sustainer and dissolver.

There is nothing superior to me. Everything rests upon me, as pearls are strung on a thread.

I am the taste of water, the light of the sun and the moon, the root syllable Aum in the Vedic mantras, the inaudible sound in ether and the ability in humans.

I am the original fragrance of the earth. I am the heat in fire. I am the life of all that lives. I am the penances of all ascetics.

I am the eternal origin of all existences, the intelligence of the intelligent, and the prowess of all powerful humans.

I am the strength of the strong, devoid of passion and attachment. I am the procreation energy which is dharmic.

Know that all states of being – be they of goodness, passion or ignorance – are manifested by me alone. I am everything, but I am independent. I am not under the modes of material nature, for they, on the contrary, are within Me.

Yet I am above all the modes and inexhaustible (though the ignorant
do not know this).

Bhagavadgita 7.4 – 7.13

Long before the Gita, the Vedas described only one Ultimate Reality with
many layers and levels.[14] There was no shift over time in these scriptures
from polytheism to monotheism, contrary to the claims of many Western
scholars who are inclined to see unity only in the monotheistic sense or
diversity only in the polytheistic sense, one supplanting the other but
never both simultaneously. If polytheism had led to monotheism in
the Vedas, as these scholars claim, the most powerful of the Vedic gods
would have been enthroned as the ultimate ruler of the universe (similar
to the Biblical commandment, 'Thou shalt not worship any other God
before me'), which never happened.

Bandhu, the Correspondence Principle

Bandhu is a concept used to explain how the whole and the parts are
held together in integral unity. All aspects of the world stem from
a common ineffable source, and what we perceive as nature is but a
pointer to a higher reality. There is interlinking among the various
faces of this reality, such as sounds, numbers, colours and ideas, and
this interlinking is bandhu. The subtle and transcendental worlds on
one side correspond with the perceptible world on the other. The term
describes the relationship of the microcosm to the macrocosm wherein
the former is a map of the latter, and paradoxically one mirrors the other.
Every entity in the universe contains within itself the entire universe.
The One manifests as many, so even seemingly disparate elements are
in fact nothing other than its forms. It is not a matter of separate parts
coming together into a synthetic structure. Parts exist only provisionally,
temporarily and relatively to the whole, never as discrete existences,
though they have distinct roles to play within the unity and add their
own light and beauty in the process.

This idea – integral unity, with the whole manifesting in the parts, and
they in turn aspiring to unite with the whole – is reflected in all facets

of dharmic systems, including in their philosophy, science, religion, ethics, spirituality, art, music, dance, education, literature, oral narratives, politics, marriage, economics and social structures. This core principle is encoded into the symbolism of Indian art, architecture, literature, ritual, mythology, festivals, and customs, all of which are intended to facilitate access to esoteric knowledge. Indian music and sacred dance have a formal grammar based on Hindu cosmology. The *Natya-shastra* (the seminal text on performing arts and aesthetics) treats 'natya' as the total art form, including representation, poetry, dance, music, make-up and indeed the whole world. It is an organic and integral view encompassing the Vedic rituals, Shaivite dance and music, and the epic tales. The eight traditional rasas (love, humour, heroism, wonder, anger, sorrow, disgust, and fear) mirror the real world and come together in pursuit of the 'purusharthas' (human goal). The same music may be performed in either temple or court settings, thereby enabling the Muslim courts to become patrons of Kathak, a Hindu spiritual dance form noted for its universal aesthetic appeal, without seeing it as a Hindu performance, which would otherwise be condemned as idolatry.

Not only does each discipline presume this unity; so does the relationship *among* disciplines. All the arts and sciences are interrelated and may be seen as manifold ways in which human nature, itself an emanation of cosmic unity, expresses itself. One discipline contains and reflects the others. Delving deeply into any one of them eventually leads to similar integral principles and structures.

Infinite freedom is paradoxically governed by the bandhu connections among the astronomical, the terrestrial, the physiological, and the spiritual, and each of these in turn is connected, in the broadest sense, with the arts, healing systems, and culture. Bandhu implies a correspondence between the whole universe and the individual consciousness; at the same time, bandhu itself lies in the higher science of consciousness, beyond the rational/objective science. The Vedic ritual altar is a representation of the cosmos, and the architecture of Hindu temples is based on physical dimensions which correspond to various astronomical metrics. The 'yantra', an important foundation of sacred geometry, represents the universe. A deity corresponds to cosmic intelligence as well as to the intelligence within a person. Rituals establish transformations based on these correspondences. In Ayurvedic diagnosis, there is a correspondence between specific points on the tongue and the entire body, and hence an expert in this field examines the tongue as part of his analysis. Bandhu accounts for the survival of dharmic spirituality, for even when certain disciplines and practices were destroyed, other disciplines encoding the same principles survived and helped revive the overall tradition.

The great strength of all these systems is the deep sense of the relatedness of things. Those raised in dharma naturally tend to look for a common element among apparently different things, to discover the reality below the appearances and to appreciate relationships among seemingly unrelated phenomena.[15]

Kapila Vatsyayan, a scholar of classical Indian art (b. 1928), has cited many examples of bandhu in the form of common metaphors. Significant symbols may be found in the Rig Veda, the *Natya-shastra* and the *Tantrasamuccya* (text on temple architecture). The seed ('bija') represents the beginnings. The 'vriksha' (tree) rises from the bija and is the vertical pole uniting the realms. The 'nabhi' (navel) or the 'garbha' (womb) brings together the concepts of the un-manifest ('avyakta') and the manifest ('vyakta'). The 'bindu' (point or dot) is the reference point or metaphorical centre around which are drawn geometrical shapes, which in turn facilitate the comprehension of notions of time and space. The 'sunya' (void) is a symbol of fullness and emptiness. From its *arupa* (formless) nature arises the 'rupa' (form) and the *parirupa* (beyond form). There is equivalence in the relationship between sunya (emptiness) and purna (completeness or integral wholeness), the paradox being that the void has within it the whole.[16]

The computer scientist and Sanskrit scholar Subhash Kak points out that there are also correspondences across many domains through special numbers and that the two forms of knowledge – 'apara' (limited/ dual) and 'para' (higher/unified) – are in fact complementary.[17] Both are sides of the one reality and correspond to the dichotomies of inner and outer worlds, ordinary and extraordinary.[18] Similarly, Vedic hymns have several layers of structure which appear to be linked to different layers of reality.[19]

From this correspondence principle, it follows that integral unity is not expressed only in terms of divinity and devotion; transcendence to such a state is also available through art. Since time immemorial in India, art has been a way to connect the manifest and the un-manifest, evoking through form the experience that is beyond form. This is evident in Kashmir Shaivism, the *Gitagovinda*, and other major traditions and artistic works. Hence, the arts are a form of yoga which can elevate the performer – and the audience – to a heightened state of consciousness. Kapila Vatsyayan has described this state as 'the progressive and sequential bond of the 'kavi' (creator, artist), 'kavya' (the art object) and 'rasika' (the connoisseur as receiver)'.[20]

B.V. Tripurari provides a good explanation of art as Krishna bhakti. Krishna is the integral unity, and the phenomenal world is nothing other than Krishna tasting his own rasa through his own shaktis. He writes:

> Krishna is rasa, aesthetic experience, and he is rasika, the greatest connoisseur of aesthetic experience. Radha is the outpouring of this internal unity of rasa and rasika ... In the external function of lila, or divine play, Krishna fully tastes himself through his primal energy, Radha. Radha gives life to Krishna as energy brings the energetic source to life. As sugarcane cannot taste itself, similarly the tasting of the Absolute (rasa) necessitates such a dynamic, non-dual Absolute. The effect of the Absolute tasting itself through its essential shaktis is the creation of the phenomenal world and all souls' apparent relationship with it. When the Absolute (Krishna) relates with the phenomenal world, this act of grace attracts all souls to unite with him, enter his divine play, and experience rasa beyond the confines of the phenomenal world.[21]

Time, Flux and Non-linear Causation

Dharmic traditions see empirical reality as transient and in flux, blurring divisions across past, present and future. Scholar Troy Wilson Organ suggests that one reason westerners have difficulty with dharmic philosophy is that the 'static categories of Western essentialism' are inadequate for discussing the 'dynamic character of Indian thought'.[22] The Western mind seeks events fixed in space and time, i.e., history, whereas the dharma traditions are comfortable with itihasa, the more flexible narrative of the past.

In this state of flux, which affects all phenomena, repetitious patterns appear as static and independent 'things', though these are illusory constructs of the limited mind. The individual person is part of the flux, of course, yet, with the aid of meditation, he or she is able to *witness* it as a detached observer. In contrast, the Western view (at least until relatively recently) has generally assumed that space-time is finite with a defined beginning and end contained in a Cartesian, deterministic grid. Such a world can be controlled intellectually and conceptually. The dissolution of boundaries and neat partitions is considered anarchic. The West seeks absolutes which it can control.

As per dharmic thought, the interconnectedness within the cosmos has causation that is non-linear and not unidirectional. The cosmos is more complex and indeterminate and may even be said to transcend ordinary space-time. Indian syllogism and logic are retrospective: the effect comes first; then, subsequently, the cause is inferred and stated. This process is referred to as 'phalahetu', which means 'effect and cause' in that particular order.[23]

In the Biblical doctrine of creation *ex nihilo*, the universe is created out of nothing and is the first cause and beginning of time. There is nothing equivalent in dharma traditions.[24] Time is without beginning. The universe is considered without beginning; prior to this universe, there was another, and before that, yet another in an infinite series of universes with no first cause. In the famous 'Hymn of Creation' in the Rig Veda, the precise origin of the cosmos is left unknown.

A parallel to the bandhu principle is the quantum mechanics notion called quantum entanglement, according to which there can be inseparability between particles at the most fundamental levels, such that if one particle of an entangled pair shifts, this effects the others instantly regardless of the distance between them. Likewise, there would seem to be a mechanism which links one realm or dimension to another and one individual to another individual even across multiple lifetimes. The part of the person which reincarnates is entangled with the past and the future and with other individuals.[25]

An object becomes associated with good or bad qualities because it is quantum-entangled with certain 'gunas'. This is why objects become desirable or undesirable. Sacred objects such as 'vibhuti' are quantum-entangled with cosmic intelligences, so that when one puts vibhuti on one's person, it is not just an ordinary material object but something that produces certain effects. Even space is not uniform with neutral units, in the Cartesian sense, but has properties which are inseparable from their contents, and this influences the humans who dwell in a given space.[26]

Time does not come in uniform units and is textured. Different periods and moments have their distinctiveness; certain hours of the day and certain days of the week are auspicious or inauspicious ('rahukala'); certain units of time ('yugas') breed certain kinds of maladies or political and religious crises (for example, Kali Yuga, or the Age of Kali, which is believed to be a time of spiritual confusion and degeneration).[27]

Thus, unlike Western metaphysics, which considers space and time as non-material entities, in Indian metaphysics space and time are 'dhatu' (substance) and effect other things. This leads Ramanujan to conclude that, 'Contrary to the notion that Indians are "spiritual", they are really "material-minded". They are materialists, believers in substance: there is a continuity, a constant flow of substance from context to object, from non-self to self – in eating, breathing, sex, sensation, perception, thought, art, or religious experience.'[28] Ramanujan's assertion that space and time are substances that are quantum-entangled with other things does not imply the Western notion of materialism, because 'substance' is ultimately Brahman's or Bhagavan's manifestation and hence inseparable from spirituality.

Dharma Logic Includes the Middle Ground

On the whole, dharma philosophers are comfortable with uncertainty and even deploy uncertainty as a logical principle. Turning to the West, we will see how Aristotle's famous Law of the Excluded Middle argues for an either/or propositional logic (which I will unpack further in this chapter). In Eastern philosophy, many more complex, though equally rigorous, understandings of logic have been put forth.

The Jains, for instance, expound elaborate theories of 'non-unique conclusions' (a principle called 'aneka-anta-vada'), which underpin their most important and fundamental doctrines. This principle refers to pluralism and multiplicity of viewpoints, the notion that truth and reality are perceived differently from diverse points of view and that no single point of view is complete. Thus, reality possesses infinite characteristics that cannot be perceived or known at once by any ordinary mind. Different people think about different aspects of the same reality, and so their partial findings appear to contradict each other. One of the branches of this system is 'maybe logic' ('syad-vada'), in which there are outcomes other than true or false. The etymological meaning of 'syad' is 'perhaps' or 'it may be so', but in the context of syad-vada it means 'in some ways' or 'from a perspective'. Reality is complex, and no single proposition can express the nature of reality fully. Thus, the term *syad* should be prefixed before each opinion or philosophical proposition, giving it a conditional point of view and thus removing any dogmatism in the statement. There are no fixed truths or events, as these depend on many contingent factors.[29]

Nagarjuna, one of the most important Indian Buddhist philosophers, also developed a sophisticated logic, and Shankara put forward the Vedantic position that our understanding is always incomplete, subject to revision and error.[30] The Vedic statement, *truth is one but sages express it in various ways*, is also a call to respect others' knowledge, which could prove to be true in the end. Indian logic has many rival schools, which accounts for the absence of any final, singular epistemology. (Appendix A gives further explanations of the Hindu, Buddhist and Jain approaches to flexible logic.)

An important feature of Sanskrit is that there are at least six ways of being different from something, as opposed to simple true/false options. The Sanskrit prefix 'a' can express at least seven types of differences: negation; approximation; absence; difference (which allows for some similarities); reduction/diminution; badness/unworthiness/impropriety/tamas; and opposite/contradiction.[31] Binary, Western, yes/no logic, on the other hand, stipulates that all answers must be one or the other, with no options, i.e., no 'maybe' or uncertainty or indeterminate state.

The Indian approach to scientific problems starts with empirical observations leading to a pragmatic recipe (algorithm), and this recipe is always falsifiable if found to contradict future measurements. It is more a working hypothesis subject to improvement through better measurement. There is nothing final about any given recipe, and all such recipes are provisional and relative depending on one's state of consciousness. In the inner sciences, this empirical methodology is turned inward with the yogi using his or her own body, in effect, as a laboratory. This empirical approach differs from the Judeo-Christian one, which is characterized more by conflict with opposing methods and the finality of doctrine.

Roddam Narasimha, a physicist, considers the Indian empirical approach to be pragmatic. He writes: 'The Greek approach may be thought of as axiomatic and model-making (*axioms* or *models* → *logical deduction* → *theorem* or *result*); and the Indian approach as that of pattern-seekers and algorithm-makers (*observation* → *algorithm* → *validated conclusion*). The Indian intellectual approach betrays a deep suspicion of axioms and models yet demonstrates great ingenuity ...'[32] He goes on to say that, contrary to popular perceptions, Indian astronomers have excelled at observation; the parameters in Aryabhata's algorithm were repeatedly fine-tuned over the centuries as observation revealed discrepancies. *Verification,* then, is very much a part of the Indian approach. The Western, model-making culture is rigid and ridden with conflicts, resulting in claims and counterclaims.[33]

Recent developments in physics and mathematics are far more compatible with dharmic logic than with the strictly Aristotelian model. Newtonian physics does not allow for the possibility of certain physical phenomena required in semiconductors, lasers, and other devices. These phenomena are based on quantum mechanics, which relies on uncertainty – a discovery that shook the foundations of Western philosophy but did not at all disturb Indian philosophers. Not even Einstein was able to reconcile himself to the uncertainty inherent in quantum mechanics, prompting him to remark: 'God does not play dice with the universe.' But Shiva and Parvati, the Hindu cosmic couple, *do* happily play dice. Indian philosophy is receptive to the uncertainty theories of physics. For the same reason, many Western pioneers of modern physics, such as Werner Heisenberg (1901–76) and Erwin Schrödinger (1887–1961), both of whom won Nobel Prizes for discovering quantum mechanics, were attracted to Hindu philosophy and rejected the Newtonian and Cartesian models. Modern physics trumped the Newtonian–Cartesian scheme in which nature can be described objectively using a set of mathematical equations; the existence of an observer is not necessary. In his book *What is Life?* Schrödinger writes:

> From the early great Upanishads, the recognition ATHMAN = BRAHMAN (the personal self equals the omnipresent, all-comprehending eternal self) was in Indian thought considered, far from being blasphemous, to represent the quintessence of deepest insight into the happenings of the world. The striving of all the scholars of Vedanta was, after having learnt to pronounce with their lips, really to assimilate in their minds this grandest of all thoughts.[34]

The Vedic notion of integral unity clearly influenced his thinking when he wrote:

> This life of yours which you are living is not merely apiece of this entire existence, but in a certain sense the whole; only this whole is not so constituted that it can be surveyed in one single glance. This, as we know, is what the Brahmins express in that sacred, mystic formula which is yet really so simple and so clear; *tat tvam asi*, this is you. Or, again, in such words as "I am in the east and the west, I am above and below, I am this entire world.[35]

According to his biographer, Walter Moore, there is a clear continuity between Schrödinger's understanding of Vedanta and his research:

> The unity and continuity of Vedanta are reflected in the unity and continuity of wave mechanics. In 1925, the world view of physics was a model of a great machine composed of separable interacting material particles. During the next few years, Schrödinger and Heisenberg and their followers created a universe based on superimposed inseparable waves of probability amplitudes. This new view would be entirely consistent with the Vedantic concept of All in One.[36]

Schrödinger wrote about his insight based on Vedanta in 1925, describing his breakthrough in reconciling multiple, simultaneous states of a system:

But it is quite easy to express the solution in words, thus: the plurality that we perceive is only an appearance; it is not real. Vedantic philosophy, in which this is a fundamental dogma, has sought to clarify it by a number of analogies, one of the most attractive being the many-faceted crystal which, while showing hundreds of little pictures of what is in reality a single existent object, does not really multiply the object.[37]

Here is another fragment of that landmark essay: 'You may suddenly come to see, in a flash, the profound rightness of the basic conviction of Vedanta: ... knowledge, feeling and choice are essentially eternal and unchangeable and numerically one in all men, nay in all sentient beings.'

Finally, Schrödinger makes an interesting analogy between Vedanta philosophy and modern physics: 'If finally we look back at that idea of [Ernst] Mach [1838-1916], we shall realize that it comes as near to the orthodox dogma of the Upanishads as it could possibly do without stating it *expressis verbis*. The external world and consciousness are one and the same thing.'[38]

John Wheeler (1911–2008), one of the foremost quantum physicists of our time, writes: 'I like to think that someone will trace how the deepest thinking of India made its way to Greece and from there to the philosophy of our times.'[39]

To the modern philosophy of science, Vedanta has made a critical contribution, to wit the notion that the observer (hence consciousness) plays a role in shaping the observed. This point was the source of the disagreement between Einstein and Tagore cited earlier. The Vedanta principle launched what has become the thriving field of Consciousness Studies in the West. Related to uncertainty are various other dharmic notions of the limits of normative logic. When, in the 1930s, Gödel's theorem demonstrated how a system of deductive logic *had* to be incomplete, classical Indian logicians were validated.

This is not to suggest that ancient Indians developed or tested the hypotheses of quantum mechanics or even Gödel's theorems, but it is worth noting that these modern discoveries are compatible with dharmic philosophy and that the metaphysical predispositions of this philosophy render it open to such implications and extensions. The ability to deal with complexity – including multiple perspectives and uncertain outcomes – is the very foundation of dharmic pluralism, in metaphysics, physics and humanities.

Not surprisingly, dharma philosophies make greater use of negation as a technique for approximating truth than do Western ones. A positive statement is rejected in favour of one or more of the seven kinds of negations noted above in order to underscore the idea that truth may be beyond simple categories. Ultimate reality is *not* merely material, *not* limited, and *not* entirely transcendent. When dealing with problems of ultimate reality, an assertion of advaita (non-duality) is preferred to an assertion of monism (oneness).[40] This negation extends to ethics. 'I do not wish to harm you' offers a richer range of possibilities than 'I wish to help you', just as 'I do not despise you' encompasses more than 'I embrace you'. Likewise, in Buddhism and Hinduism, ahimsa (non-harming) means so much more than compassion, charity, etc.

When ideas cease to be acceptable as fact, there is a tendency in dharma not to expel them outright but to accommodate them as allegory.[41] Hindus, for instance, absorb the intellectual aspects of their culture through myths and scriptures much more easily than westerners do. The historicity or logic of these myths and scriptures is irrelevant to their practical value and spiritual meaning. Diverse texts can be read together in the spirit of participating poetically in the inner meaning. In the case of the Bhagavadgita, whether or not an actual fight occurred between the Pandavas and the Kauravas on the battlefield of Kurukshetra is of less consequence than the idea of the struggle as an archetype of the eternal conflict between dharma and adharma.

Views and Relative Knowledge

Dharma philosophies explore the *limits of what can be expressed*. Reality is deemed too complex to be exhausted by a single predication or even by multiple ones.[42] Dharmic systems emphasize that truth is relative to one's perception, predisposition and conditioning, including the effects of past lives. The Rig Veda's famous statement, 'Truth is one, the wise call it by different names', affirms this wisdom in recognizing the pluralities generated by different points of view.[43] The well-known story of the elephant and the blind men illustrates just this point: Six blind men are asked to touch an object (unbeknownst to them, an elephant) and correctly identify it. The men touch different parts of the elephant and come up with entirely different conclusions as to what the object might be, with none identifying it correctly – the moral being that perspectives are relative and the whole truth is beyond any one perspective. The blindness of the men represents the relative and partial nature of all such perspectives, and their number symbolizes the five senses plus the mind, none of which alone is capable of ascertaining the truth.

The intellectual spectacles formed by our own culture and personal conditioning determine how we perceive the world. We select, group and organize the multiplicity of events in our language in order to give them coherence to the world. In Sanskrit, the closest term for philosophy is darshana, which means 'view', as in looking at a thing from a given angle. There are many views of reality depending on where one is situated and the language one is using, but total and absolute truth is never perceptible from any given view since every view is limited. It is therefore to be expected that spiritual viewpoints vary and differ from each other.

Absolute reality merely refers to a state that is final and cannot be further transcended. This is not describable by a view, and hence we refer to it as 'ineffable'. The closest we can get to it is via some combination of the following:

1. Pointers that do not describe it as such but give some sense of its nature;
2. Practical methods that are known to lead to its experience beyond cognition;
3. Metaphorical or poetic feelings that enable us to experience it in some sense; and
4. Approximate representations of it in some framework or view (though no representation could be exact or else the reality would be describable).

Ultimate freedom means freedom from all (limited) views. Therefore, whereas in the West there is a tendency to think of their contradictoriness as an obstacle, the various limited views and their truths should serve as tools for achieving this freedom. Attempts to conceptualize reality in any absolute sense are always limited by cognition and hampered by ego attachment (and the distortions that result from such attachment). Such attempts inevitably result in intolerance, selfishness, and incapacity for detached witnessing. It was for this reason that Buddha taught a provisional faith which is to be tested by the individual's personal experience. The dharma is taught so as to allow such self-testing by everyone who is spiritually inclined. Ultimately, like a raft which has been used to cross a river, it is to be discarded. Philosophy, theology and scripture can play useful provisional roles – but only as guides.

Cognitive diversity also corresponds to the capacities and interests of different viewers. Sri Aurobindo explains how this diversity of perspectives is part of the diversity of the cosmos:

> The real aim of Nature is a true unity supporting a rich diversity. Her secret is clear enough from the fact that though she moulds on one general plan, she insists always on an infinite variation. The plan of the human form is one, yet no two human beings are precisely alike in their physical characteristics. Human nature is one in its constituents and its grand lines, but no two human beings are precisely alike in their temperament, characteristics and psychological substance. All life is one in its essential plan and principle; even the plant is a recognizable brother of the animal; but the unity of life admits and encourages an infinite variety of types.[44]

The influence of perspective on truth is seen in Indian philosophy, too, where each school is a darshana, or the direct, immediate and intuitive vision of truth. However, each darshana is only one view and has to allow for the possible validity of other perspectives. Ultimate Reality in these traditions has infinite aspects, but some of those aspects can be known or experienced only in higher states of consciousness. Since reality is depicted as multilayered and multifaceted, many scholars misinterpret Hinduism as polytheistic. They do not understand that the multiple deities are but different aspects of the same integral unity.[45]

Although ultimate reality is formless and beyond conception, humans are able at least to approach it with the aid of tangible representations, such as deities. In Hinduism, each deity has a variety of alternative biographical narratives. These are not meant to be taken as literal history and might not even fit coherently into the empirical realm of linear space-time-causation. The term darshana also refers to respectful adoration of the deity in the temple (and within the devotee). Each deity is open to myriad interpretations and forms of devotion, as evidenced by the amazing variety of conceptualizations for Ganesha or Kali.[46] Since all descriptions are relative, the Supreme Being is explained as either male or female, both male and female, neither male nor female, and beyond gender altogether. The Supreme as female has many representations; indeed, only in the dharma traditions is there such an elaborate theology surrounding the Supreme as feminine.

Seen in the context of this relativity, rituals may be seen as a form of sacred theatre. All senses are used in the performance: visual objects, sounds, fragrances, actions, touch, and taste. The ritual enriches our understanding (through metaphor) and engages us in various ways – intellectual, emotional, conceptual, etc., and via paranormal access to a higher intelligence. Westerners unaccustomed to the elaborate, multifaceted content of such rituals are inclined to dismiss them as polytheistic chaos.

Thus all theistic and non-theistic representations stem from exalted experiences and are best viewed as graphic articulations and approximations rather than actual replicas of historical persons or stories.[47] They are intended to help man, with his limited faculties, to conceive of Ultimate Reality. The immense variety of representations reveals Indians' taste for symbols, for experimentation, for the artistic, and for the adventurous with a corresponding disdain for literalism and colourless depictions. The reverberations of this are felt in the prolific and colourful culture (including pop culture; for example, Bollywood).

These representations and enactments are not the result of dissent or revolt, nor do they necessarily supersede previous ones. They are but affirmations that the Supreme has innumerable forms. In dharma traditions, all systems of thought remain, to some extent, in play. The impulse is not to overturn ideas but to find ways to reconcile evolving ideas; even dissent may be integrated as a subset or partial view.[48] This provides continuity to those who choose to retain existing ways and rituals (without being made to feel primitive or obsolete), and validates, as it were, the various other ways of seeking the truth.[49]

The dharmic reservations with respect to our ability to represent divinity extend to the role of reason. As a result of past conditioning, any view of reality is relative, partial, and prone to error. Reason has been accepted as important from the beginning, though it is not by itself capable of achieving illumination or higher consciousness. Troy Wilson Organ expresses how the quest for unity across the dharma systems underpins the unity of Hindus despite all their diversity:

> Social groups are united by many different integrators: blood, language, religion, vocation, devotion, etc. But Hindus are united by a common questing for oneness. The Indian nation must cope with many divisive factors, such as more than a dozen languages, scores of religions and sects [and] thousands of caste groupings. Furthermore, the modern concept of nation does not harmonize with the Hindu emphasis on primary human relationships. Yet, there is one factor within Hinduism upon which India can build, and that is the integrating quest itself. Inclusiveness, not exclusiveness, is the principle of Hinduism. This principle is expressed by Krishna in the Bhagavad Gita when he reminds Arjuna, 'Whatever form any devotee with faith wishes to worship, I make that faith of his steady' (7:21). Hinduism is *sadhana*, the questing for the perfection in man.[50]

Indian tradition even acknowledges relative truths. These are not considered outright false or evil (in the Christian sense) but, again, a reflection of the limited cognition of the human mind. Whatever humans know is relative to contexts and cannot be simplified into canons, commandments or universal/normative rules. Both absolute and relative truths have their place. Relative truths help us to understand and cope with worldly reality in accordance with dharma. This belies the common allegation that Buddhism and Hinduism are world-negating and/or other-worldly perspectives and, as such, socially and ethically irresponsible.[51]

Freedom and Pluralism

One aspiration common to both West and East is freedom from limitations and bondage. The Western traditions emphasize the social, political and cultural dimensions of freedom in this world, as well as freedom from sin and death in the next. From a Western perspective, the dharmic traditions are passive, fatalistic and filled with despair. When we reverse the gaze, however, a different picture emerges. The dharma traditions see themselves as free from Western 'complexes', do not bear the burden of sin and guilt, and are not shackled by institutional authority, historical precedent or religious exclusivity.

Freedom to Learn from Within Oneself

The dharma traditions differ radically from the Judeo-Christian religions in that every human is considered capable, through his or her own spiritual practices, of becoming a living rishi, 'jina', 'arahat' or 'bodhisattva'. These states are the origin of many sacred texts.

Spiritual masters can thus discover new insights in ways that are inexhaustible. There will always be innumerable spiritual traditions, histories, paths, rituals, symbols, deities and communities. This explosion of original sources and texts is far greater than what is stored in the Jewish and Christian canons, commandments and prophesies. Huge libraries of scriptures document the direct empirical experiences of people from various lineages plus centuries of peer debates. Spiritual know-how is thus cumulative as opposed to substitutive, though some traditions may fade away naturally over time. There have been no incidents of institutionalized and systematic burning of books within the dharma traditions. They are an open body of knowledge without any end or finality, so there is always room for new ideas and experience. The traditions change over time, and yet their continuity enables them to encompass the ancient, modern and postmodern simultaneously and comfortably. Various traditions have also influenced and cross-fertilized each other in profound ways.

Throughout the tradition, the pursuit of truth has been inseparable from regular spiritual practice (sadhana), whose purpose is to alleviate suffering and bring illumination. This differs from the Western preference for information over transformation. Dharmic approaches to the divine reject speculation for its own sake.[52]

Dharma knowledge is classified into shruti (revealed knowledge), 'mata' (opinion or theory), 'vada' (argument or view), 'siddhanta' (proven theory), 'shastras' (systems of thought or well-established viewpoints to guide us), and smriti (historical record). When asked what the Hindu Bible is, I always respond that Hindus have a *library*, not just one book. Any complex body of knowledge requires more than one. While Judeo-Christian traditions have generated a number of commentaries on their respective scriptures, there have been attempts to freeze permanent and immutable canons in each since their inception. In dharma, no single history book is the exclusive final authority.[53] Indeed, written scripture is subordinated in Hinduism to the more direct means of oral transmission.[54] Since reason and representation are seen as conditioned and relative, there is no point in canonizing the various paths, scriptures and spiritual practices.

Freedom from Conditioning and Karma

Dharma is meant ultimately to free humans from the bonds of karma, using a variety of methods. This leads to the state known as sat-chit-ananda or 'unity consciousness', in which the practitioner spontaneously performs actions as required in his or her circumstances (which are brought about by the momentum of past karmas). Once in that state, no fresh karma is accumulated because of the absence of the ego as intentional doer of the actions. The karma of the past gradually gets depleted and exhausted.

The Buddhist equivalent of this is the realization that everything has merely a momentary episodic existence and that all these 'things' are interconnected, including every entity – past, present and future – in the cosmos. There is no physical or conceptual entity whatsoever that can be isolated. This realization liberates one from the bondage of 'things', which ultimately do not exist, and the pursuit of which inevitably causes suffering. Buddhism's transcendence from the relative world brings freedom, enabling one to achieve nirvana *in the body*.

Karma, contrary to Western misconception, is not fatalism in the sense of an external force depriving humans of free will. This misunderstanding has significantly distorted the West's understanding of dharmic civilization. In truth, the principle of karma is a constant challenge to act without attachment to the fruits. There is a whole branch of yoga called karma yoga in which the spiritual practice consists of good works. These are not performed for the sake of any deferred reward but for their own sake as a way of realizing freedom from ego-based perception in the present.

Sri Aurobindo, among others, posits that humanity is itself the stage or point in evolution at which the cosmos starts returning to Oneness. In other words, the human being is the agent of return to unity consciousness amidst the multiplicity.[55] It is ridiculous, then, to claim that Hinduism lacks agency. This worldview has important social implications. Organ writes:

> Hinduism seeks the ultimate integration in the great Upanishad affirmations 'That thou art' and 'Atman is Brahman.' Any 'that' in its essence is a 'thou'; and all are one in Brahman. 'Why should I treat my neighbor as myself?', man asks. Hinduism's answer is a most conclusive one: 'Because your neighbor *is* yourself – your Real Self.' Here may be a clue for the solution of the most important social problem of our day: how to achieve the unity of man within the diversity of nations.[56]

Freedom from History and Institutional Authority

In Hindu traditions, the state of consciousness of Jesus is achievable by each one of us and is not dependent on belief in a specific deity or historical event or institution. Nor do we have to die in order to achieve this state of consciousness; we can do so while living in this world, just as Christ presumably did. 'Dhyana', 'jnana', 'tantra' and 'bhakti' are some of the do-it-yourself methods and techniques that do not rely on external authority. There is no church, pontiff or central authority. Rather, numerous incarnations, prophets, saints and spiritual methods over several millennia have kept the traditions alive with fresh interpretations. As Sri Aurobindo puts it:

> Here is the first baffling difficulty over which the European mind stumbles; for it finds itself unable to make out what Indian Religion is. Where, it asks, is its soul? Where is its mind and fixed thoughts? Where is the form of its body? How can there be a religion which has no rigid dogmas to demand belief on pain of eternal damnation, no theological postulates, even no fixed theology, no *credo*, distinguishing it from antagonistic or rival religions? How can there be a religion that has no papal head, no governing ecclesiastic body, no church, chapel or congregational system, no binding religious form of any kind obligatory on all its adherents, no one administration and discipline? For the Hindu priests are mere ceremonial officials without any ecclesiastical authority or disciplinary powers and the pundits are mere interpreters of the Shastra, not the lawgivers of the religion or its rulers. How again can Hinduism be called a religion when it admits all beliefs, allowing even a high-reaching atheism and agnosticism and permits all possible spiritual experiences, all kinds of religious adventures?[57]

Hinduism has no standard or official (i.e., normative) theology, because there was never an ecclesiology in ancient India: no formalization of church-like institutions, no official clerical body with universal authority to canonize, normalize and make critical editions of dogma, and especially no structures to be forced on society. Even where such authoritative claims existed, they had limited jurisdiction and were vigorously challenged and hence never succeeded in retaining much control over time.[58]

No authority pronounces someone a Hindu. There is no mandatory equivalent to baptism as a point of entry, nothing which is performed by a church-certified priest or minister and makes one a member of the Christian community. Since Hinduism does not require membership in an organization, club or institution, and since it glorifies sadhus, who pursue their own independent journey, the problem of excessive institutional control has never arisen. No authority has the power to excommunicate a person from Hinduism.

There are many forms of devotional practice in the dharma traditions – performed individually or as a group, directed to a formless God or a particular deity, performed at home or in a temple. The average dharma practitioner is largely free from institutional authority, or at least there is no theological requirement for the equivalent of a church or umma.

There is a commonly held view that westerners, by and large, are individualistic whereas Asians are not, and yet, on examination, the exact opposite would appear to be the case. Westerners who practice Judaism or Christianity tend to be formal members of well-defined religious organizations which engender conformity. Many Western families have been affiliated with such institutions for centuries. Change is slow and based on consensus which forms over long periods. Individual dissent and attempts at personalizing religious practice are frowned upon. In contrast, dharma traditions are marked by individualism at the base.

No dharmic group would consider enforcing its particular tradition or set of practices on all of humanity or even on another community. No religious group in the history of dharmic civilizations has ever tried to do so - at least not for any significant length of time and not over a large territory. None of the dharma spiritual traditions is compelled by God or any other authority to convert others. The individual's spiritual journey toward enlightened living is not based on any collective action, feat or performance by one's group over any other groups. There are no infidels - only a lack of knowledge. Local governors ('jati-panchayats') have had the authority to impose fines for breach of rules and expel errant members in extreme cases, but their jurisdiction is always local and limited.

There is no privileged tribe, culture, place or time relative to God, because God is a prolific communicator, always accessible, and does not grant anyone the exclusive franchise to represent him. No community's narrative is absolute, nor is it sanctioned to undermine the narratives of others. This is how diverse worldviews, practices, paths, images and subcultures can coexist.

Nor is it necessary that there be ideological agreement in order to be worthy of respect. Shankara, for example, did not exclude people who dissented from his view from entering his circle; rather, he engaged them in dialogue. Intellectual debate and reason were never severed from religious life, faith and worship.

Freedom to Choose a Personal Path (Svadharma)

In most dharmic traditions, each individual has a unique 'svadharma' (personal dharma) or purpose in this world. This is based on his or her 'svabhava' (character) as shaped by past karma and gunas and on the context or circumstances of the person's life. Buddhists have the notion of 'upaya' (skilful means), which becomes the basis for mutual respect between those who are different. In the Jain tradition, principles of relative and multiple perspectives of truth, combined with the inherent uncertainty in knowledge, serve as protection against dogmas and universal absolutes. All of this demonstrates that dharmic spiritual practices are diverse, eclectic, and adaptable by communities, families, and individuals, and for specific circumstances.

The pursuits in life are organized into four categories with distinct ethics recommended for each: *worldly dharma* is the pursuit of righteous and ethical living, including one's relationships with family, society and the natural environment; 'artha' is the pursuit of material wealth and prosperity by ethical means; 'kama' is the fulfilment of physical desires without compromising the ethics; and 'moksha' is self-realization and liberation.

Unburdened by the belief that there is only one right path to the ultimate truth, dharma has flowered in many directions. For example, Hindus often see themselves as following one or a combination of four main paths of yoga: direct intuitive knowledge (jnana yoga), meditation (dhyana), devotion (bhakti), and perfection in work (karma). These paths are not mutually exclusive nor conflicting, and they correspond to the individual seeker's natural preferences.

Freedom of Choice of Deity (Ishta-Devata)

In Hinduism, avatars are incarnations of God. An avatar is a being who plays a role similar to the role played by Jesus in Christianity, except that the avatar is not exclusive and allows for similar claims by other traditions. Hindus, therefore, are able to accept Jesus as divine, as an incarnation of God, but not as the *exclusive* incarnation. Rama and Krishna are the two most commonly worshipped Hindu avatars. Devotion to one deity does not render the others defective, because Bhagavan's omnipresence in the cosmos provides many access points.

The various deities are attributes, cosmic processes and energies of the one Ultimate Reality, and are not gods and goddesses in the pagan sense. They manifest as either feminine ('devis', such as Lakshmi, Durga, et al.) or masculine ('devas', such as Agni, Vayu, and so on). All goddesses are facets of the one Goddess, who in turn is not subordinate to God but is God herself in the form of shakti (intelligence-energy). Devi is simply the feminine equivalent of deva and not a derivative as 'goddess' is to 'god'. The human-like images used to represent deities in Hindu and Buddhist tantra and yoga are not idols but are akin to an artist's rendering of an abstract principle. Hence the same deity may be represented in thousands of variations, including images that are not personified (such as geometric diagrams), or indeed without any images at all. In certain kinds of tantra, the deities are imagined within one's body as energies and intelligences which correspond to cosmic energies and intelligences. This is the principle of 'bandhu' at work. The divine as feminine is also worshipped as sacred geography; for instance, the river Ganga is a manifestation of Ganga devi and considered her body.

The concept of a personal deity for spiritual focus is called ishta-devata. Puja is a common ritual of worship in which a devotee invites the ishta-devata to be his or her honoured guest out of utmost love and devotion. Most Hindus believe in a direct private communion with their chosen ishta-devata without any intermediary, and most families set aside a place in their home to serve as a shrine for daily worship.

Besides visuals, the ishta-devata can actually be a mantra. Each sound in the Sanskrit alphabet corresponds to a specific divine intelligence or energy. This is why there are many mantras from which to choose depending on the individual's nature or circumstances.

Each individual's worship of his or her ishta-devata may be seen as a unique and personalized monotheism in the sense that, for the given worshipper, that deity represents the one Supreme Being. But this monotheism is not universalized and imposed on others. Only when the particular deity of a given religion gets universalized does the problem of exclusivism erupt. A Hindu would say that Christians have taken their ishta-devata (i.e., Jesus) and universalized him, then further boosted their own power by means of aggressive evangelism.[59]

The Dharmic Golden Rule

The Western golden rule says we must do to others what we want them to do to us. This is, of course, a pragmatic way to optimize the outcome for each party concerned. On a higher level, the Judeo-Christian religions assert that one should love one's neighbour as one loves oneself. The dharmic golden rule takes this a step further and says that there *is* no ultimate 'other' because each apparent other is ultimately the same as oneself. In short, love your neighbour as you love yourself because your neighbour *is* yourself. This is based on the metaphysics of integral unity discussed above.

The Bhagavadgita (2:14–15) advocates equanimity (samata) toward all because the Ultimate Reality is manifest as all beings, and all beings are in it and are inseparable from it. It clarifies (13:27) that the self is alike (sama) in all beings and that the development of character and personality (gunavikasa) is the chief means of cultivating equanimity. Sama is used here to mean ontological identity. The spirit of even-mindedness and disciplined equality (samata) generates the conviction that there dwells in each person the same spirit, and it is this that fortifies the feeling of solidarity. Arjuna is therefore told to cultivate samata (2:48).

This equanimity also permeates the attitude to skin colour in dharmic civilizations. Lord Krishna as well as Lord Rama, the two most prominent Hindu avatars, are dark, as are Kali and Durga, the most popular forms of the Goddess. Vishnu, too, is dark ('megha varna', i.e., the colour of the rain clouds), and so is Shiva. There is an explicit discussion in the Mahabharata in which varna as colour is disregarded as a criterion in preference to the criterion of gunas.

In the spirit of the same golden rule, dharmic practitioners are not asked to interfere with other faiths – an attitude sometimes mistaken for passivity. There is no requirement to proselytize, no doctrine to kill those who differ in their religious views, no teaching to destroy others' places or forms of worship, nor to denigrate them as damned or evil, nor to impose punishments or taxation of any kind on them for their religious beliefs.

It is not surprising that Hindus gave sanctuary to the early Christians, Jews and Zoroastrians who fled their homelands because of religious persecution in the early centuries following the rise of Christianity and then Islam. Zoroastrianism was a major world religion in and around Persia until the arrival of Islam. Fleeing Zoroastrians received refuge in India, and India is the only place in the world where they thrive today. Many of India's top industrialists, public officials and professionals are Zoroastrians (who call themselves Parsees). The Thomas Christians of south India trace their origins back to the early period after Jesus and have a place of respect and honour in India's pluralism. The oldest continuously operating synagogue in the world is in Cochin (now Kochi) in south India.

Had Jesus been born in India, he might well have been assimilated as another great avatar along with Rama, Krishna and others. As it is, Jesus is sometimes included in the Hindu pantheon of deities in many Indian homes and even temples (such as the Ramakrishna Mission and Paramahansa Yogananda's ashram, for example) and is promoted by many Hindu gurus as being on par with Krishna, Rama, Shiva and other deities. For a Hindu, to say 'one Lord, one church, one way' is unacceptable, naive, and completely unimaginative; it is to ignore nature's diversity, the human situation, and the abundance of divine communication that is available.

But short of rejecting its core beliefs, Christianity cannot recognize Krishna and Rama as it recognizes Jesus, i.e., as human incarnations of God, nor can it grant that Lord Shiva is ever-present as the supreme deity of transcendence, nor that Devi is God-as-Mother and also God-as-Consort to be worshipped as a manifestation of the Supreme Being. Nor can it grant that each deity has numerous forms accessible through multifaceted means and that none is under any centralized human authority or control.

It is not surprising that none of the Abrahamic religions has ever integrated with another Abrahamic religion, much less with any non-Abrahamic one. Hindus' intrinsic belief in pluralism means that many of them are blissfully unaware that their sentiments are not at all reciprocated by the Abrahamic religions, which not only reject every other deity but also consign Hinduism to paganism and the worship of false gods.

Dharmic radical pluralism is integral and not an afterthought to be overlaid on original scripture. In our modern times, Jewish and Christian religions have to compromise or modify their otherwise rigid stance under the garb of tolerance, typically to appear politically correct and avoid conflicts. Or it is perhaps part of the strategy of inculturation, designed to disarm potential converts by pretending to respect their culture only to engage in aggressive conversion at a later stage.

The pluralistic ethos of the Mahabharata, for instance, is grounded in a non-exclusivist framework including multiplicity of beliefs, concepts and ideas. This is so deeply ingrained as to make Indians psychologically comfortable with relative truths, uncertainty, ambiguity, disorder and pluralism of all kinds. The Mahabharata records numerous philosophical dialogues wherein protagonists argue across different philosophical systems, and pluralism permeates these debates. The epic includes many philosophical systems, such as Samkhya, Vaishnava and Shaiva theologies, and various non-theistic Shramana ideas.[60] Ethics, politics and sociology are debated in an atmosphere of intellectual freedom.[61] This is in contrast with Yahweh, the jealous God of the chosen people who demands unconditional obedience through His firebrand prophets and threatens to unleash His wrath if His strict rules of worship and conduct are not obeyed.

The Synthetic Unity of the West

I now turn to the Judeo-Christian traditions and seek to show that, from the dharmic point of view, they suffer from serious problems which stem from their fundamental assumptions and cosmologies. Their difficulty with others' difference creates anxiety, which is then projected outward. My premise is that Western civilization (or Judeo-Christian civilization when we wish to stress the religious and cosmological substrate) possesses unity which is at best synthetic in the sense defined in this book. This unity begins with parts that are separate and independent and brought together only through immense effort. While the West has made progress in integrating its parts, it has done so, for the most part, by deliberately bringing together extremely incompatible and fundamentally different worldviews. This process emerges from a zero-sum approach to competing perspectives, making it difficult for these perspectives to coexist and interact freely. Disparate elements must be fused such that one side prevails outright. The losing side's parts are selectively appropriated, and those that do not accord with the fundamentals are rejected and denounced.

The West, with its emphasis on individualism, is invested in the elevation of the ego. Egotism is reinforced by an emphasis on reasoning, which gives rise to either/or thinking and atomized cosmology which the ego can deal with in a controllable manner. It is through this lens that differences with the outside are perceived. When the westerner, restricted as he is to binary reasoning, looks at Hinduism, the challenge to his worldview can seem extreme and even dangerous. His response usually is to recoil and try to reduce this complex, often chaotic religion and culture into one or another conceptual straitjacket such as polytheism, caste-based hierarchy, and the like.

In order to understand the origins of this problem, we need to look at some aspects of the development of the West: first, the split between a Jewish/Christian cosmology and the classical Greek worldview, then five key developments during which the attempts at synthetic unity break down. In most instances, the worldviews in conflict are themselves synthetic rather than integral, and hence the conflicts are violent. There is a tendency for each successive stage either to digest or to eradicate prior stages because they are seen as threats. The result is a pattern of instability and discontinuity.

The Templeton Project to Re-invent the West

Before we delve into this analysis, I shall describe my experience at a world conference on science and religion in Bangalore in 2003, an experience which brought into sharp focus the fragile and inconsistent inner unity of Western thought. The Templeton Foundation, the biggest such institution in the field attempting to harmonize current science with religion (mainly Christianity), had flown in scientific luminaries, including Nobel laureates, most of whom had publicly proclaimed allegiance to Christianity. These scholars explained the ties between their personal religious beliefs and science. The then and present head of Templeton is a self-described Christian evangelical, which is ironic given that evangelicals traditionally oppose secular science in favour of literal biblical claims. Yet these speakers seemed genuinely to want to bring their faith and science together.

To accomplish this intellectual gymnastics, they had to resort to neo-Vedantic principles (without acknowledgement) that assert that consciousness is the only ultimate reality and basis of unity. These principles served as the scientific basis for their own religion no matter how much they had to stretch the interpretation of the authoritative biblical canons to make their case. Indeed, the Vedantic principles that consciousness is everything and that the material world is its manifestation have become the fashionable way to claim compatibility between religion and quantum mechanics.

But such scholars of science and religion fail to acknowledge that this view of consciousness is not at all the normative theology in the Jewish and Christian religions, and it contradicts some of their basic assumptions about the nature of the self and world and their relation to God. On this occasion, the speakers completely evaded the important distinction between divine and human consciousness, which can never be overcome in mainstream Jewish and Christian theologies. They glossed over the insistence that revelation happened only from 'above' at specific points in history and gave the impression that all religions, including Christianity, are based on quantum mechanics. Upon observing these contradictions in the opening day's speeches, I had a restless night pondering my own talk, which was to follow the next day.

I decided to set aside what I had planned to say and discussed several key questions instead: Can universal truth-claims be considered scientific if they are *contingent on a particular account of history,* especially if they depend on a historical event that could never be replicated? More to the point, what does a scientist think of claims of God's unique interventions which are space-time discontinuities and which violate or permanently change the laws of the cosmos? Can science afford to legitimize any grand narratives of human history, including the notion of an apocalyptic End Time which God is said to have revealed via his interventions? Should the scientific approach to spirituality be to prove historical narratives of one's religion, or should it be an open-ended process that also critiques the *methods* used to arrive at religious canons? Should the attempts to apply science to religion use scientific standards of inquiry to question religious dogmas and not just to legitimize certain religions? Are not many scholars invested in the religious outcomes of their inquiries?

As a physicist, I was troubled that the eminent scientists assembled had deftly abstracted out the history-centrism at the core of their religious traditions in order to make them appear scientific. In other words, they had represented their religions without any reference to historicity whatsoever, thereby altering their message to suit the scientific audience. Nobody in attendance wanted to acknowledge these concerns. So I provoked them further by asking: Are scientists with Judeo-Christian religious affiliations evading the problem of *history-centrism* in scientific discussions even though history-centrism is at the heart of their exclusivity claims?

To highlight the contrast between history-centric religions and others, I described some a-historical methods of the dharmic traditions and characterized them as first-person scientific empiricism. Then I asked: What does science have to say about truth-claims which are based on discoveries brought about by *human potential,* which can be replicated by others and which are not based on God's interventions in history via prophets? In other words, is adhyatma-vidya (based on inherent human potential) an empirical science, and if so, can it be reconciled with historically *unique* revelations?

My talk explaining the issue of history-centrism was aggressively attacked by an Indian Christian named Joseph Prabhu, an affiliate of the Templeton Foundation and a politically active leader in Hinduism studies in the American academy. But many other Indians approached me afterwards to express support, saying that I had raised 'an important issue which had to be addressed' even though it was 'not what most people wanted to hear'. Some prominent voices suggested that my history-centrism construct deserved an important place in the discourse and encouraged me to continue to show that history-centrism *cannot* be reconciled with science. This was another defining moment in my work on the central role played by history-centrism in certain religions.

The scientists present also seemed to ignore more recent developments. It is well known that the European movement known as the Enlightenment was a prolonged attack on the Christian edifice in order to allow free scientific inquiry and clip the wings of the politically powerful clergy. Christianity lost this fight against science, and its theologians are now busy repackaging their historical dogmas in science-compliant ways. Such scholars are having a remarkable impact on the reconstruction of Christianity as a 'scientific theology'. They deploy philosophical categories such as 'Whiteheadian thought,' much as earlier church theologians had appropriated Greek philosophy.

As I delved deeper, I realized that the schisms between Christianity and science have never been resolved, not even after centuries of conflict. Instead, there is merely a veneer that attempts to hide the underlying cracks. This is not the case with dharmic traditions where there is no inherent conflict in principle between science and dharma.

Because it is non-linear, dharma does not proceed along a developmental line progressing toward a climax. Rather, it spirals from a germinating point to swell in value by return and repetition. Conventional linear thought is quite inadequate to meeting the intellectual challenges of the non-Euclidean world of advanced mathematics and quantum physics. But the dharmic mind is at home in the subatomic and astronomical worlds.

The Birth of the West: Inherent Problems

Looking at the history of the West from a dharmic perspective, one begins to identify certain fundamental conceptual problems that surface from time to time and challenge the synthetic unity being claimed by westerners. These are:

1. A deficiency of the inner sciences, techniques, methodologies and theories which allow for the exploration of our inner life and consciousness.
2. Anti-intellectualism and an absence of debate, reason and cosmological exploration within the core Christian scriptures.
3. An *outward* projection of the search for fulfilment, leading to endless expeditions of imperialistic expansion and appropriation.
4. An insatiable and misguided quest for freedom without giving up the dualistic self.

Problems 1 and 2: Deficiency of Inner Sciences and of Built-in Intellectualism

A deep problem in the Western psyche, evident in its cultural history, is the absence or radical underdevelopment of adhyatma-vidya. Institutionalized Christianity has always marginalized its own mystics. Nor is there much intellectual or philosophical discourse per se in the core spiritual texts of the Judeo-Christian faiths where the emphasis is on history-centric dictates from God. Habits of inquiry, debate, reason and contemplation are not central to the scriptures but were added as an afterthought in response to critics as the tradition encountered other civilizations. The texts are not dialogical but, for the most part, poetic, legal, historical and lyrical. Philosophical ideas are implicit at points but are not central to revelation. Metaphysical speculation had to be grafted onto Biblical revelation much later via imported Greek categories. Moreover, the philosophy added is held in lower esteem than the texts of the canon.

St. Augustine (354–430), an early and influential theologian in the Christian tradition, brought Plato's sophisticated and highly developed metaphysics and philosophy into Christianity. He heavily relied on Plotinus (205–70), a Greek-based thinker, to accomplish this. Centuries later, the medieval monk and philosopher St. Thomas Aquinas (1225–74) turned to the works of Aristotle in order to introduce rational inquiry into Christianity. Both Plato and Aristotle, critical sources for developing Christian theology, were of course Greeks, not Christians, and the philosophical appropriations from Hellenism were key to bringing intellectualism to Christianity.[62] Significantly, the Church for a time regarded Aquinas's philosophical ideas as heresy and a threat to revelation. In both cases, the synthetic unity these theologians sought remained beyond reach, leaving many questions unresolved, causing anxiety, and provoking controversy among their heirs.[63] Aquinas found he could never fully express the idea of integral unity, the nature of which is mystical rather than rational.

The Protestant Reformation paved the way for a fusion of critical and scientific truths and revealed truths, and the Enlightenment sought, with only partial success, to reconcile faith and reason. These efforts, however, have often resulted either in the eradication of one side in the pair of opposites or in the perpetuation of their conflict.

Problem 3: External Projection

Alongside these running fissures in Western civilization are other, related rifts: ancient vs modern, barbarian or pagan vs civilized, primitive vs sophisticated, and polytheistic vs monotheistic. Almost all these splits have led to either the digestion of one tendency by the other, or to forced and synthetic compromises, or to the complete rejection of resistant elements. Almost always these processes have involved violent projections outside onto the other – be it individual or collective.

Rather than heed the lessons of all great teachers from Jesus to Buddha that suffering stems from identification with an isolated ego, the Western ego ferociously asserts itself with futile and dangerous attempts to manipulate the external world. The desperation of the ego is projected onto the rest of the world, forcing a unity that is artificial as well as violent. For example, the eradication of ancient Europe's old earth-based religious and holistic cultural formations (so-called paganism) in early Christian times was far more sweeping and devastating than previously believed.[64] Paganism lived on in Europe for many centuries, fuelling the Inquisition, which was especially cruel toward women. The genocide of many Native American peoples during the European conquest is a matter of record. They have been reduced to living on isolated 'reservations' at best and to museum exhibits at worst, while being celebrated with nostalgia and romantic idealization at every turn.

Great confusion arises in the Western mind when it encounters civilizations that do not fit neatly into its binary categories and absolutes in opposition. India, for instance, is, in Western terms, both civilized and barbaric, primitive and sophisticated, secular and religious. It embraces both simple village societies and a long tradition of urban culture, unified leadership and high science in everything from politics to business to physics. The West tries to come to grips with what it perceives as an impossible integration of opposites in this culture and reduce it to familiar terms in order to digest or reject a given component.

Being unable, then, to form a stable, coherent vision at home, the West has sought to ground itself by various programmes of external conquest and repression. Other cultures and peoples are seen as resources to be devoured and digested in order to fill a vast emptiness at its heart.[65]

Problem 4: The Wrong Quest for Freedom by the Western Ego

Much of Western thinking presupposes an inherent tension between self and other at both the individual and collective levels. Such tension breeds a deep-rooted anxiety about the way things are and the feeling that some external change is needed. This perceived deficiency, which some scholars argue is a particularly Western manifestation of dukkha (a dharmic principle explained in Chapter 5, page 264), may take many forms, including material, psychological and intellectual. To search outside the self for a palliative for this deficiency is one of the fundamental illusions challenged by Buddhism and several other dharmic traditions.[66]

The dualist self and its accompanying anxiety feed off and mutually antagonize each other. The stronger the ego grows, the more anxious it becomes about what it does not possess, its very nature being to remain ever discontent. Conversely, the greater the anxiety, the more powerful the self becomes as it seeks what it does not have but desperately desires. This process is indefinite and self-defeating, because it is founded on a synthetic notion of selfhood.[67]

As a result of this relentless drive, the Western self appears to get stronger over time. Because anxieties accumulate and persist, this false self or identity can collapse, but it only gets reconfigured. The fundamental problem of the synthetic self and the synthetic culture remains unresolved.

The root of this problem is that the notion of a divided self is an artificial idea based on an account of the past in which it is reified as the central player. This self always chases something into the future, missing the opportunity to be in the present moment. Only through prolonged inquiry in the present moment is it possible to discover the inner sciences and use them to manage and overcome this anxiety. But the present moment is always overshadowed by the past or the future, be it the biblical notions of Creation, the Fall of Man, Redemption, End of Time, and Salvation, or the secular notions of progress and development which follow a similar pattern. This past-and-future complex is a reified version of some grand historical narrative which veils the experience of the present moment.

One might say that the problem is twofold: (i) the self is a construct derived from the past and serves to bring coherence to its account of the past, and (ii) the present 'kshana' (moment) is sacrificed at the altar of the future in an attempt to rescue this self from its history.

The modern West is chauvinistic in its account of why freedom did not evolve in non-Western societies. The dharmic notions of freedom such as moksha, mukti and nirvana are alternatives which the West has not recognized sufficiently.[68] From a dharmic perspective, the West has been driven not by freedom but by the mandates of its self-image which require infinite expansion in a finite world. This is neither sustainable, as we now know, nor scalable to include all humanity. History points to various schemes (including colonialism and genocide) aimed at containing or undermining the non-West.[69]

Furthermore, the Hebrew prophets, Jesus included, were not much concerned about *individual* freedom; instead, they emphasized collective freedom through obedience to God. Paul employed the terminology of freedom but not in the sense that it is understood in dharmic contexts. Some of the early Greeks, such as Socrates and Plato, did emphasize the inner realm and the importance of harmony between the inner and outer, but, unlike the ancient Indians, they aligned freedom with reason and thus failed to discover yoga as a process of going deeper into the inner mechanisms and dealing with the present moment directly. They did not achieve the embodied knowing that yoga brings.

As we have seen, St. Augustine, perhaps the most influential thinker of the Christian tradition in theology, psychology and social theory, rested his views heavily on the concept of original sin, which he defined as the misuse of freedom by Adam. Original sin gave Christians the notion of individuality – but an individuality stained by sin and hence lacking freedom. The solution, a free gift of grace, is inherently deferred or postponed until the individual attains the beatific vision in heaven. Alternatively, in the Second Coming of Christ in the End Times, those saved by Jesus will attain it collectively. In either case, freedom can never be fully 'present', so anxiety persists.

The notion of sin became an explanation for how to cope with lack of contentment (or *dukkha*) in the present situation – *not* by deeper insight into the present moment, as through yoga, but by escaping from the present moment into a future that offers redemption. The postponed promise of freedom demands we submit to the institution of the church, which is God's exclusive franchise. Real freedom in the Hindu and Buddhist sense is only attainable in the present moment as a result of inner work, but this notion was often lost sight of in the West as it chased an illusory freedom lost in the past and projected into the future.

Incompatible: Christian Dogma and Greek Reason

One of the major splits in Western culture, as we saw in my encounter with the Templeton Foundation, is the one between science and religion. This tension has deep roots, especially in America, where efforts to substitute creationism for Darwin's theory of evolution point to one of the non-negotiable tenets of both Jewish and Christian faiths: the one-time creation *ex nihilo* of the universe by an external God.

It is revealing that the groups that oppose Darwin's theory of evolution most vociferously are also the loudest voices speaking for Christianity and its creation dogma. By way of contrast, not even the most orthodox Hindu, Buddhist or Jain leaders are inclined to argue against the evolution of the cosmos, or any other science for that matter. Some modern scientists with dharmic worldviews have also questioned Darwin's theory, though these questions pertain to the science behind the theory and have nothing to do with religious dogma.[70]

The Templeton Foundation's conference was but one of several recent, high-profile attempts to claim that biblical religion is fundamentally scientific. In a related vein, as we shall see, American author Ken Wilber is trying to formulate an integral philosophy that embraces (again, without acknowledgement) the Buddhist wisdom and Hindu inner sciences while slipping back into history-centric Christianity at times. Short of a profound transformation in cosmology in the West (which would entail rejection of hitherto non-negotiable beliefs such as those enshrined in the Nicene Creed), these efforts at integral unity tend to collapse rather quickly.

Hebraism and Hellenism

The split between science and religion has its origin in a split long ago described by Matthew Arnold (1822–88), the British poet and cultural historian. Arnold gives the classic and still powerful explanation of the deep divide that is irreconcilable between the biblical (Hebraic) and Greek (Hellenistic) traditions and that has persisted since the very birth of Western civilization. He writes:

> Both Hellenism and Hebraism arise out of the wants of the human nature, and address themselves to satisfying those wants. But their methods are so different, they lay stress on such different points, and call into being by their respective disciplines such different activities, that the face which human nature presents when it passes from the hands of one of them to those of the other, is no longer the same.[71]

Arnold's broad-brush dichotomy of the two parts of Western civilization is still evident today. He differentiates their respective approaches to dealing with ignorance as follows:

To get rid of one's ignorance, to see things as they are, and by seeing them as they are to see them in their beauty, is the simple and attractive ideal which Hellenism holds out before human nature; and from the simplicity and charm of this ideal, Hellenism, and human life in the hands of Hellenism, is invested with a kind of aerial ease, clearness, and radiance; they are full of what we call sweetness and light. Difficulties are kept out of view, and the beauty and rationality of the ideal have all our thoughts. It is all very well to talk of getting rid of one's ignorance, of seeing things in their reality, seeing them in their beauty; but how is this to be done when there is something which thwarts and spoils all our efforts? This something is sin; and the space which sin fills in Hebraism, as compared with Hellenism, is indeed prodigious. This obstacle to perfection fills the whole scene, and perfection appears remote and rising away from earth, in the background. Under the name of sin, the difficulties of knowing oneself and conquering oneself which impede man's passage to perfection, become, for Hebraism, a positive, active entity hostile to man, a mysterious power.[72]

Hebraism's emphasis on sin stands in contrast to Hellenism's stress on the use of intelligence to address the human condition. Arnold continues:

The discipline of the Old Testament may be summed up as a discipline teaching us to abhor and flee from sin; the discipline of the New Testament, as a discipline teaching us to die to it. As Hellenism speaks of thinking clearly, seeing things in their essence and beauty, as a grand and precious feat for man to achieve, so Hebraism speaks of becoming conscious of sin, of wakening to a sense of sin, as a feat of this kind. Of two disciplines laying their main stress, the one, on clear intelligence, the other, on firm obedience; the one, on comprehensively knowing the grounds of one's duty, the other, on diligently practicing it …[73]

Arnold goes on to say that the Protestant/Catholic split did nothing to bridge this chasm between Christianity and Hellenism, Protestantism being merely another approach to the same mindset as Catholicism and quite deficient in intellectual excellence.

The great early Christian theologian Tertullian (160–230) famously asked, 'What has Athens to do with Jerusalem?', recognizing the difficulty in synthesizing the two points of view that characterize Western culture and implying that there is a need to choose one or the other.

This split recurs in various forms throughout history – in the battle between biblical wisdom and classical Greek metaphysics in the early Middle Ages, in the tension between secular and religious art in the Renaissance, in the tension between reason and revelation in the Enlightenment, and in the culture wars between religion and science, sacred and secular, fundamentalism and humanism.

The problem is not only due to limits in Christianity. There is also a major problem on the Hellenistic side.

Aristotle: Excluding the Middle Ground

As we have begun to see, in the early Christian era the worldview of an external God controlling the universe through fixed laws was overlaid onto Greek metaphysics, and both were merged to formulate a salvation narrative catering to the Western concern for order and history. Later, European secularism continued down the same path, this time with reason, or *Logos*, as the universal principle. Reason leads to truth, and truth is singular, clear, fully apparent, completely explicable and demonstrable – free of ambiguity. Those who do not reason in this way or do not reach the same conclusions are a threat, for they invite chaos and confusion. They are 'the other'. These *non*-westerners are believed to be irrational, and whatever explanations they offer for their beliefs, rituals and customs are dismissed as such. This belief in the superiority of Western reasoning is related to the control of epistemologies based on categories of knowledge which in turn reflect the West's own peculiar history. It has had the effect of promoting exclusivism and simplistic binary categories of true/false, good/evil, self/other, and so on – leaving little room for diversity or creative growth.

This view of truth stems in part from the Western enshrinement of the classical Aristotelian Law of the Excluded Middle, which states that there is nothing between the two opposites of a proposition, thus precluding any middle ground. This is referred to as a 'bivalent', or two-valued, system. There can only be two outcomes: true or false; nothing can be simultaneously true *and* false. Although useful for making some pragmatic distinctions, this rigid principle became *essentialized* and, as such, a severe limitation on subsequent dialectical or modal thought. It is still the basis for the teaching of Western philosophy and science, and any approach that does not conform to it is rejected.

Aristotle's theory of categories endowed Western thought with the idea of permanent and ultimate essences (or substances), and used this idea in the Law of the Excluded Middle to introduce metaphysical order and precision. The ensuing traditions of Western philosophy have tended to subscribe to this rigid logic of exclusion; indeed, it has become a key principle of Western thought. Essences and exclusivism reinforce one another, both aiding and abetting intellectual control.

The Law of the Excluded Middle dictates that the principle 'P or not-P' separates one thing from another in an absolute sense. All physical and logical entities are invariant units, mutually exclusive of each other. This is not just a pragmatic criterion for distinguishing one thing from another; it is the very nature of reality in both concrete and abstract realms. The law eliminates the possibility of things being mutually dependent, interrelated and interpenetrated. It is diametrically opposed to the intertwined and fluid relationships characteristic of integral unity as discussed earlier. Not surprisingly, Western commentators dismiss such logical frameworks as the Buddhist 'catuskoti or the Jain sya-dvada as loose mystical thinking whenever they are inconveniently confronted with them.

Western thought thus privileges isolatable categories, defined rules, true/false logic, unambiguous outcomes, established authorities, and control. It is a tendency which derives from Greek thought and which is based on axiomatic models from which one makes logical deductions and thereby reaches a theorem or a result. The Western principle operates across all fields, including philosophy, science and theology. Western philosophy has been struggling to ameliorate this rigid ontology, but the underlying tendency remains inflexible. Standard IQ tests and the criteria followed in psychological and psychiatric practices are based on standard units and interchangeable parts of an Aristotelian kind.

Although a few Western thinkers have opposed or rejected exclusivist logic, they have been overshadowed, if not dismissed outright, by the force of secular absolutism.[74] It is one of the two foundations of the Judeo-Christian exclusivist ethos, the other being the exclusivist nature of history-centrism.

Five Synthetic Movements in the West

There are five historical movements in which the problems of synthetic unity and Western ego projection become clear. They are:

1. the emergence of Rome and the birth of Western Christendom;
2. the Renaissance and Reformation of the fifteenth and sixteenth centuries;
3. the Enlightenment and the birth of modern science;
4. the Oriental Renaissance of the nineteenth and twentieth centuries; and
5. colonialist expansion.

   In each of these periods, we see a breakdown of a previously unstable synthesis of classical and Hebraic values and the projection of the resulting anxiety onto others in often violent ways.

Rome and the Birth of Western Christendom

The appropriation of early Christianity by the Roman emperor Constantine (274–337) created the first large-scale mobilization of Christianity and the establishment of Christian hegemony, all within the framework of Roman imperialism. Here we begin to see some of the problems noted above surfacing, in particular: the disregard for the inner sciences as techniques for raising consciousness, the uneasy synthetic unity of intellectual metaphysics with revealed religion, and the disembodiment and external projection of the Western mind which leads to projects such as mass conversion and imperial expansion. For nearly the first one thousand years of Christianity, this Roman imperialism, either in the form of Rome itself, the Holy Roman Empire or the Roman Catholic Church, was dominant over all of Europe.

The hegemony, which remained unbroken for centuries, was driven by mass conversions to Christianity, often violently imposed from autocratic rulers. We see the violence of Western aggression based on religion in the story of Constantine's establishment of Christianity as the official state religion of Rome and in his attempts (and those of later emperors and conquerors) to promulgate it by force and mass baptism.[75]

According to an eyewitness account of the battle for control of the Roman Empire, Constantine 'saw with his own eyes the trophy of a cross of light in the heavens, above the sun, and bearing the inscription: CONQUER BY THIS'. Constantine then assembled his army and inspired them to conquer using the cross, which he described as 'a long spear, overlaid with gold, [which] formed the figure of the cross by means of a transverse bar laid over it'. His army used this cross standard and did conquer successfully, and Constantine was thus convinced of the truth of conquest by the cross.[76]

Constantine's conquest of other cultures stands in stark contrast to the very different experience of Emperor Ashoka, who ascended the throne of the Mauryan Empire in India in 270 BCE. Ashoka expanded his already large empire by invading the neighbouring kingdom of Kalinga. Although Ashoka was victorious in this horrific and gruesome war, he felt remorse for all the suffering he had caused and hence turned to Buddhism. He wrote in his Edict Thirteen that:

> The Kalingas were conquered by His Sacred Majesty the King when he had been consecrated for eight years. One hundred and fifty thousand persons were thence carried away captive, and one hundred thousand were there slain, and many times that number perished. Directly after the annexation of the Kalingas, began his Sacred Majesty's zealous protection of Dharma, his love of Dharma, and his giving instruction in that. Thus arose His Sacred Majesty's remorse for having conquered the Kalingas, because the conquest of a country previously unconquered involves the slaughter, death, and carrying away captive of the people. That is a matter of profound sorrow and regret to His Sacred Majesty.[77]

Ashoka disarmed and disbanded his army and dedicated his life to the peaceful service of Buddhism. This was a different kind of conquest, one in which the gladiator archetype surrendered to dharma, quite the opposite of Constantine's seizing the dharmic message of Jesus and turning it into a military weapon. In Kautilya's *Arthashastra*, Ashoka's feat is known as 'dharma-vijaya', or conquest through dharma, and it was elevated to a policy of statecraft and international relations and spread across Asia.

So impressive was Ashoka's example that many other Asian monarchs adopted it. Japan's Prince Shotuku, for example, used it to unify the Japanese nation and improve international relations. For this policy, the renowned historians Arnold Toynbee and H.G. Wells have called Ashoka the greatest monarch who ever lived.[78] Furthermore, when India commanded superiority in the eyes of the nations that wanted to receive its Buddhist civilization (such as China, Mongolia, Cambodia, Indonesia and Thailand), there was never any attempt to impose rulers or governance on others, or ask for taxation or tribute to any Indian nexus, or subvert the native cultures, languages and histories of those nations.[79] The contrast between this and the manner in which Western civilization has spread is stark and warrants greater attention.

The point to be made here is that the imposition of Christianity on a vast and various array of peoples with indigenous religious traditions, all lumped together under the rubric of paganism, led to a split between the religion of the clergy and military on one side and the faiths of the various peoples on the other.

Furthermore, Christianity, in the form of the Roman institution of the Church, led to a theocracy which remained in power throughout the medieval period, and its monolithic, absolute and violent nature invited constant resistance. This in turn generated further splits in the Western psyche and polity, especially the split between sacred and secular powers. The diagram below shows how history-centrism, with its lack of intellectualism and inner sciences, produced various dualisms, fears and escapist movements. The result was theocratic, absolue power.

The Renaissance and the Reformation

During the fifteenth and sixteenth centuries, there occurred a breakdown of the unstable medieval synthesis not only between sacred and secular

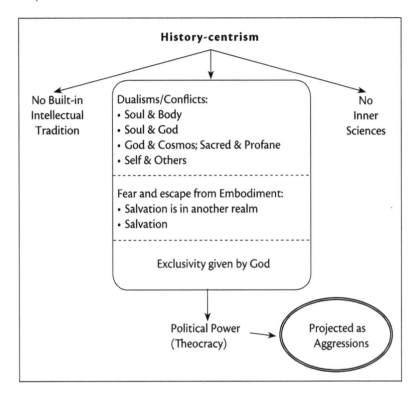

power but also between Hebraism and Hellenism. At the insistence of Luther, Calvin and their followers, the reformers emphasized a 'return to sources' (meaning the Bible), whereas the humanists in arts and letters, who were sometimes their allies, sought to revive the texts, values and ideas of the Greek classics, including a renewed commitment to reason and imagination against clerical authority.

The Renaissance was stimulated by the rediscovery of many philosophical and scientific texts of the ancient Greeks. These were transmitted through Islamic scholars who were much less resistant to Greek science than the Roman Church was.

The Protestant Reformation, which followed on the heels of the Renaissance, used new rational and scientific methods and advocated free inquiry. Still, the resulting movements were both inherently divided and in conflict with one another. For the Reformers, the goal was not freedom from history-centrism per se, but freedom from the Catholic priesthood and Roman hegemony over the means of salvation. The Reformation was saturated with Christian salvation history and would eventually continue the project of converting groups of heathens who had been 'discovered' by the colonial expansions.

Protestants, in their desire to make direct personal contact with God minus the oppressive (and expensive!) intrusions of a priestly hierarchy, did emphasize individual and spontaneous prayer and self-reflection. Nevertheless, their dualistic insistence on the otherness of God prevented them from cultivating inner consciousness as a gateway to the divine. Furthermore, since they insisted that revelation comes from an external God, and not from inner sadhana, they shunned the role of adhyatma-vidya in spiritual life. The Renaissance and Reformation increased the secularization of what hitherto had been sacred realms.

The Enlightenment and Modernism

This movement, which extends almost to the present, saw the rise of modern philosophy and an even greater distinction between sacred and secular, in part due to the triumph of disembodied reason in the work of René Descartes. Modern thought was founded on a purely disembodied reason, divorced from the inner sciences or anything like them, and based on a dualism always inherent in the West but reified at a new level by Cartesian thinking. The nation-state grew up in the shadow of this dualism and became, to some extent, the secular version of the Christendom project of the Roman Church.

The continued development of Greek reason and scientific inquiry (combined with the marginalization of Christianity) led to the Enlightenment. The supremacy of the Church was successfully challenged and significant progress made in taking Europe from the Dark Ages into the 'light' of the age of reason. Given the inherent contradictions between biblical scripture and science, however, this could only happen at a great cost, driving a wedge between the soul and the body, reason and revelation, scientific and spiritual inquiry, and the secular realm and the sacred. These opposing facets were never integrated; each was simply relegated to a prescribed jurisdiction, often living in isolation from its opposite facet.

These problems internal to the West were also ignored, because the West projected outward in a programme of expansion and conquest which was modelled on the old expansionism project of Christianity, but now joined to a new secular materialism.

The deep divides in the European outlook and the attempts to resolve them climaxed in the work of Descartes. Here the mind/body dualism inherent in the West was elevated to a philosophical absolute and became the basis for attempting to resolve the differences between Jewish and Christian faiths and disembodied reason. This was achieved, in effect, by splitting them into separate domains.

One of the most famous examples of the inherent contradictions in Western culture is Galileo's (1564–1642) conviction and imprisonment by the Church for supporting Copernicus's heliocentric view of the world. Descartes found himself caught in the crossfire between Galileo and the Church. In 1633, he had to withdraw from publishing a book because it supported Copernicus's theory.[80] Descartes the scientist believed in the machine model of the body operating under the laws of physics, but Descartes the devout Catholic believed that the soul was free to obey or disobey God's commandments and face the consequences on the Day of Judgement.

He sought to resolve the conflict by formulating a mind/body dualism, according to which the body operates on material laws, whereas the soul and mind are entirely different substances which operate as per the Church doctrines. When dealing with the mind, he examined its properties entirely apart from both body and soul. 'I think, therefore I am' (*cogito ergo sum*) became his famous motto and methodology. The realm of philosophical speculation and scientific inquiry was split from the world of spirit and living matter and took on a life of its own. By a kind of methodological fiat or truce, one was able to proceed without interfering with the other.

W.T. Jones, a historian of Western philosophy, explains how this compromise has worked:

If mind and body are completely different kinds of things, and if truths about each follow from the distinct nature of each, it is impossible for the science of minds and the science of bodies to contradict each other. Theologians, therefore, have no reason to interfere with the study of the new physics, and physicists have no reason to claim any special competence regarding spiritual truths ... There can be no conflict between science and religion, for each is sovereign in its own sphere and neither has any standing in the sphere of the other.[81]

Thus the domains of science and the Church were each defined in such a way that there was no overlap and hence no conflict. As often happens when Western culture digests foreign ideas, an untenable split occurred, separating the two sides such that each had a domain it could control. To this day, practically every school of Western psychology and philosophy accepts the Cartesian mind/body problem explicitly or implicitly as the main problem to resolve.[82]

Dharmic thought never created any such mind/body divide, politically, philosophically, or in spiritual practice. For example, *prana* is a central concept which unifies the interactive relationship between mind and body. Furthermore, prana cannot be contained in either the mind or body but spans both. It seems to have one foot in the manifest and one in the un-manifest. Prana is breath only in its most gross manifestation; otherwise, it deals with subtle energies of all levels, much like *Qi* in Chinese thought. In meditation, one experiences the teaching: 'prana is in me and I am in prana'.

In a purely mechanistic model of the cosmos, everything from agriculture to factories to social systems could be organized using Cartesian and Newtonian determinism. Descartes established the term 'laws of nature' by using it consistently. As we have seen, his achievement was to separate philosophy from theology and thereby limit the need for God in understanding the world. Newton further mechanized the cosmos as a creation of God but then made God unnecessary to its sustenance. Galileo, Kepler and Newton played decisive roles in this move away from the nebulous and undeveloped Catholic idea of the Holy Spirit as God-in-the-world, which had never been explored seriously. This trend, in conjunction with Protestantism, had the effect of reducing the divine presence within the world almost to the point of nothingness. Darwin contributed further by offering a mechanical theory for evolution.

The abandonment of God's presence in the world became an abandonment of values, because the cosmos was seen to be governed by value-free mechanical laws. This further expanded the exploitation of nature and contributed to the removal of the feminine from Judaism and Christianity, i.e., the normative laws were masculinity at work.

The Enlightenment and subsequent modernist movements sought to throw off the dogma of Christianity in favour of secular knowledge and a secular state, but here again the internal divisions and uneasy syntheses, even within the secular domain, created instability and confusion. For the scientific revolution was not free of the old history-centrism and ego projection. (This is discussed further in Chapter 6 under 'Western Secularism: Christianity's Double'.[83]) The nation state, created to advance secular, enlightened ideals, was shaped by the tension between these assumptions and science proper. The *Encyclopedia Britannica* (as a barometer of popular knowledge) explains how the secular West incorporated certain biblical ideas:

> Western civilization, even in its modern secularized forms, is heir to a long tradition of Christian patterns of thought and sensibility ... Both the 18th and 19th century Enlightenment and the Romantic versions of the idea of the progress of humanity to an ideal state of peace and harmony betray their descent from messianic-millenarian beliefs ...[84]

Stephen Toulmin, a noted cultural historian, describes the synthetic nature of the Western nation state that emerged out of all this: 'The state, created *ex nihilo,* was an artificial ordering of individual parts, not bound together by cohesion, as an organic community, but united by fear.'[85] Governance by the state was thus carried out by artificial men with artificial souls substituting for God. This required bureaucracy, which brought objectivity and reduced subjective decision making. Personal interaction was replaced by functionally motivated efficiency, and people became interchangeable parts in a social machinery and equalized by their rights and privileges. The mutuality of an organic community is replaced by an artificial ordering of parts united by fear. The local breakdown of organic communities creates what Andrea Camilleri calls 'atomized populations whose claim to humanity rests more on the assertion of human rights *vis-à-vis* an impersonal, distant and highly bureaucratized government apparatus'.[86] The atomized individuals comprising such a society are linked together only by agreements which serve their own interests - not those of society as such. The common good is simply the sum of the parts.

The Oriental Renaissance

Since the late eighteenth century, the West has undergone what some scholars (most notably Raymond Schwab) call an 'oriental renaissance'.[87] This movement, often unacknowledged but identified and explored increasingly by contemporary scholars, saw the West encounter Asian societies, and the dharmic traditions of India in particular. This encounter challenged the West and elicited some of its most problematic projections. The European encounter with Sanskrit and its sophisticated classical texts sparked one of the most vibrant and influential intellectual movements of the nineteenth century. Extensive work is needed to uncover the often deliberately concealed, or at least discounted, role played by European Indologists and their opponents in shaping the Romantic and modern concepts of the West, but the point to be made here is that the efforts to 'digest' Asian cultures and metaphysics put an even greater strain on Western synthetic unity than before. This problem is discussed in detail in my forthcoming book, *U-Turn Theory*.

As part of its programme of expansion and colonization, the West not only subsumed and digested many New World and African indigenous cultures but encountered sophisticated and cosmopolitan Asian civilizations with highly evolved and documented oral and written traditions of inquiry and achievement. Although many colonizers dismissed the latter as either primitive or morally dubious in their worship of 'false gods', others realized that there were cultural and material riches to be mined.

Europe's encounter with Sanskrit revolutionized the European study of linguistics, and its encounter with Hinduism and Buddhism deeply informed Western philosophy and challenged the Judeo-Christian traditions. Some westerners, such as the American transcendentalists: Thoreau, Emerson and Whitman, broke away from Christian orthodoxy as a result. This process continues today ever more deeply in the mainstream of the West through yoga, meditation, healing sciences, the arts, eco-feminism, philosophy, and pop culture. Although there is a popular belief that yoga and meditation can be easily assimilated into Western culture, this notion ignores the profound differences and incompatibilities between the dharmic and the Judeo-Christian traditions, especially concerning embodied knowing. The West's appropriation of Indian traditions is yet another instance of a forced or synthetic unity which has not been thought through.

Colonial Conquests

Along with the Oriental Renaissance, there has been Western colonial expansion, the violence and aggression of which are well-documented. What is frequently ignored, however, is that the motivation for this expansion and its structuring principles existed deep within the Christian worldview, even though it was undertaken in the name of secular-scientific progress and the conquering of 'backward' peoples. These conquests mostly occurred as the split between the sacred and the secular in Western culture became more and more acute. At the same time, both the sacred and the secular participated in the colonization, for although antithetical on the surface, both emerged from a religious and cosmological substrate in which strains of historical revelation and the forward march of science were mixed together.

As we have seen, the West's struggle for synthetic unity and its underlying psychic structure were projected outward in these programmes of conquest and colonization. After the break-up of the unified Christian worldview during the Renaissance and the Enlightenment, the various components came into mutual conflict but then joined together and began to expand around the world to mitigate the distress at home.

It is important to note that at about the same time when Europeans were enduring fights between and among rival institutions at home, they were starting to conquer other peoples around the world. Cultural historian David Loy analyses the psychological pressure which gave rise to these conquests: 'Psychologically we know that one personal response to increased anxiety and fear can be aggression; does the historical development suggest that the same may be true collectively? One way to secure ourselves is to expand by dominating and incorporating the other.'[88]

This outer revolution in the material realm did bring many genuine advances of enduring value, such as the removal of feudal theocracies and authoritarian ideologies (Europeans are certainly better off as a result of their achievements in modernity), but internal restlessness and discontent have demanded that Western civilization expand, quite literally, throughout the globe.[89] European expansion was followed by the rise of America as the 'new Europe' with emphasis on a Protestant and secularized version of salvation history.

In the fifteenth century, the European conquerors insisted that whatever lands they invaded were their 'discoveries' and hence their 'property' – a project which comprised gold as well as slaves, intellectual property, and assorted other riches. Christopher Columbus, still celebrated as the archetypal 'discoverer' (rather than 'conqueror') of 'new worlds', took possession of the Americas for the queen of Spain on the unimpeachable authority and legal sanction of the Pope. This bold claim was made on the basis of the *Doctrine of Christian Discovery*, which had been officially promulgated through papal decree precisely in the context of, and as a response to, Christianity's encounter with other (i.e., heathen) cultures. The latter were found to be in possession of material resources coveted by Europeans as well as spiritual and cultural treasures which the conquistadores took to be their own.[90]

Historian Steve Newcomb writes about what came to be known as the *Christian Law of Nations*, which

> asserted that Christian nations had a divine right, based on the Bible, to claim absolute title to and ultimate authority over any newly 'discovered' Non-Christian inhabitants and their lands. Over the next several

centuries, these beliefs gave rise to the *Doctrine of Discovery* used by Spain, Portugal, England, France, and Holland – all Christian nations.[91]

Note that the heathen people also came under the authority of these 'discoverers' who had the Church-sanctioned right to exploit them as property. Church theologians extended this supremacy to support the enslavement of blacks and the genocide of millions of Native Americans (among other peoples) on the basis that they were heathens. The Bible, it was argued, awarded the ownership of nature exclusively to non-heathens.

Christopher Columbus viewed the colonization of America and the conversion of its natives as necessary to fulfilling the requirements for bringing about the End Times. He tried to convince his Portuguese patrons to use their wealth from the New World to finance a new crusade to recover Jerusalem from the Muslims, because that was a precondition for the arrival of the new millennium as well.[92]

By the end of the eighteenth century, white Americans were by and large convinced they had been 'chosen' to redeem the world as God's agents in history. America was meant to be the new Kingdom of God, substituting for the church. The new approach to resolving the human condition was individual freedom defined as the pursuit of one's own self-interest as long as it could be shown to be claimed in the name of some higher purpose.

When linked to a modern programme of extreme and unbridled capitalism – with its Calvinistic insistence that the world existed to be exploited by humans who have 'dominion' over it – this projection of a Christian programme in secular form wreaked havoc on the peoples and lands of Africa, Asia and the Americas. The consequences for the earth and its inhabitants proved far-reaching and can be felt even today. By defining the conquered as pagans or primitives, Europeans were able to digest and/or synthesize their cultures and lands while completely ignoring and suppressing their various contributions to world civilization. Yet, so artificial and morally corrupt were the misappropriation and destruction of these cultures that the internal split between peoples of colour and white people became entrenched, and it continues to haunt America to this day.

The relevance of this to our thesis is that the cultural assets that are appropriated by violence and deception are then unified in a synthetic fashion, because they were not organically generated from within the cultural ecosystem nor integrated harmoniously.

4

Order and Chaos

'People from dharmic cultures tend to be more accepting of difference, unpredictability and uncertainty than westerners. The dharmic view is that so-called 'chaos' is natural and normal; it needs, of course, to be balanced by order, but there is no compelling need to control or eliminate it entirely nor to force cohesion from outside. The West, conversely, sees chaos as a profound threat that needs to be eradicated either by destruction or by complete assimilation. [...] Indians tend to be more relaxed in unpredictable situations than westerners. Indians indeed find it natural to engage in non-linear thinking, juxtaposing opposites and tackling complexities that cannot be reduced to simple concepts or terms. They may be said even to thrive on ambiguity, doubt, uncertainty, multitasking, and in the absence of centralized authority and normative codes. Westerners, by contrast, tend by and large to be fearful of unpredictable or decentralized situations. They regard these situations as 'problems' to be 'fixed'. [...] In the vast canon of classical writings in Sanskrit, we see many context-sensitive and flexible ways of dealing with chaos and difference. The search here is always for balance and equilibrium with the 'rights' of chaos acknowledged. On the other hand, in the creation stories in Genesis and in the Greek classics, there is a constant zero-sum battle between the two poles in which order must triumph.'

In previous chapters, I discussed the West's history-centrism and its struggles to force a sense of unity on an internally divided and dualistic worldview. This unity, I've argued, is fundamentally synthetic and unstable, and it tends to break down under pressure into its constituent parts. In contrast, the dharmic conception of the integral unity of the cosmos supports a more stable and relaxed approach to multiplicity and variety. This chapter explores how the West also differs from the dharmic traditions in its attitudes towards order and chaos.

Chaos arises when one experiences phenomena which do not lie within one's psychological and cultural comfort zones, resulting in a breakdown of cognition. The breaking point varies among individuals and cultures, but a few consistent patterns are discernible. People from dharmic cultures tend to be more accepting of difference, unpredictability and uncertainty than westerners. The dharmic view is that so-called chaos is natural and normal; it needs, of course, to be balanced by order, but there is no compelling need to control or eliminate it entirely nor to force cohesion from outside. The West, conversely, sees chaos as a profound threat that needs to be eradicated either by destruction or by complete assimilation.

Attitudes about order and chaos mirror the attitudes concerning certainty and uncertainty found in the two cultures. The West tends to crave assurances and certainty, partly because it insists on either/ or polarities. Western religions address the fear of death by promising salvation or damnation after this very life, whereas dharmic worldviews allow for numerous births and a gradual evolution of consciousness as paths that may undergo many turns, detours, setbacks and degrees of change.[1] Christians often favour predictable black-and-white outcomes –

such as the impending End Times and Paradise for those who subscribe to particular dogma. In such a purposeful design, it seems attractive to posit a 'war against evil' in order to completely annihilate it.

But according to Indian cosmology, there cannot be an 'ultimate war' since there is no imminent finality. Even at the end of the universe, there is always the birth of a new one, which is but one in an infinite series of universes with neither beginning nor end. The notion of a beginning-less and endless universe is daunting to most westerners, who are accustomed to fixed boundaries – the beginning and end of time, the beginning and end of the universe, objects that are finite and separate, etc.

The dharmic idea of 'burning the seeds of karma' and thereby becoming free from the effects of all past deeds implies self-realization through human striving. There is no eternal heaven or hell; there are states of existence within the same reality. They are pictured as complex transcendental realms called 'svarga' and 'naraka', respectively. One's stay in svarga or in naraka is always temporary. Svarga – or what might roughly be described in Western terms as a kind of paradise – is a place of rest and recuperation rather than our final destination; after exhausting our good karma, we return from that realm to earth to strive once again. Naraka is a place of torment and suffering for those who accumulate negative karma, but they, too, eventually return to earth. There are as many realms as there are levels of consciousness. At the highest state, we realize unity with the Ultimate Reality from which all have sprung and unto which all return. One's journey through such a multidimensional cosmos need not cause anxiety, for our ultimate essence is secure as sat-chit-ananda.

Dharma traditions, then, do not see uncertainty as evil or even inherently negative. Indeed, edifying narratives of Shiva typically show him playing dice with his consort, and both cheat playfully at times. Thus, uncertainty is not always represented as a hostile demonic force invading from without but also as that which wells up and erodes order from within. Dice is also used as a metaphor for uncertainty in the Mahabharata. Gambling has always been frowned upon as frivolous by responsible members of society who are the keepers of order. Yudhishthira, the otherwise righteous king, is addicted to dice play, and this is portrayed as a catastrophic vice. The dice game is nevertheless an obligatory and significant part of the Vedic ritual of royal consecration ('rajasuya'). The four ages (yugas) of successive decline are named after the four faces of the Indian dice (with the unlucky face, Kali, corresponding to our own chaotic time). The king's throw of the dice during this solemn ceremony suggests not only the uncertainty at the heart of cosmic order but also the power of the human ruler to determine his own yuga.[2]

The implications of these profound differences are numerous, and I explore some of them below. First, however, let us look at the way in which the West not only fears chaos but projects that fear onto India and its culture.

Indian 'Chaos' and Western Anxiety

My own casual observations confirm the idea that Indians tend to be more relaxed in unpredictable situations than westerners. Indians indeed find it natural to engage in non-linear thinking, juxtaposing opposites and tackling complexities that cannot be reduced to simple concepts or terms. They may be said even to *thrive* on ambiguity, doubt, uncertainty, multitasking, and in the absence of centralized authority and normative codes. Westerners, by contrast, tend by and large to be fearful of unpredictable or decentralized situations. They regard these situations as problems to be fixed. As we shall see, there is in fact some scholarly evidence that demonstrates this view of Western attitudes.

India often strikes the westerner as dysfunctional, defying all rational expectations and surviving only by good fortune. This impression is due in part to India's bewildering diversity, reflected in her multiplicity of communities and ethno-cultural differences – including even communities that arrived from abroad, such as the early Jews, Christians and Zoroastrians. The fact that each community has its own norms can be confusing to the Western observer who may conclude that there is no clear sense of right and wrong.

Sri Aurobindo notes this Western mindset:

> The religious thinking of Europe is accustomed to rigid impoverishing definitions, to strict exclusions, to a constant preoccupation with the

outward idea, the Organization, the form. A precise creed framed by the logical or theological intellect, a strict and definite moral code to fix the conduct, a bundle of observances and ceremonies, a firm ecclesiastical or congregational Organization, that is Western religion. Once the spirit is safely imprisoned and chained up in these things, some emotional fervor and even a certain amount of mystic seeking can be tolerated – within rational limits; but, after all, it is perhaps safest to do without these dangerous spices.[3]

As Lloyd and Susan Rudolph, scholars of South Asia at the University of Chicago, point out, 'India seen as a mirror image of the West appears otherworldly, fatalistic, non-egalitarian. It is as though we would be less ourselves, less this-worldly, masterful, egalitarian and individualistic if Indians were less what they are.'[4]

Andrew Rotter, an American historian at Colgate University, makes a similar point: 'American selves, operating largely within the categories of sexuality, race, and illness, projected onto Indian Others traits that seemed loathsome or illicit: Indians were, among other things, unsanitary, disorderly, promiscuous, and primitive.'[5]

Shortly after India's independence, another American, Harold Isaacs, interviewed assorted American academics, diplomats, politicians, missionaries, business people, members of the media and others to elicit their thoughts on the Indians and the Chinese.[6] In describing India, the Americans he interviewed used such unflattering epithets as 'teeming millions', 'teeming cities', 'swarming masses', 'mobs of people', 'hordes', and so on. One of the respondents typically remarked that India had 'millions of people; nobody knows how many there are on this human anthill'.[7] Americans associated strong smells in India with primitivism and 'filth, dirt and disease'.

A book by Katherine Mayo, *The Face of Mother India*, became immensely influential in shaping American ideas about India, and by the mid-1950s it had gone through twenty-seven American editions and sold well over a quarter of a million copies in the United States alone. Mayo greatly admired Muslims for their fighting spirit to extend their faith, and hence she specifically glorified Mahmoud of Ghazni for his violent plunders of India. She compared Ghazni to biblical figures such as Joshua, Gideon and David, because he was ready 'to throw away life itself for the honour of the One God ...' It was a horrific indictment of Hinduism, giving gory details about the abuse of girls and women, child brides, food deprivation, sati, etc.[8]

While some praised the wisdom and devotion of Hindus, most reiterated Katherine Mayo's stereotypes to conclude that Hinduism was 'a debased, hopeless sort of religion', producing 'mobs of fanatics hurling themselves into the Ganges', 'naked ascetics and scrawny fakirs on nails', and 'stupid taboos' – altogether 'a complicated, alien mess'. Gandhi called Mayo's book 'a drain inspector's report' and published a scathing criticism of it.

Furthermore, Isaacs goes on, 'the apparent sexual threat from India was [based on] ... a dangerous eroticism about the place: there were "obscene" sculptures on Hindu temples, phallic symbols everywhere, and allegedly rapacious temple priests who were said to keep prostitutes inside the walls for their own fell pleasures'.[9] These descriptions have shaped the stereotype of Indians as both immoral and undependable.

Andrew Rotter spent many years researching cultural assumptions and beliefs related to US policies towards South Asia during the Cold War.[10] After analysing the declassified writings of American political and military officials, he concluded that, overall, Indians were seen as being difficult to comprehend owing to a lack of transparency and clarity. They were also described as grotesque, smelly, disorderly, and overcrowded in a jungle-like setting. 'At the foundation of all other American perceptions was the view that India was a land of mystery, exotic and inscrutable,' Rotter writes. 'A veil seemed to hang over the country, preventing observers from seeing its features clearly ... Even those who understood East Asia, however, confessed themselves baffled by India.'[11]

India displayed none of the Western virtues of self-discipline and self-control. As Rotter puts it, 'Westerners found in Indians the very opposite of their rational self-images, exemplars of the undesirable and forbidden ... If order is the desideratum of the post-Enlightenment Westerner, the dirt and disorder of India was for the Westerner an object of loathing.'[12] In documents from the Cold War era, the US State Department declared that 'Indians, no matter how Westernized, are Asians and often totally unpredictable to Westerners'. A *Time* magazine cover story stated that 'the genius of India has ever been for myth, not rationality'. It was normal for American officials returning home from India to report incidents which illustrated 'the Indians' apparent inefficiency, irrationality, or simple peculiarity'.[13]

Americans also tended to link disorder, moral ambiguity and passivity to a lack of masculinity.[14] This is sometimes expressed metaphorically in terms of 'masculine' America wooing and capturing the 'sleepy maiden of mysticism' that is India.[15] Rotter explains:

> The Western representation of India as female conferred effeminacy on most Indian men. Caught in the enervating web of Hinduism, the majority of Indian men had been deprived of their manliness and their virility. In the context of gender, it is possible to discern *three features* that Westerners historically assigned to most Indian men. The *first* of these was passivity and its more exaggerated forms; the *second* was emotionalism; the *third* was a lack of heterosexual energy … Hindu men were passive, servile, and cowardly … They could endure anything, evidently without suffering from a sense of shame because of their inaction. They did not resist oppressors but rather regarded them with stupefying indifference … The exaggerated form of passivity was servility. This, Westerners declared, Hindu men had in abundance. Many implicitly subscribed to John Stuart Mill's observation that 'in truth, the Hindu, like the eunuch, excels in the qualities of the slave'.[16]

Emotionalism was regarded as a central Indian trait: 'Rather than deal with issues logically and coolly, Hindu men flew off the handle – just as women were allegedly apt to do. Americans claimed constantly to find verification for the cliché that the West was rational and tough; the East, emotional and sensitive.' The CIA's profile of Nehru stated that 'his character is weakened by a tendency towards emotionalism which at times destroys his sense of values',[17] and President Eisenhower believed Nehru's emotional volatility was the personification of his country.[18] India lacked reason and order.

These and other nightmarish prejudices concerning Indians may be traced to the West's perpetual misidentification and oversimplification of Hinduism as polytheistic. An impression which lingers to this day is that polytheism conditioned Hindus to think that there was no single truth, no single authority, rendering them deceitful and unreliable (as US allies) with shifting positions and policies. Westerners could not count on them to choose the side of right in a political crisis. Rotter explains that US foreign policy has always been driven by the Protestant idea of the one and only truth. In 1954, Arthur Dean, then US ambassador to the UN, told an Indian official point-blank that the United States wanted to base its policy on one of Jesus' sayings, to wit, 'He who is not for me is against me' (Matthew 12:30), and hence Dean was annoyed at Nehru's non-alignment and 'India's moral neutrality'.[19]

India's neutrality was therefore viewed as an example of her moral ambiguity and relativism – that is, as evidence that Hindus could not, and did not care to, tell right from wrong. Since, in India, God was the subject of speculation and variation, the country's foreign policy, too, was prone to vacillation. Pakistanis, on the other hand, came across as forthright, vigorous, combative (in a positive sense), and above all, monotheistic, making them similar to Americans and therefore more dependable than Indians.[20] 'The Hindu concepts of time and the cosmos … lead to relativistic foreign policy attitudes … American "itchiness" concerning non-alignment is explained in significant measure by the fact that many Americans are conditioned by religious traditions based on revealed dogma.'[21]

Rotter explains:

> Above all, the Muslims of Pakistan resembled Christians in their monotheism. Hindus believed in many gods, and thus presumably in many versions of the truth. Not so Muslims. Their God was not precisely the New Testament God, and His word came to men and women through Mohammed, not Christ. But there was no confusion about the source of the Word, and no heavenly babble beguiled Muslims and Christians: righteousness spoke with a single voice. Westerners frequently touted this similarity between Islam and Christianity … [resulting in] an understanding that predicated trust and made outsiders of those who did not share it.[22]

And he continues: 'Religious thinking helps explain the American decision, guided by [former US Secretary of State] John Foster Dulles, to forge a military alliance with Pakistan.' He notes that a Christian nation would have been the first choice but – since neither India nor Pakistan was Christian – the next best alternative to Christianity, at that time, was to go with a nation based on a prophetic faith. In Dulles's mind, Hinduism suffered from a problem similar to that of communism: lack of moral certainty. Communism had no God, and Hinduism had many gods, which made its moral compass ambiguous and confused.

In 2003, a classified report on Indo-US military relations was prepared by a team of American policy makers in the Pentagon, the State Department, the Pacific Command and the American Embassy in New Delhi. Rediff.com, an Indian–American news portal, summarized the American report, stating that India's military was competent, well-trained and sophisticated in its use of tactics and technology. However, the Americans expressed discomfort in their interpersonal relations with their Indian counterparts, reporting that Indian bureaucrats, generals, admirals and air marshals could be 'easily slighted or insulted', were 'difficult to work with', harboured 'deep-seated distrust' of Americans, and were 'obsessed' with the past rather than focused on the future. The report goes on to say that 'a number of American military officers who interacted with the Indians in the early 1990s revealed that they would much rather interact with the Pakistanis, whom they described as more accommodating, flexible and easy to work with'.[23] This is consistent with Rotter's observations that 'the Americans feel comfortable standing with "real men"' and that 'Pakistani leaders, who ate meat, drank liquor, and knew the value of a well-tuned military machine, were real men'.[24]

The overlay of renunciation philosophy, bhakti and folk religions only compounds the Westerner's impression of chaos. Chaos is entrenched in the Vedas, the Puranas and Hinduism in general for a reason: its role is to counterbalance and dilute any absolutist tendencies as well as provide creative dynamism through ambiguity and uncertainty.

The diagram that follows illustrates the images of India which prevail in much of the West through the lenses of both biblical and secular thinkers. At the top of the diagram is white culture with its view of Indian society as dangerous, possibly evil, and ripe for America's supposedly civilizing and progressive influence. The two major approaches which emanate from deep within Western culture are conservative/biblical and liberal/secular. The conservative view relies on tomes written by missionaries, whereas the liberal approach is dominated by discourses on human rights, social progress, and the like which – contrary to what these terms might suggest – are influenced by deeply racist and Eurocentric biases. Both these perceptions, in their own ways, present India as yet another chaotic place that needs to be ordered.

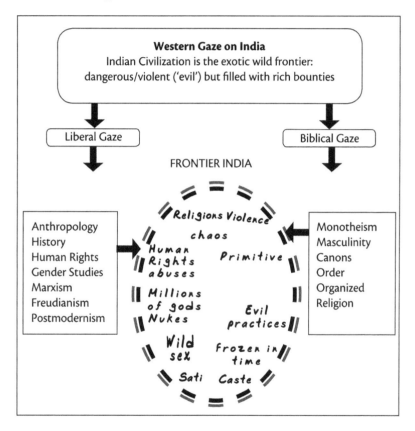

Add to all this the images and stories of naked and filthy-looking holy men, outdoor cremations, and karma mistranslated as fatalism, and India would indeed appear to be a basket case, reinforcing, yet again, the Anglo-American impression of Indians as immoral, irrational and grotesque. In fact, this is the Western impression of most non-European civilizations dating back to at least the 1600s.[25]

The different modes of cognition between Asian and Western cultures have become the subject of scientific inquiry. Recent research in cognitive science at the University of Michigan shows that Asians and white North Americans do indeed see the world differently. When white Americans are shown a photograph, for example, they tend to pay more attention to what is in the foreground, whereas Asians tend to study the background as well, taking in the whole scene. 'Asians live in a more socially complicated world than we do,' explains Richard Nisbett, the researcher who carried out the study. He concludes that Asians are more attuned to harmoniousness and complex relationships.[26]

The reductionist prejudice that *the West equals order and India equals chaos* fails to explain how Indians are able to excel not only in various spiritual practices but also in the rational fields of science, business and engineering. Western scholars are caught off-guard when confronted with evidence of sophisticated cultural and scientific achievements in the pre-Western history of the subcontinent. Many of them deal with this confusion by arguing that the achievements of the Indian past and even the comprehensive philosophies of the present are somehow *not really Indian*; hence, for instance, the view that the highly ordered and precise Indus–Sarasvati civilization is not Indian in its origins. If westerners do call something 'Indian', they try to show that it was somehow antithetical to Sanskrit-based civilization and accuse the latter of having destroyed it. Hence, too, the view that Hindu dharma did not exist prior to some conspiracy by Hindu nationalists to conjure it up during the past two hundred years. All these pronouncements are based on arguments that Hinduism lacks norms, order and central authority. As per this mindset, chaos cannot coexist with order.

Having declared Indians inferior in rationality, Western scholars find it difficult to acknowledge fully the merits of Indian systems of thought, even when the influence of these systems on the West is irrefutable. The Western mind's shift from multi-sensuous and non-sequential awareness to linear, sequential awareness is acclaimed as one of the most momentous breakthroughs in the history of humanity.[27] Indian civilization, on the other hand, has always been rooted in a multidimensional way of thinking, organizing and experiencing. And yet this synchronic Indian attitude underlies many of the recent breakthroughs of Western thought, including the 'discovery' of structuralism as an epistemological principle – a methodology that has revolutionized the study of languages and societies alike.

The West has not only failed to grasp the importance of these modes of thought; it has steadfastly resisted them on the presumption that they stem from a chaotic culture in which reason and binary logic are, for the most part, absent. As Richard Lannoy concludes:

> The tendency to condemn intuitive pattern-recognition and synaesthesia [both aspects of structuralism] as 'unscientific irrationalism' is a tragic misconception, particularly in a society like India's, which consistently displays a talent which, though long-repressed and vilified as archaic, has recently begun to regain ascendancy over the step-by-step, unilinear progression of sequential logic.[28]

Indian Comfort with Chaos

The flexibility of dharma in this respect comes in part from the emphasis on integral unity and context. All things are understood to be *inherently* held together, so one can be relaxed about plurality and not feel threatened by it. Sri Aurobindo writes: 'Unity we must create, but not necessarily uniformity.'[29] He goes on to explain that because, in dharmic traditions, unity is grounded in a sense of the integral One, there can be immense multiplicity without fear of 'collapse into disintegration and chaos'. He adds that 'nature can afford the luxury of infinite differentiation' since there is the 'secure basis' that 'the underlying immutability of the eternal' always remains unaffected.

The immutability of reality for Sri Aurobindo 'consists in an unchangeableness of being which is capable of endless formation of being, but which no differentiation can destroy or impair or minimize'.[30] This constancy has a spiritual base. He writes:

> If man could realize a perfect spiritual unity, no sort of uniformity would be necessary; for the utmost play of diversity would be securely possible on that foundation. If again he could realize a secure, clear, firmly held unity in the principle, a rich, even an unlimited diversity in its application might be possible without any fear of disorder, confusion or strife.[31]

The same fluid and interconnected relationship between order and chaos has shaped India's social, political and civil structures. What has baffled many westerners from colonial times to the present day is traditional Indian society's decentralized, self-organizing nature. This decentralized structure differs considerably from the Western preference for uniformity, centralized authority and control.

In Hindu marriages, for instance, unlike the nuptials of Christianity, the priest does not perform the rituals, nor does he have the authority to declare the couple married; he acts only as the coach. The groom and bride themselves perform the ceremony. In other words, there is no external authority declaring them man and wife. The same do-it-yourself freedom is evident in other pursuits, such as yoga and meditation. Even in formal worship, the guidelines are meant for beginners, and these give way to increasing freedom as the individual becomes self-propelled in the spiritual journey without need for external authority.

India's Kumbha Mela amply demonstrates that diversity can be self-organized and not anarchic, even on a very large scale. Held every twelve years, this is the world's largest gathering of people, attracting tens of millions of individuals from all corners of India, from all strata of society, and from all kinds of traditions, ethnicities and languages. Yet there is no central organizing body, no 'event manager' to send out invitations or draw up a schedule, nobody in charge to promote it, no centralized registration system to get admitted. Nobody has official authority or ownership of the event, which is spontaneous and 'belongs' to the public domain. Since time immemorial, numerous groups have put up their own mini-townships and millions go as individuals just to participate in the festivities.

Another example of Indian self-organization in commerce is Mumbai's dabbawala distribution service, which delivers hot meals cooked in each client's home using a network with no central node or organizer.[32] It is similar to the decentralized structure of the Internet with individual entrepreneurs functioning as local nodes dealing with their respective neighbouring nodes without any central command. Management schools have studied this structure and found it amazingly efficient, and modern delivery companies such as DHL and Federal Express have tried, but failed, to compete with it.

Creativity in Indian culture thrives on the dynamic relationship between fixed templates and improvisations. Indians generally find it easier than westerners to deal with extremes and view the space between the extremes of chaos and order as offering scope for creativity, intuition and insight. There is unity in Indian art, but it is not the unity of repetition of identical forms; it is unity in diversity. This theme is expressed in architecture, poetry, music, sculpture – indeed in every conceivable dimension of Hindu life. Several examples will illustrate this point.

In virtually all English-language writings on Indian music, a 'swara' is translated as a 'note'. This distortion has been internalized by Indians, including so-called experts. Actually, there is no Western equivalent of swara, because swara includes not just the basic note, but also a kind of melodic ecosystem which surrounds it. One scholar has remarked that 'Western musicologists who have studied Indian music can seldom make the distinctions of the graces both before and after a swara, the direction of attack, the "angle" and "curvature", because to them this is an alien idea. They think they understand swara when in reality they don't.'[33] The rhythmical timescale of classical Indian music ('tala') is based on non-linear and non-sequential pattern recognition.

Indian music ragas are never sung or played the same way each time; they reflect the mood of the performer, response of the audience, rasa of the moment, weather, time of day, season, and so forth. No two moments are alike, and no two settings are ever the same. Ragas are sung or played primarily through improvisation added to a basic melodic structure. The same raga flourishes in countless different ways thanks to this great freedom and scope for spur-of-the-moment improvisation (often called upaj in Hindustani music). Yet Indian music cannot be dismissed as random and chaotic simply because it is non-normative.[34]

The same kind of contextual sensitivity is shown in preparations of herbal medicine, as well as in medical diagnosis and prescription. Here, health is defined as the balance of opposites and involves moderating the extremes. Ayurvedic prescriptions are never pre-formulated since each individual's distinct body type needs to be ascertained before any diagnosis can be made or treatment recommended. Ayurveda's lexicon uses words like 'imbalance' rather than 'attack' (as in a 'viral attack'), etc., to describe the cause of disease. The physician prescribes a harmonious mixture in which antagonistic forces compensate for and moderate one another. Certain poisons are even used as cures in Ayurveda because toxins, too, depending on the context, have therapeutic properties. The invention of vaccination by Indians was based on the principle of using the opponent constructively to strengthen the whole system.[35] Different plants and foods contain distinct juices (rasas) which may be harmful if taken pure, but mixing and cooking can make them useful. Each individual's distinct body is assessed and corresponding juices are prescribed in the form of foods to achieve the correct balance.[36]

The best Indian chefs do not rely on written recipes or measuring tools, as this would be mechanical and devoid of rasa, yet they produce exquisite cuisine. Improvisation is also the hallmark of Indian dance, art, textiles, fashions, design, and even temple and home rituals, customs and practices. There are one thousand pillars in the famous temple at Kanjivaram, and no two are alike. Improvisation becomes more spontaneous and less deliberate as one proceeds toward greater mastery.

Advanced yogis practise in a spontaneous manner. While beginners are taught to perform yoga asanas (postures) deliberately in a set sequence, advanced practitioners have no premeditated sequence; the body seems to move of its own volition without conscious intention, and even the sense that 'I am doing' the posture fades away.[37] The ego is based on stable and coherent entities, deterministic causation, and the clutching of illusory things. It must surrender in order for the true self to emerge. Techniques the westerner might percieve as chaotic have been applied to achieve this.[38]

The festivities of Diwali and Holi symbolize the recreation of the world out of chaos through a socially creative outburst. The revellers pass from the *order* and *pattern* of everyday social life into a regenerative *temporary chaos* before returning to their respective orderly roles, rejuvenated and refreshed. The festivities symbolize rhythmical polarities: order/chaos; submission to rules/surrender to irrational impulses; division and differentiation/union and non-differentiation; obedience to taboos/transgression of taboos; discipline under the reality principle/indulgence of the pleasure principle; caste rivalry/glorification of the collective. The festival rites utilize the potency of disorder or the harnessing of the creative mind in re-establishing order.[39]

Indian art, erotica, spiritual expression, and indeed virtually all dimensions of life have sophisticated grammars that are taught as foundations of the discipline and that serve to interpret patterns and encourage improvisation. In many Hindu festivals, women across India make intricate designs with multicoloured rice powder sprinkled ceremoniously on the floor. After the ceremony, these designs get obliterated by people walking over them, causing the rice to get spread around the general area. David Shulman describes the ceremony thus: 'As the day progresses, it [the rice] will be worn away by the many feet entering or leaving the house. The rice powder mingles with the dust of the street; the sign fails to retain its true form. Nor is it intended to do so …' He goes on to say that the purpose of constructing such orderly designs is momentary only and that when they have served the moment of their usefulness, they are abandoned. That is to say, they are built not to last but to symbolize 'the momentary, unpredictable reality of the unseen'.[40]

Wendy Doniger – a leading Western authority on Hinduism whose work is particularly reductive about dharmic aesthetics – rightly explains that the smearing of the rice designs is 'a way of defacing order so that one has to re-create it'.[41] However, she goes on to suggest, incorrectly, that Hindus who try to restore temples are 'megalomaniac patrons' who 'smugly' assume that Hindu temples, art and palaces ought to last forever. Her underlying message is that the abandonment and destruction of Hindu temples by foreign domination over the past thousand years, and in contemporary times, are simply the way things are meant to be. Hindus' comfort with disorder and their creative use of it offer fine insight, but these get collapsed into her binary reductionism as disregard for order in temple architecture.[42]

Indian metaphysical flexibility is not to be confused with randomness, duplicity or lack of rigour. It is important to balance the foregoing discussion by showing the existence of order and rigour as well: the *Nyaya-Shastra* rigorously demands five steps to establish a thesis; Mimamsa has seven principles for framing a problem; there are techniques known as 'tantra-yuktis' for writing scientific texts in Sanskrit; and there are various established methodologies for debating opponents. The West's popular notion of right-brain order has thrived alongside left-brain creativity throughout Indian history, and the tension between them continues to find expression in various cultural forms.[43]

Sacred Stories

The differing attitudes towards order and chaos I have traced above manifest very clearly in the contrasting myths and foundational stories of India and the West. In the Vedas and Upanishads, and in the vast canon of classical writings in Sanskrit, we see many context-sensitive and flexible ways of dealing with chaos and difference. The search here is always for balance and equilibrium with the rights of chaos acknowledged. In the creation stories in Genesis and in the Greek classics, there is a constant zero-sum battle between the two poles in which order must triumph. Western mythologies, both Hebraic and Greek, are replete with themes that depict the negative realms as chaotic and the heavens as orderly with the two locked in perpetual struggle rather than seeking complementarities and balance. This structure underlies so much of Western culture and psychology that it can be difficult for westerners to see it unless it is reflected from an external point of view.

Vedas

In Vedic literature, numerous myths recount the creator Prajapati's efforts to beget a universe that would hold the two forces of order and chaos in equilibrium. His first attempt results in a creation which is insufficiently differentiated ('jami'), as it possesses *too much* order. This precludes integral unity because there are no sufficiently distinct components to cohere in the first place. They are undifferentiated and simply merge into each other, a state the Pancavimsa Brahmaṇa (24:11.2) refers to as a 'nightmare'. The second attempt at creation yields a universe which is too fragmented or chaotic ('pṛthak', 'nanatva'). When entities in the universe are too individualistic, scattered, separated or different from each other (pṛthak); they cannot connect. What is desired is a creation which possesses a measure of distinction and individuality but avoids the quality of jami – i.e., it would be interconnected yet circumventing the equally undesirable state of pṛthak.[44]

Prajapati recognizes that all life should be situated between these opposing excesses of too much identity difference and too much homogeneity. Ultimately, he succeeds in producing just such a universe. He does so through the power of resemblance, known as 'bandhuta' or bandhu, which was discussed in Chapter 3. The Vedas abound in attempts at finding connections among the numerous planes of reality. This serves as a cardinal principle of all Vedic thought and moral discourse.

Hinduism weaves multiple narratives around the central motif of cooperative rivalry between order (personified as devas) and chaos (personified as asuras). A key myth shared by all the dharma traditions – the 'churning of the milky ocean', or 'samudra-manthana' – shows the eternal struggle between these two poles. The milky ocean is the ocean of consciousness and creativity, which is to be churned in order to obtain amrita, or the nectar of eternal life. Two opposing sides are needed for churning. Curiously, both sides have a common father: Kashyapa (literally 'vision'). The asuras' mother is Diti (divided, limited), and so the asuras are the offspring of limited vision. The devas spring from Aditi (limitless), and they thus embody higher vision. The asuras usually have more brute strength, but both the power and strength of the asuras as well as the higher vision of the devas are needed for the churning. The to-ing and fro-ing between these archetypes is never-ending and also symbolizes the spiritual struggles within the individual.

The devas grab the tail, and the asuras, the head, of the cosmic serpent, using it as a rope which they wind around a mountain that serves as the churning stick. They engage in a tug of war, pulling back and forth to churn the primordial ocean. The dualism is between knowledge and ignorance, though the latter should not be mistaken for sin or damnation. Asuric tendencies are not considered permanent essences but inner qualities that emerge at a given point in time. Their mutual tension does not get resolved with one side defeating the other, and their stalemate produces all sorts of wondrous and beneficial objects before open conflict breaks out over questions of priority in partaking of the nectar of immortality. Significantly, nectar is produced only after a pot of poison emerges from the ocean – demonstrating yet again the interdependence between good and bad. The myth points the way to the transcendence of both order and chaos, which are brought into delicate equilibrium and ultimately subordinated to spiritual realization. The story of the Samudra-manthana is not intended to be taken literally. Indeed, the ultimate uncertainty of knowing how the universe came about is given eloquent expression in the famous 'Hymn of Creation' in the Rig Veda (X.129):

Who verily knows and who can here declare it,
Whence it was born and whence comes this creation?
The Gods are later than the world's production,
who knows whence it first came into being?
He, the first origin of this creation,
whether he formed it all or did not form it,
Whose eye controls this world in highest heaven,
He verily knows it, or perhaps he knows not.

Some of the principal Vedic divinities, especially Agni, Soma and Varuna, are asuras who have crossed over to the side of the devas at the behest of Indra but who still retain their ambivalence and sinister aspects.[45] At the end of the annual cycle – around the time of the new-year festivals – the asuras are believed to return temporarily to their demonic status. Society, at this time, dissolves into chaos (as depicted playfully during the festival of Holi) before the ordered cosmos is renewed again. In the co-operative rivalry between devas and asuras, the asuras often seem to be winning; there are frequent indications that the deepest knowledge and most exceptional powers are safeguarded by extremely ambivalent figures belonging to the camp of the asuras.[46] Such recurrent crossovers, collusions, and reversals serve to overturn and undermine the Western attitude towards chaos, which is dualistic and exclusivist: order *versus* chaos, insider *or* outsider, and so on. Richard Lannoy sums up the dynamic equilibrium found in Hinduism:

In the Hindu scriptures history is represented as a ceaseless conflict between the Dharma and Adharma — between the moral, idealistic, spiritual forces and the unregenerate forces of darkness, lust, and evil — in which the Dharma always wins. History, ethics, politics, and social speculation are blended together in a cosmic ritual scheme, with gods and culture-heroes acting as conciliatory mediators between the sacred world and the profane world. The battle between good and evil is conceived as a cosmic sacrifice for the common good, ultimately uniting gods and men in the rule of *Raja-dharma*.[47]

The Vedic concept of bandhu binds the underlying integral unity of the universe. The Vedic yajna (incorrectly translated as 'sacrifice', as discussed in Chapter 5) is the workshop where such bandhus are forged and is a metaphor for the link between life's myriad manifestations and their transcendent archetypes. Yajna, in a sense, represents the integration of chaos into order. Again, the epistemology of Vedic thought is nicely summed up in the Rig Veda (10:130.3): 'What was the archetype (rupas), what was the manifestation (pratirupas), and what was the connection (bandhuta) between them?'

The Vedic quest for links between archetypes and their manifestations holds a key to understanding the relationship between order and chaos. The rituals of the creation yajna are a metaphor for transforming the chaotic unknown by re-categorizing it and making it function as a prototype for all subsequent texts, practices and institutions. Bandhus are the bonds of interdependence.[48]

The dharmic mind sees the cosmos as an integrated whole, one which is self-organized rather than administered by an externally imposed law. If India appears to outsiders as a 'functioning chaos', it is because there is a high degree of acceptance of differences and a conscious effort at integration while maintaining autonomy. In the Rig Veda there is a remarkable insight into universal order and harmony called 'ritam', which is the ordering principle of nature. Ritam gives everything – from vast galaxies to the nucleus of an atom – its nature and course. It manifests on three levels: on the cosmic plane, as governing the course of nature; on the socio-ethical level, as justice; and within the inner realm of the practitioner. Ritam maintains balance between the micro and macro levels of existence. There is no dichotomy between ethical and cosmic order. It bridges the spheres which the West has separated, namely the sacred and the secular, spirit and nature, and so on.

The order–chaos tension results in a delicate equilibrium which makes the prevailing order not absolute but tentative, relative, porous and supple. Disorder serves as a source of creativity by preventing order from becoming fossilized. The Lord is not only the creator of the universe (as Brahma) and the maintainer of its order (as Vishnu) but also the one who ultimately dissolves it (as Shiva). The dissolution makes room for the next cycle of creation. At the spiritual level, Shiva, the Lord of Yoga, aptly assumes the appearance of chaos to facilitate the dissolution of bondage to the falsehoods in our minds – making way for new creation. This process is continual, unceasing, all-pervading and functions on both the subatomic and cosmic levels.

The notion of dynamic equilibrium between poles of opposites is found throughout the Vedic texts. The Rig Veda describes the ancient rishis as looking within their own hearts to discover the hidden connection or relationship (bandhu) between existence (sat) and non-existence (asat). Existence not only rests upon non-existence; these two poles are bound together intimately and dynamically.[49]

Lord Krishna also shows two different personalities. One is his aishvarya (organized) side, which allows for confidence, self-reliance and achievement. The other is his madhurya-bhava (sweet emotion), which is about love as opposed to orderly discipline. Hence, order is offset by love that supersedes intellect.

Biblical and Greek Mythology

Biblical creation stories and Greek myths privilege order over chaos. In the creation story in Genesis (Chapters 1–2), for instance, God creates the entire universe ex nihilo in a one-time event, complete with a whole set of mutually exclusive opposites. 'In the beginning,' the opening verses of Genesis read, 'the earth was formless and void.' This original state, as described in the Bible, is not the shunyata (emptiness) of Buddhism but rather a situation which needs to be 'fixed'. God thus intervenes, with a single dictum: 'Let there be light / and there was light' (1:3). The passage goes on to say: 'And God saw that the light was good' (1:4). Thus, God establishes the binary categories of light and dark.

Genesis then offers a whole slew of opposites: above and below; sea and dry land; sun and moon; good and evil, etc. The overwhelming impression left by this story is that of a completely transcendent God who creates a universe that is not only separate and distinct from the divine but built on mutually exclusive categories. The polarities of God/ Satan, believer/heathen, true religion/false religion, deity/idol, history/ myth, etc., which evolve later in the tradition are all, like those found in Genesis, mutually exclusive. In every case, the first option in each pair is absolutely and exclusively valid, whereas the second option is absolutely dangerous. Not only is it negative, but it must be completely eradicated to restore order, which is not a matter of balance but of conflict and conquest.

Much that is typical of Western thought originates here: a privileging of binaries and exclusive distinctions over ambiguity and formlessness, a horror of void or emptiness, a sense of deity as utterly other and outside of the normal space-time continuum. There is no indication here that anything created participates in the inner reality of the divine, nor does it seem to be the task of humans to discover or even consider higher consciousness. Instead, the task is first to make a garden ('till the earth') – a garden first conceptualized in terms of paradise but which quickly turns into a place from which humans are exiled. In this place humans are supposed to obey God's rule not to eat of the tree of the knowledge of good and evil. It is only when Adam and Eve violate this rule that they seem to become conscious, and their consciousness is fundamentally one of sin. Suddenly they know that they are naked and are therefore ashamed before God, and this deep sense of shame and alienation turns into fear of God.

The temptation to eat of the tree is akin to lapsing into a state of dualism: good versus evil. Consider also that in Genesis the serpent induces the fall from grace, and it is Eve who first succumbs to temptation – a basis for the extreme patriarchy and misogyny of the later tradition.

Contrast all this with the dharmic traditions where the serpent is a symbol not of evil but of kundalini, the primal, creative feminine life force. It is precisely by embracing and channelling feminine energy that individuals (male and female) are able to surmount dualism. Dharma philosophers would assert that dualism itself is the source of confusion preventing man from realizing the differentiated yet harmonious unity of the cosmos, a limitation of the human mind and not attributed to any disobedience of God's injunctions in the distant past.

The creation story in Genesis merits comparison with the Prajapati story, though it must be said that the latter does not occupy the same place in Hinduism that the story of Adam and Eve does in Christianity and Judaism. Prajapati's fable is just that, and it is not intended to be taken literally. Its significance lies in the elucidation of an important metaphysical and philosophical point. Indeed, most Hindus might not even know the story of Prajapati, whereas, in the Judeo-Christian tradition, the story of Adam and Eve is canonical and so central that it is among the best-known sections of the Bible. It is often (though not always) taken literally and accepted as such by millions of Jews and Christians. Evangelicals even offer this account as a viable argument against scientific accounts of the origin of the cosmos and humanity. This literalism may be repudiated by some Christians, but to call this literalism into question is to breach the very heart of the faith for many believers. Thus, what could have been viewed as just metaphorical in mainstream Christianity has become instead a litmus test for Western religious identities with none of the ambiguity, layers of meaning, or metaphysical depth of the Prajapati narrative.

The order/chaos dyad we find in Genesis was then extrapolated as the split between good and evil and God versus the Devil. Satan is a relatively minor figure in the Bible, but with the passage of time, his duel with God became the central drama in the popular imagination of the Christian religions. Satan bears responsibility for all malevolence in the world. He is the serpent in Eden whose powers of persuasion led to original sin, the voice of temptation and the dragon in the Book of Revelation, the originator of lies and promoter of evil. He will wage the final, losing battle against Jesus, thence to be cast into Hell at last. It becomes terribly important, then, to be on the right side and fight against those purported to be working for the Devil.[50]

In Hinduism, there is no equivalent of an external Satan or Anti-Christ. There is no Anti-Brahman or Anti-Ishwara or Anti-Shiva whatsoever, because good and bad are inextricably intertwined. This worldview does not condone adharma but suggests that good and bad are within oneself and may be overcome by elevating one's own consciousness, not by any external controls. Brahman includes everything, both good and bad. The negative forces are personified as a multitude of powerful intelligences –asura, rakshasa, etc – capable of producing great harm. We must recognize them, learn to cope with them, and eventually transform them through yoga to regain the state of sat-chit-ananda.[51] At the political level, for instance, rival nations would not be demonized as 'evil empires' (which is how President Reagan referred to the Soviets on numerous occasions) or as part of an 'axis of evil' (which is how President George W. Bush referred to countries that threaten the US).

That the struggle with evil is internal and not external is illustrated in the Indian narratives of devas who swallow poison rather than vanquish external enemies. In one such story, Lord Shiva himself consumes the fierce, dark and bitter poison first churned up from the ocean. He does so in order to overcome it, leaving the nectar to others. But significantly, Shiva makes this choice both out of knowledge (of the poison's deadly effect) and love (for those who might suffer harm) – not out of any dark, destructive passion. Furthermore, he is able to transmute the poison not by ejecting it but by incorporating it in himself. An equivalent story in the Book of Revelation, conceivably, might be for Christ, in his second coming, to assimilate the Devil rather than defeat him in an external struggle. Thus Christ would be setting a constructive example as opposed to demanding that all humans join him in a war against all those who side with the Devil. But, needless to say, this is but a hypothetical scenario; the good versus evil dualism of Judaism and Christianity is absolute.

In Greek culture, likewise, there are sky gods who represent order and light and who ultimately triumph over the earth gods who represent chaos and darkness. We also see one kind of order overthrown by a later, more strictly defined one. These occur in a linear sequence where the new order completely supersedes the old rather than coexisting with it to incorporate it or leaving it in some state of ambiguity. Zeus, for instance, the sky god par excellence, completely overthrows the Titans, who are much more amorphous and ambiguous deities.

The drastic either/or choices characteristic of Western thinking mirror the religious exclusivism of the Abrahamic faiths, stretching back to the first of the Ten Commandments: 'Thou shalt have no other gods before me.' Whether this was intended as a tribute to Yahweh as the premier *among* many gods or as a strict monotheistic injunction denying the existence of all other gods, it was nonetheless interpreted in the most extreme way. Immediately upon receiving the Commandments, Moses ordered the slaughter of all those Israelites who worshipped other deities. The Israelites believed that they were 'the chosen people' with a divinely mandated Manifest Destiny, and they later used this belief to justify their conquests of other nations and subsequent genocides. Mosaic Law enshrined creedal exclusivism, and consequently, the Jews have remained religiously and ethnically exclusive (though, unlike Christians and Muslims, they have no mandate to convert others).

Contextual Ethics

Westerners are especially uneasy about variation and nuance in the domain of ethics. To them, dharmic ethics can appear anarchic, impulsive, irrational and unprincipled. But the dharma has a venerable tradition of ethical theory and practice, apparently invisible to their eyes. As Sri Aurobindo puts it:

> There is no ethical idea which it [dharma] has not stressed, put in its most ideal and imperative form, enforced by teaching, injunction, parable, artistic creation, formative examples. Truth, honour, loyalty, fidelity, courage, chastity, love, long-suffering, self-sacrifice, harmlessness, forgiveness, compassion, benevolence, beneficence are its common themes, are, in its view, the very stuff of a right human life, the essence of man's dharma. Buddhism, with its high and noble ethics, Jainism, with its austere ideal of self-conquest, Hinduism, with its magnificent examples of all sides of the Dharma, are not inferior in ethical teaching and practice to any religion or system, but rather take the highest rank and have had the strongest effective force.[52]

Dharmic ethics are formulated in response to the situation and context of the problem in a way that makes Western ethics seem unduly codified, rigid, monolithic and even simplistic. A.K. Ramanujan, in his influential essay 'Is There an Indian Way of Thinking?', uses the terms 'context-free' and 'context-sensitive' to contrast the West and India in their respective approaches to ethics:

> Cultures may be said to have overall tendencies to *idealize,* and think in terms of, either the context-free or the context-sensitive kind of rules. Actual behavior may be more complex, though the rules they think with are a crucial factor in guiding the behavior. In cultures like India's, the context-sensitive kind of rule is the preferred formulation.[53]

He points out that Indian culture is like Sanskrit grammar, which is contextual in emphasis, whereas Western culture and linguistics are considerably less so. Ramanujan elaborates further:

> Various taxonomies of season, landscape, times, gunas or qualities (and their material bases), tastes, characters, emotions, essences (rasas), etc., are basic to the thought-work of Hindu medicine and poetry, cooking and religion, erotics and magic. Each jati or class defines a context, a structure of relevance, a rule of permissible combinations, a frame of reference, a meta-communication of what is and can be done ... Even the Kama-Sutra is literally a grammar of love, which declines and conjugates men and women as one would nouns and verbs in different genders, voices, moods and aspects. Genders are genres. Different body-types and character-types obey different rules, respond to different scents and beckonings.[54]

Each of these tendencies has social and political consequences. Context-free thinking lends itself to binary categories and logic, history-centric chronologies, canons, and legal codes of various sorts. This tendency is conducive to rule-based, top-down governance and control. It is easier to control things which are certain, stable and concrete, with fixed coordinates than things which are fluid and shifting. The normative logic based on Aristotle's Law of the Excluded Middle leads to thinking in terms of opposites and choices along the lines of 'us versus them'. Such reductionist discourse is useful mainly for the training of teams, be they armies, sales departments or missionaries. Control is opposed to flexibility and to sensitivity to circumstances.

Of course, the West has occasionally dabbled in countercultural revolts against normative conventions, and these have enriched its society with a new context-sensitivity.[55] In general, however, its dominant ideal is the privileging of certainty and uniformity, which it touts as universalism. Ramanujan explains this Western ethos: 'Whatever his context — birth, class, gender, age, place, rank, etc. — a man is a man for all that. Technology, with its modules and interchangeable parts, and the post-Renaissance sciences, with their quest for universal laws (and 'facts') across contexts, intensify the bias towards the context-free.'[56]

Not only is the Western conception and application of ethics independent of context; this independence itself is seen as a criterion of truth and right action. The best ethical teachings, such as the Ten Commandments or Kant's categorical imperative, are valued because they are supposed to be universally applicable in all times and places regardless of circumstances.[57] Dharmic traditions, on the other hand, have long sought to arrive at truth by balancing universal truths and acts with those that can be determined only in the context in which they occur. Dharmic cultures have thus evolved to become comfortable with complexity and nuance, rejecting notions of the absolute and rigid ideals of morality and conduct.

Dharma provides an ethical framework for the conduct of individuals and groups that enables *both* worldly pursuits *and* evolution of consciousness. Dharma is critical to the maintenance of social stability and harmony and is the ethic governing the pursuit of wealth and pleasure. Its values are founded on metaphysical and cosmic principles yet are applicable to common social life. It tries to prevent human beings from falling into crooked and unbridled impulses, desires, ambitions and egoism. The contextual nature goes hand in hand with the spirit of openness to multiple answers to complex ethical questions.

In a way illustrative of this context-sensitive quality, Baudhayana (800 BCE) – the Indian mathematician and philosopher – noted that learned men of the traditions follow the customs of their regions. He listed practices in one region which were contrary to those in another, and yet both followed shruti and smriti in their own contexts. Besides localizing ethics geographically, dharma is reflective of a variety of factors, such as: stage of life ('asrama-dharma'), occupational predispositions ('varna-dharma'), communal codes (jati-dharma), personal nature ('svabhava-dharma'), and choice of path ('sva-dharma'). Dharma also allows for exceptional circumstances when, during times of duress or emergency, one must act in ways that contradict what would normally be right action (apad-dharma). There is also sadharana-dharma (absolute/ universal), which the texts characterize as the equivalent of 'last resort', i.e., a fall-back if no context can be found to apply.

There has been no singular or central authority for issuing smritis, and numerous kings, spiritual exemplars and intellectuals have produced them.[58] A number of texts generically called smritis emerged to develop a code of conduct applicable to each of the varna and ashrama categories, and this code was updated for each time period and situation.[59] Smritis are meant to be rewritten for each era and social context, and hence modern Hindus are not bound by them. In fact, they are supposed to rewrite new smritis for current times as well as critique and amend the old ones. Indian pluralism was always based on the absence of a single absolute code applicable for all.

Different smriti texts were followed in different regions even during the same era, and new ones were formulated when historical change rendered the old rules obsolete. Diversity in codes of conduct in different religious, ethnic, and caste communities was taken for granted. When no established code seemed to apply, scholars considered the behaviour of the learned as guidelines for righteousness. Folk narratives served to explain the gist of dharma in simple guidelines and localized contexts.[60] The ruler in classical India was required to instate dharma as a facilitator only and not to impose his own practice upon others. He was meant to support diversity and implement laws differently for different contexts – taking into account place of residence, occupation, family, and other factors. Thus, different communities within the same society were allowed to practise their own codes.

Manu, a prominent compiler of ethics in ancient India, explains that the ruler must appreciate the contextual nature of dharma: '[A king] who knows the sacred law must imagine into it the laws of jati (community), of districts, of guilds, and of families, and thus settle the peculiar law of each.'[61] The great Sanskrit scholar Pandurang Vaman Kane (1880–1972) elaborates: 'Generally speaking, the king had no legislative power; nevertheless there are instances where kings created new rules, usually by recognizing existing customs. He also had residual powers to create positive law, *viz.*, in areas that were not covered by the dharma-sastras.'[62]

Even those who were countercultural, or outright heretical, had to be respected according to their own particular dharma. Kane explains:

> Narada [a great sage] states that the king should uphold the conventions of heretical sects of traders, guilds and other groups and that whatever traditional usages, activities, mode of attendance and means of maintenance were peculiar to them should be permitted to them by the king without introducing any change. Among the matters of which the king was to take cognizance and included by Narada was the transgression of usages of heretics, traders, guilds and ganas. Brhaspati [a Vedic deity] provides that in disputes among husbandmen, artisans, wrestlers, money-lenders, guilds, dancers, heretics, thieves, a decision is to be given in accordance with their conventions.[63]

There were also distinct and separate ethical guidelines applicable to rulers, which kept the rulers' powers in check. Besides Manu, there were numerous other legal theorists, none of whom had absolute authority; they codified the existing practices of the elders rather than inventing and imposing their own. The absence of Western-style normative institutions has led many Western scholars to conclude that India was never a nation as they understand the term. They find it impossible to accept that a self-organized system is viable.

Dharma may be descriptive or prescriptive, i.e., what is convention, or what ought to be, respectively. Examples of the descriptive kind are guna dharma, which refers to the natural property of anything, such as the properties of an herb without necessarily judging these properties to be good or bad. In the Upanishads, which are more prescriptive, dharma designates practice of virtue and refers more to how people ought to behave.[64]

In the Mahabharata, truth is not invariant, admitting to no nuance or context. Sitansu Chakravarti explains that there are three categories of ethics in the Mahabharata: (i) universal injunctions similar to those found in all religions; (ii) universal debts which are innate to nature, parents and forefathers, great teachers, humanity at large and all living beings; and (iii) sva-dharma, the personal spiritual path. However, none of these applies to one who has attained such spiritual heights that the domains of conventional right and wrong are transcended.

Dharma deals pragmatically with behaviour in particular circumstances rather than universal moral principles. To explain where ordinary dharma is transcended, Chakravarti contrasts the dharma of Bhisma and Krishna in the Mahabharata. The former follows normative injunctions even though he is well aware of apad-dharma, the non-normative situational dharma sometimes called for in an emergency. Krishna, on the other hand, deviates from the accepted norms when required in order to achieve his goals, which are for the overall good of humanity. For instance, he suggests killing Drona, Karna and Duryodhana by means that would be unjust under normal circumstances and indeed kills Bhisma himself – all because the Kauravas have to be defeated for the larger good of humanity. In order to build a new order where dharma prevails, methods must be used that would ordinarily be considered unjust.

This is not a case, however, of the end justifying any means. Krishna makes it clear that a non-normative or exceptional course can be followed only if one is untainted by ego and thus selfless and *sattvic* enough to know and act for the wider good.[65]

What is important in these decisions is that dharma is shown to be manifest as both pragmatic and beneficial. Hence the Buddha usually made statements that are true and useful, be they pleasant or unpleasant, as the occasion demands. Only in exceptional circumstances, to achieve compassionate and soteriological purposes, may a ruse or deception be used.[66]

Lannoy explains the principle underlying this distinction: 'Indian inclusiveness operates at a level deeper than the polarities of good and evil. It has never shown comparable insistence on the need for a choice between opposites of right and wrong, as did the Zoroastrians, the Jews, the Christians.'[67] He adds: 'In Indian ethics, good and evil are always *relative,* and a precise definition of intrinsically good or bad deeds is avoided.'[68]

There are no exact parallels to the Ten Commandments in the dharma traditions.[69] The Bhagavadgita, for instance, is not read as a book of rules or teachings, nor was it ever the law of any ruler. It does not even command, 'thou shalt do this and not that.' Rather, it explains how the system of dharma and karma operates and what the consequences of various choices can be. It is a description of natural rta/dharma. The

Gita ends with Lord Krishna asking Arjuna to act as he deems fit after having listened to the exposition of the nature and possibilities of human action that he had himself solicited. Lannoy writes:

> In the setting of India's joint family system ... the elasticity of social forms is a response to mutability: the specially Indian flavor of insistence upon relative social values, ambivalent polarities with no immutable ethics of human arbitration and choice. The Indian child learns more by observation than through explicit parental instruction.[70]

Ramanujan contrasts Western universal ethics with Indian contextual ethics, writing:

> One has only to read Manu after a bit of Kant to be struck by the former's extraordinary lack of universality. He seems to have no clear notion of a universal human nature from which one can deduce ethical decrees like 'Man shall not kill', or 'Man shall not tell an untruth'. One is aware of no notion of a 'state', no unitary law of all men ... The main tradition of Judeo-Christian ethics is based on such a premise of universalisation. Manu will not understand such a premise. To be moral, for Manu, is to particularise – to ask who did what, to whom and when ... Each class (jati) of man has his own laws, his own proper ethic, not to be universalised.[71]

However, as noted earlier, there *is* universal dharma (samanya-dharma), and it is more accurate to say that the dharma shastras give numerous recommendations within an overarching framework about individual conduct in different contexts.[72]

There are animated discussions in the Mahabharata concerning the tensions between the universal and contextual poles in Indian thought. The same tensions are codified by Manu in flexible and dialogical form, unconstrained by authoritarianism.[73] The frequently levelled charge of moral relativism against this contextual morality is inaccurate, because the *conduct* and *motive* are considered consequential in judging the ultimate value of statements. The degree of common good is the universal standard, and the well-being of all creatures, in terms of non-harming (ahimsa), is the highest truth. For the Buddha and for the sages of the Mahabharata, non-harming is the universal ideal ('ahimsa paramo dharmah') and truth, the highest dharma ('satyan paro nasti dharmah'). The contextual morality *serves* the universal morality and is an individualized expression of it. In other words, the contextual dharma applies the principles of higher universal dharma of benevolence and compassion to specific contexts.

Thus, dharmic thought offers *both* universal *and* contextual poles – not just the latter, as that would be tantamount to moral relativism. Metaphysically, the transcendent (or para) Brahman or Bhagavan is the universal that grounds the immanent (or apara) cosmic level, which is contextual. The Buddhist approximation of this universal is the web of interdependence. Similarly, there are two levels of self: the context-free Atman and the contextual self of body and mind.

This corresponds to the absolute and relative truths previously discussed. Relative truths are necessarily contextual, and only the absolute truth transcends all contexts. The universal goals of dharma get implemented via the particular context-specific dharma. The particular fulfils the universal.[74] The universal injunctions and specific prescriptions thus work together.

The relationship between these two levels of truth should not be bipolar but *bifocal.* Bipolarity implies an individual oscillating between the two levels in an opportunistic manner. For example, a person competitive and diligent in worldly affairs may try to shun responsibility for a charitable cause by citing the illusory nature of life. Thus, the absolute truth can be misused selectively when it suits individual needs. On the other hand, a bifocal approach sees both truths simultaneously at all times. Even as people conduct themselves based on the relative plane, they are aware of the absolute truth and see the relative ethics as a skilful means of attaining the absolute.

The highly contextualized path ultimately seeks freedom from all contexts; one approach is sannyasa, the life stage that is free from worldly contexts, conventions, rules, and so on. This is when the householder's context-specific dharma ends in the final stage of the wandering ascetic seeking liberation from all contexts. Thus, context-specific (relative) dharma leads up to and culminates in context-free (universal) dharma. In this manner, dharma embraces both mundane and transcendental concerns. Another radical defiance of all contextual structures is bhakti: an intense posture of surrender, it targets every bondage of jati, ritual, gender, clothing and custom, stage of life, and so on. The state of moksha – or complete liberation in this life – is the culmination of the spiritual path when one lives totally free of context.[75]

The highest manifestation of dharma is sva-dharma ('my dharma'), which is particular to a given person and situation. It is only available in the sattvic state of consciousness, and it is self-revealing and adaptive to the context in this state. At the lower (tamasic and rajasic) levels of consciousness more rigid, codified rules are prescribed. Until the individual achieves the sattvic state, the best option available is the guidance of a living spiritual master who has attained that state. The idea of self-revealing sva-dharma is alien to the Jewish and Christian mindsets, which deem the state of consciousness of the rishi to be impossible. The only source of ethics available in the Judeo-Christian religions is what has already been revealed via the prophets.

Antonio de Nicolas, a philosopher who has studied dharma traditions for many decades, explains that the dharma involves an entirely different ethic, one which is not dependent on external rules and historical revelations. He writes:

> The training for excellence is to practice the embodied technologies of decision-making, the right decisions, the wise decisions, when needed by the present dharma, context, one faces. This is the goal, the ethics of the whole program of the Avatar Krishna in the Bhagavad Gita: to train Arjuna, that fallen and disturbed warrior, to make decisions, the best ones, as needed by his present dharma (his present situation), a battle field. And this is the program of human acting, from the Rig Veda down, that Indic texts propose: an ethics of decision-making as opposed to an ethics of compliance to rules coming from the outside. There is no outside god able to make these pronouncements in Indic texts …[76]

Simplistic rules or commandments are insufficient for dealing with today's ethical situations. Nicolas notes: 'Our educational system is biased in favor of veridical decisions, decisions geared to agreements between subject and object, logical platitudes, "finding the truth" … But there are no mechanisms in education to teach any one decision based on multiple ambiguous situations, self-centered decisions, "what is best from among the possible", in the concrete situation facing the subject.' To achieve this, he says, 'new technologies need to be embodied by a subject and also by the guide, guru, spiritual director', so that a person is equipped to make the best choice among the ones available in a practical sense. Thus, the battlefield in the Gita is the human body itself.[77]

He concludes by remarking as to how veridical decision making affects society:

> It comes down to this. The West has trained its people to perform veridical agreements – this is true, this is false – but all these Western people lack the ability to make decisions in complex situations, where they have multiple choices and need the frontal lobes to view those situations.[78]

The diagram below summarizes the discussion of various kinds of dharma depending on context. The left column shows universal dharmic principles at the top. These are used as guidelines to develop context-specific kinds of dharma, shown below. The bottom of the column shows sva-dharma and reflects the individual's personal conditioning, aptitudes, predispositions, tastes and external circumstances. Again, only someone living a sattvic life of purity is able to gain direct insight into personalized right action. All others must rely on competent guidance from a living master or the lives of exemplars or spiritual texts.

The right side shows the states that are beyond contexts. At the top are states in which one is liberated from bodily desires and cognitive limitations. Hindus refer to this state as jivan-mukti or moksha. Buddhists call it shunyata. (While not identical, both claims are transcendent states liberated from bodily desires. Appendix A has more details on the relationship between these traditions.) The bodhisattva is someone who, after having achieved this state, elects to return to earth in order to help other living beings, human and other. At the bottom of the right side is the lifestyle known as sannyasa (renunciation). Such a person has abandoned social life and its norms. Hence, he or she is free from social contexts. But such a person has yet to achieve transcendence from bodily conditioning. It is a path that has not reached its destination. In this state, the person is vulnerable to temptations, and many a famous sannyasin has fallen from dignity as a result. What makes the sannyasin especially vulnerable is that his/her followers expect perfection of their teacher who may not yet have achieved it.

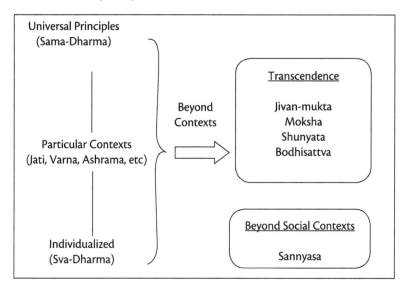

Some of the differences between contextual, non-normative Indian society and normative Western society are listed in the table below.

Non-normative	Normative
Adjudication by contextualized and jati-specific artha-shastras	Codified universal laws for society
Simultaneous continuity and change via sampradayas	Tension between Tradition, Enlightenment and Post-enlightenment
Varna and jati matrix of interdependence, fluidity and self-governance	Homogeneity and centralized management
Pluralistic and tolerant religions coexisting and interacting	Exclusivist religion replacing others through coercion
Peaceful expansion through spread of culture and thought	Violent expansion through military subjugation and genocide

Western notions of ethics cannot be used as the framework for understanding Hinduism. This does not mean that Hinduism is amoral or immoral but simply that the question of morality needs to be viewed from a wider angle.[79] In academic circles, there is a tendency to mistake context-sensitivity for moral relativism (a hodgepodge of disparate fragments).

A case in point is tantra, which, as I have mentioned above, is the set of spiritual techniques (meditation in graveyards, the eating of forbidden foods, some highly ritualized sexual practices) which are recommended for certain advanced practitioners of dharma. Tantra often runs into trouble in the West, because it utilizes transgression as the vehicle to transcend dualism in certain cases. To even begin to understand tantra, however, we must bear in mind the cultural and philosophical context in which it exists. Tantra originated as a range of bodily technologies for perfecting the individual.

Many of its practices, texts, beliefs and traditions are opposed to any normative order and serve as a form of counterculture in India. Its rejection of order takes the form even of sanctioning the deliberate violation of norms, particularly those centred on ritual purity. Over time, there occurred a healthy cross-fertilizing back and forth with Vedic and other traditions. Elements may have been borrowed from Vedic and other rituals, symbols and philosophies, and reformulated, systematized and integrated into the coherent corpus of what became known as the tantra tradition. These two poles of values and rituals coexist and mutually penetrate each other in complex ways.[80]

In dharma traditions, ethics or morality is not an end in itself, nor is it optimally imposed from without. Morality is but a preparatory means for attaining a higher spiritual state or perfection. Worldly morality may be transgressed by spiritual adepts in order to achieve the goal of spiritual liberation in a different, more effective and quicker mode. The tantric practitioners who pursue spiritual liberation through the disciplined use of transgressions must observe rigorous precepts such as not harming others, chastity, freedom from hedonistic cravings, truthfulness and so on.[81] The intensity of their self-denial would surprise the most stringent Protestant moralist. But in the end, tantra defies analysis in Western moral terms and is intelligible only from an Indian spiritual point of view. Western morality sees all transgression as *immoral* and thus worthy of rejection.[82]

The apparent contradictions between ritual and lifestyle norms and their transgressions have provided an opportunity for Western religious scholars, operating within a secularized framework, to deconstruct and debunk key components of tantra. Such condescending attitudes often denigrate the writings of scholars who are otherwise sympathetic, including some who have devoted much of their lives to its study, interpretation, and even practice.[83] While it is true that tantric practices and their rationales are opportunities for abuse, and while it is demonstrable that abuse does occur sometimes, these concerns are deviations from an extremely high, austere and ascetic set of standards and goals for achieving non-dualistic states.

Aesthetics, Morality and Truth

Given their anxiety about difference and chaos, it is not surprising that westerners are also baffled and disturbed by Indian aesthetics. Western culture privileges 'whiteness', a certain directness of speech and manner, and a clear, replicable form of art, whereas the dharmic approach relishes darkness, subtlety, accommodation, improvisation and mystery.

Furthermore, westerners assume – often unconsciously – that what is 'beautiful' (in their own, peculiar and culturally constructed sense) is also 'good' and 'true.' Likewise, that which is 'ugly' is also 'bad' and 'wrong' (and probably even politically subversive). Ever since Plato, the West has seen the three basic values of goodness, truth and beauty as inextricably connected. A judgement about one of these values tends to implicate the other two; each part of the triad is mapped unilaterally onto the rest, so that what is 'beautiful' must also be 'good' which in turn makes it 'true'.

In the Indian mind, by contrast, the domains of truth, goodness and beauty are quite distinct, and each operates relatively independently from the others. In the Sanskrit verse 'satyam-shivam-sundaram' (truth-goodness-beauty), truth (satyam) is primary, and it prevails over the good (shivam) and the beautiful (sundaram). Neither beauty nor goodness necessarily implies the presence of truth, nor, for that matter, does lack of beauty imply untruth or moral turpitude.[84]

As with so much in Western culture, the roots of its triadic complex are twofold: the biblical concept of the 'chosen people' and the classical Greek preference for lightness, symmetry and clarity of form. These two dimensions of the tradition combined to generate the conventional Western attitude toward aesthetics in terms of race, ethnic identity and physical appearance and in terms of art, literature and even music. Biblical theology and Greek influence were fused to undergird the racial stereotyping of dark-skinned peoples. Greek norms of beauty and aesthetics combined with biblical concerns about purity and exclusive lineage became the basis for evaluating other cultures, which were often depicted as ugly, savage and sexually promiscuous – with their deities and symbols viewed as asymmetrical, shadowy, threatening and grotesque.[85]

Irrational and absurd as these prejudices may seem (among other things, the original chosen people, the people of Israel, were not 'white' in the racial sense at all), they have had a virulent effect on the West's encounters with non-white peoples. They continue to inform the Western approach to India and Indians today in ways both superficial and profound. It is true that the preference for 'whiteness', symmetry, and fixed forms have been challenged in the history of Western art (especially during the Romantic movement at which time, not incidentally, India became extremely important in the Western imagination), but these challenges have only exacerbated the various splits within Western culture, which in turn lead to new impositions of order, clarity and control.

The association of beauty with truth and goodness, and of all three with Western culture, is evident even in secular thought. Kant, for instance, attacked the people of India on the basis of their art and religious aesthetics, which he found to be 'grotesque'. He wrote: 'Indians have a dominating taste for the grotesque, of the sort that falls into the adventurous. Their religion consists of grotesqueries. Idols of monstrous form, the priceless tooth of the mighty monkey Hanuman, the unnatural atonements of the fakirs (heathen mendicant friars) and so forth are in this taste.'[86]

Because of the horrible state of aesthetics in the Indian religion, he found it only *natural* that immoral customs such as the oppression of women would prevail. European man had elevated relations between the sexes beyond the physical plane to higher levels of morality, charm and spiritual inspiration. But, says Kant, the same is not true of Asia:

> Since he [the Asian] has no concept of the morally beautiful which can be united with this impulse [of sex], he loses even the worth of the sensuous enjoyment, and his harem is a constant source of unrest. He thrives on all sorts of amorous grotesqueries … he makes use of very unjust and often loathsome means. Hence there a woman is always in a prison, whether she may be unmarried or have a barbaric, good-for-nothing and always suspicious husband.[87]

Soon we shall consider some of the history of these attitudes, in particular their roots in scripture and the fusion of scripture with Greek values. But first let us remind ourselves that these attitudes persist even today and that they continue to account for some of the West's most violent and aggressive projects of domination.

When I entered the US corporate scene in the 1970s, management training seminars were being conducted that emphasized certain normative body language: a strong handshake suggested a confident and reliable individual, whereas a limp one, in Western culture, was seen as a sign of weakness and moral uncertainty. Confident eye contact (*almost* to the point of aggressiveness, but with just the right intensity and balanced by a smile) showed a person who was assertive but pleasantly in control. The term 'power lunch' entered the corporate lexicon, supported by a series of best-selling books with titles explaining what 'real men' do or do not do. 'Real women', not to be left behind, soon followed with their own similar titles.

Western lawyers advise their clients to dress formally and wear their hair in a clean 'orderly' style during court appearances, because the look is associated with morality and truthfulness. An unkempt style, on the other hand, is routinely highlighted by the media and by opponents to indicate that someone is immoral, crooked or dangerous.[88] 'Disorderly conduct' is a crime and 'disorderly' aesthetics have got a number of perfectly innocent persons into trouble. (This is ironic considering that many of the biggest crooks and criminals – including Bernard Madoff and the convicted leaders of Enron and WorldCom – have always appeared neat and orderly in public. Neither their aesthetic nor their supposed dedication to truth and reason has kept them from being immoral!)[89]

Recent trends in society and politics, combined with the globalization of popular culture, have challenged these and other perceptions of non-normative aesthetics. Black scholars have shown how black aesthetics are often depicted as being linked to evil and irrationality, and how this in turn reinforces the notion of white people as defenders of goodness and truth.[90]

In the 1950s, Elvis Presley crossed the line of what was acceptable in mainstream white society by appropriating black music for white audiences. This met with mixed reactions. On the one hand, his fans welcomed the music as positive and sexually transgressive. On the other hand, conservatives saw it as an invasion by the forces of chaos and hence dangerous. In some communities, Elvis's records were publicly burned, and the FBI ordered inquiries to find ways to control this menace. The threat of chaos eventually disappeared when whites appropriated the music so that it no longer was considered 'black'. Likewise, when jazz, the blues, rock, and other black music genres – even to some extent extremely non-normative genres such as hip-hop – were marketed, in orderly fashion, as products of the music industry, they were regarded as less threatening and became mainstream.[91] In other words, once the music became absorbed into white culture, it ceased being chaotic and dangerous.

When the US decided to capture Mexican territory during the nineteenth century, Mexicans were depicted as savages, filled with immorality and wickedness.[92] From here evolved the stereotype of the Mexican *bandito*. Today's debates about Mexican immigration involve language that may not be explicitly racist but which nonetheless embodies deep-rooted stereotypes about Mexicans' supposed lack of aesthetics, moral deficiency, and inferior reasoning. Another example is that cigarettes have become 'civilized' as a legitimate part of Wall Street capitalism whereas illicit drugs are almost wholly associated with dark or coloured races – marijuana with Mexicans; heroin with blacks; opium with Afghans; peyote with Native Americans. The 'war on drugs' thus perpetuates the mythic war between order and chaos. Thanks to the efforts of African Americans, the association between morality and whiteness has been challenged in the public sphere, though it still persists and continues to do harm.

The converse, however, is also true: Western preferences enter non-Western cultures where people try to mimic the dominant aesthetic. Western-run international beauty pageants, for instance, have increasingly influenced the standard notions of what constitutes female beauty in India. When many Indian women began to win the Miss Universe and the Miss World titles, they became role models for Indian girls. Provincial beauty pageants sprang up in most Indian states: there is now a Miss Uttar Pradesh, a Miss Punjab, a Miss Kerala, a Miss Madhya Pradesh, etc., and the winners go to the national level, and from there to international competitions. The supply chain starts locally, fed by a Miss Lucknow contest, a Miss Kanpur contest, a Miss Bhopal contest, and so forth. A high ranking in a local contest boosts a girl's social, professional and matrimonial status. To prepare for these contests, there are modelling schools all over India, even in small towns. These schools teach girls how to walk, talk and employ the body language of Western women, because the West has defined the standard of beauty for *all* women. The widespread advertising of cosmetic products that make the skin lighter is another indication that aesthetics are being defined by Western criteria.[93]

All over India, accent-training schools are being established to train the staff of call centres. The more American-sounding the accent, the higher the compensation for a young person, and this cultural influence trickles into other areas of society to the point where American phenotypes and etiquette are becoming important social markers in India!

In the West, aesthetic appeal, morality and the capacity to uphold truth have been traditionally viewed as the exclusive domain of a chosen people or a privileged line of descent. Some of this exclusivity stems from the Bible's particular emphasis on patriarchy: there is one God, the Father, and only one son who represents essence and will. In biblical tradition, the victorious heir often has to triumph over or eliminate his brothers lest the legacy become adulterated or dispersed. We see this in Genesis in the tension between Cain and Abel, between Isaac and Ishmael, and between Jacob and Esau. In each case there is conflict, sometimes violent.

The same tension emerges in the biblical story of Noah and his sons. There was a great flood after which the descendants of Noah and his wife, the only human survivors, populated the earth. Noah's three sons were Ham, Shem and Japheth. Genesis explains that Ham laughed at Noah's nudity, and as punishment for violating his honour, Noah cursed Ham's descendants to live in servitude to the descendants of the other two sons (Genesis 9:22-27). Hence, Ham embodies the 'bad' or 'impure' lineage.

In the early Christian period, this relegation of Ham to the 'bad' category became associated with darkness of skin, sexual impurity, and evil in general. In a particularly literal and obtuse application of the Greek love for what they called bright or 'shining' gods, early Christians saw *whiteness of skin* as a form of the divine privilege of light over dark and order over chaos. Thinking no doubt of Ham, Origen (an early Christian philosopher) put it directly: 'Not without merit therefore does the *discolored* posterity imitate the ignobility of the race.'[94] Ham was thus triply damned: he was 'ugly', he was 'bad' and he was unfit to propagate the 'true' line of Israel.

Until the early nineteenth century, the biblical account of how the world was populated by Noah's descendants, together with the interpretation of this story through the classical understanding of whiteness and purity, was accepted as history in much of the West. When European colonizing missions reached various other parts of the world, their missionaries and merchants encountered other cultures and wrote accounts in which they referred to them as descendants of one of the three sons of Noah, dismissing the indigenous societies' own narratives as superstition. The effect was to identify a specific branch of the descendants of Noah as populating a particular region.

In most accounts, the dark-skinned people were identified as the descendants of Ham and classified as barbaric, uncivilized and immoral.[95] The Bible was thus used to supply a theological justification for oppressing some races or lineages on account of their purported moral degradation. This identification became the basis for many pro-slavery theological arguments. The founder of the Protestant movement, Martin Luther, stated that Ham and his descendants were possessed by Satan and bitter hatred and associated them with idolatry and rebellion.[96] As recently as 1964, US Senator Robert Byrd of West Virginia tried to block the Civil Rights Act by reading the story of Noah into the US Congressional record, declaring: 'Noah saw fit to discriminate against Ham's descendants,' and therefore, presumably, so should we.[97]

Between 1517 and 1840, some twenty million blacks were captured in Africa, transported to America, and enslaved in a manner that should be considered a holocaust.[98] In 1843, a book titled *Slavery as It Relates to the Negro or the African Race* appeared in America where it immediately became a bestseller.[99] Its author justified black slavery by dramatizing how Noah had cursed Ham:

> Oh Ham, my son, it is not for this one deed alone which you have just committed that I have, by God's command, thus condemned you and your race; but the Lord has shown me that all your descendants will, more or less, be like you their father, on which account, it is determined by the Creator that you and your people are to occupy the lowest condition of all the families among mankind and even be enslaved as brute beasts going down in the scale of human society, beyond and below the ordinary exigencies of mortal existence ... and must be both in times of peace and war, a despised, a degraded, and an oppressed race.[100]

This biblical and classical racial typology (and its moral and political consequences) became well established in the West. It became a template not only for dealing with African slaves but also for encounters with many of the world's non-white people. The dilemma was always thus: where do these people fit in the history of Israel? Colonial Indologists mulled over the place of Indians in this biblical framework: were they children of Ham? Their 'grotesqueness', brown skin and incomprehensible ways did suggest that they might belong to *some* such subordinate category.

Luminaries who tried their hand at solving this puzzle included William Jones (1746–94), Max Müller (1823–1900), Brian Houghton Hodgson (1800 or 1801–94) and Bishop Robert Caldwell (1814–91).

The philologist Jones adopted the racist framework of the story of Noah and Ham as the template on which he mapped the languages of the world.[101] Jones correlated Sanskrit stories to Biblical events and used Sanskrit texts to claim that Hindus had the character of Ham.[102] This became the normative European paradigm, and later, in the second half of the nineteenth century, the same hierarchy was absorbed into secularized notions of progress, as in the work of James Mill and his son, John Stuart Mill.

Western distress at chaos and the corresponding desire to restore order are also projected onto politics, gender relations, religion and social structures. In Europe during the twelfth to eighteenth centuries, the Catholic Inquisition violently enforced its absolutist moral and theological creed. During this brutal period of European history, order was privileged over complexity, the former viewed as masculine and the latter as feminine, satanic and evil. Rulebooks provided normative mechanisms to incriminate those suspected of satanic practices. This repression lasted for many centuries, spread to virtually every corner of Europe, and resulted in the murder of millions of women (and many men as well) who were accused of witchcraft. The Salem witch trials in the eastern US in the late seventeenth century were the last gasp of this draconian project.

The European Enlightenment did leave some of these fears behind. A new and improved Christianity, purified of its mythic and superstitious elements arose, and with it a more secular and rational worldview. However, the underlying preferences and beliefs persisted and Europe's civilizing mission continued through the imposition of normative European laws and ideas. 'Rational' schemes rather than religious ones sought to eliminate chaos.

The conflation of goodness with beauty even influenced attitudes concerning nature. For instance, the potato, which is native to South America, was condemned by European settlers in the Americas on account of its lack of symmetry; it was 'ugly' and therefore linked with evil. And since its cultivation was associated with Native Americans, deemed 'immoral and uncivilized', the potato was suspicious by association and declared a dangerous food. It was only when faced with the threat of a massive famine across Europe (that could have killed as much as half the population) that farmers there decided to grow potatoes. Tomatoes, too, were banned in places like Italy on similarly superstitious grounds (whereas today it is hard to imagine Italian food without tomatoes).

Also generated during this time were philosophies of history, according to which all societies follow a universal sequence, from less order to more. Newton himself, in his 1728 work *The Chronology of Ancient Kingdoms*, developed a hierarchy of races based on ancient myths.[103] This and similar conceptual frameworks allowed the early European settlers in America to demonize the Native Americans as an evil and/or backward people living 'chaotically' in 'Satan's wilderness'. Various stereotypes were constructed around those declared uncivilized, including social irresponsibility, irrationality, and sexual promiscuity. Non-westerners were thus again seen as embodying disorder and therefore a threat.[104]

Criteria for beauty can change over time to reflect the values of the dominant culture, as in the examples of dark versus light skin and thin versus fat.[105] It is against this backdrop that we may come to appreciate how Jesus 'became white' in modern Western art. In the Italian Renaissance, the elite who sponsored works of art naturally wanted the Son of God to look like them. Since then, Jesus has been commonly portrayed with golden-brown hair and white phenotypes, when in fact he must have been dark-skinned with Middle Eastern features. His blue eyes became popular in twentieth century America as Jesus was refurbished yet again.[106]

When it came to India, it was necessary to fit this vast country, with its own complex past and religion, into the straightjacket of Western religious and political history. William Jones attempted to do just that. His overarching project, as explained by historian Thomas Trautmann, was to form 'a rational defense of the Bible out of materials collected by Orientalist scholarship ...'[107] But since Christianity was the only true religion, Jones interpreted Brahma, Vishnu and Shiva as a *degraded version* of the Christian Trinity. The degradation was the result of the pagan fall from grace. Europeans, he believed, had superior reasoning skills, compared to which Asians were 'mere children'. Jones made many compromises to the facts on the ground in order to map Indian society on to biblical ethnology. He served as an early appropriator of Hinduism but always with the goal to promote the credibility of Christianity, a stance well appreciated by his conservative Jewish and Christian readers.[108]

The diagram below shows how the triad of values encoded in Western views of truth-goodness-beauty reinforces notions of order and chaos, civilized and uncivilized. Note the rectangle containing the Civilized space in contrast with the disorderly and incoherently defined shape of the Uncivilized. To the extent that even one or two of the three qualities can be attributed to someone, all three are automatically assumed. Grotesque deities and filth in a society indicate an immoral people who lack reason. Poverty implies lack of rationality and therefore a lack of morality. Thus, the poor need to be saved from their immoral native culture. This ideology undergirds some of the rationales for the Christian project of conversion to this day.

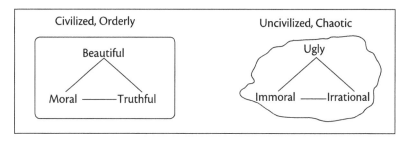

Dharmic Forest and Judeo-Christian Desert

The attitudes towards order and chaos discussed above are influenced by attitudes towards nature. The 'forest' and 'desert' are used below as metaphors to illustrate the differences between dharmic and Judeo-Christian civilizations.

In the West, the forest is often seen as a place of chaos, confusion and bewilderment; it is the 'dark wood' of Dante, the place where 'the straight way is lost').[109] The desert is the place of illumination, where truth in all its black-and-white absolutism and starkness is revealed. It is also empty, barren and flat. In contrast, the forest in dharmic traditions is a place of refuge, hospitality and profound spiritual inspiration.

Sri Aurobindo uses a forest analogy to show some essential differences between Indian and Western spiritual philosophy:

> The endless variety of Indian philosophy and religion seems to the European mind interminable, bewildering, wearisome, and useless; it is unable to see the forest because of the richness and luxuriance of its vegetation; it misses the common spiritual life in the multitude of its forms. But this infinite variety is itself, as Vivekananda pertinently pointed out, a sign of a superior religious culture. The Indian mind has realized that the Supreme is the Infinite; it has perceived, right from its Vedic beginnings, that to the soul in Nature the Infinite must always present itself in an endless variety of aspects. The mentality of the West has long cherished the aggressive and quite illogical idea of a single religion for all mankind, a religion universal by the very force of its narrowness, one set of dogmas, one cult, one system of ceremonies, one array of prohibitions and injunctions, one ecclesiastical ordinance.[110]

The forest has always been a symbol of beneficence in India, perhaps because the lush vegetation of the subcontinent (now mostly denuded) offered refuge from the heat. Some of the earliest spiritual classics of dharma are called *aranyakas*, or 'forest discourses', and their exemplars, the rishis, are known as 'forest dwellers'. Among the stages of life advocated for individuals, the penultimate one, in which the individual severs the bonds of family to pursue spiritual goals, is termed vanaprastha, which literally means 'the forest stage of life'.

The forest can be a place for balancing order and chaos. Its thousands of species of animals, plants and microorganisms are interdependent. A square foot of ground can contain the equivalent of a whole city of different life forms, including microscopic life. The microcosm, at any given level, is always connected with its enveloping macrocosm, and so these worlds-within-worlds are not separate and isolated. The forest contains enormously complex biomass that is constantly changing and evolving. Forest creatures are immensely adaptive to one another; they mutate and fuse into new forms easily.

To an Indian, a forest suggests fertility, plurality, adaptation, interdependence and evolution. The forest loves to play host and is never closed to outsiders; newer life forms that migrate to it are rehabilitated as natives. It grows organically, with new forms coexisting without destroying prior ones. It is never final and complete. Its dance is ever evolving. Indian thought, analogously, is largely process-based. For Buddhists, the interdependence of the forest mirrors the interdependence of everything in the cosmos.

The forest's diversity is an expression of God's immanence – as bird, mammal, plant, and so forth. Just as there are infinite processes in the forest, so there are infinite ways of communicating with God. Indeed, India's spiritual outlook rests on this very principle: that the divine is immanent and inseparable from life and nature in all its forms. The forest, like the human body, provides a context for the relations between the outside and the inside, between wilderness and humanity. The various dharmic texts and rituals flow into each other in complex ways that defy being ordered into so-called 'critical editions' or linear chronologies. Dharmic traditions reconfigure themselves dynamically, often creating discomfort in the Western mind, which is used to everything being in its proper place.

These traditions took root on the banks of rivers with sacred waters flowing, rivers which symbolize change and evolution. The experience of endless organic evolution was integral to the various schools of philosophy, scriptures, deities, rituals, spiritual practices and festivals. The idea of harmony arose from the forest and its interwoven-ness. Forest dwellers respect nature and do not imagine that God made the world for humanity's dominion, as their Judeo-Christian counterparts believe. Nature and its creatures are part of one cosmic family.

It is the milieu of the desert, on the other hand, that has shaped the Abrahamic faiths. The desert can be hostile and is not a place to dwell permanently or to marvel at the diversity of life. Its vast emptiness instils awe but also fear. The desert connotes starkness, a paucity of life, harsh environs and danger. The Judeo-Christian ethos is built on this sense of scarcity and fear. Nature is not supportive but profoundly threatening – an enemy to be tamed, civilized and controlled.

To overcome these circumstances, the desert dweller looks for relief from a God above. The divine is less a nurturing mother than an austere and oftentimes angry father. This God rescues him by offering strict and quick dos and don'ts. God gives him only ten commandments by which to live! In return, God expects the deepest gratitude, repentance and atonement. The desert seems to lend itself to extremes of religious experience; it is a place of repentance.

After the exodus from Egypt, Moses and his people were tested by the harsh conditions of the desert for forty years before reaching the Promised Land. John the Baptist went into the desert and practised austerities before returning with a message of repentance of sins for the people of Israel. Jesus, too, while undergoing his initiatory forty-day fast in the desert at the beginning of his public life, struggled to resist the temptations of the Devil before surrendering to God. (Contrast this image with the Buddha in a forest of bodhi trees mastering the middle way.)

Related to the metaphor of the forest is the banyan tree, beloved in myths and stories across Asia. The banyan is unique among trees in that the branches sprout first and eventually bow down to the ground and become the roots of a new tree, each providing nourishment and stability to the entire tree. The tree is a single structure but functions like a complex, decentralized organization, providing shelter and nourishment to birds, beasts and humans. Its multiple roots and branches represent multiple origins and sources – all part of the same living organism, even if the whole cannot be comprehended at one glance. Each of the separate roots feeds every trunk, and hence every leaf is connected to the entire root system. There is no centre of the tree, because its multiple roots, trunks and branches are all interlocked and inseparable. It is polycentric. Likewise, Indian civilization is a network with no central control, an open architecture intertwined internally and externally. It is naturally assimilative, and this makes it a highly efficient system for adaptation and for the fostering of diversity.

Besides being majestic and beautiful, the banyan tree is home to all kinds of life and activity. It offers shelter and shade to travellers. Monkeys make it their home. Yogis meditate under it. Village shopkeepers sell their wares beneath its canopy. Villagers gather under it, sharing community news and events. The tree is gigantic, complex and old, yet its size and complexity have coherence and grace.[111]

The desert is incapable of sustaining the banyan tree and its complexity. Turning a forest into a desert is destructive, whereas to flower a desert is to enrich it. Desert people crave greenery so much that it is their sacred colour (as in Islam). The oasis, a small life-sustaining forest in their midst, is their destination. All their notions of eternal paradise are forests. But the converse is never true: forest cultures do not crave deserts. Forest-dwelling civilizations did not turn into world conquerors looking for alternative pastures; they found contentment at home.

A forest sustains quantitatively many times the populations of deserts; hence, the ancient civilizations around the world were tiny in size compared with the Indus–Sarasvati civilization in India. The desert has fewer types of life and less multiplicity in general, and correspondingly, the desert dweller has fewer objects of cognition and so is less experienced in dealing with complex relationships and contexts.

The forest functions well as a metaphor for context-based cultures, revealing why people living in dharmic cultures are more comfortable with cognitive complexity. Of course, those who love the desert believe it can inspire awe and worship. Still, for many, it is easy to see the desert as a place of extremes – deep cold or burning heat, hunger or food, water or sand.

Western Joker and Indian Clown

A culture's myths about order and chaos become internalized and embedded in its subconscious. Its attitudes toward order and chaos then emerge, in subtle ways, in creative works that draw on archetypes, metaphors, and symbols. Modern societies express these myths through fiction, film and other media, which are helpful sources for revealing and analysing cultural differences. Hollywood has been particularly effective at projecting the Western fear of chaos in the figure of the Joker in the popular Batman movies, and I shall compare this with the figure of the clown in a number of Sanskrit poems and plays.

In the 2008 film, *Batman 3: The Dark Knight*, the character of the district attorney personifies civilization and fights all sorts of crimes that threaten order. The Joker is the antihero personifying chaos who impedes every step made by the district attorney. Towards the end of the movie, the Joker explains his philosophy to the DA: the civilized world, he says, is too concerned with plans and too predictable in following policies, rules and benchmarks. The reason he, the Joker, cannot be defeated is that he functions spontaneously in the present moment and is fearless because, having accumulated nothing material, he has nothing to lose. In fact, after stealing millions of dollars, the Joker is shown burning the mountain of money just to make the point that he is not interested in the materialistic pursuits cherished by civilization.

The movie's climax shows a defeated DA with half his face burnt and repulsive. The Joker explains that the good-looking half is the aesthetic of order which hides the ugliness beneath Gotham City (civilization) and its authoritarian control. This ugliness includes the immense corruption within the DA's own ranks and the rest of the political system that pretends to protect civilization. The DA, in the end, becomes the boss of organized crime and goes by the name Two Face. The custodian of order thus ends up becoming the chief agent of chaos. His half-handsome/half-disfigured face makes the point that order includes within it its own defeat; also, its goal can never be achieved, and it is hypocritical. This outcome presents order/chaos as mutually exclusive and irreconcilable principles.

The protagonist of the film, the superhero Batman (Bruce Wayne), is 'above the law'; he destroys the evil duo of the DA and the Joker, but he does so not by integrating either but by maintaining the myth of an incorruptible order by subterfuge. He conceals the defection of the DA and camouflages as the criminal who slays this paragon of virtue. Civilization can effectively check and perhaps even triumph over the unconstrained forces of chaos, but only by adopting the latter's tactics and assuming its apparent forms. The result is an uneasy stalemate.

Whether we side with Batman/Bruce Wayne, the disinterested philanthropist who conceals and sacrifices his own genuine virtue in order to combat evil, or throw our lot in with the anti-hero Joker as the embodiment of chaos who exposes and mocks the vacuous hypocrisy of order, the film's appeal hinges on the antithetical relationship between these two forces. The fundamental issue is never satisfactorily resolved, though the opposing claims are both rejected.

In the Sanskrit corpus of plays, chaos is personified as the figure of the clown (known as vidushaka). The clown has a privileged, though paradoxical and dialectical, relationship to the king, who upholds dharma as order.[112] The archetype of the clown is comparable with that of the Joker in the Batman film.

The handsome king representing order and the disfigured clown representing chaos are not only inseparable; they are peers and address each other as friendly equals. In the play *The Little Clay Cart* (*Mricchakatika*) by Shudraka, the friendly buffoon Maitreya actively but unwittingly furthers the harmful designs of the villain. He does so to the extent that the hero, whom he is ostensibly aiding, is almost executed on false charges of murder. Although the drama ends happily with the triumph of order over chaos, the subliminal message is that the forces of chaos must be integrated judiciously and skilfully into order if society is to function. These ideas are made explicit in the ceremonial preliminaries to the play itself. Actors representing the deva Indra and the asura Varuna get into a squabble that once again symbolizes the tension between order and chaos. The fight is reconciled and resolved by Brahma, who represents both poles and yet transcends them. When the play starts, the royal protagonist performs the role of Indra, while his antagonistic friend and counsellor becomes Brahma with a marked asuric (demonic) persona symbolically represented by his disfigurement.

The vidushaka is a transgressor whose violations of conventional order serve in fact to reinforce it. In many instances, he is planted by the ruler and helps the controlled release of disorderly forces (much like a vaccine, in which a tiny amount of bacteria is injected to build up immunity to a disease).[113] The vidushaka as 'integrated chaos' is thus the 'wild card' (joker); he is always a great brahmin presided over by the sacred Aum syllable, yet he exhibits various traits and habits which are countercultural and eyebrow-raising, such as a fondness for wine and meat, liaisons with female servants, use of a walking stick with phallic connotations, and so on. This juxtaposing of disorder in the centre of order corresponds to the creative assimilation of chaos in Hinduism.

There is thus in the Sanskrit play an underlying theme of the 'tying together of diverse threads' with equilibrium eventually restored. The principle of bandhu is ever present.[114]

From these illustrations we may see again that the Western conception of order and chaos is dichotomous; they are irreconcilable opposites, with order represented by civilization and all that is good and divine, and chaos represented by that which opposes civilization (and which opposes goodness and divinity). The Indian approach is integral, viewing them as complementary and interactive and as essential aspects of civilization, but their integration and reconciliation in a higher principle of unity is necessary for them to fulfil their function and find their complete and highest form.

5

Non-translatable Sanskrit versus Digestion

'Many Sanskrit words are simply not translatable. This non-translatability of key Sanskrit words attests to the non-digestibility of many Indian traditions. Holding on to the Sanskrit terms and thereby preserving the complete range of their meanings becomes a way of resisting colonization and safeguarding dharmic knowledge.'

Many westerners assume that the dharmic wisdom embodied in the Sanskrit language can be translated into other languages and imported into other religious and/or scientific paradigms without loss of meaning. 'Aum' can be 'Amen', 'Shantih' can be 'peace', 'Brahma' can be 'God', etc. In this chapter, I argue that this is not the case.

Ancient as it is, Sanskrit remains important for its profound creative potential. The richness of the meaning of a word is often deeply embedded in its cultural context, in the history of how that word evolved over time, and in the wider context of nuances and implied meanings that accompany its usage. A culture consists of the cumulative collective experience that is unique to its geography and history. To understand a culture is to live it. The unique experiences of different cultures are not always interchangeable, and the words used to refer to those experiences must remain intact; if linguistic categories get lost, so, over time, does the diversity of cultural experience. Many cultural artifacts have no equivalent in other cultures, and to force such artifacts into the moulds that the West finds acceptable or familiar – to appropriate them – is to distort them. This too is a form of colonization and cultural conquest.

To understand all the nuances of a word, then, it is necessary to understand the host culture. Language both reflects and shapes a culture's way of thinking, owing to its deep structures and categories. Sanskrit has certain properties which reveal the inherently contextual and unique nature of dharmic philosophy from which it arose. With Sanskrit, there is also another, deeper source of non-translatability: among its primary sounds, there are layers of connections and interrelationships forged by common underlying vibrations. The complete meaning is thus a composite of the collection, not unlike an algebraic formula.

This is why great harm is done when a foreign culture, especially a colonial one, imposes its own simplistic translations of Sanskrit. Even greater harm is done when the natives of a colonized culture adopt these foreign translations – a process that is often gradual and subtle and achieved with rewards of upward mobility offered by the dominant culture.

Integral Unity as Vibration

In order to understand why Sanskrit is unique and non-translatable and why the civilizations rooted in it differ from others, we must look more deeply into the understanding of sound and language in the Vedas. Throughout the ages, Indian rishis and grammarians have believed that primordial vibrations comprise all reality, that vibrations are the heartbeat of the cosmos. The reverberations from this cosmic 'pulsing', as discovered, constitute the alphabets of Sanskrit, which does not associate meanings with sounds arbitrarily. Human language and the concepts and objects they represent are the tangible outer manifestation of these vibrations at varying levels of concreteness.

This deep reality from which sound and form emerge was not discovered through prophets (who merely communicate God's messages) or intellectual inquiry but by direct experience in deep meditation.

A rishi is one who sees and hears the eternal truth. His (or her) extraordinary faculties enable him (or her) to experience directly the vibrations of the infinite and the concrete objects to which they correspond. The rishi does not compose hymns but *hears* or *tunes* into them. These hymns are called mantras.

Sanskrit scriptures can be understood intellectually, but some are sequences of vibrations with experiential 'meanings' and can only be known through yogic practice. Their very nature as sound makes them non-translatable. For example, no external word can fully communicate the experience of the heat and pain that fire can cause upon being burnt. The word 'burn' offers only a conceptual name for fire, not an experiential one. However, the purpose of a Sanskrit mantra lies in the effect it creates.

In this chapter, I discuss how Sanskrit reflects the dharmic belief in the integral unity of the cosmos and even how it contributes to the attainment of that unity. I also explore the uniqueness of Sanskrit, in particular how sound manifests the latent vibrations of all reality.

The same primordial vibrations bring about a myriad of physical phenomena, including our conceptions of them and their names. Hence, all differences between words, objects and thoughts are relative. The one reality becomes manifested as all the diversity we experience, comprising an integral unity. Consequently, Sanskrit words are non-translatable into other languages.

Direct Experiences and Traditions

Indian linguistic theory and rhetorical practice are highly refined, and their study and meaning are not divorced from spirituality and religious training. Many Indian traditions have tried to capture Sanskrit's primordial quality. Some rishis described their experiences in terms of shakti, or primal energy, with its pranic manifestations. Others have tried to explain the cosmos in terms of Shabda-Brahman, the vibratory supreme reality. According to the 'sphota' theory, 'dhvani' (sound) and 'artha' (meaning) are in fact a hyphenated reality – two sides of the same coin – and undifferentiated in their un-manifest essence. As sound manifests, the pairing remains, but the distinction appears more prominent until the untrained mind believes that sound and its meaning are independent.[1]

The Vedas personify this primordial vibration as Vak, a goddess who brings forth the root sounds that create all ideas, rhythmic vibrations and concrete objects. She is the generator of worlds and the material out of which worlds are made. Kashmir Shaivism teaches that there are four levels of Vak: un-manifest, subtle potential, mental image, and outer expression.[2] According to the *Shiva-Sutras*, ordinary knowledge comes from phenomenal associations, and this knowledge relates to the outer world. But the associations themselves need something to bind them together, and the energy that does so is *matrika*. Matrika strings together words and symbols, turning them into language that we can understand.[3]

In tantra traditions, every object has a phonetic sound, a built-in name. An object can sometimes have more than ten different names, but the central or 'seed' vibration ('bija-mantra'), which is the nucleus, focus and spirit of the object, remains unchanged. Therefore, if one is attuned to and unified with an object's seed vibration, one achieves a complete understanding of it. *Shabda-Brahman* is the primordial Sonic Consciousness of the cosmos. The Srimad Bhagavatam explains the un-manifest Aum and how its manifestation brings about the Vedas and all of creation.[4]

Richard Lannoy notes that the Hindu sees himself as a microcosmic organism, one that is an exact counterpart of the macrocosm, or nature. He obtains knowledge of the latter directly by immediate sensory awareness, refined through yoga. Patanjali's *Yoga-Sutras* describes this 'rtambharabuddhi' (vision, insight).[5] Indian logic, too, like the Indian approach to nature, advances not only by conceptual assumptions but by adopting multiple modes of perception. The latter have been suppressed in the West by narrow specializations. The closest Western analogy would be the scientist's description of ecological relationships wherein the environment and the organism are viewed as a single *unified* entity. Thus, says Lannoy, 'Hindus discovered, through direct cognition, the mantra system of musical incantation uniting the laws of phonetics and the physiology of sound waves.'[6]

Unity of Sound–Meaning–Object

As explained earlier, Sanskrit stems from the discovery of the ultimate essence of each object through a process mastered by the rishis. Their intuitive understanding of this unity not only enhanced their taxonomic knowledge of animal and plant life; it cultivated an empathy and innate reverence for such life (in contrast to the adherence to environmental regulations in modern society which are often the result of political or pragmatic mandates).

The following diagram shows how every object starts as a vibration that includes both the object in potential form and the sound corresponding to it. These vibrations gradually manifest and are experienced by us as separate sounds. The sound manifests further and becomes the meaning-sound pair. Thus, every object contains its inbuilt name.

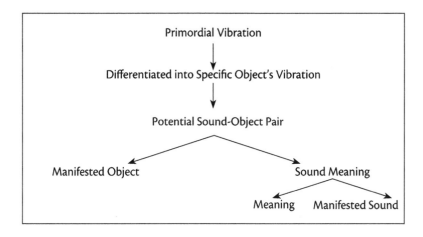

Indian grammarians are also cosmologists who see the patterns of the cosmos (ritam) as homologous with the rules of language. The term 'vyakarana' refers both to grammar and the development of speech from an indistinct stage to a fully expressed one. The various stages in the evolution of cosmic vibrations from the primordial, unified state to subtle and then gross manifestations correspond to the development of the inner self. Thus, Indian linguistics, psychology and cosmology explain, via their respective disciplines, the same reality.

Lannoy explains the priority given to this scientific method of discovery over several generations: 'The Brahmans impressed upon the minds of every subsequent generation a need to study the influence of sound phenomena on human consciousness by orientating the perceptual centers toward the inner acoustic space of the unseen. These "ancient physiologists" ascribed an ethical significance to physiological sensitivity.'[7]

The Vedic comprehension of yoga is predicated on the words that unite mind and matter. Lannoy regards the marriage of words to music as one of the great philosophical occupations of ancient India.[8]

Mantra

A mantra originates in the subtlest levels of existence, where there is silence. Upon discovering that vibrations manifest as concrete sounds and objects, the rishis explored ways to return to the source. Numerous meditation systems utilizing mantras were developed, tested and propagated to take the practitioner back to the original state of unity consciousness. Sanskrit, then, is a vehicle for achieving self-realization. It is important to note that mantras are *discovered*, much in the same way that Einstein discovered E=mc². The reality existed prior to its discovery. The same is true of mantras (which are 'a-paurusheya', or impersonal/authorless).

Each mantra is associated with the actual rishi or sage who discovered, tested and verified it. The earliest oral records clearly designate specific rishis as the 'seers' of mantras. Sri Aurobindo explains the process of discovery:

> To arrive at the Mantra he [the rishi] may start from the colour of a rose, or the power or beauty of a character, or the splendour of an action, or go away from all these into his own secret soul and its most hidden movements. The one thing needful is that he should be able to go beyond the word or image he uses or the form of the thing he sees, not be limited by them, but get into the light of that which they have the power to reveal and flood them with it until they overflow with its suggestions or seem even to lose themselves and disappear into the revelation. At the highest, he himself disappears into sight; the personality of the seer is lost in the eternity of the vision, and the Spirit of all seems alone to be there speaking out sovereignty its own secrets.[9]

Sanskrit thus provides an experiential path back to the source. It can be used as a device to reverse the trajectory of manifestation, starting with human sounds and going back to the source of creation. Suppose we could discover that from a primordial vibration, which we may refer to as A, there came a root sound, B, and that that led to a subtle sound, C, which became D. Then we could reverse the path: we could start with D (audible sound) to take our consciousness back via C (the subtle sound) and B (the root sound) to reach A (the primordial sound). This is the principle of many systems of meditation, tantra, and of various rituals.

For instance, Transcendental Meditation, as taught by Maharishi Mahesh Yogi, uses a sound called bija-mantra, which is at first chanted silently and gradually replaces all other thoughts. Only the mantra remains. Gradually, the mantra gets softer and dimmer, becoming a faint whisper within. Then that too disappears, leaving a subtle hint of its presence. The deep silence that remains is hyper-alert self-awareness, and amazing experiences of transcendence occur in this state. One has thus retraced back to the primordial source, starting with a silent repetition. Scientific research seems to support the claim that reading Vedic Sanskrit texts – even without knowledge of their meaning – produces a distinct physiological state.[10]

Hence, mantras are not arbitrary verses, nor are they to be understood only in conceptual terms. Their deepest truth is vibratory in nature, and these vibrations can take us to levels of consciousness that transcend language. One reason Sanskrit and mantras are taught in early childhood by rote (i.e., even before a child understands their meaning) is because their full effect and benefits can be experienced over the course of time. The idea that Sri Aurobindo calls 'involution' is the metaphysical basis for the subsequent evolution. The mantra is sown in the person and produces effects much like a seed that evolves into a tree. When repeated, it vibrates in every part of the practitioner's being and recreates within him the original reality from whence it came. (The important notion of involution is explained in Appendix A.)

Sri Aurobindo explains: '[The] Mantra is the word that carries the power of the godhead, that can bring [the godhead] into the consciousness and fix it there and its workings, awaken there the thrill of the infinite, the force of something absolute, perpetuate the miracle of the Supreme utterance.'[11]

Reading and writing poetry give aesthetic pleasure – a brief soaring of the imagination. A similar yet deeper experience is possible when, through chanting, the ear becomes the channel of the soul. Mantras may be thought of as energy-thought sounds. Uttering a sound word produces an actual physical vibration, and discovery of the effect of that vibration leads to the meaning associated with it. In addition, the speaker's intention, when coupled with the physical vibration, influences the end result. The sound is the carrier, and the intention gives it additional power to produce an effect.[12]

Mantras are used to evoke a spiritual frequency and bring about a particular state of consciousness. They are sound frequencies that are precisely sequenced so as to evoke the inherent shakti (potency) of vibration. Over time, the practice of chanting the mantra begins to override lesser vibrations, which become absorbed by it. After a period (which varies with individual), the chanter reaches a level where all other vibrations are stilled so that, ultimately, he is completely in tune with the energy and spiritual quality contained in the mantra. The person reciting the mantra becomes transformed in subtle ways. Also, the beneficial effects of a mantra accrue not only to the chanter but to all humanity and the cosmos at large.

Mantra energizes prana, or life-spirit energy. Some healers transfer prana to a patient. Even self-healing can be accomplished by concentrating prana on certain organs, which can have the effect of clearing away an illness. Mantra can be a part of this process. If one repeats a mantra while visualizing an ailing internal organ bathed in light, the power of the mantra can become concentrated there with beneficial effect. This is why a child is often carefully given an appropriate name so that it will internalize its name as vibration, and over time the effect of repeating the name will bring inner transformation in subtle ways.

Discovery of Sanskrit

Yogic experiences are difficult to represent accurately in any language other than Sanskrit, for, as Sri Aurobindo has noted, it is only in Sanskrit that they have been systematized.[13] Thus, Sanskrit is the 'language of yoga'. Sanskrit philosophy states that monosyllabic sounds comprising the Sanskrit alphabet are at the origin of creation. In fact, the Sanskrit phonemes themselves reveal the nature of reality. The root sound of the phoneme references its corresponding manifestation.

Among other languages, Hebrew has similar claims. The Hebrew language itself is recognized as a sacred script, and there are many mystical traditions associated with the shape and sound of its letters, including a strong sense that the letters of the name of God, rendered popularly as Jehovah or Yahweh, are so sacred and so charged with spiritual energy that they should not be spoken or written in a secular context. However, in the Jewish tradition, the source of sounds is located differently and more attention is paid to the shape and form of the written language, whereas the written form of Sanskrit came much later, and it is explicitly an oral tradition. Also, it is chiefly within Kabbalah – the mystical (and non-mainstream) practice of Judaism – that the subtleties of language and sound are understood and known. Islam, too, speaks of the special vibrations created by the Arabic of the Qur'an (which is one reason its memorization and recitation are considered spiritual practices in and of themselves). But in Jewish and Islamic traditions, Hebrew and Arabic, respectively, are usually seen as created by an external God, whereas in Sanskrit these vibrations are the Ultimate Reality itself, called *Nada Brahman*, from which 'creation' emanates.

It is important to distinguish the primordial sound/bija-mantra/ phoneme that we are discussing from what, in other languages, is called a 'word'. Shabda is commonly mistranslated as 'word', but it refers to phoneme, the smallest unit of sound-meaning in Sanskrit. Many such phonemes are combined into a sequence to create a word. In Sanskrit, there is a dictionary of meanings of individual letters or phonemes, called *ekaksharakosha*.

A word is a composite of many alphabetic sounds. In the case of English, the dictionary offers meanings for words, yet there are no meanings for primary phonemes or alphabets. They have evolved from human convention. In Sanskrit, however, each phoneme has rich meanings as a root sound, as well as specific effects on the consciousness. Thus, the potency of shabda (sacred sound) is liberating, for it is a way to gain insight into the nature of the Absolute and Consciousness.

The biblical expression 'In the beginning was the Word' would not be an accurate description of creation according to Sanskrit-based philosophies. It would be more accurate to say: 'In the beginning was the primordial sound that differentiates into multiple root sounds, which manifest further before compounding sound sequences are made possible as words.' This is to say that much has happened in the creation process before words appear, and this mechanism of vibrations prior to the appearance of words allows the person meditating/chanting to go back to the source. Only in Sanskrit do we find that each and every word can be parsed into its root sounds that contain its origin and meaning and from which it is derived.[14] Of Sanskrit, Sri Aurobindo writes:

> Every one of its vowels and consonants has a particular inalienable force which exists by the nature of things and not by development or human choice; these are the fundamental sounds which lie at the base of the Tantric bija-mantras and constitute the efficacy of the mantra itself. Every vowel and every consonant in the original language had certain primary meanings which arose out of [some] essential Shakti or force, and [these] were the basis of other derivative meanings.[15]

Sanskrit and Pluralism

Since every root sound has a distinct meaning, its signature is found in all the words derived from it. It is theoretically possible to explain the meaning of the words according to the algebraic combination of letters, syllables and roots. This transparency of rootsounds and semantics follows a natural process and gives Sanskrit the ability to discover its own history. Consequently, Sanskrit is an ever-creative language in which each word is the parent and creator of ideas. A letter is called 'akshara', which literally means imperishable or eternal. Akshara is the eternal sound, and it does not perish but reveals the whole secret of speech. Another term for letter is 'varna', which means hue or colour. Thus, every letter is heard as a sound and has a visual hue as it manifests. The rishis are said to have *seen*, and not just *heard*, the Vedas. The term for alphabet, 'varnamala', literally means 'garland of colours' or qualities or hues which the artist uses to paint reality.

Multiple Experiences of the Same Root Sound

The root sounds, depending on how they are strung and combined with others, can give rise to several words, each of which may have distinct connotations, shades of meaning, and special nuances. Since each word is discovered as the outcome of an all-inclusive yogic experience, a root sound or word often has multiple meanings, including even opposite meanings.[16]

Let us illustrate this with an example.[17] The root sound 'dih' means to gather, collect, pile up, etc. Let us refer to this as meaning #1. The experience of gathering or compiling leads to the experience of growth, increase, prosperity, and so on. So the root dih also means to increase, grow or prosper (meaning #2). When things grow, they often cover something else, so to cover is another important meaning of dih (meaning #3). Going further, this covering may be interpreted as hiding, concealing, plastering or smearing (meaning #4). Furthermore, we can get a variety of other meanings by applying prefixes and suffixes to the root word. For example, the body is called 'deha' in Sanskrit and is derived from the root dih. Why? Because it is a cover that conceals the self within (meaning #5). We can further add the prefix 'sam' to deha. Sam refers to the experience of completeness, totality and perfection (from which came the English word 'sum'). Thus, the word 'sandeha' (sam + deha) means 'perfect concealment' or doubt (meaning #6). So, in a state of doubt, the consciousness is perfectly clouded, reality is covered, truth is hidden, there is no clarity of vision, and one is confused and groping in darkness. All of these are meanings of the root dih.

The diagram below demonstrates the following: (i) A root sound has multiple levels of meaning which correspond to different but related experiences. When we analyse this closely we find that all these meanings are interdependent and not disconnected from each other. They form an integrated whole of many levels of experiences, all in a single root sound. (ii) These multiple meanings can each be used to derive words by adding other syllables using the rules of grammar.

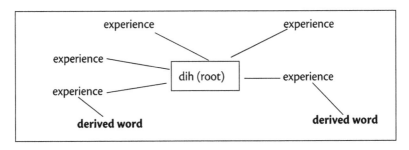

While all languages are able to create new words by combining pre-existing prefixes and suffixes, this is taken to greater heights in Sanskrit, where the process is systematic, predictable and creative. When a root sound is used to create a word, the sound undergoes transformation according to established principles. By concentrating on a new word made by an expert, the listener can parse its intended meaning. This means that Sanskrit's large vocabulary is open-ended and infinitely expandable. One may think of Sanskrit as open architecture.

New words are made (when an idea needs to be expressed) by using the root words and applying the rules of word formation. For example, when the Vedic rishi wanted to express the idea of 'wolf', he made the word 'vrika', which means 'tearer', according to its root structure. Therefore, the meaning of this word includes 'a wolf', but only among its many other meanings. On the other hand, in English, the word 'wolf' simply refers to the animal and does not bring with it a context or structure which could give rise to a family of words. In English, there is no intrinsic reason, apart from custom, to use a particular sound to refer to a particular animal (or to anything).[18] Linguistics reveals that *all* languages work similarly, yet there is a critical difference: in other languages, the *initial* posited association between the sound and the object it represents is in most cases arbitrary – unlike in Sanskrit. Words, then, evolve according to complex processes of association with other meanings and sounds. Unique to Sanskrit is the claim of the initial, primordial phoneme-morpheme association, also called 'nama-rupa' (name-form), which stems from dharmic metaphysics of the Ultimate Reality as vibration manifesting at successive levels of concreteness. The critical implication here is that just as all primordial sounds are connected back to the source in an integral unity, so are all meanings connected and interdependent, and hence all objects in the universe are inseparably unified in their ultimate sense. Everything is intertwined, and nothing is isolated.

Synonyms Are Not Redundant

Owing to the prolific outpourings by Sanskrit composers, many words have a large number of synonyms, sometimes as many as twenty or more.

A given synonym cannot be replaced by another – not only because of the typical shift in nuance within synonyms but because of the distinct root-word-sound conflation in Sanskrit. From the many possible synonyms, those which best convey the exact property being described should be chosen. A deeper analysis of each word in the list of synonyms reveals that different synonyms refer to different ways of experiencing the same object, so each synonym has a specific and definite connotation. The diagram below and the example that follows illustrate this idea.

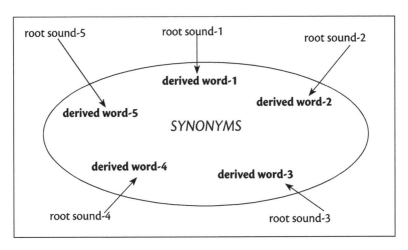

The two preceding diagrams complement each other. In the first diagram, a single root-sound spawns multiple experiences, and each of these can lead us to words containing that specific experience. In the second diagram, a single entity has numerous synonyms, each of which is derived from different root-sounds, and hence each has a different context and nuance.

For example, thirty-four words for 'fire' are listed in the *Amarakosha*, a lexicon which lists synonyms of Sanskrit words. These are: *agni, vaishvanara, vahni, vitahotra, dhananjaya, kripitayoni, jvalana, jatavedas, tanunapat, barhis, shushma, krishnavartma, shochikesha, usharbudha, ashrayasha, brihadbhanu, krishanu, pavaka, anala, rohitashva, vayusakha, shikhavan, ashushukshani, hiranyaretas, hutabhuk, dahana, havyavahana, saptarchi, srimuna, shukra, chitrabhanu, vibhavasu, shuchi* and *appittam.*

And yet none of these is redundant, because each captures a unique attribute. For example, the word vahni comes from the root *vah*, to carry, meaning 'that which carries' – hence the word is useful for conveying 'offerings to the gods'; jvalana comes from the root *jval*, to burn, and means 'that which is burning'; pavaka comes from the root *puu*, to purify, and means 'that which purifies'; shushma comes from the root *shush*, to dry, and means 'that which dries'; anala refers to 'not enough', meaning nothing is enough for fire, denoting the devouring nature of fire.[19] A competent writer must decide which of these synonyms for 'fire' is the most appropriate in a given context.

Proper nouns in Sanskrit often are *definite descriptions*. The thousand names of Vishnu (sahasra-nama) capture all the various events relating to him mentioned in the Puranas. There is a composition on Rama, sung at the Ramakrishna Mission centres, originally collected in Varanasi, wherein the sequential definite descriptions for him delineate the history of his life. Thus, we find that every syllable – and every word built of a sequence of syllables – is pregnant with meanings and acts as a node in a contextual network.

Sanskrit and Contexts

Sanskrit texts, by their very nature, require interpretation in a given context. Content cannot be separated from context or given an absolute meaning. A.K. Ramanujan explains:

> No Indian text comes without a context, a frame, till the 19th century. Works are framed by *phalasruti* verses which tell the reader, reciter or listener all the good that will result from his act of reading, reciting or listening. They relate the text, of whatever antiquity, to the present reader – that is, they contextualize it. The Ramayana and Mahabharata open with episodes that tell you why and under what circumstances they were composed. Every such story is encased in a meta-story. And within the text, one tale is the context for another within it; not only does the outer frame story motivate the inner sub-story; the inner story illuminates the outer as well. It often acts as a microcosmic replica for the whole text.[20]

The correct intonation of words, too, plays an important role in their meaning, and these were given utmost importance in traditional oral transmissions.[21] An entire meaning could be altered by a change in accent or emphasis.[22] Intonation (swara) has also endowed the language with a rich musical quality, which is why practitioners of the oral tradition in ancient India took great care in preserving texts to the level not only of syllable but also of accentuation and intonation. This made it possible to preserve all the Vedas, Upanishads and other shastras in all their original meaning and intent.

The context is also supplied by the situation, person, higher experience, and intention of the speaker. The same verse can have many meanings, and stories are nestled within one another. The framing story differs from iteration to iteration depending on the audience, and thus different contexts are provided. For example, a couple of Jain poems describe in verse the lives of seven different monks. A literal translation of these verses into any language that is not Sanskrit based would sound nonsensical and incoherent. When a word with a contextually determined meaning is reduced to only one of its many meanings, it is akin to assigning a specific constant value to an algebraic variable, thereby eliminating its usefulness as a variable.

Every word embodies a spectrum rather than a single value. For example, the word lingam is often misunderstood, because it is collapsed into only one value/meaning that is taken to be its essence. Incorrectly translated as 'phallus', this has become lingam's normative usage in Western discourse.[23] However, lingam's range of meanings includes sign, mark, spot, token, badge, emblem, and even gender. In the proposition, 'there is fire because there is smoke', the smoke is the linga. Broadly, it indicates a sign or meaning referring to something other than itself. The American flag, Statue of Liberty and national anthem are all linga for America, yet they are not redundant, because they represent different aspects of America. The logo of a company is its lingam, and there may be several linga for the same entity.

Also, meanings change over time. Hence, insisting on fixed, constant and isolated values is reductionist and distorting. Sanskrit grammar avoids both extremes – a fixed set of absolutes on one hand and randomness and arbitrariness on the other – much like a computer programming language which gives rise to an infinite variety of programs while using a precise set of rules and grammar to do so.

As a result, there is no compulsion to reconcile all the accounts of a narrative into one 'official' version (which an expansionist tradition must do in order to spread the tradition uniformly). One finds numerous versions and adaptations of the Ramayana, for example. Nor is there a felt need for the lineages of various gurus, or accounts of various avatars and other past events, to be 'organized' into a linear chronology which everyone is required to accept. The author and 'collector' (vyasa) of Sanskrit works re-contextualizes and edits the Vedic corpus anew for each yuga.[24]

The Indian word for a text is *grantha*, referring to the knot that holds the palm leaves together into a book; what this indicates is that the physical unity of the parts does not comprise some sort of critical edition independent of the context of the given reader's environment. This clearly differs from the Western tradition of constructing the canonical version of every text because that is considered its 'pure' form. There are context-sensitive designs in the Indian texts, and this manner of constructing the texts is in accord with other designs in the culture. In visual representations, there is no uniquely 'true' image of a given deity. Ramanujan writes: 'Not unity (in the Aristotelian sense) but coherence seems to be the end.'[25]

The Cognizing Self Is Part of the Context

The context is not separable from the person experiencing it.[26] This intertwining of subject–object is pervasive. Indian poetry is contextualized by a taxonomy of landscapes, flora and fauna, and also of *subjective emotions*, which Ramanujan refers to as 'an ecosystem of which a man's activities and feelings are a part'.[27]

The unity of the speaker with the environment is evident in the ease with which Sanskrit expresses action without asserting subject/object dichotomy. The ancient rishis were aware that the speaker is not the doer but an instrument. Sanskrit is structured in accordance with this idea, and being conscious of it in language can lead to the realization of the non-doer state. In most languages, the passive voice is possible only by using transitive verbs, but in Sanskrit passive expression is natural and the preferred way, and all types of verbs, transitive or intransitive, can be passive. Instead of saying, 'aham hasami' ('I laugh'), it is not at all awkward in Sanskrit to say 'maya hasyate' ('the action of laughing is being performed'). In this manner, the action and what is acted on are emphasized rather than the doer. In English, by contrast, active speech – with the emphasis on the subject performing the action in the verb – is preferred. The difference reflects two diverse attitudes: one mindset wants to be in control of action and the other, and the other does not demand credit for the same.

The *Brihadaranyaka Upanishad* (5.2) provides an illustration of this interdependence of subjective and objective context. The DA DA DA sound of three-part thunder is Lord Prajapati speaking three times to three entirely different kinds of listeners: The devatas, given to pleasure, hear the first syllable, which to them means 'damyata', or 'control'. The asuras, given to cruelty, hear 'dayadhvam', or 'be compassionate'. Humans, prone to greed, hear 'give to others'. Thus, the same utterance is heard entirely differently, depending on the change Prajapati wishes to bring about in each listener.[28]

Mysticism and the Outer World

In higher states of consciousness, rishis have inquired into the nature of external objects. This inquiry led them to develop practical taxonomies of the physical world. An example is the elaborate plant taxonomy in ancient India. According to the assessment of William Jones, published in 1795, this taxonomy was more advanced than the standard Latin-based ones used by Western botanists. Jones writes: 'I am very solicitous to give Indian plants their true Indian appellations, because I am fully persuaded that Linnaeus himself would have adopted them had he known the learned and ancient language of this country ...'[29]

According to Hindu philosophy, each and every element in creation has consciousness, which is its nucleus, or original vibration. This principle was the basis on which ancient Indian medical scientists and botanists studied plants. They combined 'pariksha' (mental investigation) with discovery by intuition to produce systematic knowledge that could be subject to peer review.[30] The thousands of names of plants available in ancient treatises are expressions of this inner contact. Naming was inseparable from realizing its essence. In Ayurveda, the names allow us to understand not only the morphological characteristics of a plant but also its medicinal properties. Ancient Indian vaidyas, or medical scientists, could discover the exact properties of plants and their multidimensional aspects without the laboratory measurement and observational facilities on which empirical science relies today.[31]

Sanskrit, Modernity and Postmodernity

Ever since the time of Jones in the late 1700s, Sanskrit scholars have contributed to the creation of linguistics in the Western academy. Colonial Indologists considered the European study of Panini's grammar a major breakthrough. Sanskrit scholars in Europe were the initial developers of modern linguistics as an academic discipline.

The West's 'father of structuralism', Ferdinand de Saussure (1857–1913), spent his academic career in Paris studying and teaching the Sanskrit grammar of Panini. Saussure's PhD was on conjugate verbs in Sanskrit, and he in turn influenced Claude Lévi-Strauss (1908–2009), the eminent anthropologist. Lévi-Strauss was only one of many Western thinkers influenced by Saussure's work, though. After Saussure's death, his students published his class notes posthumously but removed all traces and references to Sanskrit, Panini and Indian texts, replacing them with generic and universal principles that could be applied to modern European languages! The philosophical principles contained therein became known as structuralism, revolutionizing European art, sociology, history, philosophy and psychology. Structuralism was the precursor of post-structuralism, the philosophical core of postmodern thought.[32]

Until well into the twentieth century, courses in Sanskrit were a requirement for doctoral candidates in linguistics in most major universities in the West. Only after a period of intensely studying

Sanskrit in the academy (and two centuries after its discovery by the West) was the science of linguistics sufficiently Europeanized to become independent of Sanskrit.

The American poet T.S. Eliot (1888–1965) was one of the few westerners who understood both the potency of Sanskrit and its relationship to dharma. He studied the language at Harvard, where it was an integral part of the philosophical curriculum. Ultimately, he refrained from embracing either Hinduism or Buddhism as a result of his own cultural upbringing and conditioning. Nonetheless, Eliot demonstrated his insight into Sanskrit in his major poem 'The Waste Land' not only by exploring the multiple meanings of the phoneme 'DA' (mentioned above) but by ending his poem with the mantra 'shantih shantih shantih'. He had enough understanding of the claims made for Sanskrit not to attempt to translate this mantra. In her book, *T.S. Eliot and Indic Traditions,* Cleo Kearns explains that it was the poet's study of the Upanishads and Vedic texts that showed him that breath, sound and silence were at the heart of language. Eliot understood that a mantra's efficacy depends not on its meaning, per se, but on the effect that its correct utterance and accompanying breathing techniques have. While he did not use the term, he could have been speaking of mantra-shakti, or 'mantra-power', when he wrote that language works through 'syllable and rhythm, penetrating far below the conscious level of thought and feeling, invigorating every word; sinking to the most primitive and forgotten, returning to the origin and bringing something back, seeking the beginning and the end. It works through meanings, certainly, or not without meanings in the ordinary sense ...'[33]

Sanskriti, the Dharma Civilization

Sanskrit is the unifying substrate of dharmic civilization and has profoundly shaped it. Etymologically, Sanskrit means 'elaborated', 'refined', 'cultured' and 'civilized', implying wholeness of expression. Employed by the refined and educated as their preferred means of communication, Sanskrit has influenced a distinct cultural system and way of experiencing the world. Sanskriti is the term for such a culture and civilization (it may also be thought of as another term for sanatana-dharma), one that goes well beyond the borders of modern India to encompass South Asia, much of South-east Asia and East Asia. Interactions among different regions helped develop and exchange this Pan-Asian sanskriti.

Even though Sanskrit is no longer commonly spoken in Asia, it remains the underpinning of the civilizations of South and South-east Asia. Thus, even people who don't speak the language may experience its structures and principles as sanskriti. Sanskriti is the lore and repository of human sciences, art, architecture, popular song, classical music, dance, theatre, sculpture, painting, literature, pilgrimage, rituals and religious narratives, all of which embody pan-Indian cultural traits. It also incorporates all branches of natural science and technology, including medicine, botany, mathematics, engineering, architecture, dietetics, and so on. One of the stunning achievements of this repository is Panini's grammar, a meta-language of such clarity, flexibility and rigour that certain pioneers in computer science are today turning to it for ideas.

Sanskrit was also patronized by some of the Muslim rulers of India who, in some cases (in Bengal and Gujarat), had their epigraphic records inscribed in it. It was the scientific and secular aspect of Sanskrit that induced Arabs to welcome Indian scholars to Baghdad to engage in scientific discourse and translate their books into Arabic.

Sanskrit Unites the Great and Little Traditions

By the time of the great Indian poet Kalidasa (600 CE.), Sanskrit was the language of the literati and the language of choice for their ideas and works of art. It flourished as a living language across many regions before becoming eclipsed first by Persian and then by English after the military and political conquests of India. Sanskrit thus served as the spiritual, artistic, scientific and ritual lingua franca across vast regions of Asia and as a useful vehicle of communication among speakers of local languages, much as English is today. Additionally, Sanskrit was interconnected with local languages in a two-way process. The meta-structure of Sanskrit was transmitted top-down into local languages. Simultaneously, there was a bottom-up assimilation of local culture and language into Sanskrit's flexible, open architecture. Sanskriti flourished through the exchange between these two cultural streams, called the 'great' and 'little' traditions, respectively. The web of interconnectedness was woven by festivals and rituals, and scholars have used these tracers to understand the reciprocal influence of Sanskrit and local languages. Sanskrit served as a meta-language and framework of categories for the vast range of languages across Asia. While the high culture of the sophisticated urbane population (known as the 'great tradition' in anthropology) provided sanskriti with refinement and comprehensiveness, cultural contributions from the rural masses (the 'little tradition') gave it popularity, vitality and a diverse outlook.

Once information about local or regional cultural traits is recorded and encoded in Sanskrit, it becomes shared as part of sanskriti. Conversely, when elements of sanskriti are localized and given local flavour, they acquire a distinct regional identity and colour. The unity within the diversity found in South and Southeast Asia reflects this pattern.

Additionally, owing to the relationship between Sanskrit and local languages, and to sanskriti's role as the common cultural architecture, it is not necessary for everyone to *know* Sanskrit in order to absorb the embedded values and categories of meaning it carries. Similarly, a speaker of a local language would have access to the ideas, values and categories within the cultural matrix of sanskriti.

There is a rich symbiosis between the 'shastric parampara' (classical formal knowledge) and 'lokparampara' (popular and informal oral knowledge). Indeed, the latter is acknowledged beautifully and respectfully in classical texts, such as the *Natya Shastra* and literature on Ayurveda. All these cultures and knowledge systems comprise a continuum.

Many tribal practices and customs permeate the mainstream customs observed in temples. For example, in Puri's temple of Lord Jagannath, the main murtis undoubtedly express tribal motifs, and similar syncretism is found in the Meenakshi temple at Madurai. Both Lannoy and the American anthropologist McKim Marriott note that the relation between 'Little Traditions' and the 'Great Tradition' is reciprocal, i.e., they are mutually dependent and exist in harmony with each other.[34]

According to Marriott, the reciprocal sponge-like action of give-and-absorb generates a double movement: upward and downward. The former nourished the Great Tradition with the emergent elements of the village folk culture while the latter transmitted the universal, generally urban culture of the brahmins.[35]

The Puranas were a vehicle for spreading Sanskriti beyond the elites and served as an ancient form of pop culture with spiritual messages embedded in fables and tales. Vijay Nath's book *Puranas and Acculturation* explains how the Puranas integrated various social strata, jatis, dharmic sects and regions of classical India in a manner that was both decentralized and flexible.[36] These elements became a device for social mobility and enabled large numbers of tribal people to gain entry as brahmins.

The Puranas were composed over many centuries. They do not have a specific origin, nor are they attributed to a specific author. There were various compilers who functioned in a decentralized manner. In earlier stages, the writers appear to have been grounded in Vedic knowledge and possessed of considerable literary skill, and these early composers set a direction and tone for the Puranas as an innovative genre of Sanskrit literature. Later on, the process was passed on to a much wider group that was good at storytelling but had less rigor and Vedic proficiency.

As a result of large migrations from the heartland to outlying regions, new forms of cultural exchange between the migrants and locals were required. The flow of influence went both ways. One of the visible influences from 'below' was the collective singing and ritual performances which are still common in tribal communities. The interaction between sects across a varied landscape of communities and languages involved separate deities, rituals, stories, local shrines and tirthas (pilgrimage sites), and these became part of Puranic stories. The guardian deities of various local professional and artisan groups were recognized in this process. The 'agamic' (tantric) rituals became more prominent, along with specific initiations designed to formalize discipleship with a guru. The flexible frame of myth was used to assimilate deities other than Vedic ones and, over time, map these deities onto Vedic ones. In the process, some obscure deities from the Vedas gained prominence. Ganesha and

Kartikeya are examples of marginal deities who got assimilated into the mainstream.[37] In the case of Shiva, his family of deities got expanded to include 'yakshas' and 'pretas' as attendants.[38]

The Puranas popularized a larger number of tirthas and pilgrimages to them. A place recognized as a tirtha in the Puranas was believed to offer special powers for spiritual purification. Gradually, tirthas started to serve as substitutes for Vedic yajnas (rituals).[39] Such rituals were not limited to any specific varna (social class) and became even more popular than some formal dharmic rites. The local political chiefs and businesses benefited as a result of the increased popularity of their particular tirtha, similar to the impact of any tourist attraction on the local power structure and economy. It became a matter of pride and importance for a remote community to be visited by pilgrims from faraway places. Puranas also facilitated templebuilding insofar as they were the first texts with rules on temple architecture and planning.[40] Local tribal communities often got assigned important roles as functionaries in the temple, and this helped bind the temple–tribe nexus in remote areas across India.

The Puranas enriched the contextual nature of dharma by incorporating numerous local variations.[41] There is a critical difference between this process and Christian inculturation, which, in keeping with its inherent history-centrism and exclusivism, is intended to be only an interim step in the process of converting the subject to a history-centric worldview. On the other hand, dharmic osmosis across traditions has resulted in local variations being sustained over long periods without pressure to convert people to metropolitan dharmic traditions.

Both classical and popular practices share the all-inclusive epic tradition (the Ramayana and the Mahabharata), reflecting cultural integration between formal and folk traditions. Lannoy writes:

> The motley bands of professional artists, bards, wandering minstrels, and holy men who have been traveling the roads of India in unending procession since antiquity may be counted as an important element in this 'link language.' So too are the caste and sect gurus who have acquired their charisma through resolution of life's contradictions, the 'play of opposites,' the multiplicity of cultural allegiances. In the final analysis it is a single unifying power which the Indian culture-bearer utilizes to

draw together the diversity of peoples in this consistently oral society: the power of music. Social fusion is achieved through the universal appeal of melody, rhythm, and cadence ...[42]

Thus, pluralism in Hindu society is the result of peaceful coexistence among minority groups; it did not come about as a result of violent conflict aimed at achieving social change. (Unfortunately, a certain group of Western and Indian scholars insists on emphasizing conflict, which serves the agenda of vote-bank politics.) Under colonial rule, European colonizers did impose their canonized texts and theories on those whom they conquered. Worse, they completely liquidated indigenous peoples and, with them, their rich and valuable traditions of knowledge. They saw the natives as 'tribals'. Today's scholars have superimposed the same structural dichotomy in the vain hope of understanding India through divisive and conflict-ridden categories, and there has been a concerted effort to show that learned dharmic traditions are hegemonic and oppressive to the 'real' natives of India. But in India, the so-called tribals (characterized by rural life and informal knowledge systems) have always coexisted in harmony with formalized dharma systems.

Sanskriti and Pan-Asian Civilization

Across India, for instance, the stories of Krishna are adapted into numerous local subcultures. The devi has a form localized for virtually every Indian village and often for every jati. Many festivals and rituals are adapted by local people in various parts of India, and this has resulted in an astounding diversity of regional and folk traditions becoming anchored in the traditions of Hinduism.

In the Pan-Asian context, there were exchanges, mutual influences and transformations among independent cultural traditions. Such exchanges occurred when these cultures encountered each other through exploration, trade, transplantation of knowledge systems, and so on, and were, for the most part, free from any deliberate or systematic agenda from any angle. Over time, there have been attempts to reframe and actively shape the new knowledge in the local context. This is why the

Ramayana has been adapted and assimilated into many Asian cultures and languages. For instance, there is a place called Ayodhya in Thailand, and in Bali there is a 'monkey forest' where monkeys are worshipped as descendants of Hanuman, the monkey deity who worshipped and served Lord Rama.

From at least the beginning of the Common Era until about the thirteenth century, Sanskrit was the primary linguistic and cultural medium for the ruling and administrative circles from Purushapura (Peshawar) in Gandhara (Afghanistan and parts of Pakistan) to as far east as Pandurang in Annam (South Vietnam) and Prambanam in Central Java. It influenced much of Asia for more than a thousand years. Sanskriti was neither imposed by an imperial power nor sustained by any centrally organized Church ecclesiology. Thus, it has been both the result and cause of a cultural consciousness shared by most South and South-east Asians regardless of religion, class or gender.

Centuries prior to the Europeanization of the globe, the entire arc – from Central Asia through Afghanistan, India, Sri Lanka, Thailand, Cambodia, Vietnam and all the way to Indonesia – was a crucible of a sophisticated Pan-Asian civilization. In *A Cultural History of India*, A.L. Basham notes that '[by] the fifth century CE, Indianized states, that is to say states organized along the traditional lines of Indian political theory and following the Buddhist or Hindu religions, had established themselves in many regions of Burma, Thailand, Indo-China, Malaysia, and Indonesia'.[43] Years earlier, the British historian A.J. Toynbee remarked: 'India is the central link in a chain of regional civilizations that extends from Japan in the far north-east to Ireland in the far north-west. Between these two extremities the chain sags down southwards in a festoon that dips below the Equator in Indonesia.'[44]

However, unlike the violent spread of the Roman civilization which made Latin the European language for centuries, the Sanskritization of Asia was entirely peaceful, without conquest, domination, or subversion of local identities. This is not to say that political disputes and wars of conquest never occurred, but in most instances, the motive was not the imposition of cultural or religious homogeneity.

The following passage from Arun Bhattacharjee's *Greater India* elaborates on this point:

The unique feature of India's contacts and relationship with other countries and peoples of the world is that the cultural expansion was never confused with colonial domination and commercial dynamism, far less economic exploitation. That culture can advance without political motives, that trade can proceed without imperialist designs, settlements can take place without colonial excesses, and that literature, religion and language can be transported without xenophobia, jingoism and race complexes are amply evidenced from the history of India's contact with her neighbors...Thus although a considerable part of central and south-eastern Asia became flourishing centers of Indian culture, they were seldom subject to the regime of any Indian king or conquerors and hardly witnessed the horrors and havocs of any Indian military campaign. They were perfectly free, politically and economically, and their people, representing an integration of Indian and indigenous elements, had no links with any Indian state and looked upon India as a holy land rather than a motherland – a land of pilgrimage and not an area of jurisdiction.[45]

Asia's brightest students went to centres of learning in India such as Takshasila and Nalanda. King Baladeva of Indonesia was so supportive of the university in Nalanda that he made a generous donation to it in 860 CE. That a foreign king thousands of miles away in South-east Asia would wish to support a university in India underscores the importance of Pan-Asian scholarly exchange.

Early Buddhist scriptures were in Pali and other Prakrit (local vernacular) languages, but later ones were composed in what is known as 'hybrid Sanskrit'. There was a trend for using elegant Paninian Sanskrit for both verbal and written communication. The Tibetan script and grammar were developed based on Sanskrit and indeed are virtual mirror images of it.[46] Along with the spread of Buddhism to Tibet came a vast complex of cultural elements – dogmas, philosophical and metaphysical ideas, religious and spiritual practices, forms of social organization, and a rich artistic tradition.

Sanskriti has had an obvious influence on Thailand dating from 1500 CE. Sanskrit was used for public social, cultural, and administrative purposes in that country and other parts of South-east Asia. Today, Sanskrit is highly respected as the medium for validating, legitimating and transmitting royal succession and instituting formal rituals. Khmer society (in Cambodia) was highly Indianized, and the later Thai kings embraced the Indian religions and based their principles of government on Hindu practices.

China and India had a unique and mutually respectful exchange. Buddhist thought is the most notable and obvious import to China from India. The T'ang Dynasty (618–907 CE) opened the doors to Sanskriti from South and South-east Asia. The Indian influence over China reached its zenith in the seventh century when more Chinese monks and royal embassies came to India than in any other period. Nalanda University attracted large numbers of Buddhist monks from across Asia. The Chinese scholars at Nalanda studied not only Buddhism but also Vedic philosophy, mathematics, astronomy and medicine. The Chinese emperor gave liberal support to Chinese scholars studying at Nalanda. Numerous Indian texts were translated into Chinese and became established in Chinese thought.

Between 950 and 1033 CE, a large number of Chinese pilgrims visited India and absorbed the Sanskriti superstructure. They left inscriptions of their visits at sacred sites and constructed a stupa in honour of the emperor T'ai-tsong. Indian gurus and pandits meanwhile went to China where they were received with honour. The Chinese emperors appointed an official board of translators to translate Indian texts, and Indian scholars were commonly brought in to lead these efforts.

Buddhism's spread across Asia is well-acknowledged, but beyond mere religion, this pan-Asian civilization also become a fountain of knowledge in fields as diverse as language, linguistics, mathematics, astronomy, medicine, botany, martial arts and philosophy. Indian astronomers were consulted in the preparation of official calendars. In the seventh century CE, three astronomical schools known as Gautama, Kashyapa and Kumara flourished in China. That nation had already adopted the Indian theory of nine planets. Also, key Sanskrit astronomical, mathematical and medical texts were translated in the T'ang period. The distinctions between Buddhism and Hinduism in doctrines, practices and institutions were blurred and considered relatively unimportant by the receiving cultures. In China, for example, Buddhist missionaries were venerated as much for their brahmanical learning as for their monastic vows. Historians generally refer to this large-scale export of Sanskriti as the export of Buddhism, which dilutes the role of dharmic culture in general.

The arts were also centres of confluence of Chinese culture and Sanskriti and gave rise to the school known as Sino-Indian art. This school became prominent in the Northern Wei period (386–534 CE), and there are a number of rock-cut caves at Thunwang, Yun-kang and Longmen with colossal images of Buddha 60 to 70 feet high, as well as fresco paintings. The inspiration came not only from the images and pictures that were imported from India (from Ajanta and Sarnath, for example) but from the Indian artists who visited China. Indian musicians also travelled to China and even Japan to share their talent, including some who were sponsored by the Chinese emperors. Two principal types of music – Bodhisattva and Bhairo – were taken from China to Japan by an Indian musician named Bodhi during the T'ang period. Thus, sanskriti preserved the uniqueness of each culture it influenced.

Christian inculturation was part of a politico-religious design imposed from a centre located in another part of the world. This distant Christian nexus often had economic and political interests which diverged from those of the local population. The purpose of conquest was to exploit whatever served the colonizer's interests. The asymmetries between the conqueror and the conquered and between the colonizer and the colonized become cultural markers. Those who resembled the conqueror or colonizer enjoyed greater status than others. Clearly, under European rule, native converts to Christianity enjoyed better social benefits and more prestige than those from the same community who did not convert. The overriding design, easy to recognize in retrospect, was the incorporation of all peoples of the globe into a universal history – an agenda still pursued through overt conversions as well as Western universalism.

This difference between the way Sanskriti and Western civilization spread may be restated in business terms using the analogy of 'push' versus 'pull' marketing. Push marketing consists of intrusive advertising, door-to-door sales calls, tactics of intimidation, pamphlet campaigns, posters to invite prospects, junk mail solicitation (including spam), telemarketing calls, negative political campaigns and other manipulative strategies. In many instances, these methods are unethical or even outright unlawful. The spread of Christianity, and later of Islam, was achieved largely by such heavy-handed and aggressive means. To this day, Christian organizations, much like multinational enterprises, continue to set targets for conversions for every district of India (among other countries) with budgets calculated in terms of cost per conversion.[47] 'Soul harvesting', as it is officially called by the Vatican and various Protestant evangelicals, is like any multinational drive for market share.

Pull marketing is when the product demand drives the transfer without pressure or intimidation from the supplier. The consumer takes the initiative to find and approach the supplier. Common modern examples include searching classified advertising for a defined need, such as the use of yellow pages, eBay, and other sources sought out by the buyer.[48]

In the case of sanskriti, the receiving cultures found assimilation to be highly advantageous and sought out Hindu–Buddhist itihasa (narratives of the past), Puranas, symbols, rituals, doctrines, ideas of governance and aesthetics from the Indian mainland. The best evidence of this is that for more than a thousand years, the rulers of China, Tibet, Thailand, Myanmar, Cambodia, Vietnam, Sri Lanka and other nations sent their brightest students to the viharas (educational institutions) of India.[49]

Non-translatable Categories

The above discussion demonstrates why many Sanskrit words are simply not translatable. This non-translatability of key Sanskrit words attests to the non-digestibility of many Indian traditions. Holding on to the Sanskrit terms and thereby preserving the complete range of their meanings becomes a way of resisting colonization and safeguarding dharmic knowledge.

It is true that translations have played a seminal role in the growth and expansion of human knowledge throughout history. Indian stories were retold and emerged in *Aesop's Fables* in Europe; the Arabs translated Greek philosophy texts and Indian mathematics and brought new knowledge to Europe; the translation of the Bible was vital in the history of Christianity; in India, the vernacular versions of the Ramayana and the Mahabharata continue to play a crucial role in cultural exchange.

However, even in cases where the same experience is known in another culture and that culture has a word for it, the word is a mere convention and not *mantric* in its vibration effect; it does not produce the same effect as the Sanskrit mantra at levels of consciousness that are deeper than the conceptual level. In other words, conceptual equivalence is merely at the surface level of consciousness.[50]

In interfaith dialogue, Jesus is sometimes referred to as a 'rishi' or 'guru'; the Vedas or the Gita as 'the Hindu Bible'; the books of the Torah as 'Judaic Vedas'; and Hindu devotional ceremonies as forms of 'worship'. Among some Indians, too, there is a tendency to describe a guru as a 'prophet' or 'saint'. At the same time, devas are turned into Christian angels, and asuras are turned into demons. But such interchanging of terms, while reaching for similarities, inevitably ends up causing confusion and harm. Sadhana is *not* the same as belief or prayer; atman is something different from soul in the Judeo-Christian sense; prana is much more than physical breath; shakti is not synonymous with physical energy; akasha is not physical space; citta is not consciousness alone, and rasa has no equivalent in Western culture at all.

Likewise, 'surya' implies much more than the physical sun of our solar system; its meaning includes the concept of 'centre' or 'origin'. Hence, worshipping surya deva is not worship of the sun god. Similarly, agni is not simply fire in the physical sense, and only a proper understanding of it could enable one to appreciate the use of fire in rituals. Because Hindus perform rituals involving the sun or fire, there is a misleading resemblance between these rituals and those of old paganism which was superseded by the West many centuries ago.

Tantra has been misconstrued as sex and 'stridhan' as modern dowry. When the English word 'uncle' replaces the variety of native terms for distinct relationships (father's elder brother, father's younger brother, mother's brother, mother's sister's husband, and so forth), the nuanced multiplicity of bonds gets lost and replaced by a homogeneous relationship toward all uncles. Westerners might appreciate the problem if they were to imagine the terms 'mother' and 'father' supplanted by the generic 'parent'.

I am aware that important initiatives are under way, often funded by generous Western donors, to preserve and translate ancient Sanskrit texts. These efforts are laudable. They cannot substitute, however, for an understanding of the importance of Sanskrit terms and texts in the original language as resources for spiritual practice and even for social organization. Nor do these efforts even begin to rectify one of the great scandals of the modern university: the absence of Sanskrit from the curriculum – even in philosophy where it was a pillar of learning in the West not long ago.

In the following pages, I highlight some of the fundamental distinctions between Indian and Western civilizations by selecting a few Sanskrit terms which are commonly mistranslated into simplistic Western equivalents.

Brahman and Ishwara ≠ God

The word Brahman comes from the root *brih*, which means 'to expand'. The all-expansive ultimate reality which creates all, lives in all, and transcends all is Brahman. To translate it as 'God' in the Judeo-Christian sense diminishes its meaning. The 'God' whom Moses saw on Mount Sinai and from whom he received the stone tablets is not remotely the same as Brahman. This Judeo-Christian God is the creator of the universe, distinct and separate from it. Furthermore, this God is authoritative, punishes those who transgress rules, and intervenes in history at specific times and places. Brahman, on the other hand, *is* the cosmos and resides in each one of us, unrealized as atman, making us ultimately Brahman. This makes Brahman ever-present and accessible; indeed, enlightened spiritual masters who are in unity with Brahman are always among us, in every era, to serve as guides. The idea of non-dual unity with God is absent for mainstream practitioners of the Judeo-Christian faith, though it is buried among their mystics who have often been marginalized by institutionalized churches.

In much the same way, the term Ishwara is not the same as the Judeo-Christian notion of God. Ishwara has countless forms of manifestation depending on each individual's choice of form (ishta-devata). Each of the terms (Brahman, Ishwara, Brahma, Vishnu, Shiva, Devi, etc.) has rich implications which are distinct from one another. These terms (and various others) cannot all be collapsed into a monolithic concept of God.

Shiva ≠ Destroyer

Shiva is often mistranslated as 'the destroyer' and assumed to be the antithesis of Brahma, the 'creator' and Vishnu, the 'preserver'. We have seen that Brahma is not a Creator-God in the Judeo-Christian sense, nor is Shiva a destroyer-God as many writers today think. Shiva might perhaps best be described as a *transformer* who moves humanity and the universe forward in the evolution of consciousness. This evolution entails dissolution of the falsely constructed mental frame of reference (nama-rupa) and is different from destruction. The transformation brought by Shiva is a *deconstruction* process that has been misconstrued as destruction. The physical and material dissolution may also be seen as the end of a cycle – making room for fresh manifestation in the same way as one season gives way to another. The tradition emphasizes continuity, making every apparent destruction, in fact, a transformation.

Shiva is therefore also described as the lord of dance and of yoga, enlightenment and mysticism, and this is why he inspires so much more devotion than he would if he were thought of simply as 'destroyer'.[51]

Atman ≠ Soul or Spirit

The cosmological differences between India and the West are reflected in their respective views of the ultimate nature of the self. In Indian philosophy, the true nature of the self is sat-chit-ananda, which can be realized through adhyatma-vidya. In the West, on the other hand, the self is conceived of as sinful, a condition which can be alleviated only by belief in a set of history-centric revelations passed down by prophets.

In Hinduism, one's true self is known as atman. Atman is a reflection of the supreme, transcendent Self, Brahman, and as such, differs from the Judeo-Christian conception of 'soul' or 'spirit'.

Since, in the Christian view, human nature is sinful, it becomes necessary for God to intervene from without and 'save' the sinner. People may employ the inner sciences (meditation, yoga, etc.) with the aim of advancing spiritually, but this will only take them so far. At some stage, God must intervene (from outside, as it were) if the stain of sin is to be wiped clean. As I have argued, this deficiency or limitation in the soul is due to the Christian dependency on a history-centric metaphysics.

Many Christians do not like the idea that their concept of soul or spirit is limited in comparison with the atman, yet they are unwilling to relinquish their dependence on this exclusivist history which is the underpinning of precisely those limitations.

The dharmic concept of the atman is linked to the concepts of reincarnation and karma. The atman individualizes in birth, and karma is the link between one life and the next. Put another way, karma is an 'account' of one's choices in the past, and this account is carried forward at the time of death in order to influence future lives. Although the dharmic traditions have different views on the nature of the atman, they all have reincarnation and karma in common as central features.

A few early Christians (most notably Origen) did affirm reincarnation, but in doing so, they were breaking ranks with the Old Testament. As Christian theology evolved, these ideas were rejected by mainstream theology.

The reincarnation-karma theory holds that one's individual human nature is entirely the result of one's past choices. It is not a sexually transmitted condition passed on from the disobedient actions of Adam and Eve. If the notion of sin as something transmitted via sex-based birth were not a fundamental tenet of Christianity, the whole emphasis on Jesus' virgin birth would disappear. Indeed, if original sin were replaced by karma and reincarnation as the Christian explanation for the human condition, the entire history-centric enterprise would collapse along with its notions of Heaven and Hell.

Inseparable from reincarnation and karma is the idea of infinite time with no beginning or end. There is no initial state, because prior to this universe there was another one, and before that, another, and this series of universes is infinite. Judaism and Christianity, by contrast, are based on finite time with a beginning and an end. As discussed in Chapter 4, Western notions of order are derived from a belief in bounded, finite entities that are controllable. Anything that is un-bounded or infinite defies the ego's need for control and instils fear. Chaos is very difficult for westerners to accept.

While atman is without beginning (or end), the same is not true of the Western soul, which is begotten in finite time, beginning with God breathing into the dust to create Adam (Genesis 2:7). The only eternal Spirit is within God – the Holy Spirit in Trinitarian terms – and Jesus' Spirit is co-eternal with God. But the individual soul, unlike the atman, exists in finite time.

Another difference is that in Jewish and Christian traditions all individual souls belong to a realm separate not only from God but also from the world of matter. Even though spirits permeate the world, they do so as a type of entity different from the world. By contrast, the atman, being the same substance as Brahman, is not different from any other consciousness and is also the ultimate essence of the material world.

In the dharmic system, the atman resides not only in humans, but also in animals, plants and creatures of various kinds. These cumulative experiences constitute one's present psyche. The self has experienced both male and female bodies in past lives, as well as different racial, ethnic and cultural identities. All of this is radically different from the traditional Western notion of bloodlines defining one's past. My past is rooted in my own prior lives rather than in my biological father, and my future, after death, will be in my subsequent lives rather than in my children. In contrast, the Old Testament emphasizes the distinctiveness of bloodlines, giving rise to the rigid notions of race. Furthermore, in Western traditions, one's present body is the only body one has ever had. Consequently, there is greater attachment to it, which in turn can translate into attachments to race, gender, and so on. The reincarnation view is that race, sex and other forms of identity are relative to this birth only. Reincarnation loosens one's attachment to history and future successors.

Cremation, in dharma traditions, is a way of discouraging attachment to the body; hence, there is no cemetery-like place where the dead are visited and communed with long after they have died. Reincarnation theory sees death as a natural recycling, and so there are fewer obsessions with the body than in the Western tradition, which insists there is only one life to live.

Unlike the Christian soul, the atman also manifests in non-human forms such as animals, plants and nature in general, making respect for animals and the environment intrinsic and not an afterthought or optional to the theology. While there have been sporadic animal rights movements in Christianity (for instance, among the followers of St. Francis), and while ecology may be currently fashionable, these are subsequent projections in Christianity; such movements are not intrinsic to Christian metaphysics. The Bible says God gave mankind dominion over plants and animals, and the Christian motivation for stewardship and environmentalism is not derived from a belief in oneness, such as exists in dharmic metaphysics.

Vedas ≠ Bible or Gospel

The word 'Bible' is indiscriminately used in the West to refer to the sacred scriptures of other traditions. However, as used in Jewish and Christian traditions, the term refers to a specific closed canon of history-centric texts which are regarded as the normative and authentic teachings of those religions. The core of the Jewish Bible is the Torah, which contains the five books of Moses (the Pentateuch) and a number of prophetic commentaries, songs, hymns, historical narratives and wisdom writings. For Christians, sacred scripture is the Hebrew Bible (called the Old Testament) and the New Testament, which consists of the four Gospels, Acts of the Apostles, letters written to communities or individuals or churches, and the Book of Revelation. For Muslims, the sacred scripture is the Qur'an, which is seen as the corrected and perfect form of Biblical revelation, with additional, new revelations woven into it that supersede the Jewish and Christian Bible.

In all cases, these scriptures have a special canonical status: they are authoritative, and also final in certain traditions. They were given at a defined point in history, usually when the religion began to spread beyond its original homeland, to establish a canon, a textual base that would be authoritative and final. This process of forming a canon and declaring it closed happened in the Hebrew and Christian traditions in the first two centuries of the Common Era, during the period when Christianity was taking shape and the religion of Israel had to cope with the destruction of the temple and the dispersion of the people into exile.

The status of sacred scripture in these traditions differs remarkably from the status of written texts in Indian traditions. The Hebrew Bible is clearly a collection of texts written at widely different times and in different genres, but in most Christian formations it is treated theologically as if it had one single author and as if the events described literally happened. Even the famous Ten Commandments are given in the context of a specific moment in the history of Israel, a moment which is narrated at great length though interpreted variously in the three Abrahamic religions. History, in short, plays a significant role in the Hebrew Bible and in the New Testament.

Seen from a Vedic point of view, the Bible is, for the most part smriti (a written historical account) as opposed to shruti (direct enlightenment experience). The Bible entirely consists of third-party accounts, what X said to Y. A gospel is a written account of the history of Jesus' life, ministry, death, burial, and resurrection and not an account of Jesus' own first-person revelations or experiences. We might call the New Testament 'Jesus Smriti' to distinguish it from shruti.

Furthermore, the New Testament is not written in a sacred language but in a kind of popular Greek which was common throughout the Mediterranean in its time. For Christians, this language is secular, and its text merely 'points to' something else, but it does not embody, i.e., it is not literally the person of Jesus. While some fundamentalist Christians insist that that the Bible is inerrant in every detail, and the more liberal Christians hold that only the historical events of the birth, death and resurrection of Jesus are absolutely true, both camps regard the events described as the 'word' of inner truth and not the vibrations per se.

In contrast, and as discussed above, Indian scriptures are divided into shruti and smriti, i.e., a set of wisdom writings that reflect direct inner embodied knowing of the divine and a disparate group of second-order commentaries and contextual applications. The contextual nature of Indian culture has interplay between that which is constant and that which changes, between the stable patterns of reality and momentary reality.[52] Yet each is kept distinct. Shruti is inspired and timeless revelation, an eternal authorless knowledge similar to any physics formula. On the other hand, the contextual truths of smriti are ever-changing and cannot be frozen into canons. Under new circumstances, smritis – as human constructs – must be written again and again as befits time and place. Sri Aurobindo explains this requirement as follows:

> First of all, there is undoubtedly a Truth one and eternal which we are seeking, from which all other truth derives, by the light of which all other truth finds its right place, explanation and relation to the scheme of knowledge ... Secondly, this Truth, though it is one and eternal, expresses itself in Time and through the mind of man; therefore every Scripture must necessarily contain two elements, one temporary, perishable, belonging to the ideas of the period and country in which it was produced, the other eternal and imperishable and applicable in all ages and countries.[53]

Although shruti (such as primordial sounds) is authorless, the reader/listener provides the context in which it is interpreted. Smriti has two contexts: that of the author who constructs it and that of the reader who interprets it.

The Judeo-Christian religions have collapsed shruti and smriti into one book and frozen it in time without the evolving context. Again, Catholicism seems to take a more sophisticated view here than does fundamentalist Protestantism. Protestants, who in principle wish to rid themselves of the control of the institutional church and its priesthood, do not recognize tradition as authoritative and normally adopt Luther's motto: *sola scriptura* ('scripture alone' is authoritative). They have replaced an authoritarian church with an authoritarian book.

Since the Second Vatican General Council (1962–65), which laid down the template for the future of the Roman Catholic institutional church, Catholics have seen God's revelation as consisting of two strands, Bible and tradition, which some modern theologians would like to equate with shruti and smriti, respectively. But there are several reasons why the comparison can be taken only so far. For one thing, the Bible, unlike shruti, already includes a great deal of history. This makes the Bible smriti-dominated, which is consistent with the history-centric metaphysics of the Judeo-Christian traditions. Secondly, Christian tradition is specifically the experience of the Church, i.e., its history of interpretation and adaptation and not a set of records of the results of inner science.

The highly institutionalized structure of the Church means that its interpretations of scripture are controlled by a formal centralized authority. Dissent does exist, as in the present debates over homosexuality, women priests, stem cell research, etc., but it is usually initiated by groups marginalized or persecuted by the Church and takes effect slowly and after much resistance from authorities. Moreover, the various denominations of churches have become highly experienced at managing such threats over time. Challenging the core sacred text is deemed heresy or blasphemy. What would seem to be required are smritis that could be altered in response to the changing contexts of changing times. As it stands, any possibility of change rests with the same high priests and licensed ministers who maintain their power and control through institutional authority.

Since they emerged from multiple sources and are not institutionally regulated, smritis have enabled Hinduism to remain open to change without the need for violent wars or internal schisms. Westerners find it difficult to comprehend the Indian notion of sva-dharma ('my dharma', or personalized dharma), which is flexible, specific to a given space and time, and meant to be creatively discovered.

To illustrate the point more generally, the table that follows shows the comparison between the understandings of sacred scriptures in Christian and Hindu traditions:

Christianity	Hinduism
Bible is filled with historical specificity, making it smriti-laden.	Shruti does not emphasize historicity, and calls itself a-paurusheya (impersonal/authorless) and sanatana (timeless).
Christianity has only one sacred book, and its interpretation is institutionally controlled. Bible includes, if only occasionally, certain songs and expressions of what might be called bhakti or devotion (psalms), but excludes most others.	Vedas are the primary scriptures. Upanishads are relied on for high philosophical discourse. The Ramayana and Gita are far more frequently recited and cited in daily life. Bhakti saints' songs (bhajans) are the most common form of participation and these are entirely non-canonical in nature.
Until modern times, reinterpretations and changes of biblical teachings have been centrally controlled and dependent on historical authority. This has to do with an absence of embodied spirituality as a source of authority, and hence reliance on history.	New gurus have emerged from the most unexpected places, often challenging the orthodoxy with fresh interpretations which are then tested and refined in spiritual practice, thereby preventing any central authority from remaining in control continuously.

Dharma ≠ Religion or Law

The word 'dharma' has multiple meanings depending on the context in which it is used. Monier-Williams's *A Concise Sanskrit-English Dictionary* lists several, including: conduct, duty, right, justice, virtue, morality, religion, religious merit, good work according to a right or rule, etc.[54] Many others have been suggested, such as law or 'torah' (in the Judaic sense), 'logos' (Greek), 'way' (Christian) and even 'tao' (Chinese). None of these is entirely accurate, and none conveys the full force of the term in Sanskrit.

Dharma has the Sanskrit root dhri, which means 'that which upholds' or 'that without which nothing can stand' or 'that which maintains the stability and harmony of the universe'. Dharma encompasses the natural, innate behaviour of things, duty, law, ethics, virtue, etc. For example, the laws of physics describe current human understanding of the dharma of physical systems. Every entity in the cosmos has its particular dharma – from the electron, which has the dharma to move in a certain manner, to the clouds, galaxies, plants, insects, and of course, man.

Dharma has no equivalent in the Western lexicon. Colonialists endeavoured to map Indian traditions onto Christianity so as to be able to locate, categorize, understand and govern their subjects, yet the notion of dharma has remained elusive. The common translation into 'religion' is especially misleading since, to most westerners, the model of a genuine religion is one that:

1. involves worship of the divine who is distinct from ourselves and the cosmos;
2. is based on a single canon of scripture given by God in a precisely defined historical event;
3. is governed by an institution with the authority of the church;
4. consists of formal members;
5. is presided over by an ordained clergyman; and
6. uses a standard set of rituals.

All this is determined by a chain of authority tracing its credentials back to God's historical intervention in this world. As a result of its power over the discourse, Christianity has supplied many of the a priori categories and labels for the study of other religions, resulting in serious misinterpretations.

Equating dharma with worship of God creates distortion because dharma is not limited to any particular creed or specific form of worship. To the westerner, an atheistic religion would be a contradiction in terms, but in Buddhism, Jainism and Carvaka dharma, there is no place for God as conventionally defined. Even in some Hindu systems, the exact status of God is debatable. Nor is it necessary for an aspirant to visit a temple; one can achieve the same level of practice and devotion in one's own home. Indeed, one may carry the image of one's ishta-devata (chosen deity) in one's purse or pocket and never have to go to a house of worship.

In Hinduism, dharma provides the principles for the harmonious fulfilment of all aspects of life – namely, the acquisition of wealth and power (artha), fulfilment of desires (kama), and liberation (moksha). Religion, then, is only one subset of dharma's range of meanings. It may be seen as 'dharma for beginners'. For one thing, religion applies only to human beings and not to the entire cosmos; there is no religion of electrons, monkeys, plants and galaxies, whereas all of them have their dharma. Dharma is self-revealing at every moment, and since the essence of humanity is sat-chit-ananda, it is possible for them to know their dharma through direct experience. Conversely, in the Western traditions, the central law or dharma of the world and its peoples is both singular and unified, and it is revealed and governed from above. In dharmic traditions, the word adharma means non-performance of duty or unrighteousness; it does not mean refusal to embrace a given set of propositions as a belief system or disobedience to a set of commandments or canons.[55]

Dharma is also often translated as 'law', but to become a law, a set of rules has to be present, and these rules must: (i) be promulgated and decreed by an authority that enjoys political sovereignty over a given territory, (ii) be obligatory, (iii) be interpreted, adjudicated and enforced by courts, and (iv) carry penalties when the law is breached. No such description of dharma is found in the traditions.

The system of 'canon law' – that is the laws that were determined and enforced by the Church – began under the late Roman emperors. The ultimate source of Jewish law is the God of Israel. The Western religions agree that the laws of God must be obeyed just as if they were commandments from a sovereign. It is therefore critical that 'false gods' be denounced and defeated, for they might issue illegitimate laws in order to undermine the 'true laws'. If multiple deities were allowed, there would be confusion as to which laws were universal.

By contrast, in dharmic systems there is no record of any sovereign promulgating the various dharmic smritis or dharma-shastras for any specific territory at any specific time, nor any claim that God revealed such laws, nor that they should be enforced by a ruler. None of the compilers of the famous smritis were appointed by kings, served in law enforcement, nor had an official capacity in the state machinery. They were more akin to modern social theorists than jurists. None of the Vedas and Upanishads was sponsored by a king, court or administrator, nor by an institution similar to the Christian Church. The famous *Yajnavalkya Smriti* is introduced in the remote sanctuary of an ascetic. The *Manusmriti* begins by stating its setting as the humble abode of Manu, who answered questions posed to him in a state of samadhi. Manu tells the sages that every epoch has its own distinct dharma (*Manusmriti*, 1.82). In this respect, dharma is closer to the sense of law we find in the Hebrew scriptures, where Torah, the Hebrew equivalent, is also given in direct spiritual experience. The difference is that the Torah quickly became promulgated and enforced by the institutions of ancient Israel.

The dharma-shastras did not create an enforced practice but recorded existing practices. Many traditional smritis were documenting localized customs of particular communities. An important principle was self-governance by a community from within. The smritis do not claim to prescribe an orthodox view from the pulpit, as it were, and it was not until the nineteenth century, under British colonialism, that the smritis were turned into law by the state.

A subset of the dharma-shastras deals with 'vyavahara', or disputes concerning mundane civil and criminal complaints. It is only this subset that may be considered 'law' in the Western sense. *Manusmriti* (VIII.4–7) lists eighteen topics of vyavahara disputes.[56] Another important point is that even these vyavahara laws were superseded by local custom. Local tradition, being the will of the people, thus trumps normative laws. A victorious king was prohibited by tradition from imposing his own laws over a defeated people and had to respect their local laws.[57]

The reduction of dharma to concepts such as religion and law has harmful consequences: it places the study of dharma in Western hands, moving it away from the authority of practising dharma scholars; moreover, it creates the false impression that dharma is similar to Christian ecclesiastical law-making and the related struggles for state power. The result in India has been to subject dharma to the same limits as Christianity in Europe – all in the name of secularism. To treat dharma as religion remains a major blunder.

Jati and Varna ≠ Caste

The term jati (often mistranslated as 'caste') is best understood in the sense of a set, as in mathematics or a genre in literature. It applies to non-human entities as well – for example, the jati of trees, jati of rational numbers, jati of verbs, and so on. In the human context, a nation is a jati, a given religious group is a jati, gay people are a jati, the military is a jati, the employees of a given company are a jati, etc. Similarly, the word 'varna' means 'colour'. Varna also refers to the various personalities and qualities of people. An individual's varna is based on past karma and gunas, the latter being individual qualities or tendencies. This is an extensive topic of recent interest, and the reader is referred to numerous works that address it in the bibliography.[58]

Aum ≠ Amen, Allah, etc.

Nowhere is the question of non-translatability more crucial than in the English transliteration of the sound and symbol Aum. The importance of Aum has long been recognized, even in the West, where yogic practices try to preserve this original sound. Aum has been the subject of extensive and deep inquiry and practice in every system of Hinduism, including Vaishnavism, Shaivism, Tantra, Sri-Vidya, Patanjali's *Yoga-Sutra*, Sabda-Brahman, Nada-Brahman and Nada-Yoga, as well as various grammarian schools, sphota theory, etc. Numerous Vedic mantras contain Aum.[59] The same applies to Buddhism, Jainism and Sikhism.

A common yet erroneous practice, especially in 'Christian Yoga' circles, is to replace Aum with Amen or Jesus. The mantric aspect of Aum cannot be replaced by synonyms. Aum is the vibration of Ishwara, unmediated by the conditioned mind. Patanjali calls Aum a spokesperson ('vacakah') of Ishwara. Hence, the experience it brings about cannot be generated by an alternative sound such as the sound of another name for God.

When Baba Ramdev (arguably the most popular exponent of yoga in India today) visited the US in 2007, a journalist asked him a question: 'In America, some people call yoga "Christian yoga". Is that fair?' Baba Ramdev replied:

One can say 'Om' when one is doing yoga. Another can pronounce 'Allah-u-Akbar' or the name of Jesus. Yoga is a science (and is intended) for all people. It was science that discovered electricity and put together airplanes. They are not for any one group of people. It is for all people of the world irrespective of their religious beliefs. Likewise, yoga is also for all.[60]

But Baba Ramdev missed the point. Electricity is indeed a universal force, but one cannot substitute the positive pole for the negative pole or replace copper wire with another wire of different properties and expect the same results. One medicine generally cannot be substituted for another; each has its unique properties and is applicable in certain situations to produce specific results. Maharishi Mahesh Yogi explained numerous times that each bija-mantra 'is a sound whose precise effects are known'. Universal applicability means that under a given set of circumstances a specific practice produces the same results. Replacing one bija-mantra with some other arbitrary sound changes the inputs, as it were, and in science this would naturally mean a change in the outputs as well.

Unfortunately, Baba Ramdev missed the chance to explain that Aum practice is designed to dissolve nama-rupa (name and form, and the *context* of name and form) from the mind. That is the whole idea, and the scientific principle, behind mantra. Its universality lies in its ability to transcend all particular contexts. The names 'Jesus' and 'Allah' are proper nouns laden with historical context, i.e., nama-rupa. For Baba Ramdev to make any scientific equation of Aum with all these other names would require that he first study empirically the effects of chanting historically contextualized words such as 'Jesus' and 'Allah'; only then would he be in a position to determine if they are identical to the mantric effect of Aum.

Dukkha ≠ Suffering

The dharma traditions generally hold that the source of human problems is incomplete or incorrect cognition and understanding, which in turn is the result of our conditioning. Without full realization of our true nature, we imbue our world with notions of separation – of physical objects, ideas, concepts and feelings – which we insist are real. Were this not the case, our world would be too ephemeral for most of us to endure, and our need for control and security would be undermined. Believing the world to be dualistic leads to what Buddhists call dukkha (lack of contentment, or sorrow, or anxiety). While we are able to understand that physical and mental entities are made up of smaller entities, which in turn are made of even smaller ones, most people find it difficult to grasp the idea that there are no independent entities. The Bhagavadgita (12.5) addresses this very problem in verses which recommend personal devotion to Ishwara as easier and more efficacious than devotion to Brahman the formless. Western philosophers refer to autonomous selfhood as 'essence' or 'substance', but in the dharmic view, belief in such essences or substances is ignorance.

Hindu non-dualists and Buddhists both deconstruct this phenomenal reality (samsara), but with different results. The Hindu deconstruction terminates in the personal supreme being, such as Brahman or Bhagavan, wherein no separate subject remains and where no isolated categories exist. Buddhist deconstruction, on the other hand, terminates not in any supreme person but in a process among transitory entities that are interrelated in a circular/mutual manner and hence have no 'origin'. In both cases, however, there is no beginning; there is non-dualism, and separate essences are provisional and relative.

The inability of the Jewish and Christian religions to realize integral unity between human and divine is due to their insistence on absolute dualism, i.e., separation of the perceived (object) from the perceiver (subject). The ego lives dualistically in order to pursue objectives, satisfy cravings and avoid what it dislikes even though these goals are unsustainable. Since the ego believes that entities exist in and of themselves, their acquisition seems, in theory, viable. Their non-existence as separate entities is unacceptable to the ego, because that would make the ego's quest illusory, impossible and futile. The most unacceptable notion of the ego is that it is itself an artificial construction of the mind and hence an illusion. It is easy to see how the ego's sense as the separate perceiver reinforces its belief in the reality of physical, mental and emotional entities. The ego's pursuits, then, serve only to feed and strengthen the ego itself.

All dharmic systems require the individual to undergo a radical cognitive shift in order to rise above dualism so that desire for the particular (i.e., isolated essences) ceases. Avidya is the ignorant belief that separate entities have the ability to satisfy. But only by transcending the ordinary state of avidya consciousness and achieving union with the Ultimate Reality can we directly experience the ultimate. Unlike the preponderantly abstract (and disembodied) universals of Western philosophers, which are regarded as ultimately both unknowable and unattainable, the Buddha-Nature ('Buddhatta') and Brahman, or Bhagavan, are confidently declared knowable and attainable through the practices and experiences of the inner sciences.

All dharmic schools agree that the ego is afflicted with dualism; so, too, do they all disavow the essentializing and strengthening of the ego. Where they diverge is on the question of the self, or Self, in particular what happens to it after realization of its true nature. Most Hindu schools insist that the Self is the Ultimate Reality. In Advaita Vedanta, the removal of maya brings about unity with Brahman. In Sri Jiva Goswami's (1513–98 CE) interpretation, all life and matter are a form of Bhagavan and hence inseparable from him. Buddhists however insist (using various metaphysical arguments) that, since the self is inseparable from the web of interdependencies, there is no transcendent Self with which to unite. However, in all these cases, Hindu and Buddhist alike, liberation from the ego leads to the state of unified bliss (ananda). Brahman/Bhagavan is functionally analogous to Buddhist interdependence in the sense of grounding all existence without being subject to discursive thought or dualistic experience. Appendix A discusses these points further.

David Loy has developed a thesis on the history of the West as seen from a Buddhist perspective. His book *A Buddhist History of the West* explains that the West, including the various disparate parts that comprise it, is based on a flawed sense of self.[61] The self is constructed in a dualistic manner with inherent built-in tension between self and other. Using dharma principles, Loy shows that any such notion of self depends on a sense of what he calls 'lack', which corresponds to dukkha, or, in my framework, disembodiment. The psychological condition of such a separated or disembodied self is anxiety about the state of things, or rather, suspicion that there is something wrong with the way things are and that this wrongness requires some kind of external, material, psychological or intellectual change.

Dukkha is a psychological condition in which the more forcefully the self asserts itself, the more it senses the lack of what it does not possess. By its very nature, it is not self-sufficient, and its craving for external things produces its sense of lack. Conversely, the greater the dukkha, the more powerful the self becomes as the agent in charge of dealing with the problem. Loy frames the history of the West in terms of the evolution of its notion of the collective self, the various lacks/dukkha suffered by it at each stage, and the remedies that it seeks but can never obtain.

The Western idea of freedom has been defined by looking externally for a remedy for dukkha. Orlando Patterson writes that the value which the West places on freedom is 'superior to any other single complex of values conceived by mankind'.[62] But he is also aware of the futility of this pursuit:

> Since the self-existence and autonomy of such a self is an illusion, then such a self will never be able to experience itself as enough of a self – that is, it can never feel free enough. It will try to resolve its lack by expanding the sphere of its freedom, which can never become large enough to be satisfactory.[63]

Loy also suggests that moksha, mukti, nirvana, etc. are alternative notions of freedom which the West has not considered adequately or seriously enough. Among the early Greeks, Socrates and Plato did place emphasis on the inner realm and gave importance to harmony between the inner and outer. But unlike the Indians, their idea of freedom depended on reason of a disembodied kind, owing to a lack of yoga. Loy argues that the West's history of freedom has been driven by the mandates of its self-image which require infinite expansion in a finite world. He explains that the notion of sin became an explanation for how to cope with dukkha in the present situation, *not* by deeper insight through yoga but by escaping from the present moment into a future scenario of redemption. Original sin tainted Christians' notion of individuality as preconditioned by the bondage of sin.

Jesus ≠ Avatar

Christians believe Jesus alone shares complete bodily and spiritual identity with God. Attempts are often made to describe Jesus as an avatar, a Hindu term. The word 'avatar' in Sanskrit means 'descent into visible form' and refers to God descending on the earth in a human (or even non-human) form to lead us to a higher stage of perfection.

There are cognate meanings here. In both contexts, though God is omnipotent and can do and undo everything, yet he descends in a visible form in order to operate within human laws which are his own creations. By achieving an inner victory or a new realization, especially in human form, the avatar creates the capacity in consciousness for every human to achieve a similar victory or realization. In this sense, an avatar is a kind of incarnation in the same way that Jesus is in Christianity. He role-plays with deliberate and voluntary self-limitation. The avatar has infinite knowledge which he can choose to access, though ordinarily he does not, or else does so selectively. All this would apply to Jesus during his earthly life.

But the differences are insurmountable given the importance of original sin and the role of Jesus as Saviour. Antonio de Nicolas has given one of the finest explanations of the key distinction between Jesus the Saviour and the avatar of Hinduism. He explains Jesus as follows:

> The Savior image [is the mediator] between God and the sinful race of humans. We know this image also as the scapegoat, and the Substitute King: someone chosen for the occasion to be the victim of the moment for the salvation of the rest of the community. He gains immortal divinity, saves other humans, brings his Father into the scene, his followers name a Church after him, and these same followers establish a narrative, a theology, and ethics based on principles of behavior... The room left for individuals to improve their spiritual knowledge in this scheme of Savior/sinner is not great, we are, after all, sinners, born in sin, and our individual salvation is only a gift, provided we follow the rules of ethics, and not the result of any superior knowledge of God or deviation from this scheme. Judaism, Islam and Christianity are the followers and founders of the model. God and the rules of ethics come from the outside and

their mission in life is to bring all humans to surrender to this model, either through conversion or force. The individual, in this model, is an individual only in name, for after all, individual perfection consists in total surrender to the model, in letting the model become embodied in the subjects in such a way that the model, rather than the individuals, acts through each complying individual ... Wherever there is violence, the Savior model is at work.[64]

But the avatar is different:

> The Avatar model, on the other hand, has a larger range of human development than the Savior's, from the Language of possibilities of the Asat (Chaos) where all geometries of possible human forms are waiting to be born as heroes, gods, humans etc., to the Language of Sacrifice and Images, where all forms are to be sacrificed ... The gods are this side of creation and they are interior embodiments of a multiplicity of brains at work. Inner acts, rather than names, are at work. These acts are so efficient that they may create new 'gods,' new centers of action, to guide humans to make wise decisions. There are no *a priori* norms of ethics to accommodate to ...[65]

Christianity's exclusivist claim that Jesus was the *only* incarnation is unacceptable to the dharmic religions. In the dharmic tradition, each avatar comes to establish the eternal truth anew in response to the need of the time. To accept Jesus as avatar on terms established by Christianity would entail granting him exclusive status; this, in turn, would invalidate all other avatars, such as Krishna, etc.

As Sri Aurobindo explains:

> India has from ancient times held strongly a belief in the reality of the Avatara, the descent into form, the revelation of the Godhead in humanity. In the West this belief has never really stamped itself upon the mind because it has been presented through exoteric Christianity as a theological dogma without any roots in the reason and general consciousness and attitude towards life. But in India it has grown up and persisted as a logical outcome of the Vedantic view of life and taken firm root in the consciousness of the people. All existence is a manifestation

of God because He is the only existence and nothing can be except as either a real figuring or else a figment of that one reality. Therefore every conscious being is in part or in some way a descent of the Infinite into the apparent finiteness of name and form. But it is a veiled manifestation and there is a gradation between the supreme being of the Divine and the consciousness shrouded partly or wholly by ignorance of self in the finite.[66]

This God-as-Cosmos is what we call 'the world', and its divine play evolves into the immense diversity of forms; hence, the human is in fact God-as-human and no less. Cosmic evolution is the self-unveiling of Divine Consciousness. This manifestation has a purpose, and its truths are expressed in the form of multiple lines or trajectories, such as: peace, harmony, power, battle-and-conquest, knowledge-and-illumination, beauty, joy, and so on. Sri Aurobindo explains that when God-as-human 'knows itself and acts within the frame of the mental being and the appearance of birth, that is the height of the conditioned manifestation; it is the full and conscious descent of the Godhead, it is the Avatara'.[67]

For the purpose of creation, the Divine Being assumes several presiding personalities; each oversees the manifestation of particular truths. A given personality may choose to manifest as a full incarnation – in which case it is called an avatar – or as an embodiment of its particular truth – in which case it is called a vibhuti. Thus, avatar is God in visible form, and vibhuti is the manifestation of one or more of his infinite qualities. In other words, an avatar is a vibhuti, but a vibhuti is not necessarily an avatar. For example, Krishna is an avatar as well as a vibhuti, but Arjuna is a vibhuti only. Ushana, the brave king, likewise is a vibhuti.[68]

Unlike prophets, avatars do not serve as intermediaries chosen by God, nor are they absolutely necessary in order for humans to understand God's will in shaping history.

Holy Spirit ≠ Shakti or Kundalini

In the fashionable search for sameness in all religions, it is often suggested that the Holy Spirit in Christianity is the same as Shakti or kundalini in Hinduism. However, though neither faith is superior to the other, these terms represent different, even incompatible representations of divinity. Among other things, they rest on diverse cosmologies.

Early Vedic literature describes a supreme being which uses its creative power (Shakti) to manifest the universe. Shakti is subsequently systematized as the Universal Goddess with a sophisticated theology and forms of worship. The world is her manifestation. She is the matrix and primordial material substance of the universe, its consciousness and power, and the agency differentiating all forms, veiling their underlying unity in order to prevent collapse into homogeneity.

Sophisticated rituals and meditations create an awareness of and unification with the sacred presence of Shakti in everything. For instance, a popular genre of diagrams for meditation (yantra) consists of intersecting upward and downward pointing triangles that represent the ascending and descending movement of Shakti.

In Christianity, though the Holy Spirit is also 'within' the human, there is a strong emphasis on the descent from above or outside the self. Furthermore, unlike Shakti, the Holy Spirit is not seen as the essence of human selfhood or the essence of the cosmos. Christianity assumes an inherent dualism between God and creation. This necessitates historical revelations along with prophets, priests and institutions in order to bring us the truth. But Shakti, being all-pervading divine immanence, obviates dependence on any of these; its experience can be discovered by looking within using yogic practices.

Since the universe is nothing but Shakti's immanence, it may be said that eco-feminism is built into reality. Nearly every Hindu village has its own specific deity, usually a form of the Goddess. Different Hindu schools regard Shakti differently, but every masculine deity in Hinduism has his Shakti that gives him his power.

Shakti is *always* in our physical body. A Hindu text states: 'The body itself is the temple, the abode of the Goddess.' As such, she can be experienced as a series of currents, with seven focal points called chakras. A powerful psycho-spiritual concentration of Shakti known as kundalini lies dormant at the base of every person's spine. Numerous spiritual techniques can arouse kundalini and channel it upward through the chakras, in the process awakening one from the dualistic mode and moving toward unity consciousness. There is no heaven apart from this unity consciousness.

The human body is conceived differently in Christianity. Humans are on the one hand created in the image of God; yet the body is also the means of transmitting original sin and lays a person open to evil spirits. Kundalini is often represented in Hinduism as a serpent, a king cobra rising auspiciously with its hood spread. But the central myth in Christianity involves a serpent who is the embodiment of evil.

In Hinduism, the guru helps the disciple awaken his or her kundalini and integrate the experience into ordinary life. Many ashrams provide special support for kundalini awakening, which sometimes produces temporary phenomena such as shaking of the body, spontaneous expression and deep devotion. These phenomena are individual, and there is no attempt by authorities to control them except for the safety of the seeker. The most important difference is that the experience is not interpreted through a specific history as in Christianity.

Kundalini-like manifestations have occurred sporadically among Christians, but mainstream churches treat them as aberrations and even as the work of the devil. Those who have such experiences are conditioned to doubt their own sanity and are often regarded as mentally ill and even get institutionalized.[69]

In Hinduism, there is no 'evil spirit' or demonic Shakti. Shakti encompasses all polarities, being simultaneously one and many, light and dark, supportive and violently transformative; both sides of such pairs must be integrated into spirituality. Hinduism easily embraces all aspects of the divine, from the fierceness and darkness of Kali to the warm nurturing of Parvati.

If there are ever any negative effects of kundalini awakening, these stem from the individual's preconditioning and nature and are not due to external 'evil spirits'. Again, electricity is a helpful analogy. Neither inherently good nor evil, each electrical mechanism responds according to its own qualities. As a result of this attitude, Hindus have fearlessly experimented with kundalini just as scientists do with electricity.

Christianity's emphasis on the dualism between good and evil results in fear of possession by evil spirits. This fear is often projected onto 'heathen' or pagan religions, and particularly onto the Hindu Goddess Kali, whose fierceness and dark colour are shocking to westerners. The name of Jesus is sometimes invoked, or a Bible kept on hand, to get rid of such evil spirits.

Shakti is feminine and has myriad representations, none of which (when properly understood) instils a fear of chaos or evil spirits. The Holy Spirit has also at times been conceived as female, particularly in association with Sophia, the wisdom-figure of some early Old Testament hymns. But this association has usually not been embraced by mainstream Christianity. Furthermore, Christianity's most prominent female figure, the Virgin Mary, is not identical with the Holy Spirit. The Holy Spirit mysteriously incarnates Jesus in Mary's womb, but this experience is isolated and exceptional, and not possible in other humans – whereas Shakti can be experienced by everyone. There are no spiritual practices designed to elicit Mary's experience in all Christians, except metaphorically.

Many cross-cultural experts draw a parallel between kundalini awakenings and the phenomena associated with Pentecostal worship that are described as the work of the Holy Spirit. Like 'shaktipat', or guru-awakened kundalini, Pentecostal experiences can involve extreme bodily responses and can be triggered by a charismatic leader. However, such experiences are regarded with suspicion by mainstream Christianity. Indeed, the Holy Spirit has always been something of a wild card in Christian theology, opening the way to understandings that get condemned as heresies.

To contain the risk of heresies, these experiences are carefully coded within the context of the ongoing struggle for salvation from sin, a salvation available only by the grace of Jesus Christ. Unlike Shakti, the Holy Spirit is not experienced as one's inner essence manifesting through personal yoga but as an external and transcendent force invoked by communal prayer to enter and dwell within. Pentecostals are especially alert to the danger of evil or heterodox spirits, and most would dismiss, out of hand, any spiritual experience coming from someone outside the faith, making a Hindu guru especially suspect.

A further consequence of the incorrect mapping of Shakti onto a Christian framework is that the worship of a Hindu Goddess is often incorrectly equated with worship of the Virgin Mary.[70] To appreciate the metaphysical incompatibility, an example is Mahadevi in Hinduism, who is the all-encompassing female deity with all other goddesses as her forms such as Durga, Kali, Lakshmi, Saraswati, Ambika and Uma.

Sometimes called Shakti, and translated as the Divine Mother, she is the first manifestation of divine energy, the creative power from whose womb the whole cosmos and all its forms are created. She is the divine conscious force that dominates all existence. In Buddhism, she is Kwan Yin, the embodiment of compassion, Tara, the divine feminine, or Sherap Chama, the woman who, through extraordinary means, became the 'great mother' of the tradition. The worship of God as Divine Mother is a key contribution of Hinduism and certain forms of Buddhism.

The Divine Mother has numerous powers and personalities, emanations and vibhutis, and it is through these that she does her work in the universe. These emanations are the many forms and personalities which people have worshipped under different names throughout the ages. She can be seen and felt through any or all of her manifestations. Sri Aurobindo outlines the four main aspects of the Divine Mother as follows:

- Maheswari represents the personality of 'calm wideness and comprehending wisdom and tranquil benignity and inexhaustible compassion and sovereign and surpassing majesty and all-ruling greatness'.
- Mahakali represents her 'power of splendid strength and irresistible passion, her warrior mood, her overwhelming will, her impetuous swiftness, and world-shaking force'.
- Mahalakshmi represents her as 'vivid and sweet and wonderful with her deep secret of beauty and harmony and fine rhythm, her intricate and subtle opulence, her compelling attraction and captivating grace'.
- Mahasaraswati represents her 'close and profound capacity of intimate knowledge and careful flawless work and quiet and exact perfection in all things'.

'All these four aspects of the Supreme Mother have to be realized in order to make the transformation possible,' writes Sri Aurobindo. 'Once the mind and life and body are transformed by the harmony and freedom of movement of all four, then can human nature change into dynamic divine nature.'[71] One cannot simply translate one aspect into another and reduce the diversity. What this means is that an aspirant has to undergo a thorough change within before realization can begin to take hold, a change brought on with sadhana.

In the Vedic tradition, Aditi is identified as the mother of all the devatas, or the Infinite Mother. The word 'aditi' has two components: 'a' and 'diti'. The 'a' prefix here is a negation. The word 'diti' is derived from the root 'di' which means to cut, split, separate or divide, and so diti refers to separation or duality. The word 'aditi', then, refers to that which is indivisible. The undivided consciousness is aditi, the mother of all the devatas, in contrast with diti, the divided consciousness from whom all the daityas (demons) have been born.[72] Each Goddess is a form of Aditi, the infinite conscious-force. In different Hindu schools she is called by various names, such as the Will, Law, Maya, Prakriti and Shakti. She is the infinite consciousness, the source of all cosmic forms of consciousness, and all the powers are hers.

Tantra recognizes one Supreme Deity who presides over everything, and this highest deity is the great primordial Goddess. She has ten prominent personalities, called Dasha-mahavidyas, or ten great paths of knowledge.[73] These ten constitute the complete system of knowledge. Each of these goddesses governs a particular fundamental function and presides over a particular creative principle of existence.

Clearly, the way the Virgin Mary is placed and perceived by Christianity is markedly different from the way the Hindu Goddess is understood and experienced in her many manifestations.

Evangelists in south India have launched a major campaign in which Virgin Mary is used as a substitute for the Hindu Goddess. At a cathedral dedicated to her, puja-like rituals are carried out which include the use of flower garlands, sitting on the floor, burning of incense, prasad offerings, aarti, etc. Natives are made to feel that they are still within the comfort zone of their familiar ancestral faith and that this new foreign deity is actually the same thing, only in a 'modern' delivery system which is cleaner, better-financed, more charitable toward the poor, and so on. Similarly, many Christian saints get positioned by the church as rishis; Jesus is turned into an avatara or yogi, and the Bible is propagated as Veda. Some Indian teachers have even started replacing the term Shakti with Holy Spirit. All of this leaves many Hindus confused as to what, if anything, remains that is distinct and specific to their own faith.

Since the 1960s, many Christian scholars, especially women, have been interested in appropriating aspects of the Hindu Goddess to address issues within Christianity, in particular its patriarchic theology and institutions, weak ecological base, and absence of yoga and embodied techniques. While this effort is laudable, great care must be taken to ensure that core Hindu notions of Shakti are not imported as mere add-ons. Dissecting the tradition into separate parts and then digesting certain parts selectively while deleting the rest depletes and distorts the source. Shakti cannot be domesticated.

The authentic acceptance of Shakti and kundalini by Christians is much more daunting than is commonly assumed. It would entail rejecting centuries of Church inquisition against pluralistic manifestations of the divine, and it would involve reinventing Christianity with the Goddess as the Supreme Being. This would rekindle memories of paganism, polytheism and chaos, and also threaten the conventional concept of the Holy Trinity.

Prophet or Christian Saint ≠ Rishi, Guru or Yogi

'Saint' in the West is a term for someone who is holy or virtuous, and in this sense it might indeed seem to be cognate with such terms as guru, rishi or yogi, but it is not. The term 'sadhu', meaning renunciant, might be a better parallel, but even here there are problems.

Among other things, 'saint' carries specific connotations in Roman Catholic and Orthodox Christianity. It originated in the early Church.[74] In its official and proper Christian meaning, it refers to someone dead whom the Roman Catholic or Orthodox Churches recognize as being fully redeemed in heaven and enjoying the beatific vision of God in accordance with the promise of Christianity. The Catholic Church has a formal process known as canonization, which recognizes those saints who have been selected to serve as role models for Christians. There are more than 10,000 formally recognized Catholic saints, and there are many more in the Orthodox churches. Noteworthy is the fact that almost all anointed saints are men (plus a few women), and most of the early ones were martyred while spreading or defending Christianity. They are not recognized necessarily for any advancement of consciousness but for their sacrifices.

Sainthood differs from salvation, which is available to all believers instantly upon baptism and the acceptance of God into their lives and can only be forfeited by persistent sin without repentance. Sainthood – the true achievement of the beatific vision, a high level of understanding and direct contact with God – is a process achieved by witness to the truth over time, usually involving ordeals such as martyrdom, asceticism, and service to others.

Many saints were neither mystics nor theologians. Sainthood does not imply any specific experiential attainment in meditation or contemplation or any manifestation of what in Sanskrit would be called siddhis. Christians do not see saints as having any authority in the area of higher consciousness, nor is the attainment of such states a requirement of sainthood.

The main criteria for canonization are personal faith under duress and the ability to work miracles; these qualities have to be established by a formal due process, usually well after the person has been dead for some years. Miracles are important, because Catholics recognize that saints in heaven intercede for others on earth and pray for them as 'friends of God', i.e., they are intermediaries between humans and God.

The Protestant vision of sainthood differs somewhat from this model, partly out of a rejection of the excesses around the cult of the saints in medieval Catholicism. Protestants regarded these excesses as superstitious, idolatrous and indicative of corruption. Hence, Protestants resist using the term 'saint' (except very generically to refer to spiritual people), though many Protestant evangelists do claim a prophetic direct line to God. This tends to be a line to God's will, not to the sat-chit-ananda of God's being. Protestants, even more than Roman Catholics, downplay the role of human effort in achieving contact with God, which they see as entirely dependent on God's grace.

It is thus a mistake to equate the term 'saint' with guru or yogi, or even with such terms as acharya, sadhu or jivanmukta – designations in Sanskrit for persons of various levels of direct spiritual attainment. A saint is not a source of revelation through direct inner experience, like a rishi, and may or may not have attained the state of liberation in his or her lifetime, like a jivanmukta has. Furthermore, complete identity and unity with the divine is, in fact, ruled out altogether by the Abrahamic religions, which insist that God's supremacy can never be encompassed by the human being.

The term 'prophet' denotes a specific kind of spiritual leader found only in the Jewish, Christian and Islamic religions, and it has no cognate in dharma. A prophet is not a guru in the sense of someone who guides an individual disciple's sadhana toward the state of liberation. Nor is he a rishi in the sense of one who embodies unity with universal consciousness and from this state reveals universal truths. Neither is he a jivanmukta who lives in full liberation in this life. A prophet in the Abrahamic religions is someone through whom God chooses to communicate divine will on earth. He is used strictly as a mouthpiece for God. This communication may be directed at the 'children of Israel', the Christian Church, to specific nations, or to the whole human race. It is not often directed at individuals. God does not choose prophets because they are mystics or theologians. They may not even have led especially pious or ascetic lives, though they would have manifested great personal obedience and are typically moved toward deeper repentance and righteousness *after* being chosen.

A prophet is conditioned like any other ordinary human being and has not gone through life as a yogi or even necessarily as a pious person. In other words, he is usually not a contemplative or renunciant in the Indian sense. Rather, he is an actively engaged and charismatic servant of God who often challenges existing norms and authority figures such as priests and monarchs.

Prophets' opinions and personal beliefs are not necessarily correct from the point of view of mainstream theologians, who see it as their job to interpret what God really meant when he sent a message via a prophet. The prophet's own interpretation is subject to error in the eyes of theologians. The prophets themselves make it clear that the emphasis is on God's message and not on the messenger.

For example, Moses is regarded as the prophet who spoke to God face-to-face, but he is not revered as a 'saint' – much less seen as one who has obtained salvation in this lifetime. (This title would be inappropriate in any case, as it is, strictly speaking, a Christian term applied only to Christians.) In fact, he famously did not even get to arrive in the Biblical Promised Land, the site of salvation, and only saw if from afar.

A prophet's value lies in his ability to communicate with fidelity God's plan and will to human beings. That plan is not about liberating people from maya or samsara. A prophet is not a philosopher; he does not reveal the ultimate structure of reality, the nature of consciousness, or the way to attain unity with the divine. He only transmits the revelation of God's will for human action and worship. He may or may not have attained a higher level of consciousness or insight into cosmology, as many rishis did. This significant difference between prophets and rishis is concealed and glossed over when the terms are used interchangeably.

Examples of past and future prophecies are as follows: the destruction of the temple of Solomon and the exile of the Jewish people into Babylon in the sixth century BCE; the destruction of the second Jewish temple in 70 CE and the subsequent dispersion and exile of the Jews; the death and resurrection of Jesus (which mainstream Christians believe to have been prophesied by the Old Testament prophet Isaiah, among others); Jesus' future return to earth; and the view that war, famine, plague and death as portending the End Times followed by the eventual return and restoration of Jerusalem and of all peoples. Many of these are controversial and debated by scholars. But what stands out, in sharp contrast to the utterances of rishis, is that these messages are largely about specific historical or future events.

Christian groups differ widely on whether or not prophecy has continued after the acknowledged great prophets of the Hebrew Bible. Some believe prophecy ended shortly after the coming of Jesus, the ultimate prophet who delivered and embodied 'the fullness of the law'. Others argue that there is evidence – even in the Bible – that prophecy continues, and almost all Christians believe that the gifts of prophecy – healing and the deep understanding of revelation – are still manifest today. There are no absolute methods for recognizing true prophets or discerning truth from falsehood except that true prophecy does not contradict prior prophets, and believers look for miracles as evidence. False prophets constitute a major danger given the havoc they can cause, thus contributing to anxiety over historical accuracy.

In today's more charismatic and evangelical Christian formations, and some Islamic ones, and in many of the non-mainstream cults or heresies of the West, a leader will sometimes be referred to as a prophet. The title is not used in mainstream Christianity, though often a given message will be referred to as prophetic in a loose sense, meaning 'expressing or teaching the will of God for people on earth'.

Rishis, in contrast, devote their lives to attaining higher states of consciousness and certain human potentialities beyond the ordinary through disciplined practice. They achieve advanced levels of intuition and self-realization in which they see truths through paranormal vision. They believe in the limitlessness ('anantya') of experience and make constant efforts ('tapasya') to become as vast as possible, growing in consciousness from the human level to the divine. The rishi's goal of direct, unmediated knowledge of Ultimate Reality may go through stages, and it can be replicated by every human being. In the first stage, a rishi is called brahmana, or the knower of Brahman; in the second, he is called brahmishtha, or the one who lives in Brahman (not to be confused with Brahmin varna); and in the last, he is called brahmibhuta, or the one who has *become* Brahman. Becoming one with the Supreme Reality is the aspiration of the rishi.[75]

Rishis have visions of images, often symbolic, which they express in the language of mantras. They are also educators and guides; life in ancient India was largely shaped by their influence.

Rishis do not claim to be prophets of God in the Judeo-Christian sense. They are not known for their miracles, nor do they seem to be interested in them. They do not rely on sentiments or emotions. What characterize rishis are the self-realization and illumination through which they experience reality. Love, for them, is spontaneous and stems from embodying the experience of unity with all. No rishi was acclaimed for becoming a martyr, and – unlike the saints of the Church – no rishi was associated with a powerful institution. A rishi would seek out, even as a disciple, another with greater realization than his own.

It is important that this distinction be recognized by people engaged in interfaith dialogue and relationships as the imposition of a Western category onto a dharmic one, or vice versa, is unavoidably reductive.

Devatas ≠ Pagan Gods

Paganism and polytheism are often associated with a wide range of religions that were demonized and demolished, first by ancient Israel and then by the Church. Pagans have included:

- followers of the indigenous religions and cults of Canaan and the surrounding areas during the time of the Old Testament;
- polytheists of various kinds, including ancient Greeks and Romans, who believed, or seemed to believe, in numerous gods;
- medieval 'witches' (mostly women) who would invoke and utilize natural earth-related powers and whom the Church persecuted in very large numbers during the Inquisition;
- worshippers of Satan who consciously serve as enemies of Christ and simply invert Christian views and teachings by deliberate transgression;
- various other groups deemed 'heathen' by church authorities, usually shamanistic formations.

These groups were together referred to as 'pagans' or 'barbarians'. Pagans are infidels, denounced collectively as 'the other'. They are to be fought, defeated and converted to Christianity.

As Judaism and Christianity evolved and spread, they assimilated many 'pagan' and 'polytheistic' practices, symbols and ideas, giving them a new spin, as it were. The Christmas tree, for example, was borrowed from indigenous nature cults in Germany; the familiar image of Mary and the infant Jesus was probably modelled on the image of mother and child in the cult of Isis in Egypt; many of the customary traditions of Easter, such as egg decoration and the symbol of the rabbit, come from pre-Christian fertility rituals, and so on. Since inculturation involved the conversion of pagans, many of the pagan gods and objects of worship reappeared in Christian rituals in the form of saints and their relics. Also, many pre-Christian feasts and holidays got included in the Christian calendar, and religious sites were reclassified in Christian terms as part of Christian history. In many cases, this process involved forceful appropriation.

The above approach is very much in keeping with Christianity's propensity for digesting other cultures. Christianity deemed 'pagan' those aspects of the conquered religions which were rejected once the useful elements were assimilated. Even though these religions and cults were vastly different from dharma traditions, their digestion by Christianity offers insight into how Christianity approached competitors. The takeover process was often extremely violent. It resulted in the virtual disappearance of paganism and the strengthening of Christianity as a world conqueror. Christmas trees and Easter eggs notwithstanding, Christianity did not adopt the pluralism of pagan traditions but rather retained its exclusivism with greater fervour, strengthened, as it were, by the pagan elements it digested.

Devatas in Hinduism are divinities which are forms of the one Supreme Being and which simultaneously pervade everything. As such, they are the very fabric of all reality yet also transcendent and unchanging. Different Indian systems have developed their own taxonomies for expressing this idea and their own yogic practices for unfolding the innate potential for transcendence which exists in each one of us.

For example, Sri Aurobindo explains that there are three modes of Shakti: transcendent, immanent and personalized. These may be described as follows:

- Transcendent is the original supreme shakti which stands above the worlds and links the creation to the un-manifest.
- Immanent is the cosmic *Mahashakti* which creates all beings and contains, enters, supports and conducts all the processes and forces.
- Personalized is the embodied form of the above two modes of shakti, i.e., shakti in the form of various deities accessible to us, living near us, and mediating between personality and the cosmos.

Devatas are Shakti personified both as external cosmic divinities and as internal divinities within us. The inner devatas are the divine virtues we are to discover, as well as the different processes and stages on the mystical path.

The Vedas and later yogic and tantric texts call the cognitive centres 'devatas' or 'devas' (deities or, loosely, gods). They describe them as energies and even as persons. The Atharva Veda (10.2.31) calls the human body the 'city of devas' and says the body consists of eight cognitive centres. Some devas are close to the autonomous biological processes of the body whereas others are *creative* centres. The *Brihadaranyaka Upanishad* (3.9.1) refers to 3,306 devatas under thirty-three major deities, organized in three groups of eleven. All devas embody the same light of consciousness and therefore one can reach the ultimate layers of consciousness through any deva. The Yajur Veda (34.55) describes cognitive centres as actual persons called rishis, archetypal sages and seers which number seven and which reside in the body. They are also mentioned in the Atharva Veda (10.2.6). The *Brihadaranyaka Upanishad* (2.2.3) says 'the rsis [sages] are the senses'. The Vedic texts also divide the capacities of the mind into various dichotomies, such as high/low, emotion/reason, and masculine/feminine.

Abhinavagupta maps the entire range of deities onto the inner domain of consciousness. Hence, Bhairava or Shiva or Kali are fundamental structures of the consciousness of the adept yogi, whose sadhana is to discover, unfold, and explore these within. Shiva is the indescribable and paradoxical absolute consciousness within which individual consciousness takes shape as limited and contracted forms. Alongside such internal mappings of Shiva, Bhairava and Kali, Abhinavagupta's *Tantraloka* refers to various divine beings that may be seen as external to the individual. The supreme consciousness has split itself into vast numbers of divine life forms that constitute the deities within as well as the cosmos without.

Sri Aurobindo describes the dichotomy between the left and right as follows:

> The intellect is an organ composed of several groups of functions, divisible into two important classes, the functions and faculties of the right hand, the functions and faculties of the left. The faculties of the right hand are comprehensive, creative, and synthetic, the faculties of the left hand critical and analytic ... The left limits itself to ascertained truth, the right grasps that which is still elusive or unascertained. Both are essential to the completeness of the human reason.[76]

It is noteworthy that Sri Aurobindo wrote this in 1910, long before modern science came up with the idea that there are differences between the left and right hemispheres of the brain. A yogic technique of pranayama consists of breathing through the nostrils in such a way as to synchronize the two hemispheres.

So devatas are both inner and outer intelligences and powers, and yet neither aspect excludes the other. The profundity and distinctiveness are better preserved by not translating such a sophisticated notion into the simplistic (and discredited) framework of 'pagan gods'.

The word deva does not translate as 'god' in English. It is derived from the root *div* which means 'to shine' or 'to gleam'. This is not merely poetic imagination but a denotation of the actual forces of nature. Devas, then, are 'those who play in Light'. They are 'forms and personalities of one Reality', 'living realities', 'Children of Light', 'Sons of the Infinite'. Not only is the meaning of 'gods', as used in Western discourse, very different – with a much more absolute and unconditional sense than deva – but the term is burdened with the history of the persecution of pagans and heathens by European Christians (on the basis that they worshipped false gods). Thus, in Hinduism, different devatas represent different psychological states, energies and intelligences of the same reality. Therefore, one cannot replace one devata with another arbitrarily. By worshiping a particular devata, one is invoking that particular aspect of the divine. Therefore, we may worship all the devatas we wish to and experience the light and power of each using this experience as a step toward transcending all of them in order to realize the impersonal Brahman.[77]

The concept of ishta-devata (chosen deity) is unique to Hinduism and consistent with the ideal of pursuing the dharma that is best suited to one's own temperament and circumstances (sva-dharma). Hinduism is not 'polytheistic' in the sense of worshipping many gods as different ultimate entities.

Idols ≠ Murtis

The term 'idol' is loaded with negative and demonic connotations in the Abrahamic religions. The term generally refers to the graven images of false gods to which sacrifices were made in return for privileges and benefits. The Qur'an demonizes idol worshippers, as does the Hebrew Bible. Both authorize violence against them. All three religions have undergone periods in which images are purged, because they are felt to evoke idolatrous forms of worship. The reformers also felt an intense phobia vis-à-vis Orthodox and Catholic representations, which for them were associated with priest-craft and attempts to control and manipulate people through superstition and sensationalism. Nonetheless, the tendency to use such aids in worship is persistent in human religious traditions, and Orthodox churches as well as Catholicism have come to embrace these in the case of Jesus and the saints (albeit in a carefully qualified way).

In Christianity, true worship (latria) can only be to God, but images of lesser exemplars of holiness in the form of saints are tolerated as long as they are objects of reverence (dulia) and not worship. The term 'icon' is applied in the latter practice, and the term 'idol' is used for practices that elevate a material representation of a 'false god' or entity to divine status. In Orthodox churches, icons are kissed and treated with reverence, but they are not, technically speaking, worshipped. Stated more directly, what Christians revere are icons and what pagans worship are idols.

By the time Christian colonizers encountered Indian culture closely, these prejudices, biblical in origin, had become entrenched. The prominence of images and icons in popular Hinduism thus occasioned, and still occasions, a particular visceral revulsion among followers of Jewish and Christian religions. Western mischaracterization of Hinduism as polytheistic has resulted in its representations of divinity being associated with a host of 'heathen' practices and traits of pre-Christian Europe and Asia Minor. These include sacrifice to magical fetishes, lack of moral integrity, ethical instability, grotesque sexual indulgences, fatalism, and so on. The various images and devotional objects encountered are instantly and arbitrarily registered as 'idols' not 'icons'. In terms of interfaith encounters, even those friendly to visual representations, such as the early Catholic immigrants to India, were opposed to the visual representations of the divine which they encountered – especially when these involved female deities (their concept of divinity being entirely male).

The Western worldview manifests certain psychological and cultural conflicts regarding representation, especially in religion, and these have prevented the West from understanding the role icons play in Hindu and Buddhist worship. Communication has been further stymied by the asymmetry of power between rulers and the ruled, and alas many ill-informed Indians continue to perpetuate the problem by misusing terms such as 'polytheism', 'idol worship', and the like.

There is no logical reason why Indian representations of divinity could not be thought of as icons rather than idols. Indeed, the dharmic understanding of the nature and usefulness of these representations may have something to teach the West. The Sanskrit word for sacred image is murti, which means 'awakened', 'real' and 'expressive of the Divine Spirit'. 'Prana-pratishtha' is the ritual of infusing the image with prana, or divine presence. It has a parallel in Christian orthodoxy, namely the blessing and installation of an icon. Hinduism, however, goes further. Prana-pratishtha is meant to lead to a deeper, more profound, and less visually dependent way of approaching the divine. The ritual of 'visarjana', or throwing the murti of a deity into holy water at the conclusion of a festival, symbolizes non-attachment. The idea here is that one must not become attached to the physical form but instead imbue its spirit.[78]

'It is not to the stone, but to the divine person figured in the stone that the prayer is offered,' says Sri Aurobindo.[79] He further clarifies: 'Every ceremony which reminds us of the presence of the Eternal in the transient, is, if performed with a religious mind, a spiritual help and assists in the purification of consciousness from the obscuration of the senses.'[80] In a direct response to the Western practice of equating murtis with pagan idols of ancient Europe, Sri Aurobindo writes:

> Indian religion founded itself on the conception of a timeless, nameless and formless Supreme, but it did not feel called upon like the narrower and more ignorant monotheisms of the younger races, to deny or abolish all intermediary forms and names and powers and personalities of the Eternal and Infinite. A colourless monism or a pale vague transcendental Theism was not its beginning, its middle and its end. The one Godhead is worshipped as the All, for all in the universe is he, or made out of his being or his nature ... Indian polytheism is not the popular polytheism

of ancient Europe; for here the worshipper of many gods still knows that all his divinities are forms, names, personalities and powers of the One; his gods proceed from the one *Purusha*, his goddesses are energies of the one divine Force ... Indian image-worship is not the idolatry of a barbaric or undeveloped mind, for even the most ignorant know that the image is a symbol and support and can throw it away when its use is over.[81]

The common practice of equating murtis with pagan idols is reductive of the carefully nuanced and theologically sensitive tradition which surrounds murti veneration.

Yajna ≠ Christian Sacrifice

Western scholars use the term 'religious sacrifice' to refer to the ritual offering to God, or gods, of food, objects (typically valuables), living animals, or people as an act of propitiation and/or of gratitude and celebration. Sacrifice in this sense is classically understood to be a matter of the Roman religious principle 'do ut des', or 'to get you must give'. It is presumed that in response to the willing renunciation of some obvious human benefit, the deity or deities will bestow spiritual or material benefits upon the devotee.

In both the Jewish and Christian traditions (as well as the Qur'an), attitudes concerning sacrifice range from extreme ambivalence to outright rejection, as is evident in the story of Abraham and Isaac (Genesis 22.2). Abraham at first believed he was being asked by God to sacrifice his son Isaac on a mountain in the land of Moriah. Bound upon the altar and about to be slain, Isaac was spared when an angel appeared and substituted a ram. Traditionally, this story is taken to mean that, as the prophet Amos said, 'God despises your sacrifices and burnt offerings' (Amos 5:21–24).

The sacrifice of Jesus has been understood in terms of atonement theory, which was typical of ancient and medieval legal practices and mores. God sacrificed his only son to accomplish the reconciliation of God and humanity and cure the problem caused by original sin. God's justice required atonement for original sin so that humanity might be saved from damnation. But the offence to God was infinite, and human beings, limited as they are, were incapable of such a huge atonement. And so God sent his only son as sacrifice to spare humanity. The New Testament states that this sacrifice was done 'once and for all', and it is not to be repeated. (Many Muslims continue animal sacrifices as part of their popular set of religious practices.)

In the Bible, in a process which extends through the work of the prophets from ancient Israel to the early Church, the concept of sacrifice gets progressively spiritualized to mean the sacrifice of the ego. God does not require blood sacrifice, according to one of the most famous passages in the Old Testament, but the sacrifice of 'a broken and a contrite heart' (Psalm 51:17). Later, in both Judaic and early Christian traditions, this notion evolves into a belief in self-sacrifice in the form of martyrdom. In fact, the Church encouraged its followers to become martyrs by putting themselves in harm's way in order to provoke violence against themselves. Most of the thousands of saints formally acknowledged and canonized by the church were such martyrs.

Jonathan Kirsch, a scholar of religion, has shown that since the fourth century, Christians have been encouraged to act aggressively toward others for the purpose of inducing violence which could then be twisted so as to claim persecution. In *God Against the Gods*, Kirsch explains this process of glorifying martyrs:[82]

> The most zealous among them saw it as their solemn duty to make a public display of their faith even if it meant arrest, torture and death … A few of the Soldiers of Christ actively sought martyrdom by charging into the shrines and temples of the pagans, smashing the statuary, and overturning the altars, as they were instructed to do by their own scriptures: 'You shall break down their altars, and dash in pieces their pillars, for the Lord is a jealous God.'[83]

For example, a confessor who endured and survived the persecutions of pagan Rome was lionized by his fellow Christians. He was regarded as a veteran of the Holy War against paganism, a living example of what it meant to be a Soldier of Christ, and his wounds and scars were badges of honour.[84]

What is interesting is that the pagan magistrates often pleaded with Christians to show some symbolic respect toward non-Christians as this would save the magistrate from giving the mandatory punishment:

Indeed, the spectacle of men and women who went willingly and even ardently to their deaths – and, long afterward, the memory of these martyrdoms and the relics of the martyrs themselves – only stirred the fires of true belief and inspired ever greater acts of zealotry. Sometimes the pagan magistrates literally begged the Christians to make some gesture of compromise in order to save their own lives.[85]

A martyr's death was considered a 'baptism in blood', cleansing him or her of sin just as baptism in water does. Early Christians venerated martyrs as powerful intercessors, and their utterances were believed to be inspired by the Holy Spirit. The lives of the martyrs became a source of inspiration for Christians, and their lives and relics were revered. Christian chronicles of subsequent periods greatly exaggerated the persecutions. Kirsch writes that 'the most bloodcurdling examples of torture originated in the imaginations of monks who sat safely in their cells and entertained themselves by inventing extravagant and indecent fictions'.[86]

Tertullian, a second-century Christian author, wrote that 'the blood of martyrs is the seed of the Church', implying that the martyrs' willing sacrifice of their own lives helps facilitate the conversion of others.[87] Relics of the saints are still revered in the Church. The age of martyrdom led to the placement of relics in altars and influenced temple architecture. Today the Catholic and Eastern Orthodox Churches interpret the Eucharist ritual as a human sacrifice that is being remembered and re-invoked by its members (though many Protestants reject this interpretation).

Martyrs continue to be glorified today. The notorious Joshua Project, based in Denver, Colorado, is a multi-billion-dollar global organization which has the conversion of all humanity to Christianity as its stated aim. In the use of controversial tactics, the end would seem to justify the means. One such tactic is to publicize widely a list of martyrs from the earliest Christian times to the present. The lists are systematically organized by country and district. One can go to the Joshua Project's database and find names of alleged martyrs in any given district of India, a list which is updated continually. This project has become a veritable machine for generating data and misinformation about any and every Christian death that could be blamed on others. In the case of India, the Joshua Project points its finger at Hindus who comprise the dominant faith and are clearly targeted as competitors to overcome. This is particularly ironic given that Hinduism has a reputation for embracing and receiving other faiths, including Christianity. Yet when incidents of violence have occurred, it is often the Christian missionaries who cast the first stone in the form of hate speech such as 'pagan', 'idol-worshipper', 'heathen', etc. – systematically belittling Indian deities, symbols and traditions and offering whole villages financial incentives to convert. But rarely is any of this provocation ever mentioned. What is carefully documented and publicized instead are the half-truths, for example, that a Christian was attacked for merely being so.[88]

This is the continuation of the long history of valorizing Christian aggression against heathens. Martyrdom, inseparable from the notion of sacrifice in Christianity, is a dangerous concept that encourages violent death as a means to heaven. The notion of jihad is the culmination and extreme version of the very same belief that Christianity unleashed in its own history of expansion. By contrast, the only dharma tradition that formally uses the term 'martyr' for glorifying its leaders is Sikhism, which transformed into a martial sect during a specific period of Islamic rule with the intention to defend dharma from Islamic persecution. Guru Tegh Bahadur (1621-1675), for instance, became a martyr when the Mughal Emperor Aurangzeb ordered him to be brutally executed for refusing to convert to Islam.

Western scholars wrongly equate sacrifice in the Christian sense with the Sanskrit term yajna. The latter implies an 'exchange between planes of existence'. The Bhagavad Gita (3:9–16) says the devatas nurture us and we must nurture the devatas. Yajna is the thread that binds humanity to the devatas, and 'the all-pervading Brahman is ever established in yajna' (Gita 3:15). In other words, there is a reciprocal maintenance of various planes of existence, and yajna is the process of exchange with these higher levels. Creation sustains itself through yajna.[89] The essential principle behind yajna is the pouring out of one's life for the benefit of others. This is indeed part of the overall scheme of sacrifice inherent in the physical world: the minerals in the earth nourish plant life; smaller plants die and form the organic manure for trees; plants are consumed by animals for their own sustenance; animals, in turn, support humanity. Yajna is also a process that connects the manifest with the un-manifest.

Two questions arise: Did sacrifices like the ones mentioned above also take place in Indian culture? And if they did take place (regardless of the extent), are they in fact equivalent to yajna, or is yajna separate from such activities?

Concerning the first question, Indians *did* sacrifice their lives in ways that resemble the martyrs of the West (albeit not in the same sense as discussed above). Rajput women committed jauhar (self-immolation) when it became certain that the Muslim invaders had won and that their freedom, honour and very lives were at stake. The motivation was one of accepting defeat while preserving honour.[90] Another example is that of the mass suicide by Hindus who were defeated by the Dutch in Bali in 1906. The Balinese term for this act is 'puputan'.[91] But all of these were acts of voluntary surrender in the face of an invader who would undoubtedly unleash unspeakable acts of violence, pillage and rape on defeated populations. It may be viewed as defensive martyrdom at best. In contrast to the Western history of martyrdom, these were sporadic, isolated incidents; they were not part of a strategy of expansion or aggression, nor was there any centralized or systematic encouragement of martyrdom, such as citing martyrs as exemplars. Martyrdom was raised to a cult in Christendom, not in India.[92]

As for the second consideration, the explanation that follows will show that while it is true that a certain notion of sacrifice is a key element of yajna, the various other connotations normally associated with sacrifice in Western history are not applicable. Nor does the Western conception of sacrifice even begin to convey the cosmological significance of yajna, which is vast and rich.

Indian cosmology describes existence as consisting of three levels: the un-manifest, the manifest as cosmic/universal, and the manifest as individual/particular. Yajna is based on the specific cosmology of these multiple levels of existence and the mutual relationships between them.

The outer ritual is an enactment of one's inner sacrifice to the devatas, who are both within us as powers of consciousness and outside us as cosmic forces. Sri Aurobindo captures the essence of this:

> It is the One manifest as the doer and the deed and the object of works, knower and knowledge and the object of knowledge. The universal energy

into which the action is poured is the Divine; the consecrated energy of the giving is the Divine; whatever is offered is only some form of the Divine; the giver of the offering is the Divine himself in man; the action, the work, the sacrifice is itself the Divine in movement, in activity; the goal to be reached by sacrifice is the Divine.[93]

The Vedic path is not one of inaction but of surrender – that is, offering one's physical, emotional and mental actions to the divine. The overarching purpose is to counter the ego's claim to own, act and suffer as the body-mind. Yajna is a ritualistic and cognitive surrender of the ego to the fire that symbolizes the higher self. The primary elements of a yajna are the performer's inspiration ('bhavana'), learning ('svadhyaya'), rites ('karma'), offerings ('tyaga'), the deity being invoked ('devata'), and the results ('phala'). These constituents symbolize various psychological processes within us. It is, 'psychologically, a symbol of cosmic and individual activity become self-conscious, enlightened and aware of its goal',[94] says Sri Aurobindo, who elaborates:

In the ancient Vedic system there was always a double sense, physical and psychological, outward and symbolic, the exterior form of the sacrifice and the inner meaning of all its circumstances … The offering itself is whatever working of his energy, physical or psychological, is consecrated by him in action of body or action of mind to the gods or God, to the Self or to the universal powers, to one's own higher Self or to the Self in mankind and in all existences.[95]

Mistranslating yajna as sacrifice has enabled many a Western scholar to superimpose the history of human sacrifices and martyrdom, from Judaism and Christianity, onto this dharmic rite.

Karma ≠ Western Notion of Suffering

It is perhaps because human suffering is ubiquitous that every major worldview has a theory of suffering that offers an explanation and solutions. Christianity and Judaism rely heavily on the concept of original sin. This fundamental flaw in all human beings condemns them to a life of suffering on earth. Suffering arises therefore from sin, not ignorance. All humans share this original sin as a consequence of the actions of Adam and Eve, who, unable to resist temptation, partook of the forbidden fruit of the Tree of the Knowledge of Good and Evil in the Garden of Eden. As a result of this transgression, they and all their progeny (that is to say, all humans) are afflicted by original sin. Mainstream theodicy in these traditions thus traces both individual and collective suffering to that original or primal error, which is, again, an error of evil intent and choice, not just lack of wisdom or understanding.

The remedy is to be saved by an act of forgiveness by God. In the case of Christianity, only Jesus, as the Son of God, can offer others salvation precisely because he alone is exempt from original sin. (His virgin birth is crucial, for had he been born out of sexual union by human parents, he too would have been afflicted with original sin.) Christian churches thus have claimed a monopoly on Jesus' grace in order to save all of humanity.

For Christians and Jews, the original sin was the attempt to be 'like gods' (i.e., all-knowing). Hence, Christianity and Judaism have always held the quintessential Hindu idea of humanity's inner divinity to be an abomination and a sign of moral turpitude.

The European Enlightenment secularized these biblical theories of suffering and redemption through willed submission to a higher power yet retained the core elements. Georg Wilhelm Friedrich Hegel's linear theory of history claimed that non-Western civilizations lacked the West's 'spirit' and hence suffered, pending their successful rescue and absorption by the West. Later on, Marxism used the theory of class exploitation to explain suffering and proffered a solution in the form of a messianic proletarian struggle against the dominant capitalist class. Thus the Western ego, whether religious or secular, individual or collective, believes that it has a mission that requires action; it thus defines itself as the chief agent of history that marches us all toward a common grand future. Any refusal to buy into this project is punishable. Alien cultures and their spiritual traditions are problems which somehow need to be solved, usually through destruction or annexation.[96]

The dharma traditions conceive of the human condition differently. Here, the battle is not with original sin and certainly not sin vicariously assumed through the actions of others. Rather, it is ignorance which produces the chain of cause and effect and which in turn determines both individual and collective suffering. This understanding is expressed by the various theologies that have evolved around the non-translatable term karma. (Eating from the Tree of Knowledge would therefore not become the cause of sin.)

Karma is the principle by which an individual's thoughts, feelings and actions create consequences in the present and future. So, for example, an individual's efforts to cultivate intellect, aesthetic appreciation, or spiritual dimension naturally tend to contribute to advances in these respective areas. Conversely, thoughts or actions of violence, avarice or lust contribute to an increase of *these* propensities and to their fallout in this life and the next. Karma does not imply fatalism but rather a system of consequences for one's actions. Indeed, it may be rightly interpreted as the *opposite* of fatalism insofar as it offers an ethical framework of responsibility and accountability for choices that are freely made – making it possible, in other words, for humans to make and remake their lives and destinies.

Karma, then, is a psychophysical law of cause and effect. Each intentional action leaves behind a trace called samskara, sometimes described as a seed that will sprout under appropriate conditions, and the effect that is produced is called phala (fruit). The timing for the ripening of the fruit of an action is indeterminate and occurs when the appropriate fertile conditions for its exposure and resolution are in place. Repeating a given karma strengthens the samskara, which then gradually becomes a habit or tendency (vasana) and can further lead to the repetition of the action. The power of samskaras and vasanas is such that a person can fall into a default or mechanical mode of action without even being conscious of having made a choice. This is similar to the psychological notion of reinforced behaviour leading to greater bondage, though the concept has theological, philosophical and spiritual implications – not merely psychological ones. Here one's *own* actions, not someone else's (as in the case of original sin), lead to the formation of character, which in turn leads to further actions that stem from that character. Spiritual practice can enable one to burn the seeds of past karma by experiencing the fruit of past karma with surrender, not reacting or responding in a manner that would create new karma and perpetuate the cycle of action and its consequences.

Positive karma is called 'punya' and negative karma, 'paapa'. Nobody suffers for someone else's action; hence, each individual has a separate account in which the effects of his or her karma are recorded.[97] In the Samkhya system of Indian philosophy, the *individual* consciousness serves as the receptacle in which the samskaras (seeds produced by our choices) get stored. This is the basis for individuality in Indian psychology. In short, an individual's karma produces effects that amount to a deposit which is stored in that individual's consciousness.

The purpose of karma is only to reform, and it operates *only* when one thinks of oneself as being separate and independent. Once one is no longer the doer, karma ceases to accumulate (though the old 'prarabdha' of accumulated karma will continue to bring its effects).

From this viewpoint, reincarnation is the system of rebirth into another life based on one's own past karma. This explains why different persons are born into different circumstances. Karma is not a matter of God playing dice or arbitrarily assigning fate, nor is it random, nor the result of some primal collective sin. Contrary to its frequent misappropriation in the West, the karma theory is really a guide to good action and not merely a model that explains present circumstances. As the consequences of one's karma play out, the karma gets erased, but the record gets replenished with fresh karma since the ego is always making choices.

Hindus believe that each conscious being is related to God as a drop is to the ocean. All these drops are part of one coherent divine play/dance called 'leela'. There is an infinite number of individual souls in the dance, each of which makes choices and receives the consequences. Liberation is the state of freedom in which the individual ego, which is creating karma and being bound by its consequences, radically transforms and loses its separateness from the Ultimate Reality. Such a release is therefore not a physical heaven but a state of consciousness.

Earlier, I stated that cognitive error is the dharmic explanation for human suffering. There is a web of cognitive errors which cause karma to be accumulated – for example, believing the ego to be one's ultimate self, assuming that objects exist as themselves and can become the basis for pursuits and goals, grasping one's feelings and concepts as real, etc. Addressing these errors can help one disentangle one's karma and lighten the load of the ego. As the cognitive error gets corrected, one ceases pursuing obsessions.

Western scholars have incorrectly imputed a lack of individuality to Indian traditions, implying that the West alone is endowed with this trait. It is important also to remove certain misinterpretations of karma theory. The theory insists on the need to balance the inherited karma from past action (not an arbitrarily assigned fate) with personal effort (purushartha). Numerous tales from the *Panchatantra*[98] and elsewhere illustrate the folly of relying entirely on one or the other. The Indian approach to suffering is therefore neither fatalistic acceptance nor the opposite, belief in total freedom in man's present condition. The desirable attitude is pragmatic and requires differentiation between the short, medium and long terms. In the present moment, there must be dispassionate acceptance of suffering, while in the medium term one must work steadfastly to minimize it, and eventually, in the long term, one must transcend the sphere in which karma operates.

Karma ≠ Redemption

Although it is a dharmic term, karma is popular in the Western vocabulary of today. Many people sprinkle their conversations with references to karma; however, the concept itself is not easily translatable between cultures and therefore remains misunderstood. The principle of karma is similar, in some ways, to the biblical notion of justice. For example, the Bible says 'as ye sow, so shall ye reap.' Both viewpoints – the dharmic and the Judeo-Christian – stress that good or bad actions may be physical, verbal or mental, and both presume free will (though in the case of Christianity and Judaism that freedom has been compromised, if not abolished, by original sin, and in dharmic traditions it is inhibited by vasanas). Also, both are based on the notion of a just world in which justice *ultimately* will be done; both posit a universal law, an underlying cosmic principle of unfolding creation; and both suggest that no wilful actions against this creation are exempt from consequences. And yet there are important differences between the two concepts. When we fail to consider the meaning of karma in its Indian context, we run the risk of assuming that the dharmic and Judeo-Christian worldviews are one and the same.

In Judaism and Christianity, justice, while it may be approximated on earth, is finally only accomplished on the Day of Judgement when each person is held accountable for all his or her actions and thereby assigned permanently to Heaven or Hell. This is to occur, mythically speaking, at the culmination of an apocalyptic struggle known as the End Times.[99] In the karma principle, by contrast, there is no particular day of universal judgement; in fact, there is no reference to a time when the rewards and punishments will permanently end. Karma is a *perpetual* cosmic system in which consequences of all actions follow and flow back and forth, just as causation in natural sciences is continuously at work.

The Christian view of justice is similar to the interpretation of karma in the Mimamsa system: good behaviour is rewarded by enjoyment in heaven (svarga), and bad actions are punished in hell (naraka). But unlike the Christian notions of perpetual hell or eternal life in heaven, the Hindu idea is that the stay in either state is always temporary and in proportion to accumulated karma. A major difference is that these celestial stays are not able fully to exhaust all the accumulated karmas, making it necessary to be reborn in order to experience the fruits that are due to manifest under the appropriate conditions.[100] Thus, the idea of rebirth is important and pervades Indian thought.[101] Whereas in Christianity, as well as in Western secular thought (e.g., in psychology), the time span for outcomes is normally assumed to be limited to a single life-cycle, in Indian thought the cycle of causation driven by one's choices extends across lifecycles.[102] Karma theory makes rebirth an important notion: it explains why different persons are born in drastically different conditions. The Christian explanation for why humans are born unequal has to do with the inscrutable will of God.

Unlike the concept of original sin, karma theory says that it is *only our own individual past* actions (in past lives and this one) that bring us our circumstances and hold us in bondage. For example, all the passengers in an aircraft might die in a crash, but each of them individually had his death coming to him as a consequence of his own karma, so what *appears* to be collective phala is not in fact caused by collective karma. The notion of collective karma emerges only when a group of individuals collectively performs an act and hence each participant shares in the karma. But, importantly, this collective karma is not accrued due to an act by someone else – for example, Adam and Eve in the case of Christianity.[103]

For Hindus there are two problems with the Christian belief: first, the karma of a person (jiva) is non-transferrable to another person and must be experienced by the person committing it in this life or some future life or lives.[104] Also, phala cannot precede karma but always follows afterwards, so Jesus' prior suffering could not be used either retroactively (as is claimed for the Hebrew people before his birth) or to wipe out future karmas by future persons.[105]

In Christianity and Judaism, there is both collective and individual guilt, and both require expiation. The collective in question may be a whole people, such as the people of Israel, who in the Hebrew Bible are described as having sometimes fallen away from their faith and having sometimes upheld it, with rewards and punishments for the whole group as a result. The Church, at least from a Roman Catholic perspective, can also be alienated or redeemed as a collective entity. Various types of continuity with the collective over time become important. An example would be biological lineage in the priesthood of ancient Israel. Another is called 'apostolic succession' – the unbroken continuity of bishops in the Christian high church. Karma-like effects may be transmitted through these collectives quite apart from the individual sin or guilt of particular members.

For the westerner, then, the nature of the self can be constructed almost genealogically, and certainly constructed by faith or shared belief, whereas in Indian systems of karma the biological birth is a means by which the individual jiva-atman is born in accordance with its individual karmic account, and it is unconstrained in its fate by a collective identity.

In the dharmic traditions, an action is finite, as are its karmic effects, even though they may play out over long periods of time. There can be no eternal damnation for any karmic act whatsoever.[106] On the other hand, in Christianity and Islam, *damnation is forever*, and there is nothing anyone except God can do about it.[107] Again, some of the difference between the two views can be traced to the difference in cosmology discussed previously. Indian philosophy holds that time, like the cosmos, is infinite, without beginning or end, whereas biblical time started upon the creation of this one-and-only universe and will terminate at the forthcoming End Times. Most Christians picture the cosmos as having a linear history in finite time followed by eternity in Heaven or Hell. Personal actions which take place in such a timescale have eternal consequences. And this is the one and only life on earth in which to deal with sin.

As a result of this anxiety, Christians can feel driven to proselytize, often resorting to ways that run counter to Jesus' own example. Although almost every single angelic visitation in the Bible – including the angels' announcement to the shepherds of Jesus' birth, begins with the injunction 'fear not' – Christian missionaries have traditionally emphasized fear and used psychological duress, offering the 'good news' that God has given their church the exclusive remedy for the dire predicament of humankind. In Hinduism, a human can work out his or her own karma and not accumulate new karma, thereby achieving liberation over time. There is *always* another life that will be available to redress even the most atrocious deeds.

The table below summarizes these major differences:

	Time	Karma Effect (Phala)	Dependence on Historical Intervention	Psychological Implication
Christianity	Finite	Eternal	Yes	Tension, Guilt
Hinduism– Buddhism	Infinite	Temporary	No	Ease

Also, karma theory holds that human beings have the tools to break their karmic bonds entirely by their own spiritual practice and do not need divine intervention as conceived in the Judeo-Christian faiths. There is the notion of grace (God's compassion and mercy without merit), but not as a prerequisite. Human beings have the agency for their own liberation. Hence, regardless of the stature of Krishna, Shiva or Buddha, it is possible to be a good Hindu without ever having heard of them as long as one lives in accordance with dharma. In contrast, one cannot be a good Christian without knowing Jesus' history and accepting it.

In the dharma traditions, the material ego is itself viewed as the ultimate source of finitude and suffering, whereas in the Western mindset the ego always remains intact and at times even undergoes a dangerous messianic inflation.

Embodied knowing in the dharmic faiths is aimed at cleansing the ego as an interim step toward ultimately dissolving it. (Alternatively, the ultimate goal is to expand the ego so that it encompasses everything, a state known as 'purnahamta'.) Suffering spares no one and should be the impetus for higher aspirations and transmuted into a source of deep insight (prajna) and compassion (karuna). Embodied knowledge cannot be achieved by 'buying into' schemes of world redemption or through adherence to a specific cult or sect. Nowhere is this understanding better illustrated than in the life of the Buddha and the Four Noble Truths, and in the subsequent history of Buddhism – one of the most consistently peaceable religious formations in the world.[108]

The dharmic traditions are at a disadvantage in the political and psychological contest for souls and territory, because they do not proselytize. The Christian and Islamic fixation on historical revelation, schemata of salvation and damnation, and formal institutions as the exclusive bearers of divine truth has often fuelled imperialistic designs for expansion and control. The dharmic traditions, by comparison, do not have built-in mandates and justifications for aggression. They offer no infidel or heathen enemy to serve as a catalyst for mobilization, and their promises of self-realization often seem too distant and abstract for the poor, hungry, deprived and illiterate. They also have nothing like the institutional authority, control mechanisms, and organizational frameworks of Western religions.

Let us compare these traditions with respect to suffering, karma, salvation and liberation. The three columns in the table that follows demonstrate the challenges in undertaking such comparisons and in trying to make them seem equivalent. The first column states an important Christian tenet as it would be understood by mainstream Christians; the second restates this tenet as per the karma framework in the dharma traditions; and the third evaluates this tenet in accordance with karma philosophy.

	Christian Tenet	Christian Tenet Restated in Karma Framework	Indic Tenet
1	Adam and Eve's original sin condemned all humans forever to eternal damnation until the End Times unless amended by grace.	Karma of parents passed on to humans collectively for all generations to come. Phala (fruit) of karma is infinite (eternal).	Karma is not collectively transmitted. Each jiva's karma is from that jiva's own prior lives and not from forebears. All karma and phala are finite only, and never infinite.
2	Jesus suffered for the sins of all humanity, including all future humanity, to save them from eternal damnation.	Every person's karma is transferable to Jesus. Future karma of yet-to-be-born persons is potentially redeemed in advance by phala (suffering) of Jesus.	Karma is non-transferable; Phala comes after the karma, not before; it cannot be deposited in advance for future karma, nor can it be retroactive.
3	The necessary and sufficient condition to be saved by Jesus is to *believe* in the historical events of his birth, death and resurrection and comply with the biblical teachings.[109]	Mere *belief* has a karmic effect of stupendous proportions.	No *belief* by itself is able to have such a consequence of overriding all karmas.

Karma-Yoga ≠ Christian Works

'Works' is a Christian term which is similar to sadhana (disciplined spiritual practice) and karma-yoga in Hinduism–Buddhism. It refers to any conscious and deliberate spiritual practice – from charity to prayer to meditation to Bible study to participation in Christian rituals – by which the practitioner seeks to improve spiritual standing before God. In strict Protestant traditions, one cannot 'earn' salvation by any kind of effort or works, be they spiritual disciplines, acts of charity, or even self-sacrifice; for Protestants, the illusion that one can do so is one of the great obstacles to spiritual growth. As a result, there is enormous distrust among Protestants of dharmic traditions such as yoga, which suggest that people can attain salvation by works, thus implying a lack of humility and lack of understanding of the grace of God. Protestants do not deny the importance of works but regard them as the fruit of salvation and not as a means of attaining it.

Catholics mostly agree with Protestants, though they emphasize works as preparation for salvation and possibly as an aid to achieving it. For Catholics, humans are not entirely depraved (corrupt, degenerate); hence, they can aid their own salvation and attainment of the beatific vision – though the ultimate gift is still, as Protestants insist, God's to give. Hence, Catholics do have some spiritual practices which are analogous to Indian ones, such as the recitation of the rosary which is very like the Hindu japa.

Many Catholic and Eastern Orthodox traditions, such as the use of breath along with prayer and extensive monastic practices with a physical and embodied sense of spirituality, were likely borrowed from or at least influenced by India.[110] Catholics also place a higher value on ritual than Protestants do. For this reason lay Catholics, as well as the Orthodox Church and High Anglicans, generally find it easier to embrace Indian spirituality than Protestants do. Catholics are aware of the power of spiritual practices and comfortable with spiritual effort and deliberate cultivation. At the same time, paradoxically, many of them are resistant to yoga, in part because it threatens Christian exclusivism and because they understand that spiritual practices cannot be entirely separated from their theological, historical contexts and treated as neutral techniques.[111]

In order to achieve the highest aim of life, according to dharma, both personal effort and grace are necessary. An unfailing aspiration from within and supreme grace that answers from above are the two powers that come together to lead us to the highest goal. Grace can act only in conditions of light and truth, for which one's lower nature must be surrendered. This includes the mind's ideas, opinions, preferences, habits and constructions, so that the silent mind can receive true knowledge. According to Sri Aurobindo, one must 'reject desires, demands, cravings, sensations, passions, selfishness, pride, arrogance, lust, greed, jealousy, envy, hostility to the truth, so that the true power and joy may pour from above into a calm, large, strong and consecrated vital being'. At the physical level one must reject 'the physical nature's stupidity, doubt, disbelief, obscurity, obstinacy, pettiness, laziness, unwillingness to change, 'tamas', so that the true stability of Light, Power, Ananda may establish itself in a body growing always more divine'.[112] Such a total surrender of oneself must be in every movement; it is not sufficient to be in this mode occasionally, during worship or sadhana, for example.

The term 'surrender' is here used not to suggest an abandonment of responsibilities in the hope that God will do everything (the tradition would call that tamasic irresponsibility). Rather, it is meant to suggest living a life of perfection in the world. The term 'yoga off the mat' has been used to describe this way of life, as distinct from 'yoga *on* the mat', which is limited to practices in a segregated time and place only. Sri Aurobindo explains:

> Yoga may be done without the least thought for the breathing, in any posture or no posture, without any insistence on concentration, in the full waking condition, while walking, working, eating, drinking, talking with others, in any occupation, in sleep, in dream, in states of unconsciousness, semi-consciousness, double-consciousness. It is no nostrum or system or fixed practice, but an eternal fact of process based on the very nature of the Universe.[113]

The Bhagavadgita stresses karma-yoga, or liberation through action. Every action must be performed free from the ego with no desire for reward and with total sincerity; in this way, one serves as an instrument of the divine. Doing so elevates one's consciousness. It involves tapasya, which is derived from tapas whose root means to generate heat, to shine. This is the warmth of the fire of aspiration, effort, intensity, sacrifice and pain felt in the life of service and surrender. This is not seen as suffering but is accepted freely and joyfully as one's performance of tapasya for the purpose of realizing the highest aim of life. All problems and difficulties are due to humanity having forgotten this aim of life; instead people's activity is centred around the superficial ego. Tapasya refers to the constant effort and personal will to get rid of this ego, to liberate oneself from it.

Salvation ≠ Jivanmukti and Moksha

Occasionally a small group of evangelists – well-dressed and well-groomed young men and women from a local church – walks around my neighbourhood ringing doorbells to spread Christianity. I always like to invite them in, offer them chai, and engage in a relaxed conversation. Even though I went to a Catholic school and know the proselytizing game well, I pretend I'm the naive immigrant eager to ask basic questions. After a few minutes of small talk, one of them usually breaks open the topic by asking, 'Have you been saved?'

I try to look surprised and respond by saying, 'I was never condemned to begin with!' My young, charming guests usually get thrown off. They expect me to claim that I have already been saved, and their training has equipped them with the rhetorical skills to assert that their ability to save me is superior to my present faith. I usually find them taken by surprise by my posture that I do not need to be saved in the first place.

Christian salvation is a solution to the problem of Eternal Damnation caused by original sin. But that problem does not exist within the dharma traditions. Imagine someone asking you if you have been pardoned from your prison sentence, and you respond by saying that you were never condemned for any crime and that hence such a question is absurd. The implication here is that for a dharmic person to say he has been saved would imply that he accepts Christianity's fundamental tenet that every human is born a sinner and remains so until he surrenders himself to Jesus Christ. Even when the Church acknowledges other faiths as having merit, no other path can substitute for Jesus when it comes to being saved.

The closest the dharmic traditions come to salvation are the concepts of moksha in Hinduism and nirvana in Buddhism, both of which can be loosely translated as 'liberation'. But there are crucial differences between dharmic liberation and Christian salvation.

Receiving assurance of salvation is the key moment in the spiritual life of most Christians. It comes as a gift of grace, and its source lies outside the individual. It does not come as a result strictly of merit, spiritual practice, prayer or asceticism. Although these may be helpful in its attainment and even necessary in many denominations, they are not sufficient in and of themselves, because the capacity to achieve salvation is not innate in us.

In Jewish and Christian traditions, death is the consequence of sin. The freedom of the soul in Christianity entails, in the End of Time, the freedom of the body as well: there will be a resurrection of the dead in a 'glorified' physical form, and the boundary between heaven and earth will be erased or made permeable. For most people, the full realization of this salvation can come only after death.

Dharmic liberation, on the other hand, can be achieved here and now in this very body and in this very world. Moksha is similar to salvation insofar as it is concerned with freedom from human bondage, but the nature of this bondage is quite different. Moksha really refers to living in a state of freedom from ignorance, preconditioning and karmic baggage. According to the Bhagavadgita, the state where one is without desire, without ego, and beyond the drives of human nature is the first major milestone; it opens the door to further evolution and eventual liberation in the fullest sense.

Salvation, on the other hand, does not entail expanded awareness or consciousness, esoteric/mystical knowledge, or physical practices (though these may attend it). Nor is it necessarily derived from complete renunciation, as is the case in Buddhist nirvana. It can be experienced only by surrendering to the will of God, and God here is specifically the God of the Bible.

There is yet another state described in Sanskrit which has no equivalent in Christianity. One who has attained moksha may choose to remain in the world and continue to do spiritual work – that is, free from past actions (i.e., karmic bondage) and yet active in the world. This person is called jivanmukta. He or she can, at will, either turn away from the world or turn toward it and deal with it without being touched or limited by it. The Buddhist equivalent of a jivanmukta is a bodhisattva.

The New Testament calls this 'being in the world, but not of it'. There is an opening here for a potential development of a Christian jivanmukta, and St. Paul says several things about himself that would indicate he had at least tasted this state, as had other Christian saints. But the important thing is that there is no word for it in Biblical metaphysics; that is because the state was not examined, understood or cultivated through systematic techniques. The words 'saint' and 'prophet' do not suffice, nor even does 'mystic'. When Christians experienced such a state, it was not as a result of following a yoga-like systematic process; neither was it seen as bringing salvation. Hence, such a person would still be, according to the Vatican document, *Dominus Jesus*, 'in a gravely deficient situation in comparison with those who, in the Church, have the fullness of the means of salvation'.

As the evangelists leave my home, I always hope our conversation has challenged their assumptions about the people they are preaching to, and that perhaps they will re-examine the idea that all people outside of their church are in a state of spiritual deficiency. But until they do, I will continue to welcome them into my living room, offer them chai, and share with them the good news that there is no such thing as original sin.

6

Contesting Western
Universalism

'While Christianity claims a divine mandate to superimpose its
own history-centrism on the entire world, thinkers of the European
Enlightenment have also developed various conceptual absolutes and
endowed these with 'universal' status. The profound assumption is
that the shape and direction of world history are leading to a single
Western goal – be it salvation or scientific secular progress. All peoples
and cultures are forced into the various schemes put forward to
bring this about. Indeed, modern laws, regulations, conventions and
common practices are formed with this in mind (whether consciously
or not). The result has been the ongoing appropriation, by the West,
of the intellectual and cultural property of various non-Western
civilizations. This entails the dismantling of indigenous constructions
of cosmology, space, time, social relations, and indeed of the self
and its relationship to a transcendent principle. The unity of the
indigenous culture is broken into parts; these are then mapped onto
Western taxonomy, which is presented as more objective or else based
on a more correct spirituality. This is nothing less than the systematic
dispossession (an epistemic cannibalization, as it were) of the
colonized world. Once the target culture gets drained of its 'useful'
elements (as per Western needs), what is left is a lifeless husk of the
depleted culture. The victim might even get blamed as the source
and cause of its own degradation. Such a universalism fails to address
human needs; the most it can achieve is a kind of synthetic unity of
civilizations under the rubric of the West.'

One of the most important objectives of this book is to refute Western claims of universalism. According to these claims, the West is both the driver of history and its goal, providing the template into which all other civilizations and cultures must fit. This view is so deeply entrenched in the consciousness of Europeans and Americans as to form a core part of their identities. Yet, it is virtually invisible from within the Western perspective itself. By engaging in purva paksha or 'reversing the gaze', we can shed light on this view and on the ways in which it leads to the misapprehension and denigration of India and dharmic traditions.

Western universalism first achieved full-blown expression in the Romantic movement which swept Europe in the late eighteenth and early nineteenth centuries. There are four key moments, each of which directly involves India and her dharmic traditions: 1) the 'discovery' of the Orient as a spiritual and cultural, as well as material, resource; 2) the use of Sanskrit to bolster Western racial identities, especially German ones; 3) the development of a narrative of history as the unfolding of a 'universal' World Spirit manifesting exclusively in the European and American nations as opposed to Asian ones (a narrative promulgated largely by one man: Hegel); and 4) the export of this narrative back to India, with the effect that Indians came to feel a profound need to reinterpret their own past in the light of the now overwhelmingly powerful Western 'universal' myth.

As we shall see, the effects of these key moments live on, setting the terms for the encounter of the West with India and dictating many of the assumptions on which this encounter is pursued. A new storyline is developed, and the facts are interpreted and filtered to fit it. Historians make choices and manipulate the available information with authoritative certainty, and successive historians continue the process by adapting history to the needs of successive conquerors and rulers. At each stage, some facets are selected and adapted, and these become part of the collective memory and imagination. This kind of history gets embedded in people's minds in the form of symbols, narratives, tropes, identities, ancestors, places, etc. True or false, it comes to serve as the story of their collective identity.[1] While similar tendencies exist in every civilization, the West has been especially successful at imposing its accounts of history, philosophy and identity on others.

This process has required the digestion of the histories and identities of others, such that the portions deemed useful are made a part of the West. It is driven by ego anxieties which are fuelled by attempts at synthetically unifying contrasting worldviews and also by innumerable projects of expansion. As we have seen in previous chapters, Western revisionism either tries to make non-westerners minor players on the stage of Christian salvation history, or seeks to draw them into the story of how Western reason and science have triumphed over 'primitive' mentalities and cultures. Both the Abrahamic traditions and secularism are culpable in this: while Christianity claims a divine mandate to superimpose its own history-centrism on the entire world, thinkers of the Enlightenment have also developed various conceptual absolutes and endowed these with 'universal' status.

The profound assumption is that the shape and direction of world history are leading to a single Western goal – be it salvation or scientific secular progress. All peoples and cultures are forced into the various schemes put forward to bring this about. Indeed, modern laws, regulations, conventions and common practices are formed with this in mind (whether consciously or not).

The result has been the ongoing appropriation, by the West, of the intellectual and cultural property of various non-Western civilizations. This entails the dismantling of indigenous constructions of cosmology, space, time, social relations, and indeed of the self and its relationship to a transcendent principle. The unity of the indigenous culture is broken into parts; these are then mapped onto Western taxonomy, which is presented as more objective or else based on a more correct spirituality. This is nothing less than the systematic dispossession (an epistemic cannibalization, as it were) of the colonized world. Once the target culture gets drained of its useful elements (as per Western needs), what is left is a lifeless husk of the depleted culture. Victims might even get blamed as the source and cause of their own degradation.

Such a universalism fails to address human needs; the most it can achieve is a kind of synthetic unity of civilizations under the rubric of the West. Part of the problem is that the Western approach has been reductionist, and its binary categories result in violence when applied universally. For example, the binary categories of sacred/secular, monotheism/polytheism, creation/evolution, and political left/right are inappropriate starting points when trying to understand dharmic civilization. The East/West or Orient/Occident divide is also arbitrary and has come about as a result of historical events particular to what is now called 'the West'.[2]

Western academics not only produce critical editions of dharma texts but determine the very categories of the discourse, the manner in which complex words and situations are contextualized, what is included as interesting and relevant (and what is left out), which social theories and textual hermeneutics are to be used, and who the authorities are in matters of interpretation. Engaging in sweeping generalizations, the Western academy routinely passes judgement on whether Hinduism is a legitimate religion, how and when it should be discussed (if at all), and who its authorized spokespersons are. All of this causes many in the dharmic traditions to doubt the legitimacy of their culture, especially in relation to the established, prevailing taxonomy.[3]

Germany as a Case Study in Western Digestion and Synthesis

In the late 1700s and early 1800s, the leaders of what came to be known as the Romantic movement in Germany, France and England took special interest in ancient India. The theory that India was the origin of European culture started to compete against the earlier view of Europe as having a Semitic origin. This shift came about because Sanskrit was found to be close to certain major European languages – whereas Hebrew was not – and because Europeans were ecstatic about having discovered great Indian texts written in Sanskrit which could be used to reconstruct their past history. The texts of classical India indicated a civilization with great achievements in drama, religious and epic poetry, fable, advanced abstract thinking, medicine, mathematics and astronomy.

Between 1800 and 1850, virtually every major European centre of learning had established a Sanskrit or Indology department, often at the expense of downgrading Latin and Greek. This affinity with an ancient high culture prompted intellectuals to seek out a common European history. Sanskrit dominated the field of linguistics throughout Europe and the United States until well into the twentieth century, and some of Europe's most prominent historians, philosophers and other intellectuals proposed various theories to account for its profundity. However, by the middle of the twentieth century, Sanskrit had ceased to be studied rigorously, and today it faces virtual extinction in the academy.

The Renaissance and colonialism together had an uneven impact on the balance of identity politics in Europe. The French had claimed the Catholic Church and the Greco-Roman classics as their pride of heritage; the British traced their mythic lineage to Virgil's *Aeneas* and grounded their sense of nationhood, in part, on the British Empire, with India as the 'jewel in the crown'; the Spaniards and Portuguese glorified their own 'discovery' and colonization of the Americas; and the Italians held cherished memories of past Roman Empire. Such grand narratives served to boost the respective identities of rival nations and instill pride in their citizens.

Germans had no such grand claim, for they had neither a foreign empire nor a noble lineage of which to boast. The German sense of inferiority arose from the widely accepted trajectory of cultural advancement that saw civilized Europe as having begun in Greece and Israel, followed by Rome, and culminating in the major colonial powers. This positioned the French – as the inheritors of the Renaissance – at the centre of European high culture, leaving the Germans without a similar narrative. In fact, textbooks across Europe at this time depicted Germans as the barbarians who had destroyed first the Roman Empire and then the high culture of Europe in France.

It was under these circumstances that Germans felt a new infusion of pride when it became known that Sanskrit was not only the key marker of an advanced civilization but was closer to German than to any other major European language. This galvanized German intellectuals, and India became a major source from which Germans began to construct their own identity.

Germans whose works were shaped by this engagement with India included the pioneers of German Romanticism: Johann Gottfried von Herder (1744–1803) and Karl Wilhelm Friedrich von Schlegel (1772–1829), as well as the three most celebrated system-builders of German Idealism: F.W.J. von Schelling (1775–1854), Arthur Schopenhauer (1788–1860), and, of course, Georg Wilhelm Friedrich Hegel. Other prominent German thinkers of the century who were deeply immersed in Indology for much of their careers included: Wilhelm von Humboldt (1767–1835), Franz Bopp (1791–1867) and Max Müller (1823–1900). Indian thought also influenced Nietzsche's philosophical work, and Goethe was so ecstatic over Kalidasa's Sanskrit play, *Abhijnana Shakuntalam*, that he modelled the prologue of *Faust* on the conventions of the Sanskrit drama. These Germans, in turn, interacted with vibrant British and French Indologists, and this had a profound effect on what is known as modern Western thought.

This Romantic attraction for India, and for the Sanskrit classical era in particular, was always self-serving. Even at the early stages of German Romanticism, marked by immense love and respect for a mythic and perfect India, there was a tendency to superimpose Eurocentric frameworks and interests. The Indian ideas were gradually removed from their context and selectively digested into the new, emerging German framework. New origins of these Indian ideas were explored and many alternative theories proposed among prominent European thinkers.

Schlegel, for example, who was the first major German Sanskritist, started out as the great champion of everything Indian and used many ideas from Sanskrit texts to formulate a new history of ancient Germany and the West. But Schlegel suddenly converted back to Christianity and rejected his earlier thesis of India as the ancient German homeland. He tried to separate out Indian religion from Sanskrit texts in order to appropriate selectively the non-religious aspects of Sanskrit civilization into the German Christian identity. The romance for India gradually diminished, and Schlegel and other Germans began to see India as a primitive society with many evils.

Hegel's Myth of the West

But it was Hegel, among all German thinkers, who had the deepest and most enduring impact on Western thought and identity. It is often forgotten that his work was a reaction *against* the Romantics' passion for India's past. He borrowed Indian ideas (such as monism) while debating Indologists to argue *against* the value of Indian civilization. He posited that the West, and only the West, was the agent of history and teleology. India was the 'frozen other', which he used as a foil to define the West.

It was thus that Hegel attempted to construct an identity for the German people, in part through their encounter with India. As a founding father of the Enlightenment and one of the most towering figures of European thought, he developed a powerful and influential philosophy of history which included the past, present and future of all civilizations on a single template.

It is true that in the course of his education Hegel developed a strong distaste for the Abrahamic religions, perceiving their provincial, anti-philosophical aspects and the way in which so much of their wisdom was bound up in the culturally specific (and, in his eyes, primitive) milieu of the ancient Middle East. At the same time, Hegel had so deeply absorbed the history-centrism of the Abrahamic traditions and their grand salvation narrative that he essentially (and perhaps unwittingly) recreated it, though in more secular and *seemingly* more universal terms.

While breaking with religion and adopting a purely secular Greek rationality, his grand narrative mirrors, in many ways, the salvation history of Judeo-Christianity. The *Weltgeist* or World Spirit is, in effect, the protagonist of this history, and the West is extraordinary because it is destined to lead this journey while all other civilizations must follow or perish.

Hegel's World Spirit is a synthetic unity encompassing all humanity. It privileges the West, and those who do not fit into his scheme are not a part of history, though the Spirit may use them, just as plants, animals, land, etc., are used. Although all humans have a geography, not all have a history in this sense. Lack of history is due to a deficiency in agency, that is, the freedom and ability to take action and bring about change in the world. This journey of the Spirit progresses through a series of stages until it reaches the highest form of self-realization, called the Absolute Spirit (*Geist*). The Spirit produces specific forms, 'and these forms are the nations of world history. Each of them represents a particular stage of development, so that they correspond to epochs in the history of the world'.[4]

Spirit evolves from lower to higher forms; hence, Hegel places the various nations at different stages of evolution. This is God's plan, he explains: 'World history is nothing more than the plan of providence. The world is governed by God; and world history is the content of his government and the execution of his plan.'[5]

The unity he proposes is racist, with westerners (whom he thinks of as a race, to be contrasted with Africans, Asians, Native Americans, etc.) at the centre of the cosmos vis-à-vis other cultures. Conveniently ignoring whatever facts do not support the thesis, he constructs a lopsided chronology of events to show Europe and America as the twin pinnacles of human evolution. He declares this template of chronologies to be 'universal history', asserting, for example, that 'universal history goes from East to West. Europe is absolutely the *end of universal history*. Asia is the beginning.'[6] He postulates a stage called 'Prehistory' into which he lumps all those nations which are not among the chosen ones in world history. Hegel dismisses the Native Americans as 'obviously unintelligent' and speaks of them as 'unenlightened children' distinguished only by 'inferiority in all respects'. He also proclaims that India 'has no history'.[7]

Furthermore, because God is rational, 'the overall content of world history is rational and indeed has to be rational; a divine will rules supreme and is strong enough to determine the overall content.'[8] According to Hegel, only the West has been endowed with reason and thus is in the driver's seat as part of God's plan. Hegel sees the rational West as destined to be the central agent of history – like the engine of a train. Others are relegated to the past; their day is over, and so they are excluded from the future.

The Spirit is thus explicitly Western. Other cultures are either thrown away in history's dustbin, if they belong in history at all, or forced to emulate the West. Otherwise, they are trampled. World history and philosophy are seen as one single development, and the World Spirit is a single progressive movement in a linear trajectory.

Hegel has a peculiarly phobic and blind reaction to Asia in general and India in particular. He laboriously criticizes Sanskrit and Indian civilization, arguing with European Indologists with the aim of assimilating some ideas (such as absolute idealism) into his own philosophy while postulating India as the inferior other in order to construct his theory of the West. Asia's place in history is as an infant, whereas the West is mature and everyone's eventual destination.

Colonialism and Racism Justified

Hegel's linear theory of history became popular as a justification for Western colonial exploitation in the name of facilitating the progress of history. But Hegel takes the idea even further and says that for history to proceed, any act committed by the Europeans, no matter how reprehensible, is justifiable in the name of human evolution. He writes:

> Because history is the configuration of the Spirit in the form of events, the people which receives the Spirit as its natural principle ... is the one that dominates in that epoch of world history ... Against the absolute right of that people who actually are the carriers of the world Spirit, the spirit of other peoples has no other right.[9]

Colonization is thus desirable as the teleological imperative by which the superior Europeans must appropriate others. He continues:

> [S]uch a society [i.e., the West] is driven to look *beyond* itself to new consumers. Therefore it seeks its means of subsistence among other peoples which are inferior to it with respect to the resources which it has in excess, such as those of industry. This expansion of relations also makes possible that colonization to which, under systematic or sporadic form, a fully established civil society is impelled.[10]

All non-Europeans, then, are mere objects in European hands. When applying his theories to Africans, Hegel arrives at the following blatantly racist conclusions: 'It is characteristic of the blacks that their consciousness has not yet even arrived at the intuition of any objectivity, as for example, of God or the law, in which humanity relates to the world and intuits its essence ... He [the black person] is a human being in the rough.'[11]

Hegel argues it is better for Africans to remain enslaved until they pass through a process of maturation that *culminates* in their total conversion to Christianity. He says further of Africans: 'Slavery is unjust, in and for itself, for the essence of man is freedom, but he must first become mature before he can become free. Thus it is more fitting and correct that slavery should be eliminated gradually than that it should be done away with at once.' Hegel concludes his discussion on Africa with the comment, 'at this point we leave Africa, not to mention it again. For it is no historical part of the World; it has no movement or development to exhibit.'

India: Frozen Without a History

In 1828, Schlegel had already been claiming that 'Indians have no regular histories, no works of real historical science ... [All] their conceptions of human affairs and events are exclusively mythological.'[12] Two years later, Hegel himself expressed a similar view and famously described India as a land without history – in the sense of not having its own capacity to 'make history' in a conscious fashion. India, in Hegel's view, has been acted upon by world-historical actors rather than having acted herself. 'Dreams', not 'historical truth', are the natural condition and product of the Indian mind, he says.[13]

The Western spirit, conversely, is free and acting upon this freedom. For this reason, the West has superseded the East, and the relationship between them is naturally one of subordination. What the West can learn from studying India is to remind itself what it should avoid and what it must leave behind – *not* what it might adopt. He writes that it is foolish for westerners to glorify or idealize ancient India.[14]

Hegel's India is a realm of 'phantasy and sensibility'[15] that has something 'pusillanimous and effeminate' about it.[16] The Hindu lacks any sense of the 'morality involved in respect for human life',[17] and the Brahmin, in particular, has 'no conscience with respect to truth'.[18] He proffers that Indians are lost in other-worldly infinity and have not yet discovered the true nature of the finite and the particular. The Indian mind is lost in abstraction and chaos, lacking a clear sense of individuality and individual freedom. Such a society is suppressive with extremes of religiosity and wild sensuality. Therefore, India is stuck in infancy, arrested in development and incapable of maturing on its own.

Historical progress is impossible, because Indian mysticism is escapist – going backwards to the unity of Brahman – whereas the Western spirit is progressing forward to higher states of manifestation. Hegel rejects reincarnation as a crude notion leading yogis to indulge in extreme asceticism that reminds him of medieval Europeans. He finds yoga to be neither an extroverted immersion into an object, as in appreciating art or investigating something empirically, nor an inward immersion into one's personal concreteness; rather, it is an 'abstract devotion' that exemplifies what he regards as a 'negative' outlook. Moksha, he feels, is an abstract and negative liberation.

In his *Lectures on the History of Philosophy*, Hegel states that he has lost respect for Indians, because they lack coherence and are incapable of history:

> If we had formerly the satisfaction of believing in the antiquity of the Indian wisdom and holding it in respect, we now have ascertained through being acquainted with the great astronomical works of the Indians, the inaccuracy of all figures quoted. Nothing can be more confused, nothing more imperfect than the chronology of the Indians; no people which attained to culture in astronomy, mathematics, etc., is as incapable for history; in it they have neither stability nor coherence.[19]

Hegel regards colonization as India's inevitable fate: 'The British, or rather the East India Company, are the masters of India because it is the fatal destiny of Asian empires to subject themselves to the Europeans.'[20]

India, therefore, was declared 'static' and incapable of progress by itself, and it was up to the West to colonize and 'operate' on her as a doctor would on a patient – for the latter's own benefit. This view mirrored that of European colonization, which was at its peak during Hegel's time. Europe was powerful and could assert chauvinistic claims of its moral and intellectual superiority over everyone else. In all his statements about India, Hegel proudly presents himself as a 'son of the European soil'.

As the Indologist Wilhelm Halbfass (1940–2000) explains, 'Hegel had no adequate knowledge of the systematic complexity and historical variability of classical Indian thought.' Hegel was not well-versed in Sanskrit, and his polemical use of Indian culture was entirely speculative, based on his own idiosyncrasies and the specific needs of the time. He did not seem concerned about empirical validity, relying instead on wild abstractions that often made India look like a caricature.[21] All through his career, he dealt with Indian philosophy in a pejorative manner, regarding it as subordinate to European thought.

Halbfass goes on to explain how Hegel defined the course of philosophy in such a way that the Orient got bypassed:

> Hegel does provide us with an example of a very serious and comprehensive discussion of Indian thought. Yet his historical segregation of philosophy from religion, his devaluation of any form of yearning for a lost unity, and his conviction that Europe, by unfolding the 'actual,' 'real' philosophy committed to the spirit of free science, had essentially surpassed the Orient, instead contributed to a restricted use of the concept of philosophy and to a self-limitation in the historiography of philosophy.[22]

Hegel's perception of India as stagnant and lacking a history was perpetuated by Karl Marx, who described India as caught in the 'Asiatic Mode of Production'. He posited that the country was trapped in a stagnant economic state in which 'Oriental despots' wielded absolute power and governed unchanging, stratified villages. His analysis betrayed a serious ignorance of the actual economic history of India. In a series of articles written for a US newspaper, he incorrectly concluded:

> Indian society has no history at all, at least no known history. What we call its history, is but the history of the successive intruders who founded

their empires on the basis of that unresisting and unchanging society ...
From the Indian natives, reluctantly and sparingly educated at Calcutta,
under English superintendence, a fresh class is springing up, endowed
with the requirements for government and imbued with European
science. Steam has brought India into regular and rapid communication
with Europe, has connected its chief ports with the whole south-eastern
ocean, and has re-vindicated it from the isolated position which was the
prime law of its stagnation.[23]

Indian historian Ranajit Guha explains how such a segregationist view,
based on who has history and reason and who does not, served to justify
colonial rule:

The past of the 'historyless' people they had conquered proved to be
extremely useful in their attempt to convert conquest into rulership. The
East India Company's fiscal system, judicial institutions, administrative
apparatus – cardinal and formative aspects of the colonial state – relied
heavily on that past as the primary source of information required to
formulate rules and set up structures for governance. Prehistory was, in
this case, the clay used by the regime to put itself in shape. But it also
provided colonialism with space to install its own versions of the Indian
past, converting the latter into material for its edifices of colonialist
knowledge. It is thus that the 'peoples without history' in the subcontinent
got history as their reward for subjugation to civilized Europe and World-
history, just as elsewhere in realms un-redeemably sunken in Prehistory,
the colonized lacking in footwear and faith, got shoes and the Bible.[24]

Guha goes on to say:

One of the most outstanding achievements of British power in the East
was indeed the production and propagation of colonialist historiography.
It was cultivated on Prehistory's vacant plots. What was sown for seed
came directly out of post-Enlightenment European and particularly
English historical literature packaged for use in Indian schools and
universities. The product was history written by Indians themselves in
faithful imitation of the Western statist model.[25]

The humiliation and devastation of this process cannot be
overstressed:

The excluded are not ethnic or geographical abstractions. They make up the greater part of humanity with its cultures, literatures, religions, philosophies, and so forth. The philosopher goes through the lot systematically to dig them out one by one and tip them into the wastelands of Prehistory. What is discarded is not only the pasts these so-called historyless people live by in their everyday existence but also the modes adopted by their languages to integrate these pasts in the prose of their respective worlds. In this way World-history has promoted the dominance of one particular genre of historical narrative over all the others.[26]

Contesting 'Western Freedom'

Many times in his career, Hegel addressed the question of whether the arts, literature, philosophy and languages of India and China entitled these civilizations to a place in his scheme of world history, and every time he emphatically concluded that they do not. India and China, he writes,

> are lacking – indeed completely lacking – in the essential self-consciousness of the concept of freedom ... And in the Indian doctrine of renunciation of sensuality, desires, and all earthly interests, positive ethical freedom is not the goal and end, but rather the extinction of consciousness and the suspension of spiritual and even physical life.[27]

Hegel praises Greek poetry, because it depicts 'freedom of independent individuality', unlike India's Ramayana and Mahabharata, which, he believes, are inclined to 'abandon the higher demands of freedom and ethical life'.[28] This idea or condition of freedom is decisive for him and is linked to the West's being Christian. He writes that 'in the Christian age, the divine spirit has come into the world and taken up its abode in the individual, who is now completely free and endowed with substantial freedom.'[29]

Guha points out that Hegel marginalizes India and China at the same time that he praises the slave societies of ancient Greece, Rome, medieval Europe and America. It is telling that Hegel sees the East India Company's oppressive rule as 'the true valor of civilized nations' and as 'sacrifice in the service of the state'.[30]

In fact, though Hegel did not see it this way, there are many aspects of Christianity that do not accord with individual freedom, including the insistence on obedience to established and communal forms of religion. Furthermore, the role of the Church in salvation at the End Times is an obstacle to individual spiritual freedom. Contrast this with the emphasis on Indian inner science and the freedom of the individual. Two signature features of dharma traditions are unbounded freedom in choosing a path and lack of any imposed theological dogma or ecclesiastical or political authority. Such traditions cannot be dismissed as less free and individualistic than those of the West. Do not figures such as Buddha, Ashoka, and Gandhi exemplify autonomous individuals bringing revolutionary historical and intellectual change?

The notion of individualism that has emerged in the West is a relatively recent development even though it is often claimed to be derived from classical antiquity and Abrahamic theological tenets. This revisionist claim of being the exclusive and defining feature of the West – in contradistinction to the putative Oriental lack of individuality – is the result of myth-making.

German Supremacy Is Born

The very notion of a distinct West is relatively recent in history, prior to which the English, Irish, Germans, Italians, Greeks and Spaniards all saw themselves as distinct cultures mired in conflicts with each other and *not* as parts of a cohesive European civilization. Hegel ignores the fact that the West is made possible only by the rest of the world on which its very construction and sustenance depend. We also see in his work the struggle to construct a synthetic unity called 'West' out of a disparate set of cultures – not only Greek, Roman, and Israelite, but also French, German, British, Spanish, and so on.

While the West is pure, according to Hegel, some westerners are purer than others. Germany has a special destiny and Christianity is at its heart. Hegel writes: 'The Germanic Spirit *(germanische Geist)* is the Spirit of the New World *(neuen Welt)*,whose end is the realization of the absolute truth… The destiny of the Germanic peoples is that of serving as the bearer of the Christian principle.'[31]

Hegel sees the digestion of Indian civilization into Western categories as both natural and desirable. As Halbfass explains: 'The question of an adequate standpoint [i.e., epistemology] for the evaluation and comparison of different cultural traditions has been decided by the course of history itself, and it has been decided in favor of Europe. European thought has to provide the context and categories for the exploration of all traditions of thought.'[32]

This explains why Hegel opposed comparative philosophy, comparative religion, and any attempts at neutral or reciprocal understanding across the cultures; instead, European thought contains all other traditions within its structures and is the only means for integrating knowledge. Furthermore, other civilizations are rendered obsolete and redundant: the West simply assimilates or devours whatever good it 'discovers' in them. Hegel legitimizes appropriations from other 'inferior' cultures into the 'superior' West as a part of the advancement of the World Spirit.

After Hegel's death, his sweeping Eurocentric account of history and destiny was further extrapolated, culminating in the development of the Aryan identity. The term 'arya' in traditional Indian usage connotes an ethical or spiritual quality, not race, as evidenced by its frequent usage in early Buddhist texts where it clearly has an exclusively ethical and religious significance.[33] This meaning is ubiquitous in all its native contexts. The examples cited above from Buddhist sources are wholly typical and reflect an early and representative stage of the occurrence of the term. In the Bhagavadgita (2.2), Sri Krishna uses the term without implying race. The construction and invention of an Aryan race started as the theory of the mythic Indian Aryans who were Germany's ancestors and was then revised in such a way that the Germans became the Aryans themselves. Subsequently, this Aryan identity was assumed by Europeans more broadly on the basis of misapplied comparative philology. The importance of this academic fabrication cannot be overstated given that it led to Nazism in Europe and to Dravidianism in colonial India.[34]

Summary Diagram

The diagram that follows summarizes the various forces at work in the European encounter with India – both pro-India and anti-India. The left side shows the rivalries among the European identities discussed earlier. The right side shows that – at the same time that these internal rivalries occurred – there was a sense of pan-European superiority over the other races, which in turn led to genocide of Native Americans and enslavement of Africans. There had always been a demand for theories to justify this superiority and oppression over others. The lower box in the diagram shows how the Romantic movement became a sort of countercultural fashion in Europe as a reaction against the dominance of Enlightenment ideologies and the Church. Romanticism was fuelled in part by a desire to return to an idealized past when God, man and nature were in harmony. There was a search for humanity's innocent roots, often based on the popular premise that history was being guided by God who could be understood only through Christian revelation.

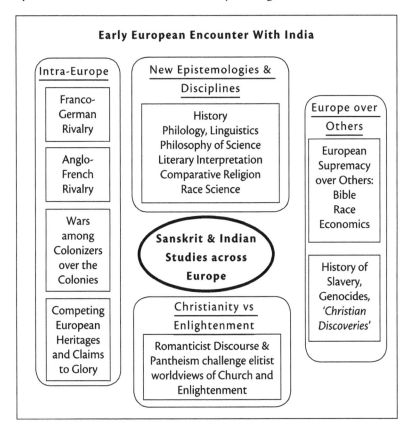

The box in the middle at the top shows how a range of disciplines and epistemologies evolved to deal with the encounter with Sanskrit.

Hegel's Legacy and Indian Civilization

Hegel was not alone in characterizing Indian thought as other-worldly. The early Romantics in the West glorified India's mystical and transcendental thought – seeing it as a rejection of materialism. The impression that Indians were escapist and unconcerned with the individual got reinforced not merely by prominent Western thinkers but also by Indian scholars who started to essentialize the mystical and transcendental in their exposition of Indian philosophy. There emerged, then, an unduly lopsided emphasis on the 'religious' nature of Indian thought. This in turn created the indelible impression among westerners that India's philosophical systems were theoretically underdeveloped as a result of her preponderant religious orientation.[35] Today, many Indian intellectuals adopt this as their own framework.[36]

Hegelian views concerning India's lack of history are at the root of much of the past dismissal of India and things Indian, and they shape attitudes towards India even today. The departments of philosophy at many Indian universities are based on Hegelian ideas and their derivatives. Once it is established in the minds of an oppressed people that they have no history of their own apart from what has been gifted to them by the oppressors, the history as written by the oppressors becomes legitimized and even glorified. Many Indians are still in the shadow of Lord Macaulay, whose notorious views on Indian culture shaped the British colonial mentality for generations. Such Indians are grateful to the colonialists for having given them a sense of history, which they are programmed to believe they lacked prior to Western rule.

The legacy of Hegel is that he blinded the West to the parochialism of its supposed 'universals' and hence consolidated the discourse on what was wrong about India. Hegel captures all cultures in his boxed-in categories of past/present, high/low, great/small. This is Reason's march forward to the realization of the Absolute in the temporal state. The degree to which Western scholarship has been influenced by his linear theory of history (including many Marxist and humanist accounts of history and the various philosophies built on such accounts) is truly amazing. His views found wide acceptance across the West and reshaped attitudes towards India.[37]

Hegel's theory of history has led to liberal Western supremacy, which hides behind the notion of providing the 'universals'. These European Enlightenment presuppositions became incorporated in the confluence of academic philosophy, philology, social theories and 'scientific' methodologies – all of which were driven by various imperial and colonial values alongside Christian theology.

These influences, then, informed Indology, and they haunt South Asian Studies today.

Common Responses to Western Universalism

Three common responses to Western universalist claims are frequently put forward. One primarily addresses the Judeo-Christian religious base of those claims while another addresses the philosophical claims. The first, discussed below, advocates secularism as the solution, i.e., the view that these interreligious issues can be resolved by avoiding reference to religion or even eliminating religious cultures from the public sphere. The second response, also discussed below, advocates a postcolonial deconstruction of all grand narratives of the kind I have discussed. The third is an escape from difference anxiety by positing that all traditions are the same or have trivial differences. All three approaches are flawed and unfortunately have been re-exported back to India in problematic forms.[38]

Western Secularism: Christianity's Double

The secular model of Western universalism is part of the artificial synthetic unity of Western civilization. The Abrahamic-messianic drive to create a materialist utopia at the end of history was met with a Marxist attack on religion. The resulting secularism implicitly includes Judeo-Christian themes and hence is not neutral with respect to the various world religions. It is riddled with Western assumptions and values about the nature of the cosmos, human identity and difference.

The whole concept of secularism itself arose from and applies primarily to societies in which religions are history-centric, politically established, expansionist, and in tension with science. This is a profoundly Western solution to a profoundly Western problem. Dharmic traditions do not have these issues since they are not history-centric and do not engage in proselytizing, nor are they threatened by scientific discoveries. Thus, secularism does not go to the root of the problem and merely offers Western ideas in a new garb.

This denatured and dry secularism, which reduces to ashes much of the richness of spiritual culture, has begun to meet with resistance. American secularists see themselves as having resolved the issues concerning Western hegemony by acknowledging and rejecting the conservative aspect of their historical religious identity and by claiming to have moved on from it. But have they? While American liberalism embraces economic and racial egalitarianism, the common requirement for religious liberalism is mere tolerance as opposed to genuine mutual respect. The idea of tolerance has become popular, but tolerance – as discussed in Chapter 1 – is a patronizing attitude and implies a position of superiority. Many liberal leaders – Hillary Clinton and Jimmy Carter, for example – are deeply Christian and yet fully aware that the core of Christianity demands exclusivity. The contradiction between Christian exclusivism and true liberalism is seldom discussed openly (and perhaps even privately).

Every American politician (right up to and including Barack Obama) must proclaim that he or she is a good Christian in order to get votes. American secular liberalism has yet to achieve genuine pluralism on the ground. It merely means that the institutions of state shall not interfere with religions, but it is worth asking whether the leaders can actually leave behind their chauvinism and exclusivism when they leave their pews and function as public officials. Christians can become true liberals only when they acknowledge and negotiate the exclusivity claims that limit them to mere tolerance and when they learn to respect and even support other faiths.

The division between secular and religious worldviews took on its prominent modern form following the French Revolution. The Catholic Church had come to be associated with the aristocracy and bourgeois conservatism, while the values of 'liberty, equality and fraternity' were thought to arise from reason alone. Reason became a tool used by liberal intellectuals against several powerful regimes, including the British Empire and the Russian monarchy.

There were efforts to construct a new and wholly artificial synthesis between religion and reason, complete with festivals and symbols. These efforts quickly collapsed, but they left a violent legacy of struggles for hegemony between Catholicism and the secular state all over Europe and the Americas. The détente between Catholicism and the secular state took many generations to achieve and never did arrive at any integral unity; rather, it was achieved by separating church and state – a principle that the American Founding Fathers advocated. It was not until Vatican II, in the 1960s, that the Catholic Church formally accepted this separation in principle.

The result was more of a political stalemate and ceasefire than a true unity. By no means did this solve the underlying problems of a divided and torn cosmology and philosophy. During the late nineteenth and into the twentieth century, Europe's greatest and most influential thinkers, Darwin, Marx and Freud, were taken to be complete secularists, while Christian theology steadily declined in intellectual prestige. Still, Christianity would not go away; it went underground only to come back in a virulent fundamentalist form, and the uneasy truce between the secular state and the religious right continues to destabilize American politics to this day.

While Christianity resists compromising its core history-centric mandates for the sake of science, many Jewish and Christian beliefs and assumptions have continued to structure this secular discourse.[39] This conflict-ridden science/religion substrate is illustrated by the curious mixture of secularism with biblical myth or superstition in the works of many famous secular Western thinkers – both in science and in philosophy. This aspect of their work is often excluded in secular discussions, but we need to retrieve these contradictions to uncover how important biblical discourse still is to Western secularism.

For instance, Francis Bacon – considered the prophet of modern Western science – sought 'a return to the state of Adam before the Fall, a state of pure and sinless contact with nature and knowledge of her powers ... a progress back to Adam'.[40] Isaac Newton was a fervent believer in the millennium and spent much of his time interpreting biblical prophecy. Thomas Hobbes's state of nature is a secularized version of John Calvin's 'natural man' without mention of God, and – in Hobbes's *Leviathan* – the Bible is cited 657 times, and there is a similar trend in his other major political works.[41] Many European socialist critiques of private property originated in interpretations of Adam's fall and God's curse upon him. Locke's theory of individual rights is rooted in the Protestant understanding of humanity's relationship with God. The unique civic society of the USA evolved out of the Puritan ambitions to create another empire for God in a new Promised Land by strict laws and suppression of dissent and by subsequent secularist reaction against them. Even Marxism, while attacking Western religion, implicitly borrowed its underlying structures and grand narrative, and these have become unstated assumptions in the secular worldview.[42]

Indian Pseudo-secularism

Another version of secularism as a way to cope with religious violence comes from Western-educated (and often Western-sponsored) Indian elites. These intellectuals denounce the dharmic point of view without adequately understanding it. They are ready to catalogue the abuses of traditional Indian society and culture (and there are, of course, legitimate concerns here) and often to collude with views that India has nothing positive to offer the world. For them, the recommended way forward for Indians is to mimic Western values and practices.

India's secularism was imported from the West, where religions are exclusivist and heavily institutionalized, but the history and circumstances of Indian society are vastly different. In India, secularism is set up to counteract communalism, whereas in Europe secularism was meant to counteract the institutional establishment of the Church.

Gandhi advocated invigorating the traditional dharmic society after India's independence. Nehru disagreed and wanted India to follow in the footsteps of the West. In this struggle for India's soul, Nehru prevailed. There occurred a shift away from Gandhi's vision of a decentralized traditional society in favour of a Nehruvian socialism that modelled itself after England and the Soviet Union.

In 1977, Prime Minister Indira Gandhi introduced an amendment to the Constitution of India whereby the word 'secular' was formally enshrined into the Preamble. The late L.M. Singhvi, who served as a consultant, refused to sign the Hindi version of the draft that translated 'secular' as 'dharma-nirapeksha' (literally meaning indifferent on dharma). Since dharma is a foundation of society, he said, the correct Hindi translation of 'secular' should be 'pantha-nirapeksha' (i.e., neutral or indifferent with reference to organized sect). Indira Gandhi agreed and (according to one anecdote) handed her pen to him, whereupon Singhvi made the correction on the final draft which is now deposited in the Rashtrapati Bhavan. This means that the government shall be neutral and even indifferent to *organized* religions. Indian academics, intellectuals, media personnel and politicians dismissed the fine and correct distinction on which Singhvi had insisted.

The two Sanskrit words with opposing meanings, nirapeksha and sapeksha, are non-translatable and important for understanding the dharmic approach to pluralism. They are introduced below:

- Nirapeksha relates to passivity and immobility where there is no effort, wish, expectation or any turn to action; it means indifference. Using pantha as the equivalent of organized religion, secularism could be stated as pantha-nirapekshata. It is the government's attitude of indifference and neutrality towards all religions and the attitude of tolerance among the various religions.
- Sapeksha literally means 'with expectation of reciprocity and mutual respect'.[43] It facilitates the principle of bandhuta (discussed in Chapter 3) in the sense of inter-subjectivity, solidarity and fraternity across paths and identities. It means unity in diversity to the extent of mutual cooperation and even mutual dependency. It is the ethos of what might be called 'positive secularism' rather than tolerance and indifference from a position of implied superiority.

Dharma itself is much more general than any sampradaya or organized religion, though it may underlie them. Among other things, it does not require membership or a particular creedal affirmation in the Christian sense; nor does it threaten freedom of thought, scientific inquiry, or the beliefs and traditions of those who do not share its understanding. I have explored its fluidity and contextual quality in Chapter 4. It is impossible to uncouple dharma from the ethics of the body, family, community, animals, nature and the cosmos at large. As we shall see, to remove dharma from the public sphere, in the Indian context, means removing its rich seedbed of cultural and spiritual resources as well.[44]

Given the mistranslation of dharma as religion (explained in Chapter 5), the Western idea of no religion in the public square has been interpreted by many Indians as no dharma in the public square. Secularized Indians have failed to appreciate that a dharma-nirapeksha society – or a society lacking dharma (as secularism has often been translated) – would be dangerously ambivalent toward ethical conduct. Nirad Chaudhuri warned against India's adopting secularism of even the highest European type, because without dharma's moral and spiritual qualities, society would become immoral and culturally debased.[45] Being irreligious still allows for ethical behaviour, but being un-dharmic equates with things like corruption and abuse. The result of importing secularism into a dharmic society has thus been disastrous in many ways.

The Western model has also been entirely misconceived by most Indian elites and political leaders. Take, for instance, the idea of separation of church and state in the United States Constitution. The Founding Fathers who drafted this document did not envision a society without religion, whether in public or private, but rather one in which many different kinds of religious expression would flourish. They would do so without state intervention or direct support, yes, but also without state regulation or suppression. The personal views of these leaders ranged from conservative to liberal. (Thomas Jefferson was deeply suspicious of Christian exclusivism and espoused a kind of perennial philosophy.) They were agreed, however, that a good society had a profoundly spiritual basis and that creed and conscience in some form were vital to the life of a democracy.

India's copycat secularism differs from American secularism in critical ways. Many American Jews and Christians publicly assert their faiths as part of what it means to be American and do not see this assertion as contradicting secularism. Indian secularism has attempted to dilute differences, seeing them as a source of tension and problems, but these interventions have sometimes had the opposite effect and made some religious identities more assertive in order to preserve their distinctiveness and thus prevent getting digested.

Postcolonial Critique

In recent years, postcolonialists, following their postmodern colleagues such as Jacques Derrida, have made many attempts to deconstruct the West's philosophical universalism. Their efforts, however, generally end in nihilism, because they do not, or cannot, escape from fundamental presuppositions such as the split between the sacred and the secular. In deconstructing grand narratives, postmodernism has ignored that it implicitly rests upon the grand narrative of secularism. Dharma philosophies and religions do not share this extreme investment in secularism and have resolved many of the dilemmas Western philosophy has encountered as a result. Postmodern philosophers, while softening on the sacred/secular split of late, have not (with a few major exceptions) been able to bring themselves to follow these dharmic approaches. That is because they stop at exactly the point where Western cosmology would have to be fundamentally abandoned.

Postcolonial scholars like to draw on their Indian identities when this gives them credibility as spokespersons, and they have indeed written devastating critiques of the West. Some have gone further and even criticized the colonized minds of Indians who have assimilated the Western categories of thinking and forgotten their own categories in the process. Hegel's project, for instance, has been thoroughly deconstructed and discredited in postmodern philosophy and postcolonial studies – and often with a good understanding of what is at stake politically and culturally.

The problem is that even these deconstructive and socially progressive analyses take place within the terms of the Western tradition from whence the problem stems in the first place. As we have seen, the postmodern critique often ends in nihilism, because it is unable to philosophize constructively. Yet there is, among these philosophers, a dim recognition that in the sophistication and dialogic character of dharmic philosophies lies the potential for a resolution to apparently insoluble problems, and several have tried to seize this potential. With a few exceptions, however, they fall short – partly because of the profound split between the sacred and the secular instilled in them and partly because they lack (and often resist) the techniques of inner science and embodied knowing that might carry them past their impasse.

Furthermore, though this is not the intention, the result of these critiques is often similar to the 'sameness' response (see below) – the difference being that, unlike spiritual sameness, here the end-state is one of indifference. In other words, after deconstructing the philosophical meta-narratives of the dominant culture, nothing is left to put in their place, whereas in true purva paksha, the dharmic notions of selfhood grounded in spirituality and religion would provide the foundation for a positive existence. This fall into nihilism, indifference and apathy happens because the crucial potential of the dharmic traditions for challenging these Western assumptions is usually under-appreciated.

Additionally, many of these Indian scholars rely directly or indirectly on Western academic institutions, publishing houses, or funding sources. In other words, they can serve as 'useful pets' of the West by supplying a measured amount of criticism and knowing where to draw the line, or else by reproducing Western self-criticisms supplied by their Western mentors.

When it comes to Hinduism specifically, they hold that tradition in considerable disdain, often relying blindly on the assumptions of the same colonial enterprise they seek to undermine. I am unaware of any of the scholars in the area of postmodernism and postcolonialism having studied Sanskrit and the dharmic theories known as siddhanta as the base for their critiques of the West. I am not the first to have criticized this group. Ronald Inden notes that such scholars have turned themselves into neocolonialists by their subconscious use of colonial assumptions in conceiving of the dharma traditions. He claims that such Indian intellectuals

> have a tendency to recuperate the older colonialist imaginings of India. Representations of the systematic mistreatment of women (patriarchy),

the exploitation of the young (child labor), domination by a parasitic Brahman caste of Aryan descent, discrimination by castes (untouchability), and the triumphalism of an atavistic Hinduism reiterate the earlier images of India as an inherently and uniquely divided and oppressive place.[46]

S.N. Balagangadhara has explained this syndrome as follows: 'These Indian scholars have to present themselves as those who remind the whites of white-guilt, and, hence, giving them a job in the academy is seen as redemption for past sins. But, as a non-Westerner, the postcolonial cannot be the West's equal.'[47]

Inspired by Western secularism, these postcolonialists have failed to undertake a fresh examination of dharma traditions and their current relevance; instead, they have imitated Western theories from the humanities and projected these onto a profoundly different tradition. Sanskrit and local vernaculars have been subverted and are now virtually extinct in some cases, because the English language and Western literature are the route to progress. Progress is sometimes defined in opposition to tradition, and those advocating tradition are often branded as puritans or fundamentalists. Many Indian scholars, following in the footsteps of westerners, have essentialized the dharmic traditions into stereotypes that I have called 'caste, cows and curry'.

There are the two kinds of Indian critiques claiming to reverse the colonial influence, and each suffers in its own way. They are summarized in the table that follows. The top left box shows the Western studies of India, into which a large number of Indian scholars have been appropriated.[48] The top right box shows those who make valuable contributions by using dharmic terms of reference to study India; however, they fail to 'gaze back' at the West using these dharmic terms – or at least not with sufficient force to make a difference. The bottom left box refers to those scholars who lash out against the West but who lack training in the use of dharmic categories and who moreover are largely dependent on the West for their careers.

More work is required to cover the material in the bottom right box, and the goal of this book is to make a contribution to that space.

	Use Western Categories	Use Dharmic Categories
Gaze at Indian Civilization	Much of colonial Indology and humanities in today's South Asian Studies.	Inden, Marriott, Ramanujan tried to champion the use of dharmic categories, but they worked within the Western system.
Gaze at Western Civilization	Postcolonialist Indian scholars who attack the West but are unwilling to stand on dharmic foundations, which they disdain.	Very rare – my goal

Naive Spiritual Sameness

Another poor response to the problem of Western universalism has been to argue that there is an underlying sameness to which all cultures and religions can appeal and that this will ensure harmony and equitable unity. This might be true if some of the religions in question did not inherently rest on exclusive claims to truth, but they do. Implicitly, Western thought and values get characterized as universal essences.

Many Indian gurus and other cultural ambassadors are responsible for promoting this view, as the misguided fashion is to focus on similarities (typically using Western universals as the common framework) and avoid what is different. It is a major crisis today that the generic replaces the particular in the way people think. There are two reasons for this: the generic evades issues of difference, and ignorance can hide behind generic statements. The failure to appreciate the size and scope of what might be called 'the dharmic difference' in the unfolding of civilizational encounters is partly due to this key misapprehension. Owing to the dharmic 'freedom from history' and its insistence on an underlying integral unity, many have been led to believe that dharma is, at base, 'teaching the same thing' as either the Abrahamic traditions or secular cognitive science or both. 'All is one,' they say, when it comes to different religious paths or visions of reality. 'What then is the problem?' And yet, these very promoters of a superficial sameness are, unbeknownst to themselves, assenting to worldviews and propositions that are simply not compatible. We have already seen how this appeal to 'sameness' is a dangerous form of denial which leaves the weaker of the various cultures wide open to aggressive digestion.

Confronted by differences, Indians often invoke familiar slogans like 'unity in diversity' or the Sanskrit phrase 'Vasudhaiva kutumbakam' (meaning 'the whole world is one family'). But a family never consists of identical individuals. One's mother, father, grandparents, brother, sister, etc., are all different persons with whom one has different relationships. Nor are all personality types in the family identical. In fact, most families also have members with negative qualities who need to be reprimanded. If anything, the family metaphor is about mutual respect for internal diversity, not for sameness.

Dharmic scholars have not developed the theoretical tools necessary to do purva paksha vis-à-vis other traditions – at least not with the same rigour with which it was done in classical times. This weakness is also linked to the fear of difference. There is an overemphasis on 'nivritti' (negation, renunciation, inaction) and marginalization of 'pravitti' (positive action, righteous worldly living). The leaders are poorly trained in communication skills, competitive analysis and strategic thinking. An overabundance of contextual freedom has turned into irresponsibility, escapism and ineptitude. Tragically, the absence of a historical canon and centralized authority, combined with reliance on embodied exemplars of adhyatma-vidya, could prove to be too idealistic in today's world, i.e., ineffectual in safeguarding the community.

As a result of these deficiencies, the guru's understanding of Western students tends to be confined to their emotional and mental states with insufficient attention paid to their identities as westerners or to any other historical and cultural influences. Hence, gurus deal with such generic psychological issues as anger, fear, desires, habits, and so forth. But there is little appreciation on the part of either the teacher or the student of deeper problems which pertain specifically to Western conditioning. Most westerners were raised and educated in such a way as to emphasize their own civilization, i.e., the Founding Fathers, Manifest Destiny, and their unique place in the world. For the student to deny or minimize these embedded attitudes and presuppositions during his interaction with the guru may be expedient and politically correct in the short term, but the long-term result is often a great deal of misunderstanding. (The onus for confronting these attitudes and presuppositions rests also on the guru.)

Conclusion: Purva Paksha and the Way Forward

'In the Mahabharata, the ceremony for the oath of a new king includes the admonition: 'Be like a garland-maker, O king, and not like a charcoal burner.' This is essentially a call for dharma-sapeksata. The garland is a metaphor for dharmic diversity in which flowers of many colors and forms are strung harmoniously for the most pleasing effect, and it symbolizes social coherence. By contrast, charcoal is a metaphor for reducing the diversity into homogeneity, burning it into lifeless ashes.'

Purva Paksha and Sapeksha Dharma

The preceding chapters have dealt with some major differences between the West and India. I have argued that these differences only come to light through a committed practice of purva paksha, or direct mutual engagement. The question that arises is: how can purva paksha contribute to the establishment of a harmonious approach to social and spiritual growth today, and on what basis can it be fairly and effectively pursued?

Here I suggest that we look to dharma for guidance, in particular to the central story told in the Bhagavadgita. In that story, the hero, Arjuna, is confronted by the mandate to advance on the battlefield, or Kurukshetra, as it is called. He balks at first, wishing to retreat from confrontation because he fears a war will do more harm than good. It takes much persuasion from Krishna, his charioteer, to get him to advance. The field before him, vast, open and visible from all directions, seems to array one side of the human family against the other and to involve the devastation of much that both hold dear. But in fact, as Krishna reveals, nothing can be lost here except illusion. Arjuna can only see this, however, by taking a stance that involves risk and a willingness to sacrifice ego in the service of dharma.

Taking this risk requires a profound understanding of the issues at stake: Arjuna is not simply fighting for his side but for justice and the broader establishment of dharma, one that is in line with the ritam (inherent nature) of the cosmos. The kingdom for which he must fight is rightfully his, as many of his adversaries acknowledge. The adversaries' fight is not due to any righteousness in their cause but to ignorance, attachment and greed. Furthermore, Arjuna is not attempting to aggrandize his own power and ego. He has already perfected himself in yoga over many years and trials and has come to a place where he can surrender these to Krishna. Nor is his course of action imposed on him from without. Rather, he is called to this engagement by his own nature and social obligations – his particular sva-dharma. In other words, it is his *duty* to engage, whereas it might not be the same for others with a different calling.

Extrapolating from this story – which is far more profound and multifaceted than can be explained here – we can deduce a few requirements and rules of engagement for effective purva paksha. For instance:

1. It must take place on a level playing field with the conditions, time and place of engagement set by mutual agreement. In other words, a genuine encounter cannot happen only under the aegis of Western institutions, using Western criteria, covered by Western media biases and conducted by protagonists who are cherry-picked by westerners.

2. The intention of the participants must not be to 'convert' each other or, conversely, sugar-coat and hence camouflage fundamental differences. The intention must be to pursue the truth.

3. The outcome of such a metaphorical duel probably cannot always be 'win-win' at the ego level. Many cherished projects and assumptions will have to be relinquished.

4. Prior to engagement, a preliminary mastery of the ego through the serious practice of adhyatma-vidya is necessary.

5. In addition to their spiritual credentials, the defenders of dharma need to be deeply informed about, and well-versed in, the traditions and theology of their opponents. Likewise, those representing the Western religions must be open to the possibility of dharma as a serious alternative to their own tradition and worldview.

This book offers an introduction to the kind of work required for this preparation. Perhaps the best public framework for such an encounter is sapeksha-dharma (discussed in Chapter 6). Sapekshata (the quality of sapeksha-dharma) itself, we remember, literally means engagement 'with reciprocity and mutual respect'. Such a framework is consistent with the principle of bandhuta in the sense of inter-subjectivity, solidarity and fraternity across paths and identities. It means unity in diversity to the extent of mutual cooperation, and even mutual dependency. This framework is the ethos of what might be called 'positive pluralism' rather than mere tolerance or indifference emanating from a position of assumed superiority.

Sapekshata stems from a belief in integral unity, which is to say that in this view difference and underlying unity are not mutually contradictory. Its opposite, nirapekshata, is closer to what the West defines as secularism, which is only a palliative developed to prevent conflicts arising from a tentative and tenuous stalemate. Secularism does not foster pan-humanness across all boundaries beyond offering the promise of material equality, and not even *that* promise has ever been realized. Sometimes, secularism is even used to promulgate divisiveness. And yet it has attained a lofty place among intellectuals.

Sapekshata is not simply a negative principle, such as the US Constitution's statement that the state should not interfere with religious practice. Rather, it is a principle of *active support for spiritual practice in diverse forms*. The pluralist character of the ancient Indian state has been attributed to dharma-sapekshata. For instance, the protection of minorities depends on the goodwill of the majority, and sapeksha-dharma is why India has an unparalleled track record of welcoming numerous kinds of communities from various parts of the world and offering them the support to prosper without any loss of identity or religious tradition.

The recent import of secularism from the West is based on substituting 'religion' for 'dharma' and adopting Western social and legal structures. This has led to divisive vote-bank politics in the name of secularism and to a counter-reaction by a segment of Hindu politicians wanting to create a Hindu 'religion' that is equally political. The chain reaction set in motion has been disastrous both for Hindus and minorities. This book, therefore, is also a contribution to the heated debate on the implications of secularism in India.

In particular, it must be stressed that sapeksha-dharma does *not* demand adherence to Hinduism. Nor does it limit its concerns to those of traditional Hindus. The notion of jati-dharma presupposes respect for each jati's separate dharma; hence, in a sapeksha-dharma system, a Muslim jati can have sharia as its jati-dharma for *internal* matters. As participants in the purva paksha, Muslims can freely advocate their legal and ethical principles in the public sphere. (Of course, injunctions like killing infidels would violate the principle of mutual respect with other jatis and thus have to be set aside.)

In the Mahabharata, the ceremony for the oath of a new king includes the admonition: 'Be like a garland-maker, O king, and not like a charcoal burner.'[1] This is essentially a call for dharma-sapekshata. The garland is a metaphor for dharmic diversity in which flowers of many colours and forms are strung harmoniously for the most pleasing effect, and it symbolizes social coherence. By contrast, charcoal is a metaphor for reducing the diversity into homogeneity, burning it into lifeless ashes. The king, in taking the oath, is being asked to exemplify supporting a coherent diversity in which highly contextual and varied culture is a unity (garland) of distinct particulars (flowers). It avoids the two extremes: incoherence of a chaotic scattering of flowers, and reductionist, homogenized universals.[2]

I offer sapeksha-dharma as an alternative to Western secularism. Secularism is perhaps better expressed as pantha-nirapeksha, which means not favouring one pantha (i.e., sect or denomination) over another. A society based on sapeksha-dharma would be expected to uphold the highest dharma rather than exercising mere tolerance or indifference. By its very nature, dharma would be sensitive to diversity among communities. Civic identity, daily life, politics and the art of government would all be maintained through multiple levels of reciprocal relationships informed and guided by this notion. It would also provide a safe framework for purva paksha since the ethic of mutual respect would trump the differences before they could turn toxic.

Also, there can be no finality or closure to dharma. It is more like an open architecture, forever unfolding and assimilating. Purva paksha, on these terms, is not a way of settling debate or of asserting unity but of allowing unity to emerge, dissolve, fall apart and be reborn from moment to moment in the unfolding of civilizational encounters.

Anticipated Western Responses

From my own serious study of Abrahamic traditions and from the dialogues and debates I have had over many years, I would anticipate the following responses from the Jewish and Christian sides.

Fundamentalist Push-back

There will be significant numbers from these religions who will reject the premise and value of purva paksha. Some of this rejection is due to provincial ignorance, fear of the unknown, psychological conditioning and even blind faith. They may also have a principled sense that adhyatma-vidya (which I regard as *a necessary condition* of engagement) is theologically false and even blasphemous in that it tries to storm heaven by 'works' as opposed to the grace of God. Many in this group adhere to the biblical taboos against the body described in Chapter 2.

Lest we underestimate this group, we should remember that it includes a large percentage of active, church-going Christians in the US, who have enormous political clout in the military, local and national governments, and even foreign policy. Many senators, congresspersons, federal and state officials, and Supreme Court justices espouse such ideas. Although not all American Christians would identify with all their positions, this is the Christian group which has the most internal consistency, elicits an impressive degree of commitment, and has recently demonstrated a capacity for organized and aggressive political action both domestically and abroad.

This is the same group that is against abortion and gay rights and that opposes the teaching of evolution in schools. A large subset of this group is also heavily invested in the conviction that the End of Time, in which those outside the Kingdom of God will be brutally annihilated, is approaching. This will be preceded by a testing of the faith in which whoever is not *for* Jesus will be assumed to be *against* him and on the side of the Devil.

For such believers, a mutually respectful engagement with dharma is tantamount to dealing with the Devil. It would be sinful to engage on any terms other than the clear intent to convert.

Open-minded within the Limits of History-centrism

Other westerners from Jewish, Christian or secular backgrounds would be interested in purva paksha and even see themselves as meeting the preconditions set out above. Many westerners have practised adhyatma-vidya and appreciate it for its physical, psychological and spiritual benefits. Many, too, have found new meaning in their own native faiths as a result of their immersion in dharmic practices. Some even view this as a legitimate and effective spiritual path.

However, a good many others in this group would be extremely unwilling to compromise the history-centrism and exclusivism which they hold to be central to their own religion. After all, the Nicene Creed, the gold standard of belief in Christianity, cannot simply be jettisoned without the faith's moorings being lost. Also difficult to overcome for many are the deep-seated fears of damnation and the personal and collective ego gratification of being identified as westerners (an identity intertwined with the Christian faith). There might be deeper and more genuine objections, too, and only rigorous purva paksha could bring these issues to light.

Many billion-dollar foundations (such as the Pew Charitable Trusts and the John Templeton Foundation) – while being sophisticated and diplomatic – are committed to spreading the influence of Christian principles in mainstream civic society and might be willing to participate in purva paksha at this level. However, I have found that they prefer not to address their history-centrism openly.

Serious Explorers into Dharma

A much smaller group of practitioners would be willing to call into question the core beliefs and historical projects of the West and even distance themselves completely from these. This group might include humanists, self-help advocates, social activists, and those who have had mystical experiences outside of conventional Western religious paradigms.

Among this group, a subset would want to explore whether Western notions at risk could be reformulated in the light of dharma so as to be less divisive. (I would place in this group such figures as the Jewish writer Roger Kamenetz and the major Roman Catholic theologians Dom Bede Griffiths and Raimondo Panikkar.)

The further subset willing to travel the farthest consists of those who advocate a wholesale translation of the essential spirituality of Judaism and/or Christianity into the dharmic paradigm. These seekers are willing to accept Jesus as an avatar on par with other Hindu avatars, and thus they are prepared to worship him on dharmic terms as their personal ishta-devata. A number of individual practitioners in the West are already quietly acting on this premise in their personal practice.

While such journeys can be quite remarkable, they are often unsustainable, because the seekers have not explicitly addressed their own cultural assumptions – in particular history-centrism and exclusivism – preferring simply to ignore these issues or set them aside. They have not fully realized the extent of the de-conditioning they may require, intellectually, psychologically and spiritually, in order to embrace a genuine dharmic perspective. Even if they can do so, there might still remain unconscious investments in Western universalism and/or worldly power. There may be a general tendency for such seekers to settle for an abstract 'perennial philosophy', or else make a 'U-turn' back to their former beliefs and religious paths. Some might 'convert' to Hinduism or Buddhism in immature and unsustainable ways.

Many will also want to capitalize, in self-aggrandizing ways, on the widespread interest in dharma in the West, assuming the guise of scholarly 'India experts' or self-help 'integral philosophers'. Rare is the Western seeker who is able to follow through on his or her quest without such a volte-face. Rarer still is the one who is able to forge a completely new and individual path of spiritual achievement.

The options and paths that open up as a result of purva paksha at this juncture are many and complex. Yet in spite of the difficulties, I would still argue that through purva paksha, individuals on all sides can articulate these various positions and explore their options.

Challenging the Leaders of Dharma

By no means is purva paksha challenging only to westerners. Those on the dharmic side will also require education and a sincere, open commitment. As explained in Chapter 1, the practice of purva paksha has largely disappeared in India over the past millennium, and recovering it will not be easy. In the eighteenth and nineteenth centuries, under successive waves of colonization, dharmic leadership either withdrew from engagement or adopted the Western paradigms. The colonizers made extensive efforts to learn Sanskrit and its corpus of texts if only for their own purposes. Unfortunately, dharma leaders were content with, and in many cases proud of, being the object of Western study and failed to reverse the gaze in order to study the West with commitment and rigour.

Swami Vivekananda did indeed explore the West, and some leaders such as Ram Mohan Roy attempted to form syncretic movements like the Brahmo Samaj. But these efforts lacked a solid understanding of Western religion, philosophy and history which is necessary for a proper purva paksha of the West. Vivekananda and others were content without a formal study of the West on dharmic terms and largely read what the West's own proponents and critics were producing, as opposed to studying the West systematically in dharmic terms. More importantly, such occasional gazing at the West was not institutionalized and perfected over time in the same manner as the West has done with respect to the study of dharmic societies. There has been no development of dharmic institutions in India comparable to Western seminaries; no places where comparative world religions are seriously taught in order to prepare future leaders with the knowledge necessary to engage with other religions. In other words, Christian and supposedly secular institutions study dharma intensively, and yet there is barely any study in the reverse direction.

Contemporary gurus and acharyas have also been disinclined to embark on a serious study of the West. Their incompetence is disguised by arrogance and superciliousness. A typical attitude is summed up in their statement: 'The truth is with us, so why should we bother to study others' ignorance?' Others betray an egoistic display of exaggerated humility by asking: 'Who am I to study other people's religions?' Still others have retreated out of despair, being overwhelmed by the challenge of confronting the West.

Additionally, since India's independence, the embrace of Western-grown secularism in India has prevented the country's universities from providing religious studies as a formal humanities discipline. The treatment of religion in the social sciences is mainly Marxist in nature, i.e., it promulgates the view that religion is a problem of backwardness to be solved with economic progress.

By failing to understand their Western students' collective identities, most gurus fail to prepare them for genuine transformation when such identities must be abandoned. It is critical that Western students be taught about the impediments in their spiritual journeys caused by history-centrist upbringing. But this requires a sophisticated knowledge of the Western psyche, paradigms and history. Since most gurus do not understand the deep history of Western disdain for embodied knowing, a large proportion of their students (after an initial period of romantic fascination) depart suddenly or else their sadhana gradually fades away. These and other problems stemming from the Western encounter with dharma are the topic of my forthcoming book, *U-Turn Theory*. In it, I explain the improvements needed on both sides of the exchange, including the necessity for gurus to have studied the West formally and extensively in order to engage with their Western students.

The precise outcome of purva paksha on both sides of the East/West divide cannot be presupposed, and the participants must remain open to all possibilities. What is needed *immediately* is a recognition of difference, and of the importance of respecting this difference. I hope this book contributes to the establishing of an open field of engagement, a Kurukshetra, on which East and West may meet on more equitable terms than in the past.

Gandhi's Sva-dharma and Purva Paksha

I wish to conclude by turning to Mahatma Gandhi, the quintessential example of someone with the audacity to assert his dharmic differences firmly but without harm or chauvinism. He was steeped in Indian cultural habits and experimented with dharma all of his life. Speaking in very simple and precise terms, he managed to alter the course of history.

His short book *Hind Swaraj*, or *Indian Home Rule*, published a century ago, is a magnificent example of purva paksha directed toward the British Empire. In it he examines British rule from an Indian perspective – including criticism of those Indian elites who had joined hands with the British. This book is one of his early writings, and it serves as a guide for spreading awareness of the problems of colonialism. Those problems have taken new forms, and so like many classics, *Hind Swaraj* has acquired a renewed and different relevance.

Hind is 'Indian' and swaraj is 'self-rule'. The British ruled India using a large number of Indians who had been appropriated to be the workers for the Empire. The police and military fighting against the Indian freedom fighters were mostly Indian soldiers wearing British uniforms and carrying the British flag. The whole civil service, including the judges, politicians and various authorities were British-controlled at the top. The average Englishman had ten, twenty or even fifty Indians working for him. In *Hind Swaraj*, Gandhi analysed the functioning of the empire and challenged Indians to stop serving a regime that was enslaving them. If they stopped serving the Empire, he argued, it would collapse on its own accord. It was not self-sustaining, in other words, but parasitic. It survived and thrived because Indians were complicit in its functioning. Too many Indians had allowed themselves to be used in the oppression of their own people.

When Gandhi turned his attention to the British way of life, criticizing its exploitative practices, hierarchies and industrialized consumerism, he was 'reversing the gaze' – quite provocatively – on another civilization he knew well from long, personal observation and study. This is precisely what I refer to as purva paksha, and my book is the result of my own lived experience and study of American ideas.

Gandhi came to the conclusion that there was in fact a deep ideological clash of civilizations between Britain and India. When a journalist asked him in England what he thought of British civilization, he said, 'That would be a good idea.'

The unsustainability of British industrialization was prominent among his concerns, making him arguably the first modern environmentalist. He noticed that the ever-increasing consumption in an industrial economy depletes the natural resources and destroys the self-sustaining villages which comprise the social fabric of India. In response to this problem, he advocated and embodied a simple lifestyle. The sum total of all of his belongings were his glasses, a pair of sandals, a pen, and a few dhotis.

Another crucial point of distinction about dharma that Gandhi stressed was the concept of truth, or 'satya' in Sanskrit. Gandhi's satya was not an intellectual proposition but a way of life that was to be actualized and embodied directly by each person. He advocated 'satyagraha', or 'truth-struggle', and insisted that it be lived, as opposed to just theorized. Hence, there was no place in his thought for the reification or codification of satya. The truth was not held in some book or set of laws; it lived in oneself and could not be separated from oneself. This philosophical distinction was at the heart of Gandhi's success. He not only advocated a sustainable society, he lived sustainably. He not only advocated the local production of whatever goods were necessary, he set the example by producing his own cloth, milking his own goat, etc.

Another fundamental difference between the civilizations presented in *Hind Swaraj* is the idea of 'ahimsa'. This term, which is often translated too simply as 'non-violence' is not the same as the Western idea of pacifism. It is much larger. 'Himsa' means harm and 'ahimsa' means non-harming. To achieve ahimsa requires activity and confrontation. To challenge the world's mightiest empire, one that caused himsa on a large scale, required great strength. Paradoxically, it takes a fighter to actualize ahimsa. Gandhi was such a fighter.

Ahimsa combined with satyagraha to produce Gandhi's ideals of sustainability and fighting against injustice. He advocated bottom-up social activism whereby the people themselves embody the change they want to see in the world. Ahimsa is not something merely to be talked about or legislated; it must be lived by individuals. But this requires a functional, sustainable society in which the people at the bottom are free to embody their satya. It was for this reason, and not just as an end in itself, that he demanded swaraj. Furthermore, himsa – properly understood – denotes *all* forms of harm. Harming the environment is himsa, as per the very deep Hindu idea that all nature is sacred. The modern eco-feminism movement, which arrived in America in the 1960s through the efforts of Vandana Shiva, is rooted in Gandhi's ideals of ahimsa. Harming animals is also himsa, and so vegetarianism is an important quality of ahimsa. Gandhi argued that, as vegetarianism has a lower impact on the environment than a meat diet, a vegetarian society is more ecologically sustainable than a non-vegetarian one.

Ahimsa also applies to cultures taken as a whole. The devastation of cultures is an important kind of himsa which is not often acknowledged in typical accounts of non-violence. For example, when the United Nations drafted its laws on genocide, they eliminated the phrases which described cultural genocide. In the officially defined UN law, cultural genocide is not prohibited. Gandhi fully understood this kind of violence and often talked about it. Cultural genocide is the systematic and complete elimination or suppression of the native religion, language, dress, way of life, customs, and/or symbols of one people by another. Even though the people in question might be given material benefits through humanitarian aid, education and medical facilities, it is himsa if there is systematic destruction of their identity, sense of history, ideas of ancestry, and relationship with nature. Stripping people of their collective notion of self is a prelude to digestion and a major part of the process of colonization. This kind of himsa goes on today under the name of 'development' wherein success is measured by the criteria of Westernization. Much of what is being called 'universal' – even in human rights discourse – is in fact cultural genocide and therefore himsa in Gandhi's sense.

Gandhi fought against this form of colonization as much as against its material and political manifestations. Although he was not against Christianity (and in fact often quoted Jesus), he opposed Christian missionaries in India. He said they should only do selfless work and not convert people. If they desired to run a school or hospital or give the poor food, these things should not become a means of conversion.

In a similar vein, Gayatri Chakravorty Spivak referred to those who seek 'to right wrongs' and those whose 'wrongs are righted' while speaking at Oxford University in a talk sponsored by Amnesty International.[3] Human rights activism, she argued, is not just about having rights but also about who is and who is not the dispenser of those rights. Western approaches to human rights tend to operate in a top-down power structure in which the empowered (such as political activists, aid workers and NGOs with access to the global media and funding) are positioned as agents and take 'the burden' and responsibility of human rights agency upon themselves. This top-down structure is incompatible with Gandhi's ideal of empowering the people to engage in their own satyagraha.

The deeper one gets into the subtlety of Gandhi's thinking, the clearer it becomes that there is disconnect between his ideals and the actions of many who look to him as their model. Many so-called Gandhians act as part of an institutional structure which causes himsa. Gandhi has become something of a brand name, and this brand does not fully align with Gandhi himself.

Gandhi believed that cultural difference is not to be erased but celebrated. This is also a very old Hindu idea. It is analogous to saying there should not be just one type of flower, or tree. The universe is built on diversity. In fact, that is what the word 'uni-verse' means: the many-in-one. Every species has subspecies and sub-subspecies, and this nesting of diversity goes on and on. This diversity is not fixed, since these entities are always in flux from one moment to the next. All of which shows that difference is the underlying principle of the universe. It stands to reason, then, that cultural homogeneity is unnatural and unfeasible. There should not be one single religion or way of life.

Gandhi was remarkably free from difference anxiety. He wore a traditional dhoti, went barefoot and bare-chested, and felt comfortable sitting on the floor. He used to milk his own goat and drink only goat milk. Even when he went to England in 1931, when King George V held a reception in his honour at Buckingham Palace, he drank goat milk. He wore the same frayed sandals that carried him on his famous march of civil disobedience to break the law banning Indians from making salt. That was his way of life. He spoke in the traditional village language and lived with the poorest people. When the world press came to interview him, they would often find him in surprising places, for example, sitting by the roadside with a poor man. He really was different and he accentuated this aspect of himself rather than downplaying or eliminating it.

One of the ways in which Gandhi protected his civilization against the himsa of cultural genocide was to use Sanskrit non-translatable words. I have already mentioned satyagraha. He referred to sva-dharma ('my dharma') as his guiding principle and to the Bhagavadgita's Kurukshetra as the battlefield where the challenges before us are fought.

Gandhi explained that the Sanskrit word swaraj does not merely denote political independence; it implies many kinds of freedom. There is a difference between 'freedom *to*' and 'freedom *from*'. In the West, freedom is conceived as freedom to own a car, to go wherever one wants, to buy what one wants, to say whatever one wants. All of that is 'freedom to' – freedom to do this and that. It is extroverted. But such a 'free' person might not be able to say that he is free *from* anger, or from desire, jealousy, habits and compulsions. That kind of freedom refers to an internal state. It actually means freedom from one's conditioned self or ego. Gandhi always worked toward achieving and embodying this state of being free from internal as well as external dependencies.

Yet another non-translatable word Gandhi used was swadeshi, meaning 'from the soil', a native product similar to the 'buy local' movement which is becoming fashionable in the West today. Gandhi's idea of swadeshi included a critique of long-distance transportation and a preference for local production and seasonal eating. This was not simply an economic preference but was related to the ideal of ahimsa. Swadeshi is better for the environment and for the health of the individual, because it is based on what one is acclimatized to use. Over time, people develop a relationship with the natural setting in which they live. Swadeshi entails eating locally grown food, wearing locally made clothes, and, where possible, buying locally made goods.

All of these ideas contributed to Gandhi's political thought. He advocated an Indian society, or samaj, based on local governance by a 'panchayat', which is the traditional decentralized system built from the bottom upwards, beginning at the village level. This idea of India conflicted directly with British rule. He was always concerned that Indians would become brown-skinned Englishmen (which unfortunately did happen to a large extent), and he always said that if India was going to adopt British civilization after independence, the British might as well stay on, as they could do a better job of it.

Unfortunately, after Gandhi's death, his quest to control the categories of discourse was lost. Many of his ideas have been translated so completely as to lose their original nuance of meaning. In his death, Gandhi has been domesticated. Gandhi has been replaced with Gandhism. This is himsa to Gandhi.

One harmful way of undermining Gandhi's ideals has come from the Hindu tradition itself. Vedanta is being misinterpreted to encourage people toward inaction, passivity and escapism by reciting lofty verses out of context. But the irony is that the people who talk the loudest about inaction and transcendence are the first to negotiate deals for their own self-centred interests. If they are parents, they want their children to do well in their exams and become materialistically successful. If they are professors, they bargain over their tenure to get the best contract. Thus, in their personal lives, they are as competitive as they can be, but when it comes to taking on the responsibility of satyagraha for society, for dharma, the Vedanta ideal of being inactive gives them an opportunity to cop out. Actually, Vedanta includes both pravitti, the path of action, and nivritti, the path of withdrawal from action. The inaction is an inward stillness even as the person is actively performing in a detached manner. It is not laziness, fatalism, or escapism.

In the popular imagination, Gandhi is depicted as passive and non-threatening. In fact, he was audacious, outspoken (what we today call 'politically incorrect'), and refused to be appropriated by any institution. Like a twentieth-century Arjuna in Kurukshetra, he attacked adharma and challenged the judges, politicians and lawyers who guarded the British Empire.

In my decade-long churning of the ocean of creativity, I have drawn great inspiration from Gandhi. His life illustrates many key points made in this book. His purva paksha of the West was challenging and audacious; he saw the inter-civilizational encounter as the kurukshetra where he performed his sva-dharma; his use of non-translatables was a strategic way of managing the discourse surrounding his culture; and his way of life demonstrated how difference may be asserted constructively while retaining respect for one's opponents at the same time. The respect, in many cases, may not have been mutual, but what is important is that Gandhi set – and lived – the example.

Appendix A

The Integral Unity of Dharma

The various dharma schools have a continuing history of debates amongst themselves, and many volumes have been compiled to document and analyse these. My goal is not to explain these systems or their relationships with one another in technical detail. Rather, I wish to highlight the ties and bonds within the vast spectrum of dharma traditions that constitute what I am calling 'the integral unity of dharma'. This unity is classically expressed in the Vedas, but it is not confined to schools that privilege the Vedas as authoritative.

This relatedness among different schools differs from the 'synthetic unity' created by fusing together independent entities that must be reconciled. Instead, it is a kind of diversity springing precisely from the wholeness that grounds it. The common attributes discussed will serve as a basis for contrasting them with the Western traditions. The purpose behind such an exercise is to highlight the unique and core ideas of dharma using the West as a foil.

Among the plethora of dharma schools, several accept the authority of the Vedas while others do not. Some like Nyaya, Vaisheshika, Sankhya and Yoga accept Vedic authority but have developed their own independent philosophies. Those that do not accept the Vedas include Buddhists, Jains, Carvaka and Lokayata (the latter two being materialist schools).

Hinduism's Integral Unity of God-Cosmos-Human

All schools of Vedanta agree that there is one Ultimate Reality that is Supreme Consciousness and that there is nothing independent of this reality. This Ultimate Reality is the raw material that turns itself into the universe.

In the Advaita-Vedantic causation theory, the world appears in Brahman in the manner of a superimposition, which is a cognitive error. The superimposition is comparable to silver in the mother of pearl or blue in the sky; the silver and the blue are not essential to these entities. There is a further stock example of the snake-in-the-rope: in the twilight, an object is mistaken for a snake, instilling fear in the person who sees it; however, in the light of day it is found to be nothing but a coil of rope, whereupon the fear evaporates. The rope was mistaken for a snake, because it was not fully visible in the twilight and also because of the pre-existing mental impression (samskara, vasana) of a coiled-up snake.

In a similar fashion, through maya, the inscrutable mysterious power of Brahman, the world and body are superimposed on the immutable Brahman, which has never in reality been anything but itself. Brahman is non-dual ('advaita'), homogenous ('nirvishesha'), and ultimately without qualities ('nirguna') or adjuncts ('upadhi'). The spider that extrudes its own web without any extraneous agency is proffered as a metaphor for Brahman as both the efficient and material cause of the universe. This metaphor is in accord with the only account of causality that is consistent with the principle of non-duality in which no external agency is admissible. The cause produces the effect without undergoing any change in its substance. The rope is not transformed into a snake (as, say, milk is into curd); the snake is merely an appearance superimposed on the rope.

The differences among the Vedanta schools have to do with their treatment of how Supreme Reality relates to the temporal or mundane world, but the unity of that reality is not in question. Adi Shankara (788–820 CE) is regarded as the foremost proponent of the school which postulates that Ultimate Reality is impersonal, while Ramanuja (c. 1055–1137 CE) – who challenged Shankara's views – is considered the leading exponent of the school which holds that Ultimate Reality is personal.

Shankara refers to the Ultimate Reality as Brahman. Although our individual selves are Brahman, maya (as the veil of illusion) leads us to experience ourselves as separate from this universal self – that is, with independent egos. This leads to two truths depending on whether the person is trapped in maya or not. This pair has been described in various ways, such as: Relative and Ultimate/Absolute; Formless Universal ('nirakara') and With-Form Particulars ('sa-akara'); the Unqualified-Universal ('nirguna') and Qualified ('saguna'). In each explanation, the relative truth – a product of maya – is impermanent, incomplete, ultimately false, and the cause of suffering.

Later, Ramanuja's school of Vishishta-Advaita ('differentiated non-dualism') challenged Shankara by setting aside the concept of maya as the reason for the experience of separation and replacing it with the idea that all particular properties, qualities and possibilities are inherent in Brahman. Universals ('samanya') and particulars ('vishesha') are inseparable; the universal offers the all-encompassing view, and the particulars offer multiplicity within it.[1] Thus, Brahman is not seen as devoid of particulars or differentiations (as was the case with Shankara). The very nature and essence of Brahman is inclusive of all existence in its many forms, as is illustrated by the relationship of the body's owner to the body. All conscious and unconscious entities make up the body of Brahman, and Brahman is the consciousness and inner controller of the cosmos, which is his body. The Absolute and Relative are thus unified.

Particular entities are not illusory but constitute the nature of Ultimate Reality as intrinsically differentiated. There is no quality-free or homogeneous substance possible. Qualities inhere in substances, and hence a substance and its qualities are inseparable. The integral unity between Brahman and the world is thus one of inseparability. In the case of a blue lotus, for example, the colour blue (quality) is inseparable from its substance, the lotus. Brahman, then, is the substance, and the individual person is a quality of Brahman – making them inseparable.

The Bhagavadgita advises us to 'see the Self in all beings and all beings in the Self'. Realizing the universal in all particulars is tantamount to achieving liberation or moksha. This cannot be achieved through mere abstract reasoning nor book learning, but only through the embodied self.

The ultimate state of liberation from contexts includes all the contexts as a subset, but the contexts are no longer a constraint. Transcendence is a state of purna (infinite fullness) that has all the contexts in it and that yet remains beyond all contexts. It is not a context-free or uniform realm.

Hinduism tends to conceptualize universals as integral unities pregnant with particulars. The relationship between universals and particulars never collapses into either pole: neither towards the other-worldly emphasis on transcendental universals (which would ignore worldly particulars), nor toward radical materialism of earthly particulars (at the expense of transcendental spirituality). This view is different from the simplistic unity stripped of particulars as is found in Western philosophy.

Ramanuja's successor, Sri Jiva Goswami, refined his system and integrated it along with Shankara's thoughts into one comprehensive view. He said the Ultimate Reality is simultaneously personal and impersonal. Instead of Shankara's view of Brahman devoid of any attributes, Sri Jiva adopted Ramanuja's view that forms and attributes are not separate essences but the very nature of Brahman.[2] Reality is endowed with multiple potencies that have no separate existence from it.

Sri Jiva further differentiates three manifestations of Reality which are experienced according to the capacity of the devotee:

Impersonal, Formless (Brahman): This is the experience of Ultimate Reality, which is indivisible, and the experiencer is inseparable from it. Those who have rejected all pleasures and seek the Ultimate Reality without specificity or form or internal variety experience this when their ardent practice leads them to realize their identity with this blissful Reality.

Personal, Form (Bhagavan): This is the experience of devotees whose senses have been imbued with devotion and desire to experience the entire universe as filled with bliss. Upon achieving transcendence, they experience Bhagavan (personal blissful quality of the Ultimate Reality). Bhagavan is revealed to the senses – both internal and external – and takes on specific characteristics for this purpose.

In-dweller within us (Paramatman): This 'super-soul' is the Ultimate Reality realized as the controller of living beings and all objects.

Just as the blue lotus is a lotus with its blueness, so also Bhagavan (B) is the Ultimate Reality qualified with all potencies and hence is the complete manifestation of the Ultimate Reality. Just as 'a lotus' is less complete in description than 'the blue lotus', because its blueness is absent, so also Brahman (A) exhibits no specific qualities and is therefore an incomplete manifestation of that Reality. The difference lies in the level of realization on the part of the devotee. The personal experience with form (B), according to Sri Jiva, is a more complete manifestation of the Ultimate Reality, whereas the attributes remain un-manifest in the impersonal. A is thus seen as a subset of B.

The distinction between A and B arises because of the two paths of jnana and bhakti. Bhakti leads to the Ultimate Reality endowed with attributes (Bhagavan), while jnana offers the same Ultimate Reality as undifferentiated consciousness (Brahman). The realization of Bhagavan thus contains the realization of Brahman in it.[3] In other words: *Bhagavan = Brahman + all attributes, qualities and essences*. If the truth of Bhagavan is realized, Brahman will naturally be understood – just as one who understands the blue lotus knows the lotus.

There is no absolute difference between Bhagavan and Paramatman, either – the latter being a partial manifestation of Bhagavan. Paramatman is the manifestation of Bhagavan as the cause of creation; he enters individuals, enlivens the bodies and all objects (including primordial/unmanifest matter called prakriti) and guides them in their functions as the inner controller.

Sri Jiva explains that the energies and other attributes of Bhagavan are inconceivable ('achintya') to the human mind and can produce results ordinarily deemed impossible (for example, the power of some mantras to cure otherwise incurable diseases). While these energies constitute Bhagavan's very essence, he also transcends them. These energies are neither different from Bhagavan nor the same. This peculiar relation of being simultaneously the same and different ('bheda-abheda') is a unique principle that also permeates Indian music, dance, sculpture, deity worship, rituals, morals, ethics, religion, and so on. The energies have distinct names, forms and personalities and are often depicted as Bhagavan's wives. This contrasts Shankara's Advaita school, which considers the quality-less, formless and nameless Brahman to be the Ultimate Reality and any personal deity – a product of maya.

Bhagavan has no material form but is experienced as existence, consciousness and bliss; however, he manifests at unlimited places in unlimited aspects simultaneously in accordance with the mood of his devotees. Besides manifesting in the material world as avatar, Bhagavan also manifests his name in the same manner. Thus, the name 'Bhagavan' is identical with Bhagavan and has the same power as Bhagavan. Even the syllables constituting the name have the power to deliver one from material bondage. Hence 'nama-japa' (or silent muttering of the Lord's name) and 'nama-sankirtana' (or congregational chanting of his name with musical instruments) link the temporal with the transcendental realm.

Those with material desires often begin worship by mistaking a lower deity for the supreme.[4] At a higher level, one considers the supreme deity as the presiding deity or as immanent in the particular deity one worships, and hence the worship is actually being directed to the supreme deity. Another, higher level of worship is to consider the deity one worships as a manifestation of the supreme deity. Sri Krishna says:

> Those whose knowledge has been carried away by countless desires surrender unto other deities and follow different religious regulations governed by their particular nature. To whichever deity they faithfully choose to worship, I alone make their faith firm. Being endowed with such faith they endeavour to worship that particular deity and thereby fulfill their desires. In fact this is all arranged by me (Gita 7.20-22).

The difference between Advaita and Vaishnavism may be summarized as follows: In Advaita, individuality is completely dissolved, whereas in Ramanuja's and Sri Jiva's system there is individuality but it is inseparable from God and is a form of God. The Advaitins believe the jiva (individual) and Paramatman are one and the same, whereas Vaishnavites believe they have eternally distinct existences. Vaishnavites cite the Gita 15.7 and assert that the jivas are not only fragments of the supreme but are eternally that, i.e., sanatana. Since there is no ultimate dissolution of the individual, it is interesting to note that liberation is lila, or divine play in which the jiva is eternally enjoying serving the Lord (as a distinct fragment of the Lord). This is the highest state of bliss, for the pure-hearted devotee accepts any condition in which he may serve the Lord – even one in which others might find him physically or materially destitute. However, in both schools of thought there is an integral unity that underlies the separate entities.[5]

Sri Aurobindo's Involution-Evolution

In the twentieth century, Sri Aurobindo drew on all schools of dharma, but his chief contribution was to expand upon the Vedic concepts of involution and evolution, which Swami Vivekananda had brought to the Western world in the late 1800s. (Vivekananda is best known in the West for having participated eloquently in the Parliament of the World's Religions in 1893 in Chicago and for his influence on several American philosophers, including William James and Josiah Royce.)

Involution, according to Vivekananda and Sri Aurobindo, is what grounds evolution. It is the mechanism by which the One manifests as many forms. Here, the undifferentiated One Reality differentiates itself and releases its latent potentialities for manifestation in diverse forces and forms, each of which is the One Reality itself, for the whole is implicit in each part.

The One Reality is both undifferentiated Oneness and its entire differentiated manifestation simultaneously, and yet it also veils its undifferentiated Oneness (withholds its manifestation) such that the diverse forms are made unaware of the implicit Oneness of which they are particular expressions.

Thus, the particular does not know that it is merely an expression of the universal. Stated differently, the parts do not know that they are not independent entities and that they are forms of the whole.

This veiling of our consciousness may be understood with the aid of an analogy. Sometimes an actor becomes so identified with the role he is playing that, for a moment, he loses awareness of his real identity. Similarly, in involution this identification of the true self with its role (part) is taken to the extreme where true consciousness is completely veiled and masked. However, since the true Absolute Self is latent within, matter itself is driven to recover its true identity through the long process of evolution – aided no doubt by higher, more conscious aspects of the Being.[6]

Sri Aurobindo explains that the Supreme Being starts off with a 'double faculty of comprehensive and apprehensive knowledge' by which it simultaneously knows both levels: One is original self-awareness in which 'all things are one being, one consciousness, one will, one self-delight and the whole movement of things a movement one and indivisible.' The second faculty is its 'action from the unity to the multiplicity and from multiplicity to unity, creating an ordered relation between them and an appearance but not a binding reality of division, a subtle un-separating division, or rather a demarcation and determination within the indivisible'.[7]

The entire cosmos is the manifestation of the One, 'continually proceeding from him into the form of himself'. It is the shakti of the One which 'repeats himself in every form of himself' and which 'reproduces there the act of self-division ...' The integral, evolutionary, self-conscious universe is nothing but God's immanence:

> In all it is the same Soul, the same divine Being; the multiplication of centers is only a practical act of consciousness intended to institute a play of difference, of mutuality, mutual knowledge, mutual shock of force, mutual enjoyment, a difference based upon essential unity, a unity realized on a practical basis of difference ... It is still his own being that the Enjoyer enjoys, even though in a multiplicity.[8]

This notion of involution is inseparable from that of the nature of the Ultimate Reality and is a major contribution to world philosophy. In Darwin's theory of evolution, there is no room for any involution, because the secular/sacred divide contradicts such a possibility. So evolution is synthetic, with the parts pre-existing separately as building blocks which happen to end up – apparently through random trial and error – into successively more evolved forms. But in Hindu philosophy, involution precedes evolution and provides the mechanism, purpose and general direction for evolution. It roots the integral unity.

It is quite natural, then, for Hindus to see the world as being self-governed by its rta/dharma. Rivers flow by means of rta (the principle of natural order) – not that they must flow, but that they simply do. It is the rta of water to seek a lower level without purpose; plants, too, are self-organized; each individual animal has the infinite capacity to govern itself; and on the human level, social structures govern themselves efficiently. The Supreme Being is involuted into matter, and hence into all forms that evolved out of matter. There is no creation/evolution conflict in such a system.

Buddhism's Approach to Integral Unity

Buddhism is also grounded in the concept of integral unity. Indeed, Buddhism demonstrates how extensively the dharmic traditions can differ from each other in matters of metaphysics while yet remaining deeply and integrally unified. (I will focus on the Madhyamika school of Buddhism to illustrate this integral unity.) Buddhism affirms one of Vedanta's key principles, which is that phenomena, as experienced by the ordinary mind, are not ultimately real when they appear as separate entities. But it offers a radical challenge to the Vedanta traditions by asserting that Ultimate Reality – conceived as Brahman or Bhagavan – is also illusory.

The Buddhist principle is that phenomena are not 'real things' that exist. It outright rejects the ultimate existence of all substances. The notion that things lack any self-existence whatsoever is called 'shunyata' (emptiness). This conclusion flows from two claims: (1) Everything is a flux of momentary instants (for which the Sanskrit term is 'kshana'), and (2) These moments succeed each other in a perpetual stream, i.e., each moment is without any separate existence whatsoever.

The claim that these momentary episodic 'existences' are all mutually caused (with no first cause or original cause or uncaused cause) is known as dependent co-arising ('pratitya-samutpada'). Since the momentary events do not endure, a different moment is a different entity. All moments in the past, present and future are causally interdependent on each other as in the metaphor of Indra's Net. This means that each one is caused by all the rest, and hence no moment exists separately by itself. All events, moments or things are linked in this way, and all phenomena affect each other directly or indirectly no matter how proximate or remote they are in time or space. There are no isolated things or processes possible – hence, no separate thing exists.

Each experience of every individual is causally linked to the entire cosmos, and so all sentient beings are interlinked. Dependent co-arising is conceived in two models: infinite linear chain reactions and circular reciprocal chain reactions. In both models, everything depends on everything else. Buddha proclaimed that this insight into causal processes linking all existence was the one truly universal law and that it operates independently without any governor. It is valid whether any Buddha appeared and gave expression to it or not.

This is the Buddhist expression of Ultimate Reality. It is not underpinned by any substance like Brahman, because Buddhists do not accept either a personal

God or an impersonal One that truly exists by itself separately from everything else. Ultimate Reality is this dance of momentary episodes.

What we commonly call 'the world' and what philosophers call 'phenomenal existence' is known in Buddhism as samsara and is merely this stream of events where no event has any separate existence. This means that no-thing has selfhood or self-nature – not even any foundation that supports the Ultimate Reality. Hence, the opening stanza in the *Mula-Madhyamaka-Karika* (a major Buddhist text by Nagarjuna, considered by many the foremost philosopher after Buddha), says: 'Neither from itself, nor from another, nor from both, nor without cause does anything arise.'[9]

The karmic law of cause-and-effect operates without recourse to a creator God or any other entity that is outside this web of mutual interdependence. Every phenomenon arises within the web of causes, so no isolated, non-contextual (independent) phenomena are possible. Even Ultimate Reality is just a term I am using to denote this infinite web of interdependence, for Buddhists emphasize that Ultimate Reality is itself empty (i.e., devoid of self-existence). Otherwise, it could be used as a sort of impersonal god and become the uncaused cause that exists separately.

This interdependent reality also includes all mental processes. The practice of insight ('vipasana') using a calm and steady mind enables the Buddhist yogi to witness the flow and interaction of mental elements. Clear comprehension ('samprajanya') allows detached observation and introspection of mental processes. When internal and external phenomena that seem to exist by themselves are observed with this keen insight, they are found to be composite (made of parts) and causal (having underlying causes). This means they do not exist independently. The process is then applied to examine the parts, and the same composite nature is discovered. The yogi's insight shows no ultimate building blocks (atoms) of any kind – be they physical, mental or emotional. Every such atom-like entity consists of other entities and processes which in turn depend on yet others. This infinite chain of dependencies on entities does not culminate in anything that exists independently (such as God).

This is expressed in the oft-quoted Buddhist axiom on emptiness: 'All phenomena are devoid of self, empty and insubstantial.' Another statement elaborates on this idea: 'All that is produced in dependence cannot be independent. And because all is non-independent, there is no self of anything.'[10] Emptiness and dependent co-arising are deemed equivalent.

Nagarjuna advanced the Buddhist principle of no essences and no substances through his critique of the notions of substance ('dravya'), being ('sat'), self-nature or essence ('sva-bhava'), characteristic ('lakshana') and causality, as well as through his critique of language. He established the following principles.

First, philosophers who have left certain assumptions and presuppositions intact have obscured the radically insubstantial and causally dependent nature of existence. The chief culprit is the notion of self-nature of persons and phenomena.

Second, by application of the logic of four alternatives ('catuskoti') of being, non-being, both, or neither to all phenomena and entities unreservedly – even to the Buddha and nirvana – Nagarjuna exposed the contradictory nature of all concepts and the limitations of language.

Third, contrary to the conventional notion that emptiness (shunyata) is the negation of all entities, he proposed that emptiness is the natural state of all existents, because they dependently co-arise and hence lack self-existence.

Finally, even the concepts of emptiness and dependent co-arising are subjected to the same critique, lest they be reified as independently existent. He proposed emptiness as the antidote for all views, not as a self-existent principle existing over and above others. Emptiness is empty of self-nature, including ideas and principles such as the emptiness principle itself.

To the critics who accused him of nihilism, Nagarjuna points out that if things were substantively existent, they could not interact. Only in the context of emptiness and dependent co-arising can there be interaction and interdependence. (See further explanation under the subheading 'The Middle Path' below.)

Buddha and Nagarjuna do not intend to establish the notion of emptiness as having any existence; otherwise it would be a 'thing' with its own self-existence. Hence, they insist that 'emptiness is empty,' meaning that the notion of emptiness is itself devoid of independent existence. In other words, emptiness is not some entity to be essentialized as a sort of transcendental realm above the phenomenal world; it is just the ultimate nature of phenomena. The classical Buddhist position on this is: 'Emptiness does not make phenomena empty, because phenomena are themselves emptiness.'[11] The ultimate truth is not another reality outside the scope of this web of interdependence but a perceptual shift from a way of thinking in terms of substances and essences to a way of thinking that no such entities exist by themselves.[12]

Buddha explains that all teachings are 'for the sake of liberation; not for the sake of grasping'[13] and should not be turned into absolutes. There is a famous statement: 'One should abandon even dharmas, not to mention non-dharmas.' The liberating views should also be abandoned like rafts that have served their purpose. Nagarjuna states: 'Those who have a view of emptiness as inherently existent are incurable.'[14] In other words, clinging to emptiness as some sort of 'state of consciousness' or a thing that exists by itself is a form of clinging to what is false.

The term dukkha is commonly mistranslated as 'suffering' in the Western sense. This translation is inadequate. Dukkha is the human condition in which one sees the world and oneself as consisting of self-existing entities. This cognitive error is responsible for our forming attachments to 'things' and desiring them. These desires are impossible to satisfy, because the things one grasps at (for satisfaction) ultimately do not exist. Since everything we perceive is interdependent with everything else, it is impossible to isolate anything and obtain it. Even the self that craves these objects and outcomes is ultimately a non-entity, and hence any attempt to satisfy it is futile. The enlightened person is freed from the afflictive emotions and sufferings caused by indulging in erroneous thinking.

Two Truths and Contexts

Since all phenomena arise in interdependence and are thus devoid of essence, they are said to exist only relatively. In the ultimate sense, they are inconceivable, because lacking self-nature makes them devoid of all individual characteristics. This such-ness ('tathata') is the Ultimate Reality devoid of any conceptual descriptions. Therefore, in order for relative existence to be comprehensible, phenomena must be understood in the context of the two truths, relative and ultimate: 'The Dharma is founded in the two truths: the truth of worldly convention and the supreme ultimate truth.'[15] The sphere of relative truth is the domain of language and concept, which is ultimately non-existent, being subject to the infinite chain of interdependence. The ultimate truth is 'peaceful, not fabricated by mental formations, not thought, without distinctions'.[16] Therefore, it is crucial to identify the contexts of statements, which could relate either to relative or ultimate truths. If this is not done, there will be confusion and contradiction.

The Middle Path

Emptiness is what makes change and action possible. Nagarjuna drives home the point that existence through essence is untenable, because change would then be impossible. In essentialist ontology, actions are not conceivable since the concept of individual, inherently existent substances precludes the interaction and interdependence that would make them possible. In other words, if phenomena were inherently existent and not empty, there would be no possibility of change, and the cosmos would be permanently frozen and immutable. Thus, emptiness and dependent arising are the true criteria for the existence of phenomenon – not self-existence. He says: 'If there is essence, the whole world would be un-arising, unceasing and static. The entire phenomenal world would be immutable.' This is Nagarjuna's death blow to all synthetic unities, because they start with separate essences and then look for unity.

For essentialists who misconstrue emptiness as nihilistic and the nemesis of action, Nagarjuna offers this rebuttal: 'If emptiness is rejected, no action will be appropriate. There would be no action which did not begin, and there would be agent without action.'[17] And again: 'if [the world] were not empty, then action would be without profit. The act of ending suffering and abandoning misery and defilement would not exist.'[18]

Nagarjuna clarifies that 'what is produced in dependence on other entities, we explain as emptiness. This is nominal existence and exactly that is the Middle Way.'[19] The Middle position is to say that phenomena are nominally existent and that neither the concept of existence nor that of non-existence applies to the reality of things. He sums up: 'To say that "it is" is to grasp for permanence. To say that "it is not" is to adopt the view of nihilism. Therefore, a wise person does not say "exists" or "does not exist".'[20]

In his first discourse, Buddha addresses the ethical implications of the Middle Path as the mean between the extremes of hedonistic self-indulgence and masochistic self-torment.[21] The philosophical counterpart to this principle eschews the extremes of affirmation and negation, one leading to the permanence view and the other – to the nihilist view.[22] This is the logic of the Middle Way, the avoidance of extremes. This understanding of dukkha, its cause, and the path to its cessation is not a metaphysical formulation; it is pragmatic, i.e., for the purpose of transformation.

The two extremes of eternally existing entities and nihilism are deeply rooted in the human psyche. They express themselves not only in ordinary life but in philosophical concepts of being and non-being – of 'is' and 'is not'. Buddha addresses the underlying psychology of the unenlightened who become afflicted with perplexity and doubt when the concepts of existence and non-existence do not correspond to the actuality of the way things come to be. To avoid the pitfalls of the extremes, one must see the dependently co-arisen nature of all phenomena.

Skilful Means: Pragmatic Use of Context

Given the Two Truths, there is a pragmatic method known as 'skilful means' which is indicative of the context-sensitive nature of the Buddhist path.[23] Buddha explains that the teachings are tailored to individual intelligence and aptitudes and to the nature of the time, place and circumstance. There is a pedagogy of gradual instruction in generosity, ethics and dharma going through stages of teachings that fit the level of the individual.

Since the sentient beings to be liberated are infinite in number, the means of liberation must also be infinite, and – since the dispositions, capacities, aptitudes and delusions of beings are infinitely diverse – the bodhisattva must also devise individual means appropriate for each case. This presents a formidable challenge to the bodhisattva, who is an enlightened master who has pledged to take birth indefinitely until every living creature gets liberated from dukkha. Mere universal compassion is inadequate when it degenerates into emotions and sentiments.

The bodhisattva must exercise his wisdom concerning the emptiness of the self-nature of persons and phenomena: there are no ultimate beings to be rescued since the ideas of a self, person and life are all conceptual constructs, the result of freezing processes into permanent substances. Yet because of his great compassion for the dukkha of sentient beings, he does not abandon a single being – even though all beings exist only at the relative level of truth. If he were to objectify the notion of 'sentient being', that would become an obstacle to helping them. He must constantly balance the ultimate truth that beings do not exist with the relative truth of his great compassion. He must apply individually appropriate remedies in the context of each individual.

Four-Way Logic

With profound philosophical skill and a razor-sharp mind, Nagarjuna developed his own approach to the problem of unity and laid the foundation for a profound understanding of how to master difference and sameness. Reality cannot be adequately described or comprehended from any partial perspective, and comprehensive knowledge requires consideration of multiple perspectives, though reality ultimately transcends any characterization. All these varieties of logic are comprehensible only within a non-essentialist and non-exclusivist framework. The laws of contradiction and the Law of the Excluded Middle are applied in Indian logic but only at times and in ways which are sensitive to context and not in an overdetermined, absolutist manner as in Western philosophy. In other words, each teaching concerning the self requires sensitivity to time, place, circumstance and interlocutor.

Nagarjuna makes a startling statement concerning the Buddha's teaching on the cardinal doctrine of no-self: 'That there is a self has been taught. And the doctrine of no-self by the Buddha as well as the doctrine of neither self nor non-self has also been taught.'[24] Thus, what seem to be diametrically opposing doctrines are all taught. Each of the extreme ends of a contradiction can have a useful place depending on the state of the individual, and neither can be absolutely rejected under all circumstances. For those extremists who are nihilistic about the self – such as the scientific materialist – the skilful means is to emphasize the conventional utility of the self-concept. Modern psychology calls this the development of the positive ego in order to prevent cognitive dissonance or fragmentation of the self that could lead to psychological illness. On the contrary, for those who tend to reify the self, the doctrine of no-self is taught as the antidote to their essentialism. Nagarjuna implies that there is a truth more profound than the extremes of self or no-self. One wonders how this could be logical, and to understand this one must go beyond the two-value true/false logic with which we are familiar.

Classical Indian logic in most dharmic philosophies – but especially in the schools associated with Nagarjuna – regards any proposition as a square involving four possibilities or extremities (the catuskoti mentioned above). The four possibilities are: true (and not false); false (and not true); both true and false; and neither true nor false. Indian logic and metaphysical systems divide each problem into these four possible alternatives – not simply true/false. Each of these four possibilities requires analysis before it can be accepted or rejected. Buddhism refined and formalized this four-alternative logic system which had existed for many centuries.[25] It is used to develop sensitivity to context and pragmatic situations. The Buddhist tetralemma (catuskoti) is used as a dialectical device to exhaust all logical alternatives. It is an approach associated with the doctrine of the emptiness of emptiness, namely, the de-reification of even the concept of emptiness. As both self and no-self are conventional designations, all that can be associated with them is likewise conventional.

Each of the four alternative views of the self may be applied both analytically and practically in order to serve as antidotes to extreme metaphysical views. However, none of these views refer to any real entity that can be found upon analysis.

Notions of Self in Hinduism and Buddhism

The Buddhist deconstruction of the self into the five aggregates of form ('rupa'), feeling ('vedana'), perceptions ('samjna'), mental formations ('samskara'), and consciousness ('vijnana') seems to annihilate subjectivity and consciousness. Its tenet of non-self ('anatman') encountered huge Hindu resistance since it is a radical departure from, and rejection of, the non-Buddhist Indian philosophical views of Self (Atman) and Purusha (Paramatman). The intense debates centred on the question of essence ('sva-bhava') and being ('sat-bhava') in this setting. The Buddhists contend that – through introspection and analysis – the self is found to be a composite and dependently arisen, and hence a contingent and impermanent phenomenon.

But there are other systems of Indian thought which advance similar non-substantialism of the psychological self (ego), though not of the metaphysical self. For instance, Patanjali propounds a psychodynamic (not merely structural) theory of empirical consciousness, advocating that the mind and mental processes are arrested ('chitta-vritti-nirodha') when the seer (Purusha) and the power of seeing are separated ('drig-drishya-viveka'). Thoughts (referred to as vrittis) come to an end when the pure consciousness of Purusha is isolated in its own being. This conception is isomorphic with the Buddhist view that the true nature of the mind is clear and luminous but obscured by adventitious defilements.

In Vedanta, too, the psychological self is a phenomenon arising from a mistaken identity; it ceases to exist, like the illusory snake-in-the-rope, when true knowledge dawns. Additionally, the Vedanta doctrine of the Atman encased within five sheaths ('pancha-kosha') has its counterpart in the Buddhist doctrine of the so-called being composed of five aggregates ('pancha-skandha').

Jainism: Multiple Perspectives and Mutual Respect

Jainism has deep roots in ancient India and exerted a strong influence for several centuries. Its worldview is different from those of other dharma traditions, though it shares the integral unity found in the Hindu and Buddhist schools.

One of the main tenets of Jainism states that reality is subjective, since it is known by relative and not absolute standpoints or perspectives. This is called 'the doctrine of nayas'. A naya is a reference point from which judgements are made.

There are seven nayas, all of which have to be exercised in order to distinguish the qualities of an object.[26] This leads to the doctrine of 'anekanta-vada', which says judgements are to be made from a variety of perspectives.

Each of these perspectives is conditioned by context and a person's background. Hence, another key tenet of Jainism is that all knowledge is only probable ('syad-vada') or partial. What we assume to be the complete truth or conventional knowledge must necessarily be prefaced with the notions of 'perhaps' or 'maybe' or 'somehow'. The implication here is that all knowledge is relative or contingent on the viewer's context, rendering absolute descriptions impossible.

Taken together, these ideas – syad-vada and anekanta-vada – are the foundations of the contextual, non-absolutist outlook of Jainism. Jainism thus is opposed to systems of thought which claim that reality has only a single determinate nature, referring to such systems as 'ekanta-vada'. Aristotelian logic and biblical exclusivism are prominent examples of this determinate nature. The many-sidedness of reality as expressed in the doctrine of nayas allows for no categorical affirmation or negation about anything since the nature of reality is too complex to be captured by a single definition or predication. The ultimate reality can only be understood by a liberated soul with the ability to entertain all possibilities simultaneously.

Critics have contended that this doctrine leads to contradictory results about any single phenomenon. The Jain's response is that contradictions can only be avoided when statements are made from multiple viewpoints yielding a comprehensive – rather than a unilateral and privileged – view. Jain logic admits that contradictory statements are inadmissible about the same thing in the same sense, at the same place and time. Discrepancies on a given thing in a given context can only exist among views from different perspectives. The Jain logician is grounded in the premise that there are no absolute essences and lays the charge of contradiction at the feet of whomsoever claims that his particular point of view is free of context and hence absolute.

Thus Jain logic, Buddhist Madhyamika logic and various Hindu systems all emphasize the context in which truths can be known. Each of these systems also offers a path to transcend the bondage of these contexts through yoga, meditation and related sadhanas. They reject unequivocally the tyranny of Aristotle's Law of the Excluded Middle and biblical exclusivism in so far as these are put forth as ultimate and absolute truths.

Appendix B

A Systems Model of Dharma and Abrahamic Traditions

Dharma metaphysics may be modelled as a meta-architecture applicable to numerous different schools which share common principles, symbols and techniques, all of which are designed to gain access to higher states of consciousness. A precise definition is impossible of course, since dharma offers a large body of theory and yogic techniques.

This book is the result of my quest, over the past two decades, to define this 'dharma architecture' in such a way that does justice to its flexibility and diversity while, at the same time, avoiding the sameness approach that denies its distinctiveness.

One can design and build any number of different kinds of computers by selecting from a vast range of components, including disk drives, screens, operating software, memory, printers, and so on. Each type of component is available from multiple vendors offering different features, e.g., there are many kinds of screens available. So there is a myriad of possible ways to configure perfectly legitimate systems depending on the combination of components one selects. And yet they all have certain *common standards and architectural principles.* This is why one can mix and match a screen from one manufacturer with a keyboard from another, for instance.

Some sophisticated consumers are the do-it-yourself types who can select and build a system from the components. Others prefer to rely on a pre-packaged system supplied by a credible supplier – known as a 'systems integrator' – who selects the components best suited for the client and puts the whole system together.

The systems integrator is the intermediary who simplifies the enormous complexity of choices and trade-offs for his target clientele. His role is threefold: (i) to select, configure and put the whole system together, (ii) to install the system, and (iii) to give it identity as a brand name.

The Hindu 'sampradaya', or an individual guru, is the systems integrator who chooses the various components which constitute a 'total system solution' for the spiritual life of a particular client. He installs this through initiation and training and provides ongoing support. Many sampradayas are like brand names in that they are characterized by, or identified with, certain symbols, manner of dress, and so on. Using this model, dharma may be seen as:

a. An open architecture for the spiritual quest as well as guidance for one's mundane living – many choices and more choices being added over time by new suppliers.

b. A variety of components that fit into the architecture based on individual choice. One can choose one's own ishta-devata and other devatas, rituals, day of the week to fast (if at all), pilgrimage sites, festivals, sacred texts, cosmological worldview, and so forth. The diversity of components that can fit into this architecture provides pluralism, and many of the components are constructed for each social context and period.

c. Pre-packaged religious systems available from sampradayas each of which provides a total-life solution. This is for the consumer who does not want to, or simply cannot, put together his or her own spiritual path from the options available.

d. A do-it-yourself option for the sophisticated practitioner which bypasses all suppliers. This practitioner has to be advanced in sadhana in order to be able to work with this option.

e. Various ongoing R&D houses (individuals or sampradayas) which periodically come out with novel ideas and practices and introduce these into the marketplace. Many innovations fail, while others succeed.

f. Like the Internet, this dharma has no centre, no owner, no founder, and alternative offerings are always subject to argumentation and change. There is no singular authority that has ever decided for all dharmic consumers what is 'right'. Nobody has been able to destroy the other options. There is no history of destroying rejected components (cf. burning books); they simply fade away when newer ones get adopted by consumers. The marketplace of consumers and suppliers has always been dynamic and nothing is resolved by the use of absolute force by theocratic rulers.

g. To participate successfully using this open architectural system does not require one to study the history of the system itself, i.e., who created the Internet, and other trivia about its beginnings.

Such a culture is a constant reworking based on numerous innovations which emerge in unpredictable ways and places. The system is self-correcting, adaptive and avoids the problems of long-term exclusivity and fixations on a specific history. The spirit of openness toward the multiplicity of possible answers to complex questions is why pluralism is deeply embedded in the notion of dharma.

The Judeo-Christian religions lack the fundamental R&D to be able to change to the same extent and to be able to offer the same choices and openness. As we have seen, they do not believe that the first principles of truth can be discovered by humans on their own; hence, their obsession with claiming historically unique events.

This closed-mindedness leads them to insist that nothing is legitimate except their own product – a monopolistic practice. They lack the tools and technologies that the dharma traditions have developed over several millennia. Whereas the dharma traditions resemble Silicon Valley innovation and freedom, the Judeo-Christian religions come across like controlled, state-supplied, monopolistic products. Like the Soviets who believed in allowing only one airline, one brand of car, one toothpaste, etc. (despite the fact that consumers have many needs), most Christians believe in allowing only one approach to religion; many in the Jewish tradition do likewise. Just as Christian institutions have discouraged or outright banned mystics (the R&D labs to discover new approaches and challenge old ones), the Soviets did not allow entrepreneurship as it threatened their monopoly.

Flexibility comes with serious challenges. There is not just one Hindu book or one Buddhist book but many, and each may offer a different solution to the same question. The following question arises: Since there is no single institutional authority to mediate such issues and provide command, on what basis is a practitioner to determine the right book to choose, the right course of action to take? The answer is that there are at least three approaches whereby a practitioner may determine the ethics for a *particular* instance: scripture, lineage (sampradaya, or guru), and personally achieving a higher state of consciousness. There are no canonized ethics, as such, that can be applied blindly as 'universal'.

It is important to establish this contextual basis of Hindu ethics (a very postmodern idea), because the main criticism levied by Christian proselytizers is that Hinduism suffers from moral relativism. This charge of relativism is often expressed in ways that could be misunderstood as positive – millions of gods, lots of scriptures, many gurus, total freedom, and so on. The contextual nature of dharma has been discussed in Chapter 4.

Notes

Introduction

1 The term 'Abrahamic religions' is often used when Judaism, Christianity and Islam are all to be referred to as a group.

1: The Audacity of Difference

1 (Friedman 2005).

2 As a recent example of such views, here is what the *New York Times* wrote: '... culture ... has only atomized lately as a consequence of the very same globalizing forces that purportedly threaten to homogenize everything. [...] Nationalism, regionalism and tribalism are all on the rise. Societies are splitting even as they share more common goods and attributes than ever before. Culture is increasingly an instrument to divide and differentiate communities.' (Kimmelman 2010: 19).

3 (Weiming n.d.). Also see (Liu 2003).

4 The scholar was Jay Garfield, and we had this discussion at the Vedanta Congress in the summer of 2009 at the University of Massachusetts, Dartmouth. A concrete example showing the importance of preserving difference is that of healing systems throughout the world. Each brings something useful to the table because of its distinct models and approaches. Western medicine, Indian Ayurveda and yoga, and Chinese medicine and acupuncture all provide unique solutions for certain types of diseases and wellness management. Yet none can be properly mapped onto another's framework without compromise. What is needed is not a cut-and-paste insertion of these practices into a Western model of medicine but an understanding of the integrity and utility of each system's own model and the philosophy behind it, so as to give it a place alongside Western systems.

5 Tolerance became a serious topic of discussion in Christianity only in the sixteenth and seventeenth centuries in response to the Wars of Religion, which started following the Protestant Reformation.

6 (Ratzinger 2000).

7 For details on the Emory Inter-Religious Council, see: (Emory Inter-Religious Council n.d.).

8 She was joined by Prof. Deepika Bahri, who had recently been appointed director of the Asian Studies Program. This was Emory's response to severe criticism of its Hindu-phobia, offered in the hope that Bahri's soft-spoken nature, Indian language skills, and Hindu name would placate Hindu parents who had protested against Emory. (Ramaswamy, Nicolas and Banerjee 2007).

9 For instance, when asked about what happened to Mahatma Gandhi after his death, theologians of some Christian denominations insist that Gandhi went to Hell because he was not Christian. For examples of such interpretations, see: (Weiss 2007).

10 The other question I asked the dean was: 'How would you balance between respect for a religion on the one hand and academic freedom on the other, especially when a professor at your university claims that Ganesha's trunk symbolizes "a limp phallus", that he has "an appetite for oral sex", and that Shiva is a "notorious womanizer"?' (For details on this anti-Hinduism scandal at her university, see: www.invadingthesacred.com.) The dean was pleasant but evasive, remarking that these important questions had to be 'considered' but that there were 'no easy answers'.

11 (Haag 2008, Oct/Nov, 2-3).

12 To take only one example, Christians, from the Spanish conquistadores to the Protestant Puritan settlers, supported and even encouraged the genocide of Native Americans. The conquistadores believed that the Native Americans were related to them in the same way that children were to adults, women were to men, and savages or wild beasts were to civilized people. Since their weakness led them to worship 'false gods' and promote heathen practices, they had to be either forcibly converted or killed outright. These projects of eradication resulted in the elimination of whole cultures. Slavery and colonization were sometimes rationalized by church officials, though, of course, economic motives were always present. Such practices are deplored today in politically correct circles, and yet the underlying religious and philosophical rationales for them remain, for the most part, unchallenged and unchanged.

13 (Balslev 1991).

14 (Balslev 1991).

15 Rorty claims that 'freedom and equality are the West's most important legacy', to which he arrogantly adds: 'I do not have philosophical backup for this claim, and do not feel the need of any.' The West, Rorty writes, 'has created a culture of social hope' which makes it 'a culture of experimentation' for bringing about 'drastic change in the way things are done'. In other words, it is politically progressive. This he contrasts with India's 'consensus that the conditions of human life are and always will be frustrating and difficult.' He goes on to describe India in patronizing tones as the 'high culture of a peaceful society' that wants to remain stuck under 'priests' and 'sages.' A visit to India convinces him that India is 'a country whose native traditions have little to do with the Western hopes of freer and more equal future generations.' (Balslev 1991: 17–25).

16 For a detailed discussion on how Indian philosophy has been marginalized in the American academy, see: (Shruti 2005).

17 Concerning Indian contributions to mathematics, Albert Einstein, a great admirer of Indian scientific achievements, philosophy and spirituality, is quoted as saying: 'We owe a lot to Indians who taught us how to count, without which no worthwhile scientific discovery could have been made.' In a similar vein, the British historian of India Grant Duff says: 'Many of the advances in the sciences that we consider today to have been made in Europe were in fact made in India centuries ago.' The influential American writer Mark Twain travelled extensively in India and spoke broadly about the achievements of ancient India. He said: 'India is the cradle of the human race, the birthplace of human speech, the mother of history, the grandmother of legend, the great grandmother of tradition. Our most valuable and most constructive materials in the history of man are treasured up in India only.' The popular American historian Will Durant echoes Mark Twain's admiration for Indian achievements in his *Story of Civilization*: 'India was the mother of our race and Sanskrit, the mother of Europe's languages. India was the mother of our philosophy, of much of our mathematics, of the ideals embodied in Christianity, … of self-government and democracy. In many ways India is the mother of us all.' For these and other quotations on the same theme, see: (sciforums.com 2001).

18 (Balslev 1991: 53).

19 (Todorov 1999: 308).

20 Even today the Catholic Church sees itself as the new embodiment of Israel, the chosen people, with a mandate to establish the kingdom of heaven worldwide, even though this mandate is currently understood to recognize the separation of church and state. Furthermore, the Catholic Church has a history of violent, as well as non-violent, repression of heresy. The political dimension

inherent in such evangelizing is especially apparent in the intimate and ongoing collusion between the churches and secular state power.

21 The Vatican Directive Prot. N. 802/69 dated 25 April 1969, *Twelve Points of Inculturation*, applies officially in India. The Kerala church has a new curriculum in every seminary for training its clergy which includes symbolic use of the Hindu tradition of sanyas, bhajans, the *gurukul* system and *Varnashram*. The church calls this 'Indianization' (Anathkrishnan 2007).

22 (Pearson 1990: 123).

23 In his Annual Letter of 1651, Father Antony Proenca pleaded with his readers: 'Among my readers, there will surely be some who could procure for us some lotion or ointment which could change the colour of our skin so that just as we have changed our dress, language, food and customs, we may also change our complexion and become like those around us with whom we live, thus making ourselves "all to all", *Omnia Omnibus factus*. It is not necessary that the colour should be very dark; the most suitable would be something between black and red or tawny. It would not matter if it could not be removed when once applied; we would willingly remain all our lives the "negroes" of Jesus Christ, A.M.D.G. [to the greater glory of God].' (Shourie n.d.).

24 (Samuel 2008). This Bible is called the New Community Bible.

25 (Malhotra and Neelakandan, *Breaking India*, 2011: 111–124).

26 There are many examples in popular culture of Indian mimicry due to inferiority complexes. *The Times of India* did a survey on the level of sexual satisfaction among its readers. Interestingly, the results were expressed in terms of 'world standards' on such things as frequency and ways of having sex. In their radio discussion on the survey, one female anxiously asked, 'Sir, how are we doing compared to world standards?' Critics have pointed out that auto manufacturers in India use Western anthropometric data, including details such as height, weight and key physical specifications of people who are likely to drive, or be driven around in, a car. In the absence of gathering Indian population data, car makers such as Maruti Suzuki India, Mahindra and Mahindra and Tata Motors rely on mannequins based on US, Japanese, European or Korean specifications. The American size of 6 ft and 75 kg does not suit Indian drivers in terms of brake and clutch operations. Women's dress size standards in Indian metropolitan cities are European or American sizes, and likewise for shoe sizes. Even in describing weather, many Indians writing in English refer to hot sunny days as 'nice days' and rain as 'bad weather', an attitude reflecting the context in England where it is often rainy and the sun hardly shines, but out of context for hot climates where rain is a blessing and a celebration by nature and culture alike. The use of first, middle and last names by Indians of today has replaced

the traditional use of village name or jati name. The adoption of the Western calendar has similarly undermined the native festivals that corresponded to the Indian seasons and the agricultural roles performed, such as planting and harvesting. The lure of Hollywood Oscars overrides native criteria for popularity and success among many new elite movie producers of India. This follows the trend in written works by Indian authors who often cater to Western tastes and stereotypes about Indians. Organizations such as the South Asian Journalists Association (SAJA) cater to Indians' complex of feeling ignored. They make a big thing of Indians being invited by, included in, and even investigated by the American establishment as a mark of 'having arrived on the world stage'. I have discussed this issue of whiteness complexes among Indians in various articles, and there is extensive literature on the wider subject of whiteness written by American scholars, both black and white. See (Malhotra, *Whiteness Studies and Implications for Indian-American Identity* 2007). Many Indian intellectuals have a Hegelian fear of being left out of history, an issue taken up in Chapter 4. Later on, Karl Marx modified this linear history into stages defined by class structures. To qualify for the revolutions leading to utopia, his system demanded that the starting point be a feudal system, and from there his class struggle system would move society forward. This led many Indian historians and social scientists to work hard at characterizing Indian society as feudal, in order not to be left out of history.

27 In a separate volume titled *U-Turn Theory,* I cite numerous examples of this kind of digestion of Indian civilization into the West and illustrate the effect of such a process over time.

28 There are numerous examples where the conquering civilization gets significantly modified. Early Christianity digested pagan and pre-Christian traditions, and this brought Christmas and the mother/son icon and various other rituals and symbols into Christianity. The conquest of the Native Americans by Europeans introduced new agricultural foods into the rest of the world, including potatoes, tomatoes and corn. Similarly, Islam's expansion into India allowed it to serve as the bridge between India and Europe, because Islamic scholars translated major treatises on Indian mathematics, astronomy and botany and retransmitted these to Europe, adding fuel to the scientific revolution. European colonization of India brought cross-cultural fertilization, as the Europeans learned steel and textile manufacturing, agriculture, medicine and shipbuilding from India.

29 Hegel is a good example of such a thinker, as explained in Chapter 4.

30 It is interesting to note that in the early UN debates on the legal definition of genocide, the notion of cultural genocide was proposed initially

but then dropped, and only physical genocide was declared a crime. See Article 7 of the 1994 draft (later this article was deleted): (Draft United Nations Declaration on the Rights of Indiginous Peoples 1994).

31 Readers who need a brief overview of the dharma philosophies mentioned in this section might benefit by reading Chapter 3 first and, for a deeper look, Appendix A.

32 Besides the US and the European Union, jurisdictions which remain highly nationalistic include Russia, China, Japan and the Arab states. Each has an overriding grand narrative rather than multiple competing narratives, as in the case of India.

33 (Sardar 1998).

34 (D. Horowitz 1967).

35 (Malhotra and Neelakandan, *Breaking India*, 2011) For a short article, see: (Malhotra, *We, the Nation(s) of India*, 2009).

36 The same scholars promote the divisive and separatist movements on behalf of Dalits, Dravidians and minority religions by constructing elaborate histories, religions, linguistic models and political identities for them. The methodology is not being used to deconstruct minority identities in the same way. For instance, one could question whether a genuine Dalit identity exists at all, given that this is a recent category and those said to belong to it are from thousands of separate jatis across hundreds of miles of distance, with little if any historical contact and no commonality of religion, language or customs. In other words, contrary to the ideals of deconstructing boundaries, in the case of Dalits, Dravidians and certain other groups, their boundaries have been recently constructed using imported theories. This practice is rife in the field known as subaltern studies.

37 (Said 1979).

38 (Marriott 1990).

39 (Ramanujan 1990).

40 (Fox 1986: 20). Subjecting Western epistemologies to the scrutiny of Western viewpoints and ways of knowing introduces what sociologist Richard Fox has called a measure of 'epistemic parity'.

2. Yoga: Freedom from History

1 (Sri Aurobindo: 'On Himself', *SABCL* Vol.26, p.68). This is true even of Sikhism, which has a defined historical lineage of gurus but which does not claim that they are intermediaries in the individual practitioner's self-realization of liberation.

2 For example, ethnographic studies in Nepal, Orissa and other regions reveal that Puranic stories served as generic templates, which were localized for each place, time and context. Into these, tribal deities were incorporated, thus becoming part of the Hindu–Buddhist mainstream. These deities had narratives, songs and rituals, and a special relationship with each locality. This assimilation of communities respected cultural specificities and was never just a ploy to gain a foothold so as to erase local traditions later.

3 (Lannoy 1971: 292).

4 (Aurobindo, *Collected Works of Sri Aurobindo: Essays on the Gita*, 1997: 15).

5 This occurred around Diwali, after the events of 11th September 2001, as part of the state governor's programme to give state employees exposure to the major religions being practised in New Jersey. I was the featured speaker on Hinduism ('Diwali Celebration', 2001).

6 In Hinduism, for instance, the loss of history would never be permanent, as time is cyclical. The narrative goes as follows: After the dissolution of the universe, a new universe is manifested, and the first living being, Brahma, is self-born from a lotus flower which grows out of Vishnu's navel. After meditation for 1,000 celestial years, there manifests in his heart the Vedic knowledge and the knowledge for recreating the universe. This is when creation takes shape. Thus, the highest knowledge is again recoverable (but, it should be stressed, only by qualified persons).

7 An excellent example is the 'Pratyabhijna' doctrine of 'self-recognition' which its Kashmiri founder, Utpaladeva (early tenth century CE), promulgated explicitly as a new and easy method open to all (despite its hidden philosophical sophistication and claims to fulfil all the doctrines that came before). There was thought to be no contradiction between its being revealed by a human being for the first time in a specific place and the timeless validity of its core insights and teaching. Nor is there an undue sense of catastrophe over a particular tradition being irremediably lost over time.

8 (*The New Oxford Annotated Bible with Apocrypha: New Revised Standard Version*, 2010).

9 Ronald Inden wrote a book to illustrate that Indian history can be accurately discovered in reliable records. (Inden, Walters and Ali, *Querying the Medieval: Texts and the History of Practices in South Asia*, 2000).

10 In contrast to the approach to Indian antiquity, the West has a well-established discipline of biblical archaeology in the academy, and in the popular imagination, history is propagated in such places as the History Channel on television. For decades, serious scholarship has been seeking physical evidence

to match biblical references. In the West, this endeavour is highly respected, whereas in India comparable efforts tend to get dismissed as chauvinism.

11 (Aurobindo, *Letters on Yoga*, 1970: 425–27). He is referring to the popular stories about Krishna, saying that these do not occur in space time and that they are *always* occurring and available for us to actualize on earth.

12 Sri Aurobindo wrote on the historicity of Krishna and Jesus as follows: 'The historicity of Krishna is of less spiritual importance and is not essential, but it has still a considerable value. It does not seem to me that there can be any reasonable doubt that Krishna the man was not a legend or a poetic invention but actually existed upon earth and played a part in the Indian past. Two facts emerge clearly, that he was regarded as an important spiritual figure, one whose spiritual illumination was recorded in one of the Upanishads, and that he was traditionally regarded as a divine man, one worshipped after his death as a deity; this is apart from the story in the Mahabharata and the Puranas. There is no reason to suppose that the connection of his name with the development of the Bhagavata religion, an important current in the stream of Indian spirituality, was founded on a mere legend or poetic invention. The Mahabharata is a poem and not history, but it is clearly a poem founded on a great historical event, traditionally preserved in memory. Some of the figures connected with it, Dhritar Parikshit, for instance, certainly existed and the story of the part played by Krishna as leader, warrior and statesman can be accepted as probable in itself and, to all appearance, founded on a tradition which can be given a historical value and has not the air of a myth or a sheer poetical invention. That is as much as can be positively said from the point of view of the theoretical reason as to the historic figure of them, but in my view there is much more than that in it and I have always regarded the incarnation as a fact and accepted the historicity of Krishna as I accept the historicity of Christ' (Aurobindo, *Letters on Yoga*, 1970: 425–27).

13 Raimundo Panikkar (1918–2010), a recognized authority on both Hindu traditions and Roman Catholic theology, provides a perspective on the relationship of time, history and culture different from that proposed in Judeo-Christian religions. The vision that a people has of its own history, argues Panikkar, suggests how their tradition understands their past and assimilates it into the present. But a people's attitude to its history is determined less by written interpretations of that past than by their ways of life and how they relive or revisit it. India, for instance, has lived her memories of the past more through her epics than through the written records or documents of history. The lack of interest in literal historiography can be frustrating and upsetting to the Western mind. But the same Western mind, retorts Panikkar, fails to see that its own myths precisely are taken as history. (Panikkar 1979).

14 An award-winning book, *Lies My Teacher Told Me: Everything Your American History Textbook Got Wrong* (Loewen 1995), gives numerous examples of outright fallacious history which is taught in US schools and accepted as true by the public, especially as it pertains to centuries of encounters with Native Americans and African–Americans.

15 (M. King 1964: 147).

16 An arguable exception would be the Western 'stages' of civilization, such as archaic, magical, primitive, traditional, medieval, modern, and so on. These may not even be accurate in understanding Europe, yet they are being universalized and applied to all other civilizations. India does not neatly fit into these stages; it always has had many of the qualities of all such stages. For instance, Auguste Comte's Law of Three Stages of Knowledge states that knowledge in all branches necessarily passes through theological (animistic), philosophical (speculative) and scientific ('positive') stages. Each subsequent stage is superior, and old knowledge is always obsolete. He concludes that the West is ahead of, and superior to, all other civilizations. For more analysis, see the following article available on the Internet: 'Word as Weapon: The Polemically Charged Use of Terminology in Euro-American Discourse on Hinduism' (Morales 2002).

17 (Guha 2002: 71-72).

18 Not all Christians believe in this part of the Bible, which was controversial even when the canon was formed. Although it seemed a genuine vision from a highly authoritative source (John of Patmos), it inflamed dangerous sentiments and was susceptible to misapplications.

19 (Gibbs 2002: 46-47). *Also see:* (Biema 2002).

20 (Gibbs 2002: 42). *Also see:* (Biema 2002).

21 (Thurman, *Inner Revolution* 1999).

22 (Ibid.: 211-212).

23 (Ibid.: 275-277).

24 (Ibid: 176).

25 Avidya should not be equated with original sin in Abrahamic traditions. Avidya implies no particular failure of morality or disobedience to an external deity, but rather a cognitive limitation, to be overcome by each individual even if it takes many lifetimes to do so; sin is a state of moral corruption which does indeed lead to moral blindness but needs to be addressed by repentance in the practitioner and forgiveness from the divine.

26 Anindita Balslev refers to this form of scientific inquiry as 'second-order empiricism', a unique achievement of Indic traditions. (Private communication).

27 (Wallace 2002: 12).

28 (Wallace 2002: 13-14). Another Western scholar who has specialized in bringing dharmic principles and meditation to modern cognitive psychology is Eleanor Rosch Heider, professor of psychology at the University of California, Berkeley. For an overview by her, see: (Rosch 1997).

29 The insistence on apostolic succession in the Church is supposed to guarantee transmission directly from person to person back to the first disciples of Christ, and this may appear to be an exception here. But in fact it functions more as a support for institutional claims than as a way of guaranteeing an embodied transmission of spiritual experience.

30 The Indian notion of body is that it is the integral being: the physical, emotional, mental, psychic and spiritual bodies and many intermediate *pranic* bodies or parts and planes of the being, all interlinked with each other, with the atman seen as both transcendental and immanent in the self.

31 Initially, there were seven rishis known traditionally as belonging to the 'Northern list' (possibly referring to the stars in the northern constellation of Ursa Major): Gautama, Bhardwaja, Vishvamitra, Vashishtha, Kashyapa, Angiras and Jamadagni. Later, another list of seven rishis evolved, which is known as the 'Southern list' (possibly referring to the stars in the southern constellation of Carine): Bhrugu, Angiras, Marichi, Pulastya, Pulaha, Kratu and Atri.

32 Dattatreya is an interesting example of someone who combines many subtypes. He is worshipped as a supreme deity by millions of Hindus. Originally a semi-divine rishi, he is ascribed great integrative force in the *Markandeya Purana* where he figures as the essence of Brahma, Vishnu and Shiva. His enormous fame as a great guru and yogi establishes links with Buddhism (identified as Devadatta in the syncretic milieu of Nepal) and Jainism (as Digambara; identified with Tirthamkara Neminatha). Dattatreya co-mingles even with popular Sufi saints from the medieval period onwards. The three-faced Dattatreya icon of the guru, yogi and avatar (divine incarnation) stands as an impressive paradigm of the eclectic and integrative quality of dharma and its ahistorical quality.

33 *Anguttara Nikaya* (1.18).

34 *Digha Nikaya* (1.3).

35 This is also different from the Western secular notion of a set of propositions based solely on reason, which exist independently of any consciousness. In Indian thought, the possibility of truth being ultimately independent of consciousness and separable from it does not arise. Everything that appears to be unconscious is also only *a form* of consciousness and is situated within consciousness itself and is not apart from it.

36 Certain Indian ascetic groups also treat the body in a similar manner, but this is seen as a means to transcendence, not an innate evil caused by something akin to original sin.

37 The foundational texts of Indian ethics involve animal stories (the original source of Aesop's fables and later those of Lafontaine) taught to children to illustrate simple moral precepts within concrete pragmatic contexts. What is particularly striking is that there are often tales that illustrate diametrically opposite moral lessons. For example, one demonstrates that even an injured tiger cannot change its carnivorous nature, whereas another shows how a crow is able to overcome its nature in order to befriend a mouse. Indian children were thus taught contextual ethics without being forced to assimilate rules of moral conduct by catechism.

38 Furthermore, these transgressions may be contrasted with the rigid unforgiving (but nevertheless often transgressed) morals prevalent in Judeo-Christian ethics, as well as with the nihilistic relativism of postmodern ethics.

39 Modern Bible scholarship amply demonstrates this. A major example is what is called the 'Johanine comma', an emendation in the text of one of the New Testament letters to emphasize the doctrine of the Trinity, which was known but went unremarked for years until the Higher Criticism (the school of Bible interpretation generated by German historicism) discovered it and made a point of it in the nineteenth and twentieth centuries.

40 Textual hermeneutics and the intellectual discrimination it fosters ('bauddha-jnana' in Kashmir Shaivism) operate within the context of the transmission ('from mouth to mouth' or 'mukhat mukham') of embodied knowledge ('paurusha-jnana').

41 In certain Christian understandings, especially that of Vatican II, the Church is absolutely and unconditionally the embodiment of Christ. See the work of the great Jesuit theologian, Henri De Lubac (Lubac 1988).

42 The Shankaracharya mathas are a rare exception of institutionalization that succeeded for a long time. But the Shankaracharya institutions do not control Hinduism in the same manner that the various churches may be said to control Christianity.

43 Actually, Abhinavagupta turns this insight on its head and treats the founders of the various traditions, including the Buddha, as not mere persons ('paurusheya') but as embodiments of such eternal knowledge.

44 I am indebted to William Pinch for reviewing an early version of my history-centrism thesis and sending me the following counter-example in an email in 2004: 'I am in general agreement with your emphasis on historicity in the Judeo-Christian-Islamic traditions ... But I see historicity as emerging

in Indic traditions as well, particularly among the bhakti saints – and I don't see this as a response of Western impact. You say that "Indians who claimed enlightenment using the ahistorical methods were glorified and honored as spiritual leaders during their lives, and often developed massive followings", and then turn to the bhakti saints and more recent figures as examples. A look at the *Ramanandi sampraday*, arguably the largest ascetic/monastic community in India (and certainly the largest Vaisnava order) and the crucible of most north-Indian bhakti hagiography, would appear to undercut this assertion, as would the Dasnami, the Saiva counterpart to Ramanandis. Both communities developed mass followings well after the *samadhis* of their founders – the Ramanandis in the sixteenth/seventeenth century, the Dasnamis in the fourteenth/fifteenth century. Those texts *(Sankaradigvijayah* and *Bhaktamala)* are fundamentally historical narratives. This is not to say that the method of enlightenment is not at work as well in these communities, but it is to say that history matters in a serious way to them.' In response to Pinch, I maintain that these examples merely show a history of lineages. They are not history-centric, because they do not claim *God's unique intervention* for all humanity through their specific lineages.

45 Among other things, because Vedic cosmology has always been much more time-and-space-oriented than Western cosmology (at least until recent science extended the vision of the latter), the dharmic sense of what constitutes an epoch or period in time – a 'kalpa' – is much greater. Human events are often dwarfed in this expanded view.

46 A few examples will make this clear: (i) Gödel's theorems demonstrate that all the truths of common mathematical systems cannot be written in any language. Linguistic expression, including statements made in mathematics, is limited in the set of truths it could possibly state. (ii) Wittgenstein's theory of language as a game is built on problematizing the meanings of sentences and the limits of what may be represented. (iii) The quantum uncertainty principle applies to the uncertainty built into the state of all physical systems. (iv) Kant considered his transcendental realm and the notion of the noumenon to be outside the mind's capacity. (v) Various postmodernist philosophers refute any mental representation of an objective ultimate reality.

47 (Wallace 2002: 11-12).

48 Christianity's direct experience of God is called the 'beatific vision', which can only be achieved after death. The *Catholic Encyclopedia* defines it as: 'The immediate knowledge of God which the angelic spirits and the souls of the just enjoy in Heaven. It is called "vision" to distinguish it from the mediate knowledge of God which the human mind may attain in the present life.

And since in beholding God face to face, the created intelligence finds perfect happiness, the vision is termed "beatific".' The vision implies a parent–child relation to God – not the classic dharma notion that we *are* God playing this human role. Besides, this beatific vision is available only after one dies and goes to heaven, not before. The Bible says God 'dwells in unapproachable light, whom no one has even seen or can see' (1 Timothy 6:16). Only in heaven does he reveal himself to us *face to face* (1 Corinthians 13:12; Matthew 5:8; Psalm 17:15).

49 (Wallace 2002: 3) cites the following: (Butler 1967, Burnaby 1991, Eckhart 1979).

50 (Wallace 2002: 3-4).

51 (Ibid.: 4).

52 (Wallace 2002: 12) cites the following: (James 1950, 416–24).

53 (Wallace 2002: 5-6).

54 The nature of this atonement is expressed in Bible verses such as: 'He himself bore our sins in his body on the tree, that we might die to sin and live to righteousness' (1 Pet 2:24) and 'For Christ also died for sins once for all, the righteous for the unrighteous, that he might bring us to God' (1 Pet. 3:18). There are variations of substitutionary theory, but they generally hold that atonement in Christ's death occurs in place of some consequence for humanity.

55 In the Judeo-Christian religions, every person can, to some extent, gain access to and know God. But the historical prophets' unique and extraordinary role is unavailable, which renders their historicity critical. There are many other (lesser) prophets who continue to emerge, but these do not create or alter the mandatory canons on which authority is based.

56 Jesus does say to those who claim superior knowledge of God through their biological and historical connection to Abraham: 'Do you not realize that God can raise up children to Abraham from these stones.' However, it is not the same thing as saying that yoga by itself (i.e., human 'purushartha', or effort) suffices. In other words, the dependence on God to do it would remain even after considering Jesus' remark.

57 A prominent theoretical physicist at Princeton's Institute for Advanced Studies made the counter-argument to me that the Big Bang was a unique event in which physicists believe, thereby making physics also history-centric. However, this argument is flawed: physicists believe in the Big Bang Theory not as a premise of physics (in the sense that Christians believe in Jesus' historicity as the premise for Salvation). Rather, the Big Bang Theory is a conclusion which is scientifically derived, based on physical laws and empirical evidence which is verifiable today. Hence, the Big Bang Theory does not make physics history-

centric: it is a result of physical theory and not a prerequisite belief or cause of it. Those who regard it as evidence of history-centrism are mixing causes and effects. However, the religious historicism that defines the individual's mission in the world in relation to God has in many ways been transposed onto, and still propels, the evolutionary approach to life on earth within a cosmic history extending from the Big Bang to some unknown destination.

58 In the context of his elaborate discussion of the nature and meaning of tradition ('agama'), Abhinavagupta, who is a great Hindu admirer of the Buddha, claims that the Buddha is ultimately not a historical person but rather a perennial ('a-paurusheya') spiritual principle which anyone can become, as it were, with proper effort. We see here the de-historicizing thrust deliberately at work within the core of the dharmic tradition.

59 This is a 1975 ecumenical version. (Creeds n.d.).

60 At least since the second Vatican Council (1962–65), official Catholic doctrines has held that God operates through every spiritual tradition, though not with the fullness found in Jesus (cf. the official conciliar document *Lumen Gentium*, Chapter II, Article 19). So one can tolerate other faiths, even respect them to some extent, but eventually they serve merely as preparation to become Christians in order to be saved.

61 A good example would be the split between the Roman Catholic and Orthodox Churches regarding the proper date of Easter, perhaps the most important liturgical event in the Christian calendar.

62 See especially the various works of René Guénon (1886–1951) which focus on aspects of initiatory paths and transmission and examine the problems posed by Christianity. These differences in tradition and context have been typically ignored or downplayed by Indic scholars, who have devoted entire theses to developing and emphasizing the similarities between, say, Shankara and Meister Eckhart.

63 Meister Eckhart, an exemplar of Christian mysticism, was not in any way interested in politics or the acquisition of power, unlike the more worldly priests. His one idea was the unity of the divine and the human, which seems natural from the dharma perspective but which was a threat to the church's dogma of a strict dualism between the human and the divine (a dogma which justifies a hierarchical ecclesiastical power structure). Eckhart was declared a heretic and persecuted by the church. At some point between 1327 and 1329, he died mysteriously while in church custody (Blakney 1941: xxiv).

64 For examples of how the West's claims to mysticism, inner sciences and spirituality in general have benefited from Indian influences, see the following works: (U. King 1980: Bruteau 1974; Overzee 1992; Coward, *Jung and Eastern*

Traditions 1985; Coward, *Yoga and Psychology* 2002; Clarke 1997; Olson 2002; McEvilley 2001; Federici 1995; Kearns 1987). Also, (Roy, Pothen and Sunita 2003; Parkes 1987; Rajasekharaiah 1970; Wolters 1982; Pai 1985).

65 Here is how Eugene Taylor of Harvard describes Western mysticism: 'Indeed there is an unbroken tradition of mysticism which can be said to embody forms of meditative practice in the West – from the NeoPlatonists such as Plotinus, through the medieval mystics both early and late – Johannes Erigena, St. Bonaventure, John of the Cross, St. Teresa, St. Bernard of Clairvaux – followed by such personalities as Robert Parsons, Margaret Mary Alacoque, and Emanuel Swedenborg, to modern Christian contemplatives such as Teilhard de Chardin and Thomas Merton, and now Shlomo Carlbach, Bede Griffiths, and David Steindl-Rast.' Taylor then explains that the kind of meditation that is now spreading in America is distinctly Asian: '[M]editation per se should be taken as a uniquely Asian phenomenon which, wholesale, has only recently come to the attention of the West. In its new Western context, particularly in the United States, however, it has undergone significant reformulation. In the U.S. it has become indigenized, so that now one can say that Asian forms of meditation have become thoroughly Americanized. (E. Taylor n.d.). Because of the weakness of an indigenous discourse of spiritual exploration in the West, Indian yoga and adhyatma, or the body of yogic techniques of spiritual realization of oneness with God, have had a major impact on contemporary Western paradigms, a matter I discuss extensively in my forthcoming book on the 'U-Turn Theory'.

66 For example: (a) The notion of the stream of consciousness in James's psychology is derived from the Buddhist characterization of consciousness metaphorically styled as a stream ('sota'). James's notion of a psychodynamic constellation of mind and mental states is patently the Buddhist conception of a central mental event ('mano, citta') accompanied by satellite mental states in ever-changing configurations. The Buddhist conception of mind and mental events posits (based on introspection, not speculation) a solar-system model of mind. (b) Furthermore, James's signature idea of pragmatism, especially as applicable to metaphysics, is borrowed from the very anti-speculative methodology which is a cardinal and signature Buddhism. James's pragmatic axiom is closest to the Buddhist notion of 'artha-kriya', elaborated on by the Buddhist logic school of Dignaga and Dharmakirti. This is the central deconstructionist tenet of the Madhyamika school. James was under the tutelage of the Sri Lankan Buddhist scholar Anagarika Dharmapala (see note on Anagarika Dharmapala) and acknowledges his debt to him openly, though

accounts of this are rarely acknowledged by present-generation biographers of James or historians of philosophy.

67 Anagarika Dharmapala (1864–1933) was a Sri Lankan (then Ceylonese) lay Buddhist who founded the Mahabodhi Society in 1891 to recover Buddhist management of the site of the Buddha's enlightenment at Bodh Gaya. He worked diligently for the revival of Buddhism in India and the restoration of its sacred sites. He has the distinction of being the first Buddhist scholar to teach on four continents: Asia, Europe, North America and Australia. He shared the honour of being invited to the World's Parliament of Religions in Chicago in 1893 with Swami Vivekananda, a watershed event in the introduction of Buddhism and Hinduism to the West. As a visiting scholar at Harvard during James's tenure, he exercised a significant influence over James, who acknowledged as much on a number of occasions in his article 'Yoga Psychology in the Schools: Some Insights from the Indian Tradition' (Salmon n.d.).

68 A compelling argument can be made that the system (theory-praxis) found in Patanjali's Yoga-Sutra offers greater depth and consistency than the tenets of Husserl's phenomenology. Also, Husserl's notion of 'lifeworld' may simply be equivalent to atman (god as embedded in the individual self) as understood in *Dvaita Vedanta*. Westerners like to describe it as a 'fundamental [belief] uncovered by Husserl', simply ignoring Indian traditions (Husserl 1999). These two systems are appropriately contrasted because they are comparable in their claims to have developed theories and methodologies, specifically epistemologies and praxes, adequate for grounding and comprehending all common sense and third-person scientific knowledge on one hand, and on the other, all metaphysical knowledge. Therefore, one should acknowledge Patanjali as one of the world's earliest systematic scholars of the mind sciences. His Yoga Sutra contains an elaborate theory and framework for understanding the mind, various practices for achieving specific states, and descriptions of what the practitioner experiences at each stage. But even prior to Patanjali, many Indian texts were based on the systematization of extensive inner experiences resulting from disciplined practices. Subsequently, many traditions emerged, each based on a systematic exploration of the mind.

69 Much of this resistance takes the form of what I have called the U-Turn, an initial immersion in one or another dharmic perspective followed by a relapse into more familiar contexts.

70 Many dharmic traditions, including primarily Hindu ones, stress the purity of the body and the need for cleansing. For the most part, however, this purity does not have to do with any imputed original sin, or indeed sin of any kind.

71 The Pratyabhijna school of bhakti mysticism, for example, explicitly justifies image worship as a deliberate projection of the creative Self onto an external support to facilitate meditation and inner transformation. See Chapter 5 on the difference between images in dharma and idolatry.

72 (Second Hindu–Jewish Leadership Summit Declaration, Israel 2008).

73 Ethnographic reports, especially those by Christian missionaries in India, of involuntary 'possession' during village festivals and other religious occasions, have served only to reinforce such stereotyped perceptions of Hindu spirituality as a whole, even of yogic techniques which are a mode of self-purification.

74 In Judaism, the *Shekinah* is the female principle of God, but the elaborate philosophy, practice and lineages of this spiritual practice and tradition are lost. At the same time, it is to be acknowledged that the dharma ideal is too often not implemented by society, as for instance, when women are not allowed in certain temple spaces.

75 Susan Jeffords has argued that American notions of masculinity have remained *opposed* to femininity, and hence the feminine qualities are to be discarded or at least contained in order for the masculine qualities to manifest properly (Jeffords 1989: xii).

76 There are other body fetishes peculiar to Christianity. In many biblical interpretations, the human body is to be resurrected at the End Times and shall live forever in Heaven along with one's family and friends. The resulting cohesiveness within a given group and anxiety towards others have perhaps been a factor in the scandalous fact that the American church remains far more racially segregated even today than businesses, government or schools. Also, many Christians believe that fixing up the body before burial, locating the dead body in a good cemetery, etc., are all worth the effort because we will all live happily forever in Heaven in these bodies. Bereavement often entails accepting that one's departed relative has entered Heaven where he waits for the rest of the family to rejoin him – sort of like one member of a tour group going ahead of the others to make the arrangements and then wait for the rest to join up. A relative of mine who converted to Mormonism is desperately trying to convert not only his children in the US but also his parents and relatives back in India, as he is convinced that this will ensure that the family is joined happily in Heaven.

3. Integral Unity and Synthetic Unity

1 (Organ 1970: 339).

2 Translation: 'That is purna. This is purna. Purna comes from purna. Take purna from purna, still purna remains' (*Brihadaranyaka Upanishad*, 5.1.1).

3 The Australian philosopher David John Chalmers refers to the 'hard problem of consciousness', which raises the question of how consciousness can arise out of inanimate processes comprising the chemistry of the brain. This question has persisted despite numerous speculative theories.

4 David Loy also explains that the differences between Advaita Vedanta and Madhyamika Buddhism are not of such a kind as to make them incompatible. (Loy, Nonduality: *A Study in Comparative Philosophy*, 1988).

5 It is important here to underscore *panentheism* (with the *en* in the middle) which is not to be confused with 'pantheism' (without the 'en' in the middle). The former signifies the immanent nature of God without a transcendent spirit, whereas the latter is nature worship characteristic of many pagan faiths, at least as characterized by their opponents. Panentheism refers to the world as God and at the same time God remaining transcendent. This dual character of God is central to integral unity. God is the unchangeable transcendent and also everything that exists, and hence ever in flux. Charles Hartshorne, a prominent philosopher and theologian, introduced the term 'panentheism' into the Western lexicon after his detailed study of Hindu metaphysics in the 1930s (especially Ramanuja and Sri Jiva Goswami).

6 Mahayana Buddhism denies any such bifurcation: 'There is no specifiable difference whatever between nirvana and the everyday world; there is no specifiable difference whatever between the everyday world and nirvana.' (*Mulamadhyamikakarika*, 25:19)

7 (Organ 1970: 104).

8 Christian theologians hold that immanence was always there; the essence of Jesus as immanent pre-exists his incarnation as one member of the eternal trinity of God. His incarnation merely manifested it. In mainstream Judaism and Islam, God is most often seen as transcendent *but not immanent*.

9 Sri Aurobindo writes: 'The pairs of opposites successively taken up by the Upanishad and resolved are, in the order of their succession: 1) the Conscious Lord and phenomenal Nature, 2) renunciation and enjoyment, 3) action in nature and freedom in the soul, 4) the one stable Brahman and the multiple movement, 5) being and becoming, 6) the active Lord and the indifferent Akshara Brahman, 7) vidya and avidya, 8) birth and non-birth, 9) works and

knowledge.' (*The Collected Works of Sri, Aurobindo*: *Isha Upanishad*, Vol. 17, 2003, p. 85)

10 The West's synthetic unity may be linked to the premise of nominalism as conceived by William of Ockham (1288–1348), one of the church's major figures of medieval thought. The theologian Servais Théodore Pinckaers (1925–2008) explains: 'For Ockham, there is absolute separation between God and the world. God created the world, but he remains a stranger to it. There is no symbiosis between the world and God. The two realities are isolated in their respective existence. Moreover, this is nothing but the consequence of the radical insularity of all beings' (Pinckaers 2005: 141).

11 The mantra is: 'brihaddhi jaalam brihatah shakrasya vaajinivatah' (8.8.6). 'ayam loko jaalamaasit shakrasya mahato mahaan' (8.8.8). It was later adopted by the Mahayana Buddhists in the third-century scriptures of the *Avatamsaka Sutra* to illustrate the principle of mutual interrelatedness and interpenetration of parts and wholes. The formal logic of this principle was further worked out between the sixth and eighth centuries in the Huayan school of Chinese Buddhism known as Kegon in Japan.

12 Michael Talbot started as a science fiction writer who later integrated many Indian ideas which he had learned via the works of other westerners such as physicist David Bohm, neurophysiologist Karl H. Pribram, and psychologist Stanislav Grof. All three had studied Indian thought for decades and later claimed originality in their 'independent' discovery of the nature of reality. Grof termed this 'holographic'. Talbot's most influential non-fiction books were *Mysticism and the New Physics* (1993), *Beyond the Quantum* (1988) and *the Holographic Universe* (1992).

13 (Hofstadter 1999).

14 'Purusha evedam sarvam yad bhutam yacca bhayam' – 'Purusha is all this, all that was, and all that shall be' (Rig Veda III.90). 'Pado asya vishva bhutani tripadasya'mritam divi' – 'He is immanent in all this creation and yet he transcends it' (Rig Veda X.90.3).

15 According to some systems, there are 8,400,000 forms of flora and fauna, yet the emphasis is on the sense that one living unity comprises all these multiple living forms.

16 (Vatsyayan, *The Square and the Circle of Indian Arts*,1997).

17 For instance, the number 360, the nominal day count of the year, shows up as the 360 bones of the infant (which later fuse into the 206 bones of the adult); and various multiples of 360 include the *Garbha Upanishad*'s statement that the body has 180 sutures and 900 sinews, and the *Brihadaranyaka Upanishad*'s mentioning that the number of 'nadis' (subtle nerves for the flow

of prana) is 72,000. Another central Vedic number is 108: The chain of 108 links is held together by 107 joints, which is the number of marmas, or weak spots of the body in Ayurveda. The *Natya-Shastra* speaks of the 108 karanas (movements of hand and feet in the vocabulary of dance.) There are 108 beads of the rosary ('japamala'), a tradition of the 108 names of divinity, and the number 108 appears in many other settings in the tradition, including temple architecture (Kak, 'Ritual, Masks, and Sacrifice', 2004).

18 (Kak, *The Gods Within*, 2002, 100-101).

19 In their book *The Complementary Nature*, J.A. Scott Kelso and David A. Engstrom compile numerous instances of complementarity across the sciences, humanities and arts, all the while referring to recent Western discoverers as 'pioneers' and to earlier Western thinkers as 'originators'. There is scarce mention of dharmic sources apart from vague and superficial references to 'eastern wisdom'. The authors do not bother to cite instances of Western thinkers (such as T.S. Eliot) who, by their own admission, were clearly influenced by dharmic culture or philosophy. Moreover, the terminology used is a combination of new-age and archaic Greek/biblical jargon (Kelso and Engstrom 2006).

20 Writing in (Dehejia 1996: vii).

21 (Tripurari 1998: 20-21). A different perspective is offered by Harsha Dehejia, a scholar who interprets Indian art as a non-devotional means for transcendence, calling this the advaita (non-dualism) *of art* (Dehejia 1996). He distinguishes between art as an expression of devotion to a personal God (that is to say, the artist as 'bhakta') and art that uses rasa as an expression of the movement toward transcendence (the artist as 'rasika'). Bharata, the ancient writer of *Natya-Shastra*, made this distinction implicitly between art in devotional and non-devotional ways, and later on, Abhinavagupta made it explicit. Thus, it can be said that classical Indian texts do not require worship as a criterion for attaining 'ananda', or the bliss of transcendence. In the sixteenth century, Sri Jiva Goswami introduced the category of 'bhakti-rasa' to clarify the distinction by emphasizing devotion to a personal deity. Thus, the equivalent of the secular/sacred distinction is available in the distinct approaches to ananda via art and devotion. The key point of difference with the West is that in dharma both art and devotion are based on common notions of integral unity with bandhus linking the manifest and unmanifest. This is why I disagree with Harsha Dehejia when he calls Indian aesthetics 'secular', for what is lost in secularism is the principle that all rasas are forms of one rasa and the ultimate rasa is a state of unity-consciousness, and also the related idea that all 'rupas' (forms) are a concretization of 'purusha'; in other words, the integral unity of forms that is accessible as rasa is lost in the strictly secular model. Western secularism

lacks the un-manifest/manifest cosmological principle that makes the advaita of art possible. What happens is that the bandhu principle is compromised by many westerners who decontextualize the dharmic source and relocate it in a secular frame.

22 (Organ 1970: 172).

23 In Sanskrit grammar, temporal connectives and the dynamic relation of acts are seldom lineally articulated. A sequence of connected events, while it may be perceived linearly, is not valued in the same way as a *non-linear pattern* outside history (Lannoy 1971: 289).

24 In Samkhya theory, effects are latent in the cause. In Vedanta, Brahman becomes the world through a process of self-emanation. In the Buddhist doctrine of 'dependent arising', all effects are traced to prior causes, and the infinite series of prior causes consists of interdependent entities, each with momentary existence only.

25 Each Hindu deity is not an isolated, localized historical person but is present here and now as well. The rishis discovered these deities as cosmic intelligences and also discovered (or programmed) the mantras that allow humans to become quantum-entangled with them. Humans are linked with devatas; our unconscious and conscious layers are linked with one another. The genders, varnas, ashrams and jatis are templates which are interconnected in this way. Mantras are programs which tap into the cosmic memory, as it were. Rishis have done a lot of intense spiritual practice called 'tapasya' to uncover the reality and then develop a path through which we can link up to it as well.

26 Houses (containers) have mood and character and affect the fortune and moods of the dwellers. The village soil produces crops for the people but also affects their character. Richard Lannoy, a scholar of Indian civilization, explains: 'Food is believed to transmit certain qualities in the nature of the donor and the cook, besides (in the case of meat) "toxic" essences passed on from the psycho-physiological system of an animal violently killed. Westerners, even when vegetarian, are regarded by the inmates of Brahman ashrams as not only polluting because of their imperfect dietary system, but [as] spiritually "retarded", because they have absorbed "toxic" substances through heredity, "bad" karma ...' (Lannoy 1971: 151).

27 (Ramanujan 1990: 51). Also, musical instruments such as the veena have to be made on an auspicious day by members of a particular jati or family after observing certain austerities; the gourd from which it is made must come from specific places. The gunas of the substances affect the quality of the instrument, and hence of the music (Ramanujan 1990: 52-53).

28 (Ramanujan 1990: 52-53).

29 This idea is also admirably articulated in *Twenty Stanzas on Mere-Representation* (*Vijnaptimatrata-Siddhi Vimsika*) by the Buddhist philosopher Vasubandhu (Anacker 2002).

30 In Nagarjuna's system, logic has four modes, each of which qualifies and extends the other. Starting with the classical dharmic technique of negation that ultimate reality is 'not this/ not that', Nagarjuna adds that it is also '*not not* this/*not not* that'. This aphorism points to a subtle yet spiritually potent way of understanding at once the relativism of phenomena and their non-trivial status, both the absoluteness of the divine and its resistance to reification.

31 (*A Concise Sanskrit-English Dictionary*, 1990).

32 (Infinity Foundation n.d.).

33 Hence, the history of Western science and religion is filled with allegations of fraud. Narasimha writes: 'As an aside, we may note that strong belief in models has an interesting concomitant, namely the notion of *fraud*. The history of Western science is shot through with the idea of theories and models *and* of fraud. Ptolemy himself was accused of fraud; so, in more recent times, were Galileo, Newton, Mendel, Millikan and a great variety of other, lesser known figures. I believe the reason for this can be traced to faith in two-valued logic, namely the idea that answers to questions have to be either *yes* or *no*; models have to be *true* or *false*: there are no other options. Scientists often encounter situations where there may be discrepancies between model and observation. If the discrepancies are large, the theory would of course be quickly rejected, but the crucial cases are those in which the discrepancies are small but not negligible. If the scientist falls in love with the model, he is tempted to ignore inconvenient observations which do not agree (as many of the names mentioned above did at one time or the other) or else stretch the model in bizarre ways (as Newton did with the speed of sound). If, on the other hand, observation is the starting point and one has no great faith in any particular physical model (which was the prevailing norm of Indian scientific thought), the question of fraud does not arise. Indian scientists, even classical ones, do not appear to have accused each other of fraud. This could not have been mere politeness, as they did make charges of ignorance and even stupidity against each other (as Brahmagupta did against Aryabhatta, for example). We could say that fraud is the besetting sin of a model-making scientific culture' (Roddam Narasimha, 'The Revolution of Modern Science,' a presentation at a symposium in Delhi).

34 (E. Schrödinger 1992: 87).

35 Moore, Walter J., *Schrödinger: Life and Thought* Cambridge University Press (1992). pp.170-73.

36 As quoted in 'The Mystic Vision' as translated in *Quantum Questions: Mystical Writings of the World's Great Physicists* (1984) edited by Ken Wilber, Shambala Publications, Boston.

37 'The Mystic Vision' as translated in *Quantum Questions: Mystical Writings of the World's Great Physicists* (1984) edited by Ken Wilber, Shambala Publications, Boston.

38 See (E. Schrödinger 1964).

39 In a foreword to (Jitatmananda 1986).

40 (Organ 1970).

41 The slaughter of the horse in the Ashvamedha Yajna was interpreted allegorically in the Aranyaka texts. There was to be no actual sacrificing of the horse: each limb of the horse became an allegory of meditation upon nature. He who mediated on the dawn was, as it were, meditating upon the head of a horse; the sun worshipper was, as it were, adoring the eye of the horse; the air was the life of the horse, etc.

42 For example, Sri Jiva Goswami's Vedanta is called 'achintya-bheda-abheda', meaning inconceivability of difference/non-difference. This expresses the impossibility of reducing the ultimate truth to fit within the limits of human knowledge. Jain 'syadvada' logic and Buddhist 'catuskoti' logic make these presuppositions much more explicit.

43 'Ekam sad vipra bahudha vadanti' (Rig Veda, 1:164.46).

44 (Aurobindo, *Collected Works of Sri Aurobindo: The Human Cycle, The Ideal of Human Unity, War and Self-Determination*, 1997: 423-425). The practical situation today is such that Sri Aurobindo advocates applying 'the minimum of uniformity which is sufficient', until such time as individuals have evolved to make any external imposition unnecessary. In the same writing, he says: 'We shall find that a real spiritual and psychological unity can allow a free diversity and dispense with all but the minimum of uniformity which is sufficient to embody the community of nature and of essential principle. Until we can arrive at that perfection, the method of uniformity has to be applied, but we must not over-apply it on peril of discouraging life in the very sources of its power, richness and sane natural self-unfolding.'

45 For example, some Hindu philosophical systems describe three levels of Reality as material ('adhibhautika'), deity ('adhidaivika') and transcendent ('adhyatmika'). Using these levels, the river Ganga is considered holy, and the way it presents itself to one's senses is at the adhibhautika level. But Ganga is also Ganga Devi (Goddess Ganga), a deity worshipped in temples, and this is at the adhidaivika level of experience. Beyond both these is the adhyatmika, or

spiritual, form of Ganga as Lord Vishnu's consort and yet non-different from Vishnu. This last level is beyond our ordinary sensory realm.

46 Sri Ganesha is the deity of categories and also the deity of auspicious beginnings, implying that categories emerge in a fresh beginning and are not preset absolutes. In the beginning come the categories; this is why Ganesha is worshipped at the start of any new activity.

47 In Chapter Eleven of the Bhagavadgita, Krishna grants Arjuna's request to see His universal form. Krishna states that it is not possible to see it with ordinary eyes, and thus He confers divine vision on Arjuna to enable him to see the universal form.

48 When a treatise attempts to find shortcomings in an opposing view, it does so authentically, without unfair allegations or misrepresentations, unlike what frequently happens in modern fights between rivals. Thus, even when an original text has become lost, one can recover its positions because of the way opposing treatises have depicted it in their purva paksha. Such a tradition, without purging anything along the way, becomes increasingly more complex as it proceeds.

49 For example, *Sarva-darshna-sangrahah*, a text written in the traditional style, depicts all the darshanas in an ascending order, each leading on to the next as a more sophisticated version, without absolutely falsifying what has been superseded.

50 (Organ 1970: 90).

51 In response to such allegations, one must point out that a famous intellectual of the Advaita Vedanta tradition, Madhavacharya, played a key role in establishing the Vijaynagar kingdom and created a strong ground for the Hindu dharma in the face of the Islamic invasion, and he was helped by his brother, Sayabacharya.

52 Although this is true, by and large, of the Indian spiritual systems, there are others, such as *Nyaya*, which find delight in speculation for its own sake. Karl Marx also criticized philosophers for being too theoretical; he thought the purpose ought to be to change the world. However, his was strictly an external pursuit which did not offer the means to enhance the inner being.

53 Sikhism does have a single book, but its worldview is not closed as this is not a history-centric book but rather a book of inspirations and principles. Sikhism does not claim historical uniqueness of its ten gurus and respects the legitimacy of other religions' exemplars. Sikhs openly acknowledge their borrowings from Hinduism and Islam.

54 The Veda was restricted from being written down. Only in modern times has it been published in book form.

55 'Man represents the point at which the multiplicity in the universe becomes consciously capable of this turning and fulfillment' (Aurobindo, *The Upanishads*, 1996).

56 (Organ 1970: 93).

57 (Aurobindo, *Indian Spirituality and Life* 1919).

58 The Western ones were vigorously challenged, too. The Reformation challenged the whole concept of priesthood and abolished its establishment, eventually separating it from state power completely for its followers. But these challenges have been rarer and involved immense violence and struggle. Such movements did not overturn the heavily institutionalized structure.

59 In this respect, Jewish monotheism differs from Christian and Islamic versions. Jews regard the commandments from God as second-person speech, i.e., directed specifically at *them*, and hence *particular to them*. But Christians and Muslims claim the instructions delivered to them via prophets to be third-person speech and hence universal commands for all humanity. While the commands apply universally, the 'adhikara', or authority, to propagate and enforce them was given specifically to Christians and Muslims, respectively. So the adhikar was handed down in second-person speech specifically to them, directing them to serve as God's agents for enforcing the universal edicts.

60 'Shramanas' were itinerant ascetics and free-thinkers who pursued the quest for liberation and enlightenment (moksha-marga) without acknowledging the supremacy of Vedic revelation. The founders of Jainism and Buddhism were styled 'shramanas'. In Buddhist discourses ('sutras'), non-Buddhists often refer to the Buddha as the 'shramana' (Pali: 'samana') Gautama. Sometimes 'shramanas' and 'brahmanas' are contrasted; however, the shramana ranks included many free-thinking 'brahmanas'.

61 Even when Indian thought differentiates between, on the one hand, Veda-based ('astika') mystical and proto-scientific empirical systems (such as Vaisheshika and Samkhya), and on the other, the non-Vedic based ('nastika') systems of Jainism and Buddhism, the underlying ethos is to try to integrate old tenets into the new ideas and in the worst case to leave them alone rather than abolishing them.

62 Augustine Aurelius, Bishop of Hippo (354 CE–430 CE), is considered the most influential early Christian theologian after St. Paul. He was one of the most prolific Church writers and dealt with a vast range of theological issues facing the Church in his day, and this had a big influence on the politics of Rome. He started out as a well-known orator who had studied the philosophies of Plato and who was also heavily influenced by Plotinus. Augustine then became a Christian at age 32. Eight centuries later came the next big leap in theology

from Aquinas. It is widely accepted that Aquinas used Aristotle to formulate his entire Christian theology. Jewish scholars in Toledo, Spain, under Islamic rule, had translated Aristotle's works, and this triggered a need for a Christian response. Aquinas's theory of knowledge is not a vision of divine truth (contrary to what one expects from a rishi) but rather a Christianized revision of Aristotle's philosophy. It is ironic that Christian Rome contributed to the destruction of the Greek libraries. These documents were preserved by Islamic scholars, and it was these old Greek manuscripts that became available to Europe at the end of the Crusades. Thus began the appropriation of Greek pagan intellectual works to construct what is now called Christian theology. While scholars know all this and write about it, the common westerner is shielded from these facts and taught that Christian theology is internally inspired.

63 Thomas McEvilley has explained the likely Indian origins of some aspects of Greek thought. For instance, he says the Western intellectuals' cover-up of the likely Indian origins of Plotinus protects Western identity and historicity: 'Translations of his work may have a churchy kind of ring. The view of Plotinus as a kind of proto-Christian theologian may express, at least in part, a dread of finding possible Indian origins for the texts whose influence was to contribute to shaping the thought of Thomas Aquinas, Nicolas of Cusa, Meister Eckhart, and many later Western thinkers. So it is not only that "to admit oriental influences on [Plotinus] was tantamount to besmirching his good name," but even more, it would also besmirch that whole aspect of the Western tradition that flowed from him. If Plotinus had passed massive Asian influence into the Western tradition, there would be little point to calling it Western tradition' (McEvilley 2001: 550).

64 For a harrowing account of the violent conquest of paganism by Christianity in the early medieval period, see: (MacMullen 1999). Paganism is a general term for the earth-based and shamanistic religions that lie at the ancient base of many societies. These religions typically engage with what they see as many spirits and energies, not all of them necessarily divine in the absolute sense. They tend to worship nature. These faiths became the target of aggressive Christianity after Constantine.

65 Although conquest and conflict are by no means absent from dharmic traditions, these conflicts stemmed from an entirely different psychology and political programme than did the huge colonial endeavours of the West.

66 For an extended view of this analysis, see the work of cultural historian David Loy's *A Buddhist history of the West*.

67 A good discussion of these ideas, from a Buddhist point of view, may be found in (Loy, *A Buddhist History of the West: Studies in Lack*, 2002). David

R. Loy analyses this Western penchant for solving deep internal divisions by projecting itself on to the external world.

68 One such typically self-congratulatory account is Orlando Patterson's statement that the West's value of freedom is 'superior to any other single complex of values conceived by mankind' (Patterson 1992, 402-403).

69 (Loy, *A Buddhist History of the West : Studies in Lack*).

70 The dharma traditions are not free from ideological tensions, but it is unthinkable to imagine a 'war' between science and dharma; the underlying cosmologies and paradigms would embrace and enable both.

71 (Arnold 1869: 94). This was Arnold's influential analysis of the deep conflict between the biblical and Greek traditions.

72 (Arnold 1869: 94-95).

73 (Arnold 1869: 95).

74 Even the development of modal logic touted as an exclusively Western breakthrough in philosophy has failed to mitigate this pervasive categorical thinking. With the recent development of many-valued logics in the West, attributed to such figures as Lucasiewicz and Lobochevsky, the view that Aristotelian logic is the only valid logic is no longer universally held among academics. However, Aristotelian logic continues to exert influence on the Western mentality. Even the earlier influence of Kant's *deontological ethics* reflects the Judo-Christian theological decrees mandating an inflexible morality regardless of context.

75 James Carroll's book *Constantine's Sword* explains how institutionalized Christianity emerged in the fourth century after Jesus (Carroll 2001).

76 Carroll writes: 'The emperor constantly made use of this sign of salvation as a safeguard against every adverse and hostile power, and commanded that others similar to it should be carried at the heads of all his armies, (Carroll 2001: 175).

77 (V.A. Smith 2009: 171).

78 (Wells 1922).

79 (sciforums.com 2001).

80 (Robinson 1976: 249).

81 (W.T. Jones 1969: 176).

82 Kant's transcendental ego caused further harm by removing the spiritual self and making it inherently inaccessible and impossible ultimately to know.

83 Not only were such famous scientists as Issac Newton, Francis Bacon and John Locke profoundly and explicitly Christian and deeply influenced by Christian worldviews, notions of time and the like, but the new secular giants,

Freud, Marx and Darwin, were implicitly Judeo-Christian in their history-centrism, their sense of time as linear, and their assumption that the Western ego is the normative paradigm for all.

84 Some examples of secularism disguising biblical assumptions and ideas are: Francis Bacon (1561–1626), considered the prophet of modern Western science, sought 'a return to the state of Adam before the Fall, a state of pure and sinless contact with nature and knowledge of her powers … a progress back to Adam' (Loy, *A Buddhist History of the West : Studies in Lack*, 59). Newton was a fervent believer in the millennium and spent much of his time interpreting biblical prophecy. Thomas Hobbes' (1588–1679) state of nature is a secularized version of Calvin's 'natural man', without God being mentioned, and in his *Leviathan,* the Bible is cited 657 times; there is a similar trend in his other major political works (Loy, *A Buddhist History of the West : Studies in Lack*, 127). Many European socialist critiques of private property originated in interpretations of Adam's Fall and God's curse upon him. John Locke's (1632–1704) theory of individual rights is rooted in the Protestant understanding of man's relationship with God. The unique civic society of the USA evolved out of the Puritan ambitions to create another empire for God in a new Promised Land by means of strict laws and suppression of dissent. Even Marxism, while attacking Western religion, implicitly borrowed its underlying structures and 'grand narrative', and these have become unstated assumptions in the secular worldview. See: (Eliade 1987: 206-207) and ('Eschatology' 1992).

85 (Toulmin 1990: 211-212).

86 (Camilleri 1994: 24).

87 See (Schwab 1984).

88 (*Loy, A Buddhist History of the West : Studies in Lack*, 109).

89 (Malhotra, 'American Exceptionalism and the Myth of the Frontiers', 2009).

90 In 1452, forty years before Columbus's historic voyage, Pope Nicholas V issued to King Alfonso V of Portugal the 'bull' (i.e., an edict with the legal authority of the Vatican) known as *Romanus Pontifex*, in which he declared war against all non-Christians throughout the world and specifically sanctioned and promoted the conquest, colonization and exploitation of non-Christian nations and their territories. Since non-Christians were considered less than human (and hence lacking souls), even wholesale genocide was condoned. In this edict, the Pope directed Portugal's king to 'invade, search out, capture, vanquish, and subdue' all those who the King's men saw as 'pagans … and other enemies of Christ'. The Pope's directive was to 'reduce their persons to perpetual slavery, and to apply and appropriate … [their] possessions, and goods, and to convert

them …' This doctrine was subsequently reinforced by a later Pope in order to legitimize Columbus's conquests. European nations upheld and implemented the doctrine as the legal and moral basis for colonialism (Davenport 1917: 20-26). When Columbus first arrived on Guanahani Island, he performed a ceremony in order to take possession of the natives' land for the king and queen of Spain. Pope Alexander IV issued a new bull, *Inter caetera,* of 3 May 1493, reinforcing this doctrine of discovery. Like the judgments of the US Supreme Court, these papal bulls stand to this day despite the attempts of the North-American Indians who have been agitating against them and trying to have them repealed.

91 (Newcomb n.d.).

92 (Loy, *A Buddhist History of the West: Studies in Lack,* 59)

4. Order and Chaos

1 'The Indian idea of oneness of life leads to an open-ended sense of perfectibility, to less anguish in the face of time and a less fanatical will to achieve everything in a single lifetime' (Lannoy 1971: 227).

2 Gambling, like many other expressions of chaos, is frowned upon as a vice in the disciplined life of a normal Hindu, and this is why Yudhishthira is severely castigated, even by his own wife, Draupadi, for this otherwise inexplicable addiction. Nevertheless, the Diwali tradition is for everyone to play dice and other games of chance, even gamble with money. Such days of exception, inserted into the calendar of Hindu festivals, are also part of Holi. What is destructive, threatening and to be avoided in 'normal' life is nevertheless to be integrated into the larger cultural framework, drawing on ritual and myth. Also, the Bhagavadgita (16.6 and 18.40) explains that everything is composed of the three gunas (i.e., not good/evil).

3 (Aurobindo, *Collected Works of Sri Aurobindo: The Renaissance in India,*1997:191).

4 (Rudolph and Rudolph 1967: 9). Rudyard Kipling, a great lover of India's wilderness and native culture, wrote sarcastically, mimicking the fantasies of his ignorant British audience: 'India, as everyone knows, is divided equally between jungle, tigers, cobras, cholera, and sepoys' (Kipling 1987). Regardless of what he intended, such images travel over time and get re-contextualized and reconfigured by others into the stereotypes we are describing here.

5 (Rotter, *Comrades at Odds: The United States and India,* 1947-1964, 2000: 35)

6 *Scratches on Our Minds* came out in 1958. Paperback editions of the book, re-titled *Images of Asia*, were published in 1962 and 1972. M.E. Sharpe did a paperback version with the original title restored in 1980. It is now out of print (Isaacs 1980). I have summarized and excerpted from Andrew Rotter's comments on the book. See (Rotter, 'In Retrospect: Harold R. Isaacs's Scratches on Our Minds', 1996: 177-88).

7 Quoted in (Rotter, *Comrades at Odds: The United States and India, 1947-1964*, 2000: 10).

8 (Mayo 1935). Mayo influenced several generations of American policy makers when she wrote that the Muslim 'is the purest of monotheists ... He worships One God and Him only, Omniscient, Omnipresent, Omnipotent ... and the Ten Commandments of Moses are embedded in his law.' The Hindu, by contrast, 'is the most elaborate of Polytheists. He worships millions of gods, some by acts that are cardinal offenses against any moral code of civilized humanity.' Another sensational novel in America depicted 'barbaric India, land of languor, intrigue, strange appetites, exotic women, cruel and scheming men'! In the Hollywood movie, *Gunga Din*, the thugs do horrible atrocities in Kali's name, and Steven Spielberg's blockbuster movie *Indiana Jones and the Temple of Doom* features Hindu worshippers eating monkey brains, having male-slaves, and drinking Kali's blood (Rotter, Ibid.:201-04).

9 (Rotter, 'In Retrospect: Harold R. Isaacs's Scratches on Our Minds', 1996: 177-88).

10 (Rotter, *Comrades at Odds: The United States and India, 1947-1964*, 2000).

11 (Ibid.: 8).

12 (Ibid.: 12).

13 (Ibid.: 18).

14 'Americans held gendered stereotypes of Hindu men and women: Men ... were weak. They were also cowardly, treacherous, emotional, flighty, and given to talk rather than action. They refused to stand up to evil, preferring to compromise with it, mediating disputes instead of taking the one right side in them, failing utterly to behave like ... "true men". Hindu men, Americans concluded, were effeminate. Not so Hindu women, who had admirable backbone, but with it the less admirable quality of ruthlessness and a regrettable penchant for emasculating men' (Ibid.: 191).

15 (Rotter, Ibid.: 191).

16 (Rotter, Ibid.: 192). This view was also echoed by Abbe Dubois, who wrote extensively on Hindus' lack of aesthetics, morality and courage: 'Their [Hindus'] want of courage almost amounts to deliberate cowardice. Neither

have they that strength of character which resists temptation and leaves men unshaken by threats or seductive promises, content to pursue the course that reason dictates. Flatter them adroitly and take them on their weak side, and there is nothing you cannot get out of them' (Dubois 2002, 188).

17 (Rotter, Ibid.:, 194).

18 (Rotter, Ibid.: 22).

19 (Rotter, Ibid.: 238-239).

20 (Rotter, Ibid.: 235-236).

21 Harrison, Selig S., quoted in (Rotter, Ibid.: 220).

22 (Rotter, Ibid.: 229).

23 (Bhushan 2003).

24 (Rotter, Ibid.: 219).

25 For a fuller analysis of the history of this mindset, see (Malhotra, 'American Exceptionalism and the Myth of the Frontiers', 2009).

26 (Associated Press 2005).

27 (Lannoy 1971: 280).

28 (Ibid.: 422).

29 (Aurobindo, *Collected Works of Sri Aurobindo: The Human Cycle, The Ideal of Human Unity, War and Self-Determination*, 1997: 423).

30 (Aurobindo, *Collected Works of Sri Aurobindo: The Life Divine*, 2005, 353-355).

31 (Aurobindo, *Collected Works of Sri Aurobindo: The Human Cycle, The Ideal of Human Unity, War and Self-Determination*, 1997: 423).

32 (Dabbawala n.d.).

33 Personal email communication from Dr Rajan Parrikar.

34 (Organ 1970: 18-19). The following two excerpts from Troy Wilson Organ's, *The Hindu Quest for the Perfection of Man,* explain how dharma is expressed in music: 'It would be a great mistake to dwell upon the multiform nature of Hindu philosophy and miss the common theme running through the systems. Indian music is a helpful analogy of Hindu philosophy. In classical Indian music the musicians start with a raga, i.e., a melody composed of notes in a specific order and with specific emphases, and a tala, i.e., an organized group of beats on which the rhythm structure is based. Raga corresponds approximately to scale in Western musical theory; tala corresponds to measure. The musicians are challenged to weave a woof consistent with the given melodic and rhythmic pattern. Whereas a concert of Western music is a re-creation of an original creation, a concert of Indian music is a creation within the framework of the raga and the tala. Raga and tala constitute the invariable; the musicians supply the variable. Indian music thus is a revealing of the pluralities within

oneness; it is the manifold manifesting of the Cosmic Oneness. So is Indian philosophy. The primary texts of Hinduism, the Vedas and the Upanishads, supply the raga and the talas. This is the speculative insight that Reality is the integration of values.' Organ goes on to say, 'In Indian music creativity demands the deliberate variegation of the effects of beauty within *raga* and *tala*: variety within structure, freedom within law, liberation within discipline, plurality within unity, many-ness within one, diversity within simplicity, many-foldness within the single, finite within the infinite, relative within the Absolute, the informal within the formal, particularity within universality, unpredictability within predictability, pluralism within monism, variegation within evenness, creativity within staticity, difference within sameness, change within the unchanging, flux within stability, novelty within the established, movement within the unmoved, alternation within the unalterable, *jiva* within *atman*.'

35 'Vaccination, unknown to Europe before the eighteenth century, was known in India as early as 550 A.D.' (Durant 1997: 531-32). Also: 'The ancient Chinese knew of preventive inoculation against smallpox, which they probably got from India' (Garrison 1913: 52).

36 (Zimmermann 1999: 128-129).

37 Swami Kripalu (after whom the Kripalu Yoga Center in Massachusetts was named) was videotaped many times in such spontaneous flows of asanas.

38 For example, a technique called 'chaotic breathing' is meant to break mental patterns. Some mantra techniques use the principle that vak (sound/thought) has four levels, and silent inner speech (madhyama) can lead spontaneously to pashyanti, wherein the patterned mind is deconstructed and one experiences a heightened state of alertness without content or sense of time or self.

39 (Lannoy 1971: 194).

40 (Shulman 1985: 3-4).

41 (Doniger 2009: 682).

42 Doniger is placating the lobby that does not want Hindus to reclaim their temples (taken over by invaders) by arguing that such a demand is somehow un-Hindu. Of course, as a proud collector of Indian art, Doniger would not want to allow her own vast collection to be re-appropriated on the same basis. Nor would she want her intellectual property taken over without recourse in this way.

43 Nyaya Shastra's five steps to establish a thesis are: pratijna (hypothesis), hetu (causal element), udaharana (data or example in support), upanaya (verification or experiment), nigamana (conclusion). The *Mimamsakara's*

principles for framing a problem are: upakrama (introduction), upasamhara (hypothesis), abhyasa (general outline of the hypothesis), apurvata (indication of originality), phala (purpose behind this framing), arthavada (argument in support of the solution or refutation of opponent), and upapatti (establishing the conclusion). The tantrayuktis are enumerated in various texts such as *Arthashastra* of Kautilya (third century BCE), *Sushrutasamhita* of Sushruta (fifth century BCE), *Charakasamhita* of Charaka (second century BCE), *Ashtangahridaya* of Vagbhatta (third century CE) and *Vishnudharmottara* purana (fourth or fifth century CE). In addition to these ancient texts, there is another, titled *Tantrayuktivicara*, which exclusively deals with thirty-six devices for presenting scientific texts. A work called *Anvikshiki* has been attributed to Medhatithi Gautama and was preserved in Charaka schools. It deals with three themes, one of which is sambhasha or vadavidhi (methods of debate). One such system included: pratijna (issue or proposition to be debated), sthapana (the case including reason, example, application and conclusion), pratisthapana (a counter-propositions or 'holes' in the case), hetu (sources of knowledge), upanaya (application); nigamana (conclusion), uttara (rejoinder), siddhanta (tenet established after examination by experts), and samshaya (doubts and uncertainty).

44 This analysis is based on (B.K. Smith, 1989: 51-54).

45 The crisscrossing between the two sides has been interpreted by some with the theory that asuras as a whole were more ancient divinities that had somehow fallen from grace (like the Titans of ancient Greece) with the rise of the devas. In early Iranian religion, their roles are reversed, with the devas becoming the 'demons', or rather the gods of a hostile civilization.

46 Some examples: (1) Brihaspati, the purohita (ritual performer) and guru of the devas constantly competes with his counterpart among the asuras, Shukrachraya, but it is the latter alone who holds the key to the secret of immortality. Thus Brishaspati's own son, Kacha, has to become Shukra's disciple and trick him into revealing the secret for the benefit of the devas. (2) Some of the most revered father-figures (the brahmin preceptor Drona, the wise Vidura, the patriarch Bhishma, et al.) in the Mahabharata all remain in the camp of the demoniac Kauravas. Ultimately, Krishna instructs Arjuna to seek spiritual wisdom and instruction in statecraft from the dying Bhishma even after having facilitated the slaying of the latter. Conversely, Bhima, who is Arjuna's elder brother, betrays many savage and demonic traits which the epic highlights by having his birth coincide with that of the villain, Duryodhana. (3) Sri Rama has to perform penance for his slaying of Ravana, who is not only a brahmin but a great devotee of Shiva.

47 (Lannoy 1971: 294).

48 (B.K. Smith, 1989: 220). The ritual includes the sprinkling of sand (representing chaos) around patterned baked bricks (representing order) and the murmuring of inarticulate (anirukta) sounds amidst the well-articulated (nirukta) speech and chants. The finite thus remains grounded in the un-manifest and non-ordered potentialities of the infinite. The syllable Aum is considered anirukta par excellence, signifying everything by signifying nothing.

49 'At that time, there was neither existence nor non-existence, neither the worlds nor the sky. There was nothing that was beyond. There was neither death nor immortality. There was no knowledge of the day or night' (Rig Veda, X. 129).

50 Much of the Judeo-Christian myth of the Devil is not biblical but a reflection of the influence of folklore and earth-based religions. The myth does reinforce the inherent dualism, however.

51 For example, Ravana was very knowledgeable, wise, and a worshipper of Shiva, and he achieved great spiritual powers, but he is classified as asura because his ego and arrogance took over and led him to adharmic conduct.

52 (Aurobindo, *Collected Works of Sri Aurobindo: The Renaissance in India*, 1997: 148).

53 (Ramanujan 1990: 44-47).

54 (Ibid.: 52-53).

55 The West has also developed 'situational ethics' at certain points. Wittgenstein's notions of meaning against class-logic, searches for 'native categories' in anthropology, and holistic medicine, are also akin, in varying degrees, to Indian perspectives. Postmodern thought in the West has gone to great lengths to deconstruct normative categories, but in the absence of the notion of purna (or Brahman), the end-result, as I have said elsewhere, is narcissistic and nihilistic, or leaves a vacuum that is eventually appropriated into some normative framework.

56 (Ramanujan 1990: 54)

57 Universal Western ethics also tend to be abstract and therefore difficult to put into practice. Kant's categorical imperative is an example: one teaches a child to say 'please' and 'thank you' rather than the abstract principle of 'be polite'. The process of learning does not depend on apprehending universal categories.

58 However, smritis cannot be rewritten by just anybody, as this requires authority. There are people called 'shastrakara', or people who write shastra, but that is a high platform on which to be. The ordinary man does not have the adhikara, or authority, to produce shastra. What is more realistic in the

modern era is that existing dharma shastras should be adapted by practitioners to modern circumstances. No new smritis need to be written from scratch, but commentaries on existing ones could proliferate and create change.

59 The four varnas are the spiritual and intellectual leaders (brahmana), leaders of governance (kshatriya), those engaged in commerce (vaisya), and workers (shudra). The four asramas are: student in youth (brahmacharya), householder in adult life (grihasth), the transitional stage of pre-retirement (vanaprastha), and renunciation in old age (sannyasa).

60 Various smriti texts were used by kings as guidelines for the judicial systems in their kingdoms. In the late 1700s, the British, in order to rule in India, applied their penchant for canonized, universal laws and devised normative laws for India, which they termed 'Hindu Laws'. They became the first in India's long history to try to homogenize Hindu laws across the vast land. While these Hindu laws were derived from various Indian smritis, the latter, by their very nature, were always intended to be flexible, context-sensitive and open to revision and rewriting. By canonizing (as it were) the smritis at a particular moment in history and by presuming certain contexts to be universal, the British not only grossly misinterpreted the essence of Hinduism but stymied its social evolution as well. Unfortunately, even after independence, the same static Hindu laws have prevailed and hardened into what is now commonly accepted as Hindu laws. The British put great effort into this project; they made a number of attempts to engage the assistance of teams of pandits. They were simply unable to accept the contextual nature of laws, as that notion of contextuality was alien to their own ethos of uniformity and because it would not enable them to control the Indian public. The British-developed Indian criminal code is based on Roman and British traditions, but their judicial system followed the guidelines of the smritis in civil matters such as succession, adoption, marriage and divorce, and so on. Muslims, Christians and tribal communities were allowed to follow their respective traditions in such civil matters. The notion of a uniform civil code in Indian law would, under a system similar to Manu's, have to be limited to certain types of laws that are general but would have to allow jati-specific laws for affairs that are internal to a given jati.

61 (Manusmriti, 7.41).

62 (Scharfe 1989: 221-22).

63 (Kane 1930: 882).

64 For example, Taittiriya Upanishad (1.11) says: 'Speak the truth. Practice virtue (dharma) ... Let there be no neglect of study and teaching. Let there be no neglect of the duties to the devatas and the fathers ...'

65 cf. (Chakravarti 2006).

66 For example, in the *Discourse to Abhaya* (*Abhaya-Kumara-Sutta*) there are statements classified according to their truth-value, utility (non-utility) and pleasantness (or unpleasantness). The intention is to ascertain what kinds of propositions are approved or asserted by the Buddha. In terms of the possibilities of being true (bhutam, taccam) or untrue (abhutam, ataccham), useful (atthasamhitam) or useless (anatthasamhitam), pleasant for others (paresam piya manapa) or unpleasant for others (paresam appiya amanapam), we get the eight following possibilities: (1) true useful pleasant; (2) true useful unpleasant; (3) true useless pleasant; (4) true useless unpleasant; (5) false useful pleasant; (6) false useful unpleasant; (7) false useless pleasant; and (8) false useless unpleasant. It is worthwhile quoting the text in order to get the context of this teaching: 'The Tathagata does not assert a statement which he knows to be untrue, false, useless, disagreeable or unpleasant to others (no. 8). He does not assert a statement which he knows to be true, factual, useless, disagreeable and unpleasant to others (4). He would assert, at the *proper time,* a statement which he knows to be true, factual, useful, disagreeable and unpleasant to others (2). He would not assert a statement which he knows to be untrue, false, useless, agreeable and pleasant to others (7). He would not assert a statement which he knows to be true, factual, useless, agreeable and pleasant to others (1).' For an extensive discussion of this topic, see (Kalupahana, 1992: 45-52). For an even more technical exposition, see (Jayatilakee, 2004: 338-68).

67 (Lannoy 1971: 96, 227)

68 S.N. Balagangadhara has extensively argued for this non-normative nature of dharma and its difference from Western religion. Sarvepalli Radhakrishnan (1888–1975) points out that 'the human race is not divided into the kingdom of Ormuzd and the kingdom of Ahriman [the good spirit and the evil spirit in the Zoroastrian religion]. In each man are these two kingdoms of light and darkness' (Radhakrishnan, *The Bhagavad Gita,*1948: 335).

69 The oft-made parallel between the yamas and niyamas in Hinduism and Buddhism and the Ten Commandments is inappropriate for precisely these reasons. A better parallel might be made with Jesus' Sermon on the Mount, which is more like a discourse on dharma than a set of codified laws.

70 (Lannoy 1971: 85).

71 (Ramanujan 1990; Marriott 1990: 44-47).

72 For instance, in *Manusmriti* the morality prescribed for all people includes 'contentment, forgiveness, self-control, abstention from impurity, control of the sense-organs, wisdom, knowledge of the Self, truthfulness, controlling anger, cultivation of curiosity, and abstention from injuring creatures'. These are clearly

universal principles or ideals (called samanya-dharma). The text then details the implementation of the samanya-dharma tailored to a variety of contexts, rather than applied homogeneously: A teacher and priest must not kill, but a soldier or policeman is allowed to do so under the right circumstances (i.e., in the line of duty, to protect society). The injunction to non-injury is specified for the brahmana as well as for the student (3,177), and for the ascetic forest-dweller (vana-prastha) this is likewise enjoined (75), as well as the practice of friendship and compassion towards all living creatures, and liberality to all (8). Furthermore, although there is an explicit preference expressed for adhering to one's own sva-dharma, a crossover is explicitly recommended under certain circumstances, if the overarching universal principle calls for it. For example, in chapter 4 of *Manusmriti*, a brahmana or kshatriya is permitted to engage in trading in certain situations but must avoid agriculture since this involves an unacceptably high degree of harm to animals and insects. The *universal ethic* of compassion to all living beings is repeatedly emphasized, even in times of distress, i.e., when the *context* does not override it. A vaishya may, in times of distress, adopt a shudra's mode of life on a temporary basis and relinquish it as soon as possible.

73 Here are some examples of universal dharma: 'Abstention from injury, truthfulness of speech, justice, compassion, self-restraint, procreation with one's own wife, amiability, modesty, patience – the practice of these is the best of all religions as taught by ... Manu himself' (Santiparva, 21.11-12). 'Refusal to appropriate what is not given, charity, study (of the scriptures), penance (tapas), abstention from injury (ahimsa), truth, freedom from wrath, and worship of the gods in sacrifices – these are the characteristics of virtue' (Santiparva, 37.10). 'Abstention from injury, by act, thought and word, in respect of all creatures, compassion, and charity, constitute behavior that is praiseworthy. That act or exertion by which others are not benefitted or that consequence of which one has to feel shame should never be done' (Santiparva, 124.65-6). 'Righteousness (dharma) was declared for the advancement and growth of all creatures. Therefore, that which leads to the advancement and growth of all creatures is righteousness. Therefore, that is righteousness which prevents injury to creatures' (Santiparva, 109.9-11). '... I know morality, which is eternal, with all its mysteries. It is nothing else than that ancient morality which is known to all, and which consists of universal friendliness, and is fraught with beneficence to all creatures.' 'That mode of living which is founded upon a total harmlessness towards all creatures or (in the case of actual necessity) upon a minimum of such harm, is the highest morality' (Santiparva 262.5-6). The following are some examples of contextual dharma: 'That which is virtue may, according

to time and place, be sin. Thus, appropriation (of what belongs to others), untruth, and injury and killing, may, under special circumstances, become virtue. Acts that are (apparently) evil, when undertaken from considerations connected with the gods, the scriptures, life itself, and the means by which life is sustained, produce consequences that are good' (Santiparva, 37.14). 'Might is not always meritorious and forgiveness also is not always meritorious... Therefore, men should never exhibit might in excess or forgiveness in excess' (Vanaparva, 6.8 ff). 'There where falsehood would assume the aspect of truth, truth should not be said. There again, where truth would assume the aspect of falsehood, even falsehood should be said' (Santiparva, 109. 4-5). 'It is always proper to speak the truth. It is better again to speak what is beneficial than to speak what is true. I hold this is the truth which is fraught with the greatest benefit to all creatures' (Santiparva, 329.13). 'In seasons of distress, a person, by even speaking an untruth, acquires the merit of speaking the truth, even as a person who accomplishes an unrighteous act acquires, by that very means, the merit of having done a righteous act. Conduct is the refuge of righteousness. You should know what righteousness is, aided by conduct' (Santiparva, 259.6). As may be evident from these quotations, the absolute standard of morality and righteous conduct must be moderated or compromised at times, depending on emergency, exigency and necessity (as in distress), and in the service of an even higher standard of truth than relative truth and untruth. That higher standard accords with universal compassion and non-injury. Thus: 'That mode of living which is founded upon a total harmlessness to all creatures (or in the case of actual necessity) upon a minimum of such harm, is the highest morality' (Santiparva, 262.4-5). See: (Radhakrishnan, *A Source Book in Indian Philosophy* 1957).

74 For example, in the Buddhist *Dhammapada*, the Buddha makes the following universalist credo of Dharma: 'Hatred ceases by non-hatred, not by means of hatred. This is an eternal law (sanatana dharma)' (*Dhammapada*,1,v). The emphasis on the eternality of the ethical principle of not opposing hatred with hatred is a patently universalist ethical principle.

75 Ramanujan elaborates on this: 'Where kama, artha and dharma are all relational in their values, tied to place, time, personal character and social role, moksha is the release from all relations. If brahmacharya (celibate studentship) is preparation for a fully relational life, grhasthasrama (householder stage) is a full realization of it. Vanaprastha (the retiring forest-dweller stage) loosens the bonds, and sannyasa (renunciation) cremates all one's past and present relations. In the realm of feeling, bhavas are private, contingent, context-roused sentiments; vibhavas are determinant causes; and anubhavas, the consequent

expressions. But rasa is generalized; it is an essence. In the field of meaning, the temporal sequence of letters and phonemes, the syntactic chain of words, yields finally a "sphota", an explosion, a meaning which is beyond sequence and time' (Ramanujan, 1990: 54).

76 (de Nicolas 1986).

77 (Ibid.: 1986).

78 (Ibid.: 1986).

79 Furthermore, the Western scholars engaged in this are not formally qualified as psychologists, and there is inadequate due diligence and supervision of their work by psychology experts. There has often been an 'anything goes' Wild West attitude of using pop psychology in interpreting Tantra. The licence to 'tantricize' Hinduism as a whole, and in a cavalier manner to boot, is more common among American than European scholars. It is natural for certain well-placed and influential American scholars to champion their own hermeneutics, because this empowers them as the new authorities on the vast theatre of Hinduism. The more esoteric, sensational and complex their theories become, the more their role as intermediaries in the cross-cultural encounter becomes secured. Other academicians have gone to the extent of claiming that the traditional Tantra practitioners' view is ill-conceived and obsolete, and does not correspond to any reality. André Padoux, French specialist on Kashmir Shaivism and Abhinavagupta's tantric works, makes this type of claim in his opening essay in the collective volume *The Roots of Tantra* (Padoux, 2002: 23-24).

80 Although the Vedic sacrifice is performed by brahmins typically for the upper strata, tantric sadhana (practice) is an individual discipline of the mind-body and its transmission has been available to everyone irrespective of caste. Certain tantricized sects, such as the Pashupatas and Kapalikas, were composed of those who had renounced worldly pursuits; however, they were not averse to the cultivation of siddhi (power) and even espoused radical sensuality. Tantra's worship of deities is not a subservient prayer to an external God but rather a pursuit to gain personal access to the deities' powers. At the level of the Tantra adept, the cosmic symbolism holds esoteric meaning within one's inner experiences. But, for Indian householders, the same symbolism pervades popular festivals and pilgrimages without necessarily having the same esoteric meaning that it has in Tantra (i.e., it has more popular significance). In *Srimad Bhagavata*, Lord Krishna recommends a blend of both in Kaliyuga (*Srimad Bhagavata*, 11.2749, 11.1137).

81 There are stringent moral standards to maintain self-discipline, conquer selfish desires and egotism, and prevent cruelty and exploitation of others in

Buddhist Tantra or *vajrayana* as well as in Shaiva Tantra. These codes are the root and branch vows which enjoin a morality grounded in a compassionate motivation (bodhichitta) to cherish others more than oneself. Tantric morality is premised on the balance of wisdom and compassion (prajna-karuna), or alternatively, wisdom and skilful means (prajna-upaya). In the traditionalist Tantric worldview, only the most disciplined and unselfish are really qualified for the higher practices. A dissolute and licentious tantric practitioner is pejoratively called a 'beast' (pashu) in the Shaiva-Shakta tantric schools.

82 (Hiltebeitel 1989).

83 Thus André Padoux, who did his doctoral research under his personal guru, Lilian Silburn, refers to Abhinavagupta as being unaware of his contradictions, because he is an Indian (i.e., caught up within the very system he is attempting to describe objectively). This remark was apparently not intended for Indian audiences, for it was removed from the subsequent English translation of his French thesis.

84 As a result of this, Indian narratives are filled with what Westerners would consider ethical and ontological contradictions. Dharma, or right action, is a domain of its own, and is not necessarily related to aesthetics or even necessarily to conventional morality. It is interesting that the aesthetics of the king are glorified as rupa (good-looking), whereas the sadhu/tantrika is another kind of exemplar, who is not a-rupa (neutral looks) but vi-rupa (bad looks). Dharma is not related to rupa (aesthetics) but a separate domain. Indian logicians and grammarians do not bring in beauty or morality.

85 Origen of Alexandria (185–254 CE), one of the founding fathers and prominent theologians of the early Church, wrote that the Egyptians went into bondage because 'Egyptians are prone to degenerate life' and sinking to vices. 'Look at the origin of the race and you will discover that their father, Ham, who had laughed at his father's nakedness deserved a judgment of this kind and that his son, Chanaan, should be servant to his brothers, in which case the condition of bondage would precede the wickedness of his conduct.'

86 Kant, Immanuel. 'Observations of the feeling of the Beautiful and Sublime'. Quoted in (Eze 1997: 55).

87 Ibid. Kant made sati seem like a normative practice which could be used as the basis for making sweeping conclusions: 'The despotic sacrifice of the wives in the very same funeral pyre that consumes the corpse of husband is a hideous excess' (Eze 1997: 55).

88 I remember a local Princeton policeman, originally from India, giving advice to some Indian teenagers to stay out of trouble by avoiding drugs, gangs, etc. One of the kids avoided direct eye contact with him, and the policeman

reprimanded him, 'When stopped by a police officer, *make sure you look directly and confidently at his eyes and with complete certainty in your tone.* If you don't do this, police officers are trained to suspect that you have something to hide.' He explained that it was important to have a strong and positive body language, with chest out and not hunching or looking scared. He pointed out that Indians are often misunderstood, because they have a very different body language than white Americans.

89 This is not to say that Indians are not corrupt. The point is that in India there is not the same kind of conflation of morality, aesthetics and reason, and hence one finds a wider spectrum of each independently of the other two.

90 In the 1930s, when Theodor Adorno criticized whites for defining jazz as black music, the prevailing white-dominated discourse did view jazz as 'primitive and perhaps even dangerous, its refinement best left to whites' (Steinman 2005: 117). Record companies forced black groups to adopt frontier names such as 'The Jungle Band' and 'Chocolate Dandies', and they were given labels like 'Ethiopian Nightmare'. Mainstream critics described jazz as degenerate and something of which to be wary. Only when practised and marketed by whites did it become mainstream.

91 Adorno explained capitalism's appropriation of black music into 'commodities' and 'confusing parodies' which were 'manufactured by the fashion industry' (Steinman 2005: 118).

92 See (Kagan 2006; Slotkin 1985).

93 I have discussed this syndrome more widely in various articles. See, for instance: (Malhotra, 'Whiteness Studies and Implications for Indian-American Identity', 2007).

94 Goldenberg explains the use of the term 'discolored' in this passage by analysing Origen's approach to skin colour: 'One must ask why Origen chose to mention the Egyptians' skin color while describing their bondage … The answer I think can be deduced from Origen's extensive exegetical treatment of dark skin elsewhere in the Bible. He explains the dark color of the maiden of Son 1:5, saying darkness is due to prior sinful condition … "black because of the ignobility of birth", (Haynes 2002: 68).

95 Haynes further explains: 'For over two millennia, Bible readers have blamed Ham and his progeny for everything from the existence of slavery to serfdom to the perpetuation of sexual license and perversion to the introduction of magical arts, astrology, idolatry, witchcraft and heathen religion. They have associated Hamites with tyranny, theft, heresy, blasphemy, rebellion, war and even deicide' (Haynes 2002: 67).

96 (Haynes 2002: 68).

97 (Haynes 2002: 2). Also see: ('What's up with the Biblical Story of Drunken Noah?', 2005).

98 As Haynes points out, for tax purposes, slaves were counted as property along with domestic animals. The US Congress passed a bill asking the US Census Bureau to count each slave as three-fifths of a person. Indeed, by the eighteenth century, as slavery became a central institution of the European economy, the Hamitic myth was entrenched and governed the discourse on race relations and justification of slavery. The advocates of slavery included respected professionals such as doctors, lawyers, politicians, clergymen and professors who based their position on the Curse of Ham as historical fact (Haynes 2002: 66). Some extreme pro-slavery advocates went to the extent of tracing the black race as descendants of the cursed Cain, the first murderer in Biblical mythology. More importantly, even converted Africans themselves accepted this version of their history as taught to them by Europeans. Thus, the slave and black poetess Phyllis Wheatley wrote in 1773: 'Remember Christians, Negroes black as Cain/ May be refined and join the angelic train' (Goldenberg 2003: 178).

99 (Haynes 2002: 107).

100 (Priest 1852: 94) cited in (Haynes 2002: 247). This book was reprinted three times in New York, from 1843 to 1845 and had six editions in Kentucky from 1852 to 1864 (Haynes 2002: 247). The book was called *The Bible Defense of Slavery* and its author was venerated. Troup Taylor, another Christian, wrote a pamphlet that also became famous and saw many reprints. Titled *The Prophetic Families, the Negro: His Origin; Destiny and Status* (T. Taylor 1895), it explained how the curse on Ham was passed on through Canaan to the entire negro race: 'Canaan who is certainly the father of the negro family, was adapted to a destiny suited only to an inferior people. The prophecy begins by saying "Cursed be Canaan; a servant of servants shall he be unto his brethren"... Let us see how literally the prophetic law embraced in this verse has been fulfilled by the negro and negro alone' (T. Taylor 1895: 20-21).

101 Earlier Islamic scholars had concluded that Indians were black descendants of Ham but that they were the first nation to have cultivated the sciences, and hence Allah ranked them above some white and brown peoples. See, for instance: (i) The eleventh-century work translated in (Andalui 1991). (ii) Shem is named as the ancestor of Arabs and Persians; Ham, as the ancestor of Indians; and Japhet, as the ancestor of Turks, Chinese and Russians, in the 1768 work by Muhammad Qasim Hindu Shah Firishta (Firishtah n.d.). (iii) A later work places Akbar in the lineage of Japhet, whom it regards as the most just of Noah's sons, while Ham had sons named Hind and Sindh. (Beveridge 1902, Reprint 2010).

102 (Sugirtharajah 2005: 148, 150).

103 (Newton 2009). Later, Bryant (in 1774-76) evolved this further in his three-volume series titled *Analysis of Ancient Mythology* (Byrant 2003). The sons of Ham included Egyptians, Greeks, Romans and Indians. These descendants of Ham had invented the arts but then declined into idolatry.

104 (Slotkin 1985).

105 From the Egyptian paintings to the Ajanta caves, art history shows a diversity of ideas about human beauty, reflecting the prevailing view of that time and place. When one examines the women models in the Renaissance paintings, most of them are pale, overweight by today's standards, and without cosmetics or jewellery. By today's standards of Madison Avenue fashion, few of the Renaissance models would get jobs even as ordinary models. The dominant culture during the Renaissance did not exert much physically, as that was a marker of the labour class, whereas the elite today espouse exercise as a value. The European elite in prior centuries avoided the sun, while the poor worked in the fields, but today the rich boss is out playing golf and getting tanned or going to beach resorts, and it is the blue-collar worker who is indoors in a sweatshop.

106 A very early Greek text by John Chrysostom has Jesus with dark blue eyes, though this depiction did not become popular in the mainstream until relatively recently.

107 (Trautmann 2004: 42).

108 Trautmann explains the Hindu images which are so prominent on Sir William Jones's statue in St Paul's Cathedral: 'The scene as a whole, therefore, is presented not under the aspect of a depiction of pagan idolatry but as a benign, independent record of the truth of the Biblical story of the universal flood' (Trautmann 2004: 80).

109 *The Divine Comedy*, 'Inferno', Canto 1

110 (Aurobindo, *Collected Works of Sri Aurobindo: The Renaissance in India* 1997: 186). I am indebted to Dr Lokesh Chandra who, during our conversations in the 1990s, suggested the terms 'forest civilization' and 'desert civilization'.

111 The jati called baniya, prevalent in northern India, often sold groceries and other merchandise under such a tree, and British writers of the seventeenth century started to refer it as 'banyan', naming it after the community conducting its business underneath its shade. The traditional Indian school was often held under a banyan tree, and this is still the case in remote areas.

112 F.B.J. Kuiper's magnum opus *Varuna and Vidûshaka: On the Origin of the Sanskrit Theater* argues for the (asura) Varuna-identity of the Hindu joker. It grew out of his primary work on the centrality of balance between order/chaos, gods and demons, in Vedic religion (Kuiper 1979).

113 It is important to bear in mind that the Hindu sages were keenly aware of these connections and theorized them in multiple ways.

114 (Lannoy 1971: 399). Lannoy argues that this art form usually conforms to a tragicomic mould in keeping with the conception of the Hindu universe as a conjunction of complementary forces morally opposed to each other.

5. Non-translatable Sanskrit versus Digestion

1 Katyayana, the Sanskrit grammarian and mathematician of the third century BCE, stated that shabda (speech), artha (meaning) and their mutual relation are eternal (nitya). He believed that the word-meaning relationship was not a result of human convention but was eternal. Although the object that a word refers to is non-eternal, the substance of its meaning remains unchanged, like a lump of gold used to make different ornaments, and is therefore permanent. According to Patanjali, spotha (meaning) is the permanent aspect, while dhvani (sound) is its temporary aspect. The Sanskrit author Bhartrihari, on the other hand, regarded shabda as indivisible, unifying cognition and linguistic usage, and ultimately identical with Brahman. Shabda-Brahman is both the underlying cause of the articulated sounds and the linguistic expression of their meaning. Language philosophy was debated between the naturalists of the Mimamsa school led by Kumarila, who held that shabda designates the actual phonetic utterance, and the Sphota school, led by Mandana Mishra, who identified sphota and shabda as a mystical 'indivisible word-whole'.

2 The Indian conception of the relation of the macrocosm to the microcosm is also expressed in the tantric system as the four layers of vak (vibration) which comprise a tangled web. From the grossest to the subtlest, these are as follows: (1) Vaikhariis what we conventionally experience externally. Here things are separate and relate as independent entities. For example, verbalizing a mantra as audible sound is at the vaikhari level. (2) Madhyama is the subtler level of cognition, where the mantra is in the mind as a thought but not verbalized aloud. (3) The next more subtle level is pashyanti, which is in the subconscious mind where these entities are inter-contained and inter-defined and not really separable at all. This is when the mantra disappears, leaving only a very mild presence but without form. (4) Para is the ultimate reality, where there are no separate entities and only an ocean of possibilities from which the aforementioned levels arise to manifest difference. The mantra is absent and there is silent but heightened awareness.

3 (Kak, *The Gods Within*, 2002: 151).

4 *SrimadBhagavatam* 12.6: Verses (40-41). The Supreme Self perceives this unmanifest, subtle sound outside of the physical sense of hearing and power of vision. The complete Vedic sound one employs is an elaboration of the 'omkara', which appears from the soul in the ether. Of the self-originating Brahman and Paramatman, it is the direct expression. It is the eternal seed of the Vedas that is the secret of all mantras. (42) The three sounds [A, U and M] of the alphabet beginning with A originated from that sound. They are fundamental to the threefold aspect of material existence, namely, the gunas, as well as to the names of the Vedas, destinations of lokas, and states of consciousness [avasthatraya]. (43) The mighty unborn Lord Brahma created from it the different sounds of the total collection of vowels, sibilants, semivowels, and consonants as they are known by their short and long measures.

5 Patanjaji's *Yoga-Sutra* (I.48-51). Such enlightenment/understanding is saturated with harmony, order and righteousness. Whatever one has learned or heard from external sources is outside of the consciousness, but this special realization is of a different category. This spontaneous self-awareness completely transmutes the entire being and there is total change. All other habits and tendencies are overcome by it. When even this special realization (with the seed of fragmentation still present in it) gets transcended, *everything* is transcended, and the seeker has, as it were, come full circle. The Reality realizes itself, without the need for the separate individual even in his subtlest state. This indeed is the enlightenment in which there is no seed at all for the manifestation of duality.

6 (Lannoy 1971: 273-74).

7 (Ibid. 275).

8 Pure, ecstatic contemplation of phonetic sounds reverberating on the ether in the sacred chant is comparable to the contemplation of geometrical forms and mathematical laws by the Pythagoreans. 'Only the Pythagorean master can hear the music of the spheres: only the perfect Hindu sage can hear the primordial sound – *nada*. One system exalted numbers, and the other, words'(Lannoy 1971: 276).

9 (Aurobindo, *Collected Works of Sri Aurobindo: The Future Poetry*, 1997: 38).

10 An example of such a study was reported in the article titled '*Physiological patterns during practice of the Transcendental Meditation technique compared with patterns while reading Sanskrit and a modern language*', published by the Psychology Dept., Maharishi University of Management, Fairfield, Iowa. It claims: 'This study tested the prediction that reading Vedic Sanskrit texts, without knowledge of their meaning, produces a distinct physiological state.

We measured EEG, breath rate, heart rate, and skin conductance during: (1) 15-min Transcendental Meditation (TM) practice; (2) 15-min reading verses of the Bhagavad Gita in Sanskrit; and (3) 15-min reading the same verses translated in German, Spanish, or French. The two reading conditions were randomly counterbalanced, and subjects filled out experience forms between each block to reduce carry-over effects. Skin conductance levels significantly decreased during both reading Sanskrit and TM practice, and increased slightly during reading a modern language. Alpha power and coherence were significantly higher when reading Sanskrit and during TM practice, compared to reading modern languages. Similar physiological patterns when reading Sanskrit and during practice of the TM technique suggests that the state gained during TM practice may be integrated with active mental processes by reading Sanskrit' (Travis, et al. 2001).

11 (Aurobindo, *Collected Works of Sri Aurobindo: The Future Poetry*, 1997: 313). This is a paraphrase of Anjali Jaipuria, 'Mantric Poetry', presented at National Seminar on Philosophy of Indian Poetics & Value-Oriented Education, 24-26 January 2003, Sriperumbudur, India.

12 In texts such as *Sringaraprakasha* of Bhoja (Chapter 7) and *Durghatavritti* of Sharanadeva, the authors declare that intonation has an important role to play in revealing the intention of the speaker, and it helps in the interpretation of texts in the right manner. Bhoja has given several divisions and subdivisions of intonation and their importance. In *Sringaraprakasha*, each category of intonation has been illustrated with examples from Sanskrit literature.

13 (Aurobindo, *Collected Works of Sri Aurobindo: The Synthesis of Yoga*, 1999, 11-12).

14 Dr Sampadananda Mishra of the Sri Aurobindo Society, Pondicherry, India, has theorized that reciting certain Sanskrit alphabets gives an experience of pranayama. 'It is as if the alphabet is breathing,' he remarks.

15 (Aurobindo, *Hymns to the Mystic Fire*, 1996: 449).

16 For example, the word ushas in the Vedas has both light and darkness as its meanings. The experience of light is not complete without the experience of darkness, and so the word meaning 'light' also expresses the sense of 'darkness'.

17 I am indebted to Dr Sampadananda Mishra of the Sri Aurobindo Society, Pondicherry, for providing this example.

18 For more details, see: *Sanskrit and the Evolution of Human Speech* by Dr Sampadananda Mishra, pp. 119-124 (unpublished).

19 Again, I am indebted to Dr Sampadananda Mishra of the Sri Aurobindo Society, Pondicherry, for providing this example.

20 (Ramanujan 1990: 48).

21 The correct method is prescribed by the Vedanga called Siksha, which covers enunciation (ucharana), tone (swara), duration (maatra), pitch (balam), evenness (samam) and compounding (santhanam). These rules, designed to ensure clear, lucid and effective pronunciation of mantras, require that the sounds be properly audible and not mumbled or overemphasized; nor should they be uttered in a casual manner or in a staccato fashion, nor delivered too fast or too slow or with a shaking of the head. The sounds should have been orally learnt from a teacher and should be orally chanted with concentration and understanding and never read from a written script.

22 In his *Mahabhashya* (1.1.1), Patanjali gives a beautiful example to illustrate this point. Indra killed Trishira, the son of Tvashta. This enraged Tvashta, who set about avenging his son's death. For this he conducted a sacrifice with the intention of bringing into life a powerful being that could kill Indra. He had recited repeatedly 'indrasatrurvarddhasva', meaning 'may the killer of Indra grow stronger',But, unfortunately,Tvashta recited the mantra with the wrong accentuation. As a result, the word indrashatru, meaning 'the killer of Indra' ('indrasya shatruh') gave the sense 'he whose killer is Indra' ('indrahyasya shatruh') and ultimately the being that came out of the sacrificial urn was killed by Indra. Tvashta could not get the desired result, and all his efforts proved futile because he accented incorrectly. Erroneous intonation or accentuation, then, can bring harmful results or no result at all.

23 See (Ramaswamy, Nicolas and Banerjee 2007), for details on this example and the controversy surrounding it.

24 (Sullivan 1994: 377-401).

25 (Ramanujan 1990: 50).

26 Epistemologically, there are many theories in Indian philosophy which emphasize the contextual nature of subject–object relationships. One sophisticated theory is propounded in the Vijnaptimatrata philosophy of the Yogachara school of Buddhism, according to which all erroneous cognitions are said to arise in the form of bifurcation of subject and object (grahya-grahaka-vikalpa) in what is more fundamentally a non-dual experience (advaya-vijnaptimatrata) in which duality discrimination (dvaya-vikalpa) is introduced as an inveterate tendency to dichotomize. The general Buddhist theory of 'dependent arising' ('pratitya-samutpada') also emphasizes the mutually dependent nature of the subject-object (nama-rupa) relation.

27 (Ramanujan 1990: 50).

28 These three 'das' comprise a model conversation policy, an intense desire to preserve the equilibrium, and a subsistence ethic designed not to upset the social ecology. This institutional framework is rooted in the exchange of

services and social reciprocity called the 'jajmani' system wherein the law of karma operates as the ethical correlative. See: (Lannoy 1971: 194-95).

29 (W. Jones 1795: 237-312). Westerners consider Carolus Linnaeus (1707–78) to be the father of modern taxonomy.

30 This method was also used by The Mother, Sri Aurobindo Ashram, to give spiritual names to hundreds of flowers. She explained how she discovered the significance of a given flower 'by entering into contact with the nature of the flower, its inner truth. Then one knows what it represents' (Mother 2003: 230).

31 Dr Sampadananda Mishra of the Sri Aurobindo Society, Pondicherry, has provided the following examples to show how the various names of a plant reveal the different aspects of its truth. The modern botanical description of guduchi or tinosporacordifolia is that it is a climber with long offshoots; rich in foliage, in sap; the leaves of which are used as vegetables; its mature stem is black green in colour; it has no thorns; it has a bitter taste; it promotes good health and imparts longevity and is benevolent in action; cattle love to eat its leaves; it is capable of rejuvenating itself from the cut bits of the stem; and its fibrous shoot was used in surgery for suturing. Now let us look at the different names of this plant given by the ancient Indian Acharyas. The very name guduchi is derived from the root gud, which means 'to guard or protect or preserve'. This indicates the high potentiality of the plant. The names amritavalli, amritavallari, amritalata, somavalli and somaltika indicate that this is a weak-stemmed plant. The name mandali indicates that the stems of this plant entwine in a circular fashion; kundali indicates that the stem gets entangled while it twines; nagakumari indicates that the stem has a twining nature comparable to that of young snakes; tantrika points out the spreading nature of the plant; tantri indicates the tough rope-like nature of the plant; chadmika refers to its thick foliage; vatsadini indicates that its leaves are eaten by the calves; shyama refers to the black green colour of its stem; dhara indicates that the young stems of this have slight longitudinal grooves; chakralakshana indicates the appearance of the stem in cross-section; vishalya indicates that the plant has no thorny or irritant appendages; the names china, chinnaruha, chinnodbhava and chinnangi refer to the undying nature of the stem or stem bits; abdhikahvaya refer to the richness of sap in its stem and leaves; amrita indicates that the persons using this plant would live a long and healthy life; soma refers to the powerful action of the plant as an elixir; the names rasayani, vayastha and jivanti refer to the rejuvenating nature of the plant; jvarashini and jvarari refer to the specific use of the plant in fevers; bhishakpriya and bhishakjita signify that this plant is the favourite of the physicians; vara indicates that it is the best among medicines; soumya

and chandrahasa indicate its nature of benevolence in action; devanirmita, amritasambhava and surakrita indicate the divine origin of the plant. These examples show that the ancient Indian rishis did not create multiple names for one plant just out of their fanciful imaginations; the names corresponded to their various experiences in the process of discovering the complete nature or truth of a plant.

32 Richard Lannoy, who researched this history, points out that Indians were structuralists several thousand years before Claude Lévi-Strauss lost all sense of time and became totally absorbed in tracing the labyrinthine geological strata of the Cévennes and long before structuralist physics was developed with the aid of non-numerical, computerized pattern-recognition (Lannoy 1971, 280).

33 (Eliot 1964: 118-19). Kearns explains that Eliot's use of 'shantih shantih shantih' to end *The Waste Land* showed his deep appreciation of the sound and breath effects involved, and that the closest Christian equivalent, 'the peace that passeth understanding', would be a feeble translation. Yet Eliot omits aum at the end. This was the final threshold dividing Indic and Western tradition which Eliot did not want to cross (Kearns 1987: 228-29).

34 (Lannoy 1971: 166).

35 (Ibid).

36 (Nath 2001).

37 (Ibid.: 98).

38 (Eck 1982: 69).

39 According to *Skanda Purana* (II.8.6.81-84), by taking a bath in the place where Sarayu and Ghaghara meet, the pilgrim receives punya (merit) equivalent to a thousand Ashvamedha Vedic rituals, etc.

40 For example, the *Linga Purana* (I.77.8-25) refers to different styles of temple architecture.

41 For example, in the *Markandeya Purana* (XIX.10), drinking liquor is not disapproved of, and meat and liquor are mentioned as acceptable offerings to Lord Dattatreya.

42 (Lannoy 1971: 193).

43 (Lamb 1975: 442-43).

44 As quoted in (Bhattacharjee 1981: 199-200).

45 (Bhattacharjee 1981: 1-3).

46 There is synergy between Sanskrit and Prakrit. A tinge of Prakrit added to Sanskrit brought Sanskrit closer to the language of the home, while a judicious Sanskritization made Prakrit into a language of a higher cultural status. Both processes were simultaneous and worked at conscious as well as subconscious levels. As an example of this symbiosis, one may point to various Sanskrit texts

in medieval India which were instruction manuals for spoken or conversational Sanskrit by the general public.

47 For examples of such projects, read (Malhotra and Neelakandan 2011)

48 There can certainly be abusive practices in pull marketing; the mere fact that the buyer takes the initiative does not preclude unethical conduct on the part of the seller. Likewise, not all push marketing is unethical but can be easily co-opted by the aggressive ego.

49 (Lamb 1975).

50 Another distortion in translation is the loss of families of words. We have seen that the synonyms for a given object are like a family. But when these are separately mapped on to another language they no longer comprise a family.

51 Monier Williams gives 'in whom all things lie' as the primary meaning of Shiva, derived from the root *śi*. Other important meanings of the word are 'auspicious', 'kind', and so on. Shiva is also 'a-kala', i.e., beyond time, and 'sada-shiva', the eternal who stays on despite and beyond destruction.

52 The Vedic term ritam means truth defined as a repeated pattern of events, something like universal laws of science. This is distinguished from satyam, which is absolute truth. While empirically observed patterns of repeated events are open to verification, as well as falsification, satyam, based on transcendental experience, is absolute and independent of contingencies of empirical observation (which David Hume spoke of in the eighteenth century).

53 (Aurobindo, *Collected Works of Sri Aurobindo: Essays on the Gita*, 1997: 4).

54 (*A Concise Sanskrit-English Dictionary* 1990). In specific systems there are also other meanings, such as, for instance, in Jaimini's *Mimamsa* aphorisms (1.1.2).

55 It has been pointed out that the Hindu school of Purva Mimamsa does demand commandment-style obedience. This system consists of mechanical reciting of mantras in the right way so as to achieve the desired result, and it interprets the Vedas as including 'vaidhi' (commandments) among its verses. Jaimini originated the Purva-Mimamsa school by compiling earlier interpretations, the main thrust of which was that the slightest deviation from the correct procedure of the yajnas (temple ritual) would not only be futile but counterproductive. Language had to be purposeful, and purely descriptive language was worthless. In his book *Vidhi Viveka*, the eminent scholar Mandana Misra discusses the Purva-Mimamsa claim that dharma is to be known only from the Vedic injunctions. See: (Natrajan 1995). However, it is refuted by

Vedanta and Tantra and replaced by what is called Uttara Mimamsa. Buddha, Mahavira and Krishna were all opposed to the purva-mimamsa way. Krishna (in Gita 2. 42-6) criticizes the 'veda-vada-ratahs', or the persons who have superficial knowledge of the Vedas, and for having the wrong bhava. He emphasizes the importance of knowing the higher purpose of rituals as opposed to the mechanical performance of them. Sri Jiva refers to two kinds of bhakti: vaidhi-bhakti is based on scriptural compliance whereas raganuja-bhakti is based on feelings of love from the heart. The latter is far superior. Thus, Purva Mimamsa is seen as having a role for beginners and is superseded by Uttara Mimamsa. Also, even at the Purva Mimamsa stage, vaidhi was never a set of commandments against others but was intended as a set of instructions to help the individual raise his or her own consciousness in order to transcend, as it were, the need for commandment.

56 Interestingly, these laws do not pertain to jatis, varnas, etc., in other words there are no civic or criminal laws as such pertaining to castes.

57 For a detailed account on why Dharma is not law, see: (Sharma 2005).

58 See, for example, Sharma 2005.

59 Some examples from the Vedas are as follows: *Chandogya Upanishad* (2.23.2-3): 'As leaves are held together by a spike, so all speech is held together by Aum. Aum is the world-all.' *Taittiriya Upanishad* (1.8): 'Aum is Brahman. Aum is the whole world.' *Katha Upanishad* (2.15-17): 'The word which all the Vedas rehearse, and which all austerities proclaim, desiring which men live the life of religious studentship – that word is Aum. That syllable is Brahman. That syllable indeed is the supreme. Knowing that syllable, whatever one desires is his.' *Mandukya Upanishad* (1-12) explains that Aum is divided into four components: 'A', 'U' and 'M' correspond to the three states of consciousness, namely and respectively, waking, sleeping and deep-sleep. The fourth is the 'turiya' state, which transcends all these. Thus Aum is the Self (Atman). *Maitri (Maitrayaniya) Upanishad* (6.22) explains that Aum is both the way to understand Ultimate Reality as well as the means to transcendence in order to attain it. Aum is equated with 'Shabda-Brahman'. *Maitri Upanishad* (6.28) compares Aum with the raft for crossing to the other side of the space in the heart. *Svetasvatara Upanishad* (1.13-14) explains the use of Aum as sound for meditation. 'Both the universal and the individual Brahman are to be found in the body by the use of Aum. By combining one's body and the Aum sound for practising *dhyana,* one may see the deva within oneself.'

60 (G. Joseph 2007).

61 (Loy, *A Buddhist History of the West : Studies in Lack* 2002).

62 (Patterson 1992: 402-03).

63 (Loy, *A Buddhist History of the West : Studies in* Lack 2002, 9).

64 (de Nicolas 1986).

65 Ibid.

66 (Aurobindo, *Collected Works of Sri Aurobindo: Essays on the Gita*, 1997: 13-14).

67 Ibid.

68 This is based on the Bhagavadgita's view. The Puranas and some other Vaishnava traditions do not make a clear distinction between vibhuti and avat*a*ra, and there is a tendency to apply the name 'avatar' to anyone who has risen above the ordinary level of human consciousness or has some special divine power. But the Bhagavadgita is specific about avatars and says that there can be infinite numbers of vibhutis, or ones with special qualities and powers of the divine, but the Supreme descends in human form as an avatar for a specific purpose.

69 *Kundalini Rising: Exploring the Energy Awakening,* by Gurmukh Kaur Khalsa and Dorothy Walters. Sounds True, 2009.

70 The Virgin Mary has long been the object of both devotional and scholarly interest, and recent years have seen a proliferation of studies on traditions of worship of Hindu goddesses. Despite the parallels between the two, however, no one has yet undertaken a book-length comparison of these traditions. In *Divine Mother, Blessed Mother*, Francis Clooney offers the first extended comparative study of Hindu goddesses and the Virgin Mary (2005). Clooney is almost unique in the field of Hindu studies as a Christian theologian with the linguistic and philosophical expertise necessary to produce sophisticated comparative analyses. Building on his previous work in comparative theology, he sheds new light not only on these individual traditions but also on the nature of gender and the divine.

71 (Aurobindo, *The Mother* 1995, 54).

72 'The Gods are born from Aditi in the supreme Truth of things, the Dasyus or Danavas from Diti in the nether darkness; they are the Lords of Light and the Lords of Night fronting each other across the triple world of earth, heaven and mid-air, body, mind and the connecting breath of life' (Aurobindo, *Collected Works of Sri Aurobindo: The Secret of the Veda* 1998, 232). Also: 'Aditi is the infinite Light of which the divine world is a formation and the gods, children of the infinite Light, born of her in the Ritam, manifested in that active truth of her movement guard it against Chaos and Ignorance. It is they who maintain the invincible workings of the Truth in the universe, they who

build its worlds into an image of the Truth' (Aurobindo, *Collected Works of Sri Aurobindo: The Secret of the Veda* 1998, 475).

73 The names of these ten personalities appear differently in different Tantras, though the most popular and widely accepted names are: Kali, Tara, Tripurasundari, Bhuvaneshwari, Tripurabhairavi, Chhinnamasta, Dhumavati, Bagalamukhi, Matangi and Kamalatmika. At the start of each cycle of creation, Kali emerges as Time, and Bhuvaneshwari as Space; the flaming word supreme turned toward manifestation is Bhairavi; the perceiving word is Tara; the expressed word is Matangi; the primordial luminous desire is Sundari; the delightful beauty is Kamala; Chhinnamasta combines light and sound in her thunderclap; and Bagalamukhi stifles the free flow of things.

74 Some linguists feel that it was an adaptation of Sanskrit 'santah', with the root word 'sat'. In Hindi it is 'sant'. In support of this, one notes that saints emerged prominently in Catholicism, and hence this was not something adopted from Judaism.

75 'Tat paramam Brahma-veda Brahma-ivabhavati' ('The knower of that ultimate Brahman becomes Brahman, nothing less'), *Mundaka Upanishad*, 3/2/9. There are seven types of rishis: srutarshi, kandarshi, paramarshi, maharshi, rajarshi, brahmarshi and devarshi.

76 (Aurobindo, *The Hour of God: Selections from his Writings*, 1995, 218).

77 An example of worshipping numerous devatas for specific qualities is the following aphorism by Sri Aurobindo: 'Be wide in me, O Varuna; be mighty in me, O Indra; O Sun, be very bright and luminous; O Moon, be full of charm and sweetness. Be fierce and terrible, O Rudra; be impetuous and swift, O Maruts; be strong and bold, O Aryama; be voluptuous and pleasurable, O Bhaga; be tender and kind and loving and passionate, O Mitra. Be bright and revealing, O Dawn; O Night, be solemn and pregnant. O Life, be full, ready and buoyant; O Death, lead my steps from mansion to mansion. Harmonise all these, O Brahmanaspati. Let me not be subject to these gods, O Kali' (Aurobindo, *The Hour of God: Selections from his Writings*, 1995, 85).

78 This view of the worship of images is consistent with the 'smarta' schools of Hinduism. This is distinct from Vaishnavism where the image is seen as a living being ('archa-vigraha') because the Lord has entered it after the necessary rituals, and hence it is not a mere symbol. But in either case, it is not an idol in the Western sense of that term.

79 (Aurobindo, *Collected Works of Sri Aurobindo: Essays in Philosophy and Yoga* 1998, 247).

80 (Aurobindo, *The Upanishads* 1996, 278).

81 (Aurobindo, *Collected Works of Sri Aurobindo: The Renaissance in India* 1997, 192).

82 (Kirsch 2004).

83 Ibid.: 108-109.

84 Ibid.: 115.

85 Ibid.: 15-16.

86 (Ibid. 2004: 113).

87 (Salisbury 2004).

88 See: Breaking India.

89 Rig Veda (I,164,35) says that yajna is the very navel of the universe. It was Lord Prajapati who first fashioned yajna, and through it he wove into one fabric the warp and weft of the three worlds (Rig Veda I,164,33-35).

90 One prominent incident in the sixteenth century is described as follows: 'For it is an Indian custom that when such a calamity has occurred, a pile is made of sandalwood, aloes, etc., as large as possible, and to add to this dry firewood and oil. Then they leave hardhearted confidants in charge of their women. As soon as it is certain that there has been a defeat and that the men have been killed, these stubborn ones reduce the innocent women to ashes... As many as three hundred women were burnt in the destructive fire of those refractory men' (Allami 1977, 472).

91 'Puputan' is a Balinese term that refers to a mass ritual suicide in preference to facing the humiliation of surrender ... [In] 1906, an overwhelming Dutch force landed at Sanur beach ... [and] the Raja, dressed in traditional white cremation garments [and] magnificent jewelry ... [led a procession of his] officials, guards, priests, wives, children and retainers [and] began killing themselves and others... the Dutch open[ed] fire with rifles and artillery. Women mockingly threw jewelry and gold coins at the troops ... Approximately 1,000 Balinese died' ('Puputan' 2011).

92 While not linked to the concept of yajna, it has been suggested that the Bhagavadgita, too, incites violence, especially when Lord Krishna urges Arjuna to fight his close relatives in order to fulfil his dharma. But before rushing to declare these wars as equivalents, several critical differences must be noted. Arjuna declares his reluctance to fight as he has nothing to gain, whereupon and Krishna educates him on the inner state of the warrior – consisting of detachment, self-mastery, transcendence of ego, and devotion – as a critical prerequisite of action. In the Bhagavadgita it is dharma (as righteousness) and not one's specific brand of religion that is paramount and worth fighting for. In the Abrahamic traditions, the son, or the warrior, must be *willing* to die for the self-proclaimed 'true' faith, often in place, or on behalf, of his forefathers. This

willingness could, of course, testify to a transcendence of ego, but that is not stressed in the usual transmission and teaching of this story in the Abrahamic traditions. While Hinduism has had its share of militant wars, immolations and sacrifices, it has nothing like the violent history of martyrdom which we see in early Judaism, Christianity and Islam. Nor does martyrdom offer the ticket to salvation or entry into paradise. Arjuna's liberation would depend, the Gita makes clear, on a lifelong treading on the path of dharma and not on a single act of self-immolation, no matter how worthy and defensible the cause.

93 (Aurobindo, *Collected Works of Sri Aurobindo: Essays on the Gita* 1997, 120).

94 (Aurobindo, *Collected Works of Sri Aurobindo: The Secret of the Veda* 1998, 278).

95 (Aurobindo, *Collected Works of Sri Aurobindo: Essays on the Gita* 1997, 119).

96 Hegel's philosophy of history is the self-conscious expression of an attitude that operates implicitly across the whole culture, and this remains Christian even when translated into secular theories regarding the end of history.

97 One person may, indeed, suffer from someone else's hatred or anger, or get a positive surprise from someone. But it is the recipient's own past karmic debt that has created such circumstances, and the other person doing the act is merely a vehicle for what was coming anyway through one means or another. So there are two separate accounts involved here: the person doing the act and the one to whom it is being done. The doer, by this act, is creating fresh karma in his account, as it were. The recipient suffers a consequence of past karma in *his* account. Each account is with the cosmos and not with another individual. The cosmos may deploy an individual as the vehicle or may bring about situations that are not directly brought about by any individual, say, an accident or earthquake or an epidemic.

98 *Panchatantra* is the Sanskrit collection of animal fables, probably compiled in the third century BCE. Buddhist prose fables are interspersed with wise sayings in verse. The work is attributed to Vishnu Sharma.

99 The Biblical book of Revelation, Chapters 6–18, describes the End Times prior to the Second Coming of Christ. The world will be devastated, millions of people will perish, and the most evil person in all history will be ruler of the entire world. The Second Coming of Christ puts all this to an end.

100 The dialogues in *Katha Upanishad* explain the temporary nature of such stays in heaven/hell, and their difference from moksha, which is permanent.

101 The idea of rebirth is embedded in a hierarchy of innumerable forms of life. Some texts estimate 8.4 million forms of life all the way from 'Brahma the creator to a blade of grass'. Some interpretations assume that the jiva-atman (soul) starts at the lowest forms of life and naturally evolves to the human form where it has the free will to be able to bring about progress.

102 The accumulated samskaras, or traces, that ripen across a series of life cycles are called samcitakarma.

103 There is nothing equivalent to the collective guilt, suffering and redemption found in Christianity.

104 In Hinduism, there is a similar concept of receiving grace from one's guru whereby a guru can diminish negative phala by assuming the negative karma of a disciple. However, such transfers are rare and local, and never on a universal scale such as the claim of Jesus transferring all karma of all humanity, including those born thousands of years after him.

105 The Bible speaks of Jesus' sacrifice as ongoing forever, a perpetual flow of blood until the end of time, which would have to be the case if his death on the cross were a metaphysical as well as physical one, and thus never really over as is insisted in the faith. So this discrepancy is not insurmountable theologically.

106 That the Indian spiritual traditions posit infinite time and finite karma does not mean that there is no sense of urgency to the spiritual quest or that that attitude is carefree or casual. Quite the contrary. The moksha-marga discourse which abounds in the spiritual literature of all dharma traditions includes urgent admonitions for those who are qualified by dint of discrimination (viveka) and detachment (vairagya) to strive for liberation in the present life (jivanmukti). In the Indian traditions, however, this urgency is within the context of individual sadhanaand the realization that the liberation path (moksha-marga) may stretch over several lifetimes and the final goal not achieved in the present life. The efforts made toward the realization of the goal in anyone life persist as tendencies (samskaras) in the psyche (chitta) and their karmic potential will be activated in subsequent lifetimes.

107 According to Dante, the gates of Hell carry the message: 'Abandon hope, all who enter here' ('Lasciate ogne speranza, voi ch'entrate').

108 The Four Noble Truths are: (1) Dukkha is inherent in the ordinary human condition. (2) The cause of dukkha is attachment. (3) Cessation of suffering is attainable in human life. (4) The way to achieve this is through the eightfold path.

109 This is explicitly true of Catholics and Mormons, as well as Protestant evangelicals, Pentecostals and members of mainline denominations such as

Baptists, Southern Baptists, Presbyterians, Methodists, Calvinists, etc.

110 The subject of Western appropriations of Indian spiritual traditions is covered in my forthcoming series of books on 'U-Turn Theory'.

111 (Malhotra, *A Hindu View of Christian Yoga* 2010).

112 This whole paragraph is based on (Aurobindo, *The Mother* 1995, 1-41).

113 (Aurobindo, *Collected Works of Sri Aurobindo: Essays Divine and Human* 1997, 18).

6. Contesting Western Universalism

1 Homer, for example, does this backward projection to construct Greek prehistory using civilizations that were non-Greek (such as Hittites, Anatolians, etc.). Similarly, the book *Black Athena* shows how African civilization was co-opted in the Egyptian historians' workshop, and later this Egyptian civilization got co-opted into Greek civilization. What is called Roman Art was often the art of non-Roman peoples conquered by Imperial Rome and hence named after the new owners. Christianity selectively borrows from Judaism's Old Testament, and Islam selectively borrows from the Bible. The 'pagan' category was created by collapsing immense diversity and context in pre-Christian Europe, Egypt, Greece, Persia, Hittite, India, Africa, Latin America, and just about everywhere else

2 The origins of the separation of East vs. West goes back to the truce called by the Pope in the fifteenth century between Spain and Portugal by legitimizing their right to plunder on either side of the longitude passing through the Azores islands in the Atlantic ocean.

3 Indian mimicry of British Victorian laws enacted under colonial rule has led to a contemporary controversy about gays. In traditional Indian society, there are no normative sexual categories of 'gay' and 'straight', and therefore being gay is neither banned nor formally sanctioned. It is simply left ambiguous and indeterminate for individuals to figure out for themselves in their own contexts. In the traditional Indian approach, the Western categories of gay/straight are not mutually exclusive, nor are they the permanent essences of a person. From such a perspective, questions such as whether a gay person is 'allowed' to be Hindu appear strange.

4 (Hegel, *Lectures on the Philosophy of World History*, 1982: 64).

5 Ibid.

6 (Hegel, *Samtliche Werke*, 1955: 243); quoted in (Dussel 1995: 20).

7 As Edward Said points out, Asia and Africa were often declared 'static, despotic, and irrelevant to world history (Said, *Culture and Imperialism*, 1993: 198).

8 (Hegel, *Lectures on the Philosophy of World History*, 1982: 30).

9 Cited in (Dussel 1995: 24).

10 (Hegel, *Enzyklopadie Der Philosphie*, 1952: 151).

11 (Hegel, *Lectures on the Philosophy of World History*, 1982: 138).

12 (Schlegel 1859: 120).

13 (Hegel, *The Oriental World: India*, 1956: 140–41, 162–64).

14 See (Clarke 1997: 65–67).

15 (Hegel, *The Oriental World: India*, 1956: 109).

16 Ibid., 149.

17 Ibid., 150.

18 Ibid., 164. This series of quotes is paraphrased from (Kearns 1987, 92–94).

19 (Hegel, *Lectures on the History of Philosophy*, 1995: 125–26).

20 From (Hegel, *Lectures on the Philosophy of World History*, 1982), Quoted in (Droit 1989: 189).

21 Hegel read translated works of India and sought advice from the noted Sanskrit linguist F. Bopp in Germany, but his most important references were the writings of British colonialists, such as William Jones, F. Wilford and J. Mill. Toward his final years, Hegel seemed to become more open to treating Indian philosophy as legitimate. Earlier he had claimed that India had to be 'excluded from the history of philosophy' because 'real philosophy begins only in Europe.' Hegel softened this stance somewhat after reading Colebrooke's articles on Samkhya and Nyaya-Vaisesika, regretting that these systems had been misunderstood by Europeans as 'religion' rather than philosophy. But even after this new insight into India, he continued to insist that Indian philosophy was disconnected from the historical process of progress because it lacked the idea of the autonomous individual self as a concrete agent of historical change. He was emphatic that Indian thought is a generic and vague mysticism that annuls all individuality and discourages initiative. His influence on other Enlightenment thinkers has been such that holistic ideas are dismissed as confusion. Although there is much talk currently of holism in philosophy and of a unified theory of knowledge, the binary dialectic using a sharp distinction of categories remains the predominant characteristic of Western thought.

22 (Halbfass 1988: 146).

23 (Marx 1853). This was the final article in a series on India. See: (Halbfass 1988: 137–38).

24 (Guha 2002: 44–45).

25 Ibid. Some other examples of social sciences propagating these same prejudices can be found in: Weber's *The Religions of India*; Karl Wittfogel's *Oriental Despotism*; modern psychoanalysis of India by Carstair's *The twice born*; Mussaief-Masson's *The Oceanic Feeling*. Indian culture is depicted as pathological under such theories.

26 (Guha 2002: 48–49).

27 (Hegel, *Lectures on the Philosophy of World History*, 1982: 142).

28 (Hegel, *Aesthetics*, 1975) quoted in (Guha 2002: 38).

29 (Hegel, *Lectures on the Philosophy of World History*, 1982: 131).

30 (Guha 2002: 40–41).

31 (Hegel, *Lectures on the Philosophy of World History*, 1982: 341).

32 (Halbfass 1988: 96).

33 'Arya' is often the first member in the appositionally defined compounds (karmadharaya-samasa) such as 'Arya-Dharma: Noble Dharma','Arya-Pudgala: Noble /Holy Person','Arya-Sravaka: Noble/Holy Disciple','Arya-Marga: Noble/ Holy Path', and 'Arya-Sangha: 'Spiritual Community'.

34 (Malhotra and Neelakandan, *Breaking India*, 2011).

35 Such notions are reinforced by studies such as (Radhakrishnan, *Eastern Religions and Western Thought*, 1997), the title of which reflects the emphasis.

36 Among the Indian champions were Sarvepalli Radhakrishnan and T.R.V. Murti. Radhakrisnan's *An Idealist View of Life* (2009), and Murti's transcendentalist interpretation of Nagarjuna's deconstruction philosophy in his translation of the Mula Madhyamika Karika in *The Central Philosophy of Buddhism*(1960), are typical examples of this emphasis.

37 Many other European philosophers began simply to ignore Indian thought or else dismiss it as trivial. Halbfass lists a representative sample of works on the history of philosophy which ignore Indian philosophy except perhaps for some short, dismissive remarks which are assumed to be self-evident (Halbfass 1988: 153-54). James Mill, whose multi-volume history of India became the defining work on India for half a century, Lord Risley who developed and enforced hierarchical caste categories in India through the census every decade, and Max Weber, the pre-eminent Western sociologist of his era, were each very heavily influenced by Hegel's views on India. The same mindset has persisted among Western intellectuals to this day. For instance, it is evident in the writings of Jean Gebser, a well-known twentieth-century thinker who is often cited by westerners claiming to be devotees of Sri Aurobindo and other Indian gurus. They have been pursuing what they regard as East–West integration but in a

very Hegelian framework of world history, which enshrines the imperative of a Western-dominated future (Gebser 1985).

38 A similar failure to address the problem of false Western universalism accrues to the common notion among successful Westernized individuals that the forces of capitalism and globalization will eventually bring a level of economic prosperity that will make the question of religious and cultural identities moot, a matter of fashion, as it were, or of personal preference that has little or no impact on the public sphere. This again is a dangerous form of denial, for as we have shown in the early chapters of this book, globalization is at base an imposition of Western values and modes of being in disguise; it's very presuppositions – that the world is 'progressing' toward some millennial goal of prosperity, that rampant acquisition and expansion are the only possible engines of development, and that the world is a set of resources to be exploited purely for the good of humans – are all versions of Abrahamic myth of history and its secular scientific alternative. But what has never been addressed in a satisfactory manner is how the Western model of progress can be scalable to cover all seven billion humans on the planet without human or environmental exploitation.

39 *Encyclopaedia Britannica* explains how the secular West has incorporated certain biblical ideas: 'Western civilization, even in its modern secularized forms, is heir to a long tradition of Christian patterns of thought and sensibility...Both the 18th- and 19th-century Enlightenment and the Romantic versions of the idea of the progress of humanity to an ideal state of peace and harmony betray their descent from messianic-millenarian beliefs...'('Eschatology', 1992).

40 (Loy, *A Buddhist History of the West : Studies in Lack*, 2002: 59).

41 (Ibid.: 127). Similarly, Western theories of human rights in vogue today, including the doctrine enshrined in the UN charter on human rights, are based on the debates among Christians in prior centuries. When John Locke, a British philosopher, started talking about 'natural rights' in the eighteenth century, he was reflecting an earlier debate within Christianity. Thus, Christian ethics and other ideas got dressed up in secular language. In psychology, it could be argued, the notion of the development of the self is a complex secularization of the Christian notion of soul.

42 Mercea Eliade's deconstruction of modern Marxism as Judeo-Christian myth is very interesting: 'Marx enriched the venerable myth by a whole Judeo-Christian messianic ideology: on the one hand, the prophetic role and soteriological function that he attributes to the proletariat; on the other, the final battle between Good and Evil, which is easily comparable to the apocalyptic

battle between Christ and Antichrist, followed by the total victory of the former. It is even significant that Marx takes over for his own purpose the Judeo-Christian eschatological hope of an absolute end to history;...' (Eliade 1987: 296-97). Similarly, *The Encyclopaedia Britannica* explains: 'Marxist Communism, in spite of its explicit atheism and dogmatic materialism, has a markedly messianic structure and message... Some of the analogies between Marxism and traditional Christian eschatology have been described, in a slightly ironical vein, by the English philosopher, Bertrand Russell, who contends that Marx adapted the Jewish messianic pattern of history to socialism in the same way that the philosopher-theologian St. Augustine (AD 354–420) adapted it to Christianity. According to Russell, the materialistic dialectic that governs historical development corresponds – in the Marxist scheme – to the biblical God, the proletariat to the elect, the Communist party to the church, the revolution to the Second Coming, and the Communist Commonwealth to the millennium... The similarities are founded on actual historical contacts... and also on the fact that they are variations of the same social dynamics and of a basic myth...'('Eschatology', 1992).

43 See (Tilak 2009).

44 Gopalrao Joshi was a Maharashtrian who converted to Christianity in the early twentieth century to get the benefit of sending his wife Anandi to the US for a master's degree in medicine. When asked to take oath as a witness in a court of law by placing his hand on a Bible, Gopalrao refused. He said that as a Hindu he can go to any temple; and starting to go to Jesus' temple makes no difference, and insisted on taking oath by placing his hand of the Gita. In other words, Christianity is a sect, a sampradaya, and he did not want to give up dharma even as a Christian.

45 (Chaudhuri 1987: 881).

46 (Inden, *Imagining India*, 1990: xii).

47 Personal communication. Some of the prominent names that come to mind are: Vinay Lal, Gayatri Chakravorty Spivak, Ramachandra Guha and Partha Chatterjee.

48 For a recent example of many such discussions among Westernized Indian youth and my response to them, see: (History-Centrism vs. Non-History-Centrism, 2010).

Conclusion: Purva Paksha and the Way Forward

1 Mahabharata, XII.72.20.
2 Scharfe 1989: 221.
3 Spivak, 2004.

Appendix A: The Integral Unity of Dharma

1 In Vedanta, as in Kashmir Shaivism, universals (samanya) and particulars (visesha) are inseparable – the universal serving as the unity view and particulars as the multiplicity view of the very same reality. The universal is seen in and as every particular, and each particular is nothing other than a mode of the universal.

2 To appreciate this, we must first understand that there are three types of differences possible: (i) differences between two objects belonging to the same category (sajatiya), (ii) differences between two objects belonging to different categories (vijatiya), and (iii) differences within the same object, either among its various parts or between its form and its essence (svagata). The impersonal school categorically denies all three differences in Brahman, and this makes Brahman devoid of all forms and attributes. Ramaanuja does not accept the first two differences but accepts the third one, since inherent in Brahman are form and attributes that are built into its unity and are not separate essences.

3 Although the complementarity of jnana and bhakti are generally advocated as the manifestations of the cit-shakti, there is a difference between Sankara's Kevala-advaita and the Vaishnava Vedanta schools in general as to the relative superiority of jnana and bhakti. For Sankara, bhakti is preparatory or prerequisite to jnana; i.e., bhakti leads to brahma-jnana or cognitive realization of the attributeless (nirguna) Brahman. Thus, there is the popular saying bhakti jnanam mata, meaning 'bhakti is the mother of jnana'. In other words, devotion culminates in knowledge. On the other hand, the devotional schools of Vaisnava Vedanta, such as the Achintya-bheda-abheda of Sri Jiva Goswami, consider the personal (Bhagavan) as higher than the impersonal absolute (nirguna-brahman), and knowledge (jnana) may be said to culminate in bhakti. Jnana is not demeaned and is generally considered complementary to bhakti, and eventually jnana is superseded or sublated by bhakti (Bhagavadgita, 7.19).

4 Lower deities are functional and meant for managerial affairs of the universe.

5 According to *Srimad-Bhagavatam* (3.29.13), 'a pure devotee does not accept any kind of liberation – salokya, sarsti, samipya, sarupya or ekatva – even though it is offered by the Lord.'

6 Sri Aurobindo explains this as follows: 'The material existence has only a physical, not a mental individuality, but there is a subliminal Presence in it, the one Conscious in unconscious things, that determines the operation of its indwelling energies ... We see then all the powers inherent in the original self-existent spiritual Awareness slowly brought out and manifested in this growing separative consciousness; they are activities suppressed but native to the secret and involved knowledge by identity and they now emerge by degrees in a form strangely diminished and tentative.' (Aurobindo, *Collected Works of Sri Aurobindo: The Life Divine*, 2005: 570-71).

7 (Aurobindo, *Collected Works of Sri Aurobindo: The Life Divine*, 2005: 277).

8 Ibid.: 150.

9 (*Mula-Madhyamaka-Karika*, 1, *Pratyaya-Pariksha*). Translation by Dr Laul Jadu Singh.

10 *Four Hundred Stanzas* by Aryadeva (*Catuh-Shataka-Shastra-Karika*, XV1, 23).

11 Quoted from the Kasyapa Chapter of the *Arya Ratnakuta Sutra* in (Lopez 2004, 353). Also, the *Essence of the Perfection of Wisdom* (*Prajna-Paramita-Hridaya Sutra*) famously states this principle: 'Form (rupa) is emptiness (sunyata), emptiness is form, form is not different from emptiness nor emptiness from form. What is form, that is emptiness, what is emptiness, that is form, and so it is for feeling, perception, dispositions and consciousness (the remaining aggregates).'

12 To reify the two truths in terms of two different ontological orders (of existence as pertaining to phenomena and noumena) would be to err in the direction of essentialism. This makes Buddhism radically different than Kantian and other Western idealism. Seen from a Buddhist view, the Kantian blunder is to reify two distinct ontological orders of existence, phenomenal and noumenal.

13 This statement, found in many places in the Pali canon in the original Pali is: 'nissaarana atthaya, na gahahana atthaya'; in Sanskrit: 'nihsarana arthaya', 'nagrahana arthaya'.

14 (*Mula-Mamadhyamika-Karika*, XIII, 8). Translation by Dr Laul Jadu Singh.

15 *(MMK,* XX1V, 8). The worldly conventional truth is called samvritti-satya/ loka-vyavahara. The supreme ultimate truth is called paramartha-satya.

16 (*MMK, Atma-Bhava-Pariksha* 8).

17 (*MMK, Arya-Satyani-Pariksha* 38). Translated by (Garfield 1995: 317).

18 (*MMK,* XXIV, 37). Translated by (Garfield 1995: 72).

19 (*MMK,* XXIV, 39). Translated by (Garfield 1995: 72).

20 (*MMK, Svabhava-Pariksha* 10). Translation Dr by Laul Jadu Singh. Nominal existence is referred to as prajnapti-sat.

21 It opens on this very theme: 'These two extremes are not to be resorted to by one who has gone forth from the world. What are the two? That conjoined with the passions, low, vulgar, common, ignoble and useless, and that conjoined with self-torture which is painful, ignoble, and useless. Avoiding these two extremes, the Tathagata has gained knowledge of the Middle Way, which gives sight and knowledge and which tends toward calm, insight, enlightenment, nirvana' (Opening verse of *Setting in Motion of the Wheel of Dharma [Dharma Chakra Pravartana Sutra]*).

22 *The Kaccayana Vacchagota Sutta* presents concisely the principle of Dependent Arising as a philosophical Middle Path.

23 Skilful means is called upaya-kaushalya.

24 (*MMK, Atma-Bhava-Pariksha*). Translated by (Garfield 1995, 72).

25 Nagarjuna employs both positive and negative forms of the tetralemma. In this way, the positive-negative distinctions indicate the different perspectives of the two truths (relative-conventional and ultimate). An example of the positive tetralemma from the conventional perspective is the four alternative positions on the self. This is not an irrational exercise by Nagarjuna but simply an explanation of how, from the perspective of conventional truth, the self-notion is valid in a verbal-pragmatic way. However, from the perspective of the ultimate truth, the self does not exist. The positions that (1) the self exists conventionally but is empty and (2) the self therefore and ultimately does not exist are equivalent in meaning though apparently contradictory. Nagarjuna's negative tetralemmas are more complex since, by means of these, he explores the limits of expressibility and the paradox incurred when one attempts to characterize reality from the ultimate perspective. An example of the negative tetralemma is: '"Empty" should not be asserted; "nonempty" should not be asserted. Neither both nor neither should be asserted. These are only used nominally' (*MMK,* XXII, 11). In this example, Nagarjuna discusses what is inexpressible from the ultimate perspective: namely that nothing, even that phenomena are empty or its negation, can be asserted from the ultimate perspective. Ostensibly nothing

can be said, but skilfully Nagarjuna has the final word: he has characterized the ultimate reality in principle beyond characterization. That the relationship between the two kinds of tetralemmas may generate a higher order of paradox also means that the two truths, apparently contradictory, are ultimately equivalent and non-dual when duality discrimination (dvaya-vikalpa) ceases. See the discussion in (*MMK*), and (Chandrakirti 2004: 285–324).

26 Technically, these are called sapta-bhangi. The seven possible forms of statement which are formally expressed are: (1) a thing is, (2) it is not, (3) it is and is not, (4) it is indescribable, (5) it is and is indescribable, (6) it is not and is indescribable, and (7) it is, is not, and is indescribable.

Index

Bibliography

A Concise Sanskrit-English Dictionary. Delhi: Gian Publishing House, 1990.

Allami, Abu-al-Fazl. *Akbarnama.* Vol. 2. Delhi: Rare Books, 1977.

Anacker, Stefan. *Seven Works of Vasubandhu.* Borehamwood: Motilal Banarsidass Publishers , 2002.

Anathkrishnan, G. '"Sanyas" lessons for Christian clergy'. *timesofindia. indiatimes.com.* 21 October 2007. http://articles.timesofindia.indiatimes. com/2007-10-21/india/27990022_1_sanyas-priests-yoga (accessed 4 May 2010).

Arnold, Matthew. *Culture and Anarchy; an Essay in Political and Social Criticism.* London: Smith, Elder & Co., 1869.

Associated Press. 'In Asia, the Eyes Have It.' *Wired.* 23 August 2005. http:// www.wired.com/culture/lifestyle/news/2005/08/68626 (accessed 8 April 2011).

Aurobindo, Sri. *Collected Works of Sri Aurobindo: Essays Divine and Human.* Vol. 12. Pondicherry: Sri Aurobindo Ashram, 1997.

———. *Collected Works of Sri Aurobindo: Essays in Philosophy and Yoga.* Vol. 13. Pondicherry: Sri Aurobindo Ashram, 1998.

———. *Collected Works of Sri Aurobindo: Essays on the Gita.* Vol. 19. Pondicherry: Sri Aurobindo Ashram, 1997.

———. *Collected Works of Sri Aurobindo: Isha Upanishad.* Vol. 17. Pondicherry: Sri Aurobindo Ashram, 2003.

———. *Collected Works of Sri Aurobindo: Record of Yoga II.* Vol. 11. Pondicherry: Sri Aurobindo Ashram, 2001.

———. *Collected Works of Sri Aurobindo: The Future Poetry.* Vol. 26. Pondicherry: Sri Aurobindo Ashram, 1997.

———. *Collected Works of Sri Aurobindo: The Human Cycle, The Ideal of Human Unity, War and Self-Determination.* Vol. 25. Pondicherry: Sri Aurobindo Ashram, 1997.

———. *Collected Works of Sri Aurobindo: The Life Divine.* Vols 21-22. Pondicherry: Sri Aurobindo Ashram, 2005.

———. *Collected Works of Sri Aurobindo: The Renaissance in India.* Vol. 20. Pondicherry: Sri Aurobindo Ashram, 1997.

————. *Collected Works of Sri Aurobindo: The Secret of the Veda.* Vol. 15. Pondicherry: Sri Aurobindo Ashram, 1998.

————. *Collected Works of Sri Aurobindo: The Synthesis of Yoga.* Vols 23-24. Pondicherry: Sri Aurobindo Ashram, 1999.

————. *Hymns to the Mystic Fire.* Twin Lakes: Lotus Light Publications, 1996.

————. 'Indian Spirituality and Life'. *intyoga.* 1919. http://intyoga.online.fr/isl01.htm (accessed 4 April 2011).

————. *Letters on Yoga.* Twin Lakes: Lotus Light Publications, 1970.

————. 'Second letter in 'The Mother'.' *intyoga.* http://intyoga.online.fr/mothr02.htm (accessed 4 April 2011).

————. *The Hour of God: Selections from his Writings.* Delhi: Sahitya Akademi, 1995.

————. *The Mother.* Twin Lakes: Lotus Light Publications, 1995.

————. *The Upanishads.* Twin Lakes: Lotus Light Publications, 1996.

Balslev, A.N. 'Cross-Cultural Conversation; Its Scope and Aspiration'. In *Cross-Cultural Conversation*, edited by A.N. Balslev. Atlanta: Scholars Press, 1996.

————. *Cultural Otherness: Correspondence With Richard Rorty.* Shimla: Indian Institute of Advanced Study and Munshiram Manoharlal, 1991.

'Beatific Vision.' *The Catholic Encyclopedia.* http://www.newadvent.org/cathen/02364a.htm (accessed 30 March 2011).

Beveridge, Henry. *The Akbarnama of Abu'l-Fazl.* Delhi: Low Price Publications, 1902, Reprint 2010.

Bhattacharjee, Arun. *Greater India.* New Delhi: Munshiram Manoharlal Publishers Private Limited, 1981.

Bhushan, Ranjit. 'Uncle's Grand Slam!' *India Outlook.* 16 June 2003. http://www.outlookindia.com/printarticle.aspx?220412 (accessed 10 April 2011).

Biema, David Van. 'The End: How It Got That Way'. *Time*, 1 July 2002, pp. 46-47.

Blakney, Raymond Bernard. *Meister Eckhart, a Modern Translation.* New York: Harper & Row, 1941.

Bruteau, B. *Evolution toward Divinity: Teilhard de Chardin and the Hindu Traditions.* Wheaton: Theosophical Publishing House, 1974.

Burnaby, John. *Amor Dei: A Study of the Religion of St. Augustine.* Norwich: The Canterbury Press, 1991.

Butler, Dom Cuthbert. *Gregory and Bernard on Contemplation and the Contemplative Life.* London: Constable & Co. , 1967.

Byrant, J. *New System or an Analysis of Ancient Mythology.* Whitefish: Kessinger Publishing, 2003.

Camilleri, Joseph. 'Human Rights, Cultural Diversity and Conflict Resolution.' *Pacifica Review* 6, no. 2, 1994, pp. 17-41.

Carroll, James. *Constantine's Sword: The Church and the Jews: a History.* Boston: Houghton Mifflin, 2001.

Chakravarti, Sitansu. *Ethics in the Mahābhārata.* Delhi: Munshiram Manoharlal, 2006.

Chandrakirti. *Introduction to the Middle Way.* Boston: Shambhala, 2004.

Chatterjee, A.K. *The Cult of Skanda-Kartikeya in Ancient India.* Calcutta: Punthi Pustak, 1970.

Chaudhuri, Nirad C. *Thy Hand, Great Anarch!: India, 1921-1952.* London: Chatto & Windus, 1987.

Clarke, J.J. *Oriental Enlightenment.* New York: Routledge, 1997.

Clooney, Francis X. *Divine Mother, Blessed Mother : Hindu Goddesses and the Virgin Mary.* Oxford: Oxford University Press, 2005.

'Congregation for the Doctrine of the Faith.' *Wikipedia, the Free Encyclopedia.* http://en.wikipedia.org/wiki/Congregation_for_the_Doctrine_of_the_Faith (accessed 4 May 2010).

Coward, Harold. *Jung and Eastern Traditions.* Albany: SUNY Press, 1985.

———. *Yoga and Psychology.* Albany: SUNY Press, 2002.

'Creeds'. *Catholic Wiki.* http://www.catecheticsonline.com/wiki/index.php?title=I_Believe (accessed 5 April 2011).

'Dabbawala'. *Wikipedia, The Free Encyclopedia.* http://en.wikipedia.org/wiki/Dabbawala (accessed 28 April 2010).

Dallmayr, Fred, 'Modes of Cross-Cultural Encounter'. In *Cross-Cultural Conversation,* edited by A.N. Balslev, Atlanta: Scholars Press, 1996.

Davenport, F.G. *European Treaties Bearing on the History of the United States and its Dependencies to 1648.* Vol. 1. Washington, DC: Carnegie Institute of Washington, 1917.

de Nicolas, Antonio T. 'The Philosophical Foundations of Neoconservatism.' *World & I,* September 1986.

Dehejia, Harsha V. *The Advaita of Art.* Delhi: Motilal Banarsidas, 1996.

'Diwali Celebration'. State of New Jersey Department of the Public Advocate, 2001. http://www.state.nj.us/rpa/Diwali%20Celebration.htm (accessed 6 April 2011).

Doniger, Wendy. *The Hindus: An Alternative History.* New York: Penguin, 2009.

'Draft United Nations Declaration on the Rights of Indigenous Peoples'. United Nations High Comissioner for Human Rights, 1994. http://www.unhchr.

ch/huridocda/huridoca.nsf/%28Symbol%29/E.CN.4.SUB.2.RES.1994.45.
En?OpenDocument (accessed 5 April 2011).

Droit, Roger-Pol. *L'Oubli de L'Inde, Une Amnésie Philosophique.* Paris: Presses
Universitaires de France, 1989.

Dubois, A.J. *Hindu Manners, Customs and Ceremonies: The Classic First-Hand
Account of India in the Early Nineteenth Century.* Mineola, NY: Dover
Publications, 2002.

Durant, Will. *The Story of Civilization: Our Oriental Heritage.* New York: MJF
Books, 1997.

Dussel, Enrique. *The Invention of the Americas.* New York: Continuum,
1995.

Eck, Diana. *Banaras: City of Light.* New York: Knopf, 1982.

Eckhart, Meister. *Sermons & Treatises.* Vols. I-III. Longmead: Element Books
Ltd., 1979.

Eliade, Mircea. *The Sacred and the Profane : The Nature of Religion.* San Diego:
Harcourt, Brace, 1987.

Eliot, T.S. *The Use of Poetry and the Use of Criticism: Studies in the Relation of
Criticism to Poetry in England.* London: Faber & Faber, 1964.

Emory Inter-Religious Council. http://www.religiouslife.emory.edu/life/
council.cfm (accessed 29 April 2010).

'Eschatology'. In *Encyclopedia Britannica.* Chicago: Encyclopedia Brittanica,
1992.

Eze, E. C. *Race and Enlightenment: A Reader.* Hoboken: Wiley-Blackwell,
1997.

Fanon, Franz. *The Wretched of the Earth.* New York : Grove Press, 2004.

Federici, Silvia, ed. *Enduring Western Civilization: The Construction of the
Concept of Western Civilization and its 'Others'.* Santa Barbara: Praeger,
1995.

Fox, R. *Gandhian Utopia: Experiments with Culture.* Boston: Beacon Press,
1986.

Friedman, Thomas L. *The World is Flat : a Brief History of the Twenty-first
Century.* New York: Farrar, Straus and Giroux, 2005.

Garfield, Jay L. *The fundamental wisdom of the middle way : Nāgārjuna's
Mūlamadhyamakakārikā.* New York: Oxford University Press, 1995.

Garrison, Fielding Hudson. *An Introduction to the History of Medicine.*
Philadelphia: W.B. Saunders Company, 1913.

Gebser, Jean. *The Ever- Present Origin.* Athens: Ohio University Press, 1985.

Gibbs, Nancy. 'Apocalypse Now'. *Time,* 1 July 2002.

Goldenberg, D.M. *The Curse of Ham: Race and Slavery in Early Judaism,*

Christianity, and Islam (Jews, Christians, and Muslims from the Ancient to the Modern World). Princeton: Princeton University Press, 2003.

Guha, Ranajit. *History at the Limits of World-History*. New York: Columbia University Press, 2002.

Haag, J. 'From Tolerance to Respect'. *Sacred Journey, The Journal on Fellowship of Prayer*, 2008, Oct/Nov: 2-3.

Halbfass, Wilhelm. *India and Europe, An Essay in Understanding*. Albany: SUNY Press, 1988.

Harris, R., ed. *Neoplatonism and Indian Thought*. Norfolk: SUNY Press, 1981.

Haynes, S. R. *Noah's Curse: The Biblical Justification of Amercian Slavery*. Oxford: Oxford University Press, 2002.

Hegel, G.W.F. *Aesthetics*. Oxford: Clarendon, 1975.

———. *Einleitung in die Geschichte der Philosophie* . Hamburg: F. Meiner, 1962.

———. *Enzyklopadie Der Philosphie*. Oxford: Clarendon Press, 1952.

———. *Lectures on the History of Philosophy*. Lincoln: University of Nebraska Press, 1995.

———. *Lectures on the Philosophy of World History*. Cambridge: Cambridge University Press, 1982.

———. *Samtliche Werke*. Hamburg: F. Meiner, 1955.

———. 'The Oriental World: India'. In *The Philosophy of History*. New York: Dover, 1956.

———. *The Philosophy of History*, rev. ed. New York: Colonial Press, 1900.

Hiltebeitel, A. *Criminal Gods and Demon Devotees*. Albany: SUNY Press, 1989.

'History-Centrism vs. Non-History-Centrism.' *Nirmukta*. 15 July 2010. http://nirmukta.net/Thread-History-Centrism-vs-Non-History-Centrism (accessed 29 March 2011).

Hodder, Alan D. *Thoreau's Ecstatic Witness*. New Haven: Yale University Press, 2001.

Hofstadter, D.R. *Godel, Escher, Bach: An Eternal Golden Braid*. New York: Basic Books, 1999.

Horowitz, David. *Containment and Revolution: Western Policy towards Social Revolution: 1917 to Vietnam*. London: Blond, 1967.

Horowitz, I. *The Rise and Fall of Project Camelot: Studies in the Relationship between Social Science and Practical Politics*. Cambridge: M.I.T Press, 1967.

Husserl, Edmund. *The Essential Husserl : Basic Writings in Transcendental Phenomenology*. Bloomington: Indiana University Press, 1999.

Inden, Ronald. *Imagining India.* Oxford: Blackwell, 1990.

Inden, Ronald, Jonathan Walters, and Daud Ali. *Querying the Medieval: Texts and the History of Practices in South Asia.* New York: Oxford University Press, 2000.

Infinity Foundation. 'Indic Mandala.' http://www.infinityfoundation.com/mandala/indic_mandala_frameset.htm (accessed 28 April 2010).

Isaacs, H.R. *Scratches on Our Minds: American Views of China and India.* Armonk: M.E. Sharpe, 1980.

James, William. *The Principles of Psychology.* New York: Dover, 1950.

Jayatilakee, J.N. *Early Buddhist Theory Of Knowledge.* Delhi: Motilal Banarsidas, 2004.

Jeffords, Susan. *The Remasculinization of America : Gender and the Vietnam War.* Bloomington: Indiana University Press, 1989.

Jitatmananda, Swami. *Modern Physics and Vedanta.* Mumbai: Paras Prints, 1986.

John Berkman and Craig Steven Titus, eds. *The Pinckaers Reader: Renewing Thomistic Moral Theology.* Washington D.C: Catholic University Press, 2005.

Jones, W.T. *A History of Western Philosophy,* 2nd ed. New York: Harcourt, Brace & World, 1969.

Jones, William. 'Botanical Observation of Select Indian Plants'. *Asiatic Researches* 4 (1795): pp. 237-312.

Joseph, George. 'Yoga has nothing to do with religion. It is not Hinduism'. *Rediff.* 17 July 2007. http://specials.rediff.com/news/2007/jul/17slide1.htm (accessed March 29, 2011).

Joseph, J. 'Of Insults, Obsessions and Distrust'. *Rediff, India Abroad.* 23 April 2003. http://www.rediff.com/news/2003/apr/23josy.htm (accessed 28 April 2010).

Jung, C. *Memories, Dreams, Reflections.* New York: Vintage Books, 1965.

Kagan, Robert. *Dangerous Nation.* New York: Alfred A. Knopf, 2006.

Kak, Subhash. 'Ritual, Masks, and Sacrifice'. *Studies in Humanities and Social Sciences.* Indian Institute of Advanced Study, 11 (2004).

———. *The Gods Within.* Delhi: Munshiram Manoharlal, 2002.

Kalupahana, D.J. *A History of Buddhist Philosophy.* Honolulu: University of Hawaii Press, 1992.

Kamat, J. *Roman Catholic Brahmin! A Biography of Robert de Nobili.* 'Kamat's Potpourri'. 2 October 2002. http://www.kamat.com/kalranga/people/pioneers/nobili.htm (accessed 4 May 2010).

Kane, Pandurang Vaman. *History of Dharmaśāstra.* Poona: Bhandarkar Oriental Research Institute, 1930.

Kearns, Cleo McNelly. *T.S. Eliot and Indic Philosophy.* New York: Cambridge University Press, 1987.

Keesing, R. 'Exotic Readings of Cultural Texts'. *Current Anthropology* 30 (1989): p. 4.

Kelso, J.A. Scott, and David A. Engstrom. *The Complementary Nature.* Cambridge: MIT Press, 2006.

Kimmelman, M. 'D.I.Y. Culture'. *New York Times*, 14 April 2010: p. 19.

King, Magda. *Heidegger's Philosophy: A Guide to His Basic Thought.* New York: Macmillan, 1964.

King, Ursula. *Towards a New Mysticism: Teilhard de Chardin and Eastern Traditions.* London: Collins, 1980.

Kipling, R. 'Yoked with an Unbeliever'. In *Plain Tales from the Hills*. Oxford: Oxford University Press, 1987.

Kirsch, Jonathan. *God Against the Gods.* New York: Viking Compass, 2004.

Koestler, A. *Darkness at Noon.* New York: Macmillan, 1941.

Kuiper, F. *Varuna and Vidûshaka: On the Origin of the Sanskrit Drama.* Amsterdam: North Holland Publishing Co, 1979.

Lakoff, G., and M. Johnson. *Philosophy in the Flesh: The Embodied Mind and Its Challenge to Western Thought.* New York: Basic Books, 1999.

Lamb, Alastair. 'Indian Influence in Ancient South-East Asia.' In *A Cultural History of India*, ed by A.L. Basham. London: Oxford University Press, 1975.

Lannoy, R. *The Speaking Tree: A Study of Indian Culture and Society.* London: Oxford University Press, 1971.

Liu, Henry G.K. 'The Race Toward Barbarism'. *Asia Times.* 9 July 2003. http://www.atimes.com/atimes/China/EG09Ad01.html (accessed 3 April 2011).

Loewen, James. *Lies My Teacher Told Me: Everything Your American History Textbook Got Wrong.* New York: New Press, 1995.

Lopez, Donald S. Jr, ed. *Buddhist Scriptures.* London: Penguin, 2004.

Loy, D.R. *A Buddhist History of the West : Studies in Lack.* Albany: SUNY Press, 2002.

———. *Nonduality: A Study in Comparative Philosophy.* New Haven: Yale University Press, 1988.

Lubac, Henri de. *Catholicism: Christ and the Common Destiny of Man.* San Francisco: Ignatius Press, 1988.

MacMullen, R. *Christianity and Paganism in the Fourth to Eight Centuries.* New Haven: Yale University Press, 1999.

Malhotra, Rajiv. 'A Hindu View of Christian Yoga'. *The Huffington Post.* 8 November 2010. http://www.huffingtonpost.com/rajiv-malhotra/hindu-view-of-christian-yoga_b_778501.html (accessed 11 April 2011).

————. 'American Exceptionalism and the Myth of the Frontiers'. In *The Challenge of Eurocentrism: Global Perspectives, Policy, and Prospects*, edited by R.K. Kanth. New York: Palgrave Macmillan, 2009.

————. 'We, the Nation(s) of India'. *Tehelka*. 17 January 2009. http://www.tehelka.com/story_main41.asp?filename=Ne170109we_the.asp (accessed 5 April 2011).

————. 'Whiteness Studies and Implications for Indian-American Identity'. *rajivmalhotra.sulekha.com*. 26 April 2007. http://rajivmalhotra.sulekha.com/blog/post/2007/04/whiteness-studies-and-implications-for-indian-american.htm (accessed 5 April 2011).

Malhotra, Rajiv, and Aravindan Neelakandan. *Breaking India*. Delhi: Amaryllis, 2011.

Marriott, M., ed. *India Through Hindu Categories*. New Delhi: Sage Publications, 1990.

Marx, Karl. 'The Future Results of British Rule in India'. *New York Daily Tribune*, 8 August 1853.

Mayo, K. *The Face of Mother India*. New York: Harper & Brothers, 1935.

McEvilley, T. *The Shape of Ancient Thought: Comparative Studies in Greek and Indian Philosophies*. New York: Allworth Press, 2001.

Morales, Frank Gaetano. 'Word as Weapon: The Polemically Charged Use of Terminology in Euro-American Discourse on Hinduism'. International Forum for India's Heritage. 2002. http://ifihhome.tripod.com/articles/fgm001.html (accessed 30 March 2011).

Mother, The. *Complete Works of The Mother: Questions and Answers 1953*. Vol. 5. Pondicherry: Sri Aurobindo Ashram, 2003.

Murti, T.R.V. *The Central Philosophy of Buddhism*. London : Unwin Hyman, 1960.

Nath, Vijay. *Purānas and Acculturation*. Delhi: Munshiram Manoharlal Publishers, 2001.

Natrajan, Kanchana. *The Vidhi Viveka of Mandana Misra, Understanding Vedic Injunctions*. Delhi: Indian Books Center, 1995.

Newcomb, Steve. 'Five Hundred Years of Injustice: The Legacy of Fifteenth Century Religious Prejudice'. Indiginous Law Institute. http://ili.nativeweb.org/sdrm_art.html (accessed December 8, 2007).

Newton, Isaac. *The Chronology of Ancient Kingdoms*. Green Forest: New Leaf Publishing Group, 2009.

Nikam, N.A. *Some Concepts of Indian Culture: An Analytical Interpretation*. 2nd ed. Shimla: Institute of Advanced Studies, 1973.

Olson, Carl. *Indian Philosophers and Postmodern Thinkers*. Mumbai: Oxford University Press India, 2002.

Organ, T. W. *The Hindu Quest for the Perfection of Man*. Athens: Ohio University Press, 1970.

Overzee, Ann Hunt. *The Body Divine: The Symbol of the Body in the Works of Teilhard de Chardin and Rāmānuja*. Cambridge: Cambridge University Press, 1992.

Padoux, A. 'Opening Essay'. In *The Roots of Tantra*, edited by R. Brown and K.A. Harper. Albany: SUNY Press, 2002.

Pai, P.S. *T.S. Eliot, Vedānta and Buddhism*. Vancouver: University of British Columbia Press, 1985.

Panikkar, Raimundo. *Myth, Faith, and Hermeneutics : Cross-Cultural Studies*. New York: Paulist Press, 1979.

Parkes, Graham, ed. *Heidegger and Asian Thought*. Honolulu: University of Hawaii Press, 1987.

Patterson, Orlando. *Freedom*. New York: BasicBooks, 1992.

Paul VI, Pope. 'Lumen Gentium'. *The Holy See*. 21 November 1964. http://www.vatican.va/archive/hist_councils/ii_vatican_council/documents/vat-ii_const_19641121_lumen-gentium_en.html (accessed 30 March 2011).

Pearson, M. *The Portuguese in India*. Hyderabad: Orient Longman, 1990.

Pinckaers, Servais. *The Pinckaers Reader: Renewing Thomistic Moral Theology*. Washington DC: Catholic University Press, 2005.

Priest, J. *Bible Defense of Slavery: Or the Origin, Fortunes, and History of the Negro Race*. Glasgow: Kessinger Publishing, 1852.

———. *Slavery as It Relates to the Negro or the African Race*. Albany: C. Van Benthuysen and Co, 1843.

'Puputan'. *Wikipedia*. 10 April 2011. http://en.wikipedia.org/wiki/Puputan#cite_note-1 (accessed 11 April 2011).

Radhakrishnan, Sarvepalli. *The Bhagavad Gita*. New York: Harper & Brothers, 1948.

———, ed. *A Source Book in Indian Philosophy*. Princeton: Princeton University Press, 1957.

———. *An Idealist View of Life*. New York: HarperCollins, 2009.

———. *Eastern Religions and Western Thought*. Oxford: Oxford University Press, 1997.

Rajasekharaiah, T.R. *The Roots of Whitman's Grass*. Madison: Farleigh Dickinson University Press, 1970.

Ramanujan, A. 'Is there an Indian way of thinking? An informal essay'. In *India through Hindu Categories*, edited by M. Marriott. New Delhi: Sage Publications, 1990.

Ramaswamy, K., A.D. Nicolas, and A. Banerjee. *Invading the Sacred: An Analysis of Hinduism Studies in America.* Delhi: Rupa & Co, 2007.

Rao, Satyanarayana. *Myths and Deities, Some Aspects of Hindu Iconographic Traditions.* Madras: New Era Publications, 1993.

Ratzinger, Joseph Card. 'Dominus Iesus'. *The Holy See.* 6 August 2000. http://www.vatican.va/roman_curia/congregations/cfaith/documents/rc_con_cfaith_doc_20000806_dominus-iesus_en.html (accessed 5 April 2011).

Robinson, D.N. *An Intellectual History of Psychology.* New York: Macmillan, 1976.

Rosch, Eleanor. *Transformation of the Wolf Man.* 1997. http://cogweb.ucla.edu/Abstracts/Rosch_97.html (accessed 8 September 2010).

Rosenberg, E.S. 'Gender'. *Journal of American History (77)*, 1990: p. 119.

Rotter, A.J. *Comrades at Odds: The United States and India, 1947-1964.* Ithaca: Cornell University Press, 2000.

Rotter, A. J. 'In Retrospect: Harold R. Isaacs's Scratches on Our Minds'. *Reviews in American History, 24*, 1996: p. 1.

Roy, Sumita, Annie Pothen, and K.S. Sunita. *Aldous Huxley and Indian Thought.* New York: Sterling Publishers, 2003.

Rudolph, L., and S. Rudolph. *The Modernity of Tradition: Political Developments in India.* Chicago: University Of Chicago Press, 1967.

Said, Edward. *Culture and Imperialism.* New York: Vintage Books, 1993.

———. *Orientalism.* New York: Vintage Books, 1979.

Salisbury, Joyce Ellen. *The Blood of Martyrs: Unintended Consequences of Ancient Violence.* New York: Routledge, 2004.

Salmon, Don. 'Yoga Psychology In The Schools: Some Insights from the Indian Tradition'. Infinity Foundation. http://www.infinityfoundation.com/mandala/i_es/i_es_salmo_yoga_frameset.htm (accessed 30 March 2011).

Sampath, G. 'Why did Hinduism never become an "organised" religion like Christianity or Islam? - Interview with Wendy Doniger'. *dnaindia.* 4 October 2009. http://www.dnaindia.com/lifestyle/report_why-did-hinduism-never-become-an-organised-religion-like-christianity-or-islam_1294838 (accessed 4 May 2010).

Samuel, Dibin. 'Indian Bible Draws Fire Over Hindu References'. *The Christian Post.* 11 August 2008. http://www.christianpost.com/news/new-indian-bible-draws-fire-over-hindu-references-33769/ (accessed 5 April 2011).

Sardar, Ziauddin. *Postmodernism and the Other: The New Imperialism of Western Culture.* London: Pluto Press, 1998.

Scharfe, Hartmut. *The State in Indian Tradition.* Leiden: Brill, 1989.

Schlegel, F. *The Philosophy of History in a Course of Lectures.* London: Henry Bohn, 1859.

Schmidt, L.H. 'Commonness across Cultures'. In *Cross-Cultural Conversation,* edited by A.N. Balslev, Atlanta: Scholars Press, 1996.

Schrödinger, E. *What Is life? with Mind and Matter, and Autobiographical Sketches.* Cambridge : Cambridge University Press, 1992.

Schrödinger, Erwin. *My View of the World.* Cambridge: Cambridge University Press, 1964.

Schwab, Raymond. *The Oriental renaissance : Europe's Rediscovery of India and the East, 1680-1880.* New York: Columbia University Press, 1984.

'sciforums.com.' *INDIA's contributions to the world.* 13 November 2001. http://www.sciforums.com/India-s-contributions-to-the%20world-t-4567-html (accessed 4 May 2010).

'Second Hindu-Jewish Leadership Summit Declaration, Israel'. Hindu Dharma Acharya Sabha. 2008. http://www.acharyasabha.org/index.php?option=com_content&task=view&id=41&Itemid=41 (accessed 6 April 2011).

Sharma, Shashi S. *Imagined Manuvad: The Dharmashāstras and Their Interpreters.* Delhi: Rupa & Co., 2005.

Shourie, A. 'The Roman Brahmin (n.d.)'. *The Arun Shourie Site.* http://arunshourie.voiceofdharma.com/articles/roman.htm (accessed 29 April 2010).

Shruti, ed. *Indian Philosophy at University of Hawaii.* Delhi: Vidhi Vedika Heritage, 2005.

Shulman, David. *The King and the Clown in South Asian Myth and Poetry.* Princeton: Princeton University Press, 1985.

Slotkin, Richard. *The Fatal Environment: The Myth of the American Frontier in the Age of Industrialization, 1800-1890.* Norman: Univrsity of Oklahoma Press, 1985.

Smith, Brian K. *Reflections on Resemblance, Ritual, and Religion.* New York: Oxford University Press, 1989.

Smith, V. A. *Asoka, the Buddhist Emperor of India.* Ithaca: Cornell University Library, 2009.

Spengler, O. *The Decline of the West.* Vol. I. New York: Oxford University Press, 1991.

Spivak, Gayatri Chakravorty. 'Righting Wrongs'. *The South Atlantic Quarterly* 103, no. Number 2/3, Spring/Summer (2004): pp. 523-581.

Steinman, Clay. 'Beyond Eurocentrism: The Frankfurt School and Whiteness

Theory'. In *Globalizing Critical Theory*, edited by Max Pensky, pp. 115-137. Oxford: Rowman & Littlefield, 2005.

Sugirtharajah, R.S. *The Bible and Empire: Postcolonial Explorations*. Cambridge: Cambridge University Press, 2005.

Sullivan, Bruce M. ' The Religious Authority in the Mahābhārata: Vyāsa and Brahmā in the Hindu Scriptural Tradition'. *Journal of the American Academy of Religion* 62 (1994): pp. 377-401.

Talbot, M. *Mysticism and the New Physics*. New York: Penguin Books, 1993.

————. *The Holographic Universe*. New York: Harper Perennial, 1992.

Taylor, Eugene. 'Mysticism'. *Purify Mind*. http://www.purifymind.com/ MeditationIntro.htm (accessed 5 April 2011).

Taylor, T. *The Prophetic Families and the Negro: His Origin, Destiny and Status*. Atlanta: The Foote & Davies Printing Co., 1895.

The New Oxford Annotated Bible with Apocrypha: New Revised Standard Version. New York: Oxford University Press, 2010.

Thurman, Robert. *Inner Revolution*. New York: Riverhead Trade, 1999.

Tilak, Shrinivas. *Reawakening to a Secular Hindu Nation: M.S. Golwalkar's Vision of a Dharma-sāpeksha Hindurashtra*. Charleston: Booksurge, 2009.

Todorov, T. *The Conquest of America*. Norman: University of Oklahoma Press, 1999.

Toulmin, Stephen. *Cosmopolis: the Hidden Agenda of Modernity*. New York: The Free Press, 1990.

Trautmann, T.R. *Aryans And British India*. New Delhi: Yoda Press, 2004.

Travis, F., T. Olson, T. Egenes, and H.K. Gupta. 'Physiological patterns during practice of the Transcendental Meditation technique compared with patterns while reading Sanskrit and a modern language'. *The International Journal of Neuroscience* 109 (July 2001): pp. 71-80.

Tripurari, B.V. *Aesthetic Vedanta: The Sacred Path of Passionate Love*. Eugene: Clarion Call , 1998.

Vatsyayan, Kapila. *The Square and the Circle of Indian Arts*. New Delhi: Abhinav Publications, 1997.

Wallace, Alan. 'Why the West Has No Science of Consciousness: A Buddhist View'. Infinity Foundation. July 2002. http://www.infinityfoundation. com/indic_colloq/persons/person_wallace_alan.htm (accessed 30 March 2011).

Weiming, Tu. *Tu Weiming*. http://www.tuweiming.net/ (accessed 5 April 2011).

Weiss, Jeffrey. 'Who goes to hell?'. The Ross Institute. 6 January 2007. http:// www.rickross.com/reference/fundamentalists/fund211.html (accessed 10 January 2010).

Wells, H.G. *A Short History of the World.* New York: Macmillan, 1922.

'What's up with the Biblical Story of Drunken Noah?' *The Straight Dope.* 27 January 2005. http://www.straightdope.com/columns/read/2194/whats-up-with-the-biblical-story-of-drunken-noah-part-2 (accessed 9 April 2011).

Wolters, Albert M. 'A Survey of Modern Scholarly Opinion on Plotinus and Indian Thought'. In *Neoplatonism and Indian Thought,* edited by Baine R. Harris. Norfolk: International Center for Neoplatonic Studies, 1982.

Yogananda, P. *The Second Coming of Christ.* Los Angeles: Self Realization Fellowship, 2004.

Zimmermann, F. *The Jungle and the Aroma of Meats: An Ecological theme in the Hindu Medicine.* Delhi: Motilal Banarasidas Publishers, 1999.

Acknowledgments

This book has been reincarnated several times and became significantly different each time. During the decade-long churning I went through that culminated in this book, I approached numerous experts in specific areas of specialization for their critical feedback. I knew that I was developing novel ideas and approaches to interpret many old philosophies, and this required constant dialogue with competent scholars to make sure that I did not deviate too much from the established schools. Such experts' inputs helped me reconsider many of my arguments, the areas of emphasis, and the organization and the overall thrust of the book.

For instance, Don Wiebe, a leading academic scholar of the philosophy of religion, took a considerable amount of time and sent back a long critique from a scientific approach to the study of religions, going chapter by chapter and point by point, playing devil's advocate. Francis Clooney, a Jesuit and a Professor of Religion at Harvard, raised numerous theological points that led me to sharpen my arguments. Dr Shrinivas Tilak studied an early draft and suggested numerous resources to help my thesis. Dr Sunthar Vishvalingam helped edit and make substantial inputs on certain areas such as the comparison between the Jokers in the two traditions' literatures. Dr Laul Jadu Singh verified my interpretations of Buddhism and added valuable new ideas. Dr Satya Narayan Das, a renowned scholar of Jiva Goswami's Vaishnavism and Vedanta, read through the entire draft, making critical suggestions, and we had multiple brainstorms as part of my churning process. Krishna Kirti Das added further insights from the Vaishnav perspective, commenting on my treatment of that tradition. Dr Sampadananda Mishra served as my expert advisor on Sri Aurobindo and we had numerous discussions in person and by phone over a long period.

Dr Larry Seidel helped edit certain portions at an earlier stage before they were incorporated into this book. Dr Anand Paranjpe, an acclaimed scholar of Indian theories of psychology, provided extensive criticisms after reading the entire draft, and these led me to rewrite some portions. Swami Tadatmananda, Professor Ramakrishna Puligandla and Dr Sitansu Chakrabarti each provided helpful comments using their expertise in Indian philosophy. Professor Makkhan Lal and numerous others also read the drafts and provided helpful feedback.

I wish to especially thank Dr Cleo Kearns who went through multiple iterations of the drafts, pointing out issues pertaining to the Judeo-Christian perspectives, organizational chronology and clarity, and helped me rewrite critical portions to improve the drafts. At times I felt that we were having a Dharma–Christianity purva paksha on very detailed technical issues and this was very helpful. Anita Vasudeva of Roving Writers played an important role as overall critic providing constructive suggestions that led to the rewriting of several portions. She was also instrumental in convincing HarperCollins to publish this book. Shefali Chandan went through the entire manuscript in detail and argued with me on where, why and how the presentation must be improved for mainstream readers. She made substantial improvements in the writing style. Kent Hayden brought in solid arguments as a Christian theologian. I thank Thom Loree for painstakingly copyediting every sentence for language, style and grammar.

I thank V.K. Karthika, publisher, HarperCollins India, for agreeing to publish the book on such a tight schedule, and Shantanu Ray Chaudhuri for editing and ensuring its overall quality on a timely basis. I thank Shuka Jain for her excellent cover design.

The funding for the finalizing of this book during 2011 included a grant provided by Uberoi Foundation. For this, I thank Professor Ved Nanda, Katherine Nanda, Anu Bhatia and Manohar Shinde, and as well Bal Ram Singh, Director of Center for Indic Studies, University of Massachusetts, Dartmouth. Additionally, I thank Raghu Rao for providing funds towards the promotion of the book in the US.

Lightning Source UK Ltd.
Milton Keynes UK
UKHW040852021222
413231UK00014B/259/J